HINDI HINDU HISTORIES

SUNY series in Hindu Studies
Wendy Doniger, editor

~ CHARU GUPTA ~

Hindi Hindu Histories

Caste, Ayurveda, Travel, and Communism in Early-Twentieth-Century India

SUNY PRESS

First published by Permanent Black D-28 Oxford Apts, 11 IP Extension, Delhi 110092 INDIA, for the territory of SOUTH ASIA.
First SUNY Press edition 2024.
Not for sale in South Asia.

Cover image: Swapnil Dwivedi/Unsplash
Cover design by: Anuradha Roy

Published by State University of New York Press, Albany
© 2024 Charu Gupta
All rights reserved
Printed in the United States of America

No part of this book may be used or reproduced in any manner whatsoever without written permission. No part of this book may be stored in a retrieval system or transmitted in any form or by any means including electronic, electrostatic, magnetic tape, mechanical, photocopying, recording, or otherwise without the prior permission in writing of the publisher.

Links to third-party websites are provided as a convenience and for informational purposes only. They do not constitute an endorsement or an approval of any of the products, services, or opinions of the organization, companies, or individuals. SUNY Press bears no responsibility for the accuracy, legality, or content of a URL, the external website, or for that of subsequent websites.

For information, contact State University of New York Press, Albany, NY
www.sunypress.edu

Library of Congress Cataloging-in-Publication Data

Names: Gupta, Charu, author.
Title: Hindi Hindu histories: caste, ayurveda, travel, and communism in early-twentieth-century India / Charu Gupta.
Description: [Albany] : [State University of New York Press], [2024] | Series: SUNY series in Hindu Studies | Includes bibliographical references.
Identifiers: ISBN 9798855800661 (hardcover) | ISBN 9798855800678 (ebook) | ISBN 9798855800654 (paperback)
More information available at https://lccn.loc.gov/2024000343.

for

Maa

even in your absence
your boundless love and wisdom
continue to be my lifeline

Contents

Figures	xi
Abbreviations	xv
Note on Translation and Transliteration	xvii
Acknowledgements	xix
INTRODUCTION: VERNACULAR FREEDOMS AND LIFE NARRATIVES	**1**
Malleable Circuits of the Vernacular	7
Hindi and Hindu: Negotiating Language, Literature, and Religion	15
Self-Writing, Life Histories, and Sexual Embodiments	23
Utopian Desires of Freedom	32
Trajectory of Chapters	35

I: SANTRAM BA (1887–1988)

1 READING SELF, RESISTING CASTE, REIMAGINING MARRIAGE	**40**
Life History and Caste: Self and Collective Identities	44
Familial and Social Roots: Caste Discrimination, the Arya Samaj, and Hindi	48
A History of the JPTM and Anticaste Thought	56
Transgressive Intimacies: Championing Intercaste Marriages	68
2 CAST(E)ING AND TRANSLATING SEX: VERNACULAR SEXOLOGY FROM THE MARGINS	**79**
Vernacular Print Cultures and Sexology in Hindi	83

Translating Marginality into Authority: Marie Stopes and the Sanskrit Sex Classics — 88
A Heterosexual Ethics: Conjugal Desires, Brahmacharya, and Birth Control — 99

II: YASHODA DEVI (1890–1942)

3 PROCREATION AND PLEASURE: WOMEN, MEN, AND AYURVEDA — 112
Popular Health Literature, Biomedicine, and Ayurveda — 118
A Gendered Ayurvedic Authority on Domestic Health — 122
A Moral Sexologist: Reproduction, Intercourse, and Masturbation — 129

4 KITCHEN PHARMACY: CULINARY RECIPES AND HOME REMEDIES — 146
The Politics of Food and Health in Colonial UP — 149
A Robust World of Cookbooks and Home Remedies — 154
Food Recipes and Cookbooks — 155
Recipes for Home Remedies — 158
Menu for a Hindu Nation and the Ingredients of Gendered Embodiments — 162
The Educated Housewife as "Ghar ka Vaid" — 172
Food for Freedom: The Political Economy of Home Remedies — 177

III: SWAMI SATYADEV PARIVRAJAK (1879–1961)

5 FANTASY, FITNESS, FASCISM: MASCULINE VERNACULAR HISTORIES OF TRAVEL — 184
Travel Writing: A Passion for Hindi — 194
Admiring the West: Beauty, Pleasure, and Physicality — 202
A Dialogue between East and West, Slavery, and Freedom — 207
"Perfect" Bodies: Masculinity and the Idolisation of Hitler — 214

6	**FASHIONING A HINDU POLITICAL SANYASI: AUTOBIOGRAPHY AND SECTARIAN FREEDOM**	**220**
	Anatomy of a Hindu Ascetic: Sexual Constraint and Masculine Virility	225
	Egoism and Eulogising Self	229
	Conceptualising an Exclusionary Freedom	232
	Segmented Freedom and Nationalism: Hindu Sangathan and Muslims	234
	Gandhi and Godse	239
	Vindicating Assassination	242

IV: SATYABHAKT (1896–1985)

7	**A "MARGINAL" HISTORY OF VERNACULAR COMMUNISM**	**248**
	Historical Antecedents, Hindi and Communism	252
	The First Communist Conference and Satyabhakt's Marginalisation	262
	Idioms from Below and Communist Writings	269
8	**HINDU COMMUNISM: APOCALYPSE AND UTOPIAN RAM RAJYA**	**284**
	An Eclectic Hindu Worldview	289
	Indian Traditions and Hinduism in Dialogue with Communism	293
	Apocalyptic Predictions and Future Prophecies	298
	Communism as a Utopian Ram Rajya	303
	Glossary	312
	Bibliography	318
	Index	359

Figures

1.1	Santram BA (from Santram, *MJKA*, 1963 edn).	40
1.2	Jacket front of *MJKA* (from Santram, *MJKA*, 1974 edn).	41
1.3	Jacket front of Satnam Singh's version of the *MJKA* (from Singh, *Santram BA*, courtesy Samyak Prakashan, Delhi).	46
1.4	Poster celebrating Santram's birthday (from Birsa Ambedkar Phule Students' Association [BAPSA], JNU).	47
1.5	An issue of *Yugantar* (from *Yugantar*, June 1932, cover).	55
1.6	Cartoon entitled "Ponga Pandit" in *Yugantar* (from *Yugantar*, October 1933, 6).	61
1.7	Intercaste marriage performed by the JPTM (from Madhu Chaddha, granddaughter of Santram).	71
1.8	Santram with his second wife, Sunder Bai, 18 February 1954 (from Madhu Chaddha).	73
2.1	One of Santram's many books on sexology (from Santram, *Kama Kunj*, cover).	91
2.2	The advertisement for *Kama Kunj* in *Madhuri* (from *Madhuri*, March 1930).	95
3.1-i and 3.1-ii	Yashoda Devi and Sri Ram Sharma, both in 1921 (from Samir Sharma, great-grandson of Yashoda).	116
3.2	Post Box address for letters to Yashoda Devi (from Yashoda, *Dampati Arogyata*, 673).	117

FIGURES

3.3-i and 3.3-ii	Illustrations relating to the cure of leukorrhea and venereal disease (from Yashoda, *Dampati Arogyata*, 412, 455).	131
3.4-i and 3.4-ii	Illustrations of female genitalia (from Yashoda, *Dampatya Prem*, 386; idem, *Nari Sharir*, 111).	131
3.5	Yashoda with helpers (from Samir Sharma).	132
3.6	"Vivah, Vigyan, Kamashastra: Anand Mandir" (from Yashoda, *Dampatya Prem*, cover).	133
3.7	The happy outcome of conjugal love (from Yashoda, *Dampatya Prem*, 251).	134
3.8	Sample representation of monogamous conjugal bliss (from Yashoda, *Dampatya Prem*, 148).	135
3.9-i, 3.9-ii, and 3.9-iii	The aftermath of male adultery and torture of a woman by a tyrannical husband (from Yashoda, *Dampatya Prem*, 164, 508).	142
4.1-i and 4.1-ii	Sample illustrations showing recipe columns (from "Pak Shiksha", *Chand*, September 1929, 120; "Bhojan", *Sudha*, March 1933, 188).	156
4.2	Advertisement for *Pak Chandrika* in *Chand* (from *Chand*, July 1930).	157
4.3	Illustration accompanying column on home remedies (from "Gharelu Dawaiyan", *Chand*, May 1929, 98).	161
4.4	The ideal kitchen (from Gupt, *Pakprakash aur Mithai*, inside page).	165
4.5-i, 4.5-ii, 4.5-iii, and 4.5-iv	A series showing women serving and men eating (from Bhagwandas, *Ras Vyanjan Prakash*, 4–7).	168
4.6	Reading recipes, following recipes (from Gupt, *Pakprakash aur Mithai*, cover).	169
4.7	The cover of one of Yashoda Devi's books (from Yashoda, *Pradar Rog Chikitsa*).	176

4.8-i and 4.8-ii	Women sharing medical knowledge and preparing remedies (from Yashoda, *Dampati Arogyata*; idem, *Nari Dharmashastra*, back cover).	179
4.9	Yashoda Devi's house in Allahabad, 1930 (from Samir Sharma).	180
5.1	Satyadev in 1907 (from *Saraswati*, February 1907, 56).	185
5.2	Satyadev in 1911 (from Satyadev, *Amrica Bhraman*, inside cover).	186
5.3	The jacket of one of Satyadev's many travelogues (from Satyadev, *Europe ki Sukhad*).	192
5.4-i and 5.4-ii	Two sample advertisements put out by Satyadev (from *The Leader*, 10 February 1912, 2; *The Leader*, 14 March 1912, 2).	207
5.5	Satyadev's passport (from L/PJ/7/12023, IOR, BL).	208
7.1-i and 7.1-ii	Satyabhakt in middle age and as an old man (from Satyabhakt, *Gorilla*, 1; "Index of Photographs, No. 55", 1974, ACH, JNU).	249
7.2-i and 7.2-ii	Two books by Satyabhakt – *Bolshevism Kya Hai* and *Karl Marx* (from Satyabhakt, *Bolshevism Kya Hai*; idem, *Karl Marx*).	270
7.3-i and 7.3-ii	A list of books available in Satyabhakt's bookshop (from F. 7, Acc. 299, PMML).	273

Abbreviations

Deptt	Department
JPTM	Jat-Pat Torak Mandal
Judl	Judicial
Home Poll	Home (Political) Department
IOR, BL	India Office Library and Records, British Library, London
MJKA	*Mere Jeevan ke Anubhav*
NAI	National Archives of India, New Delhi
PMML	Prime Ministers' Museum and Library, New Delhi
NNR	*Native Newspaper Reports of UP* (also called *Selections from Vernacular Newspapers* and *Notes on the Press*)
PAI	*(Secret) Police Abstracts of Intelligence of UP Government*
SKM	*Swatantrata ki Khoj Mein arthat Meri Atm Katha*
UP	The United Provinces of Agra and Oudh (later known as Uttar Pradesh)
VSPM	*Vichaar Swatantrya ke Prangan Mein*

Note on Translation and Transliteration

ALL TRANSLATIONS FROM Hindi to English are my own. I have not used diacritics and opted instead for a phonetic representation of sound. Recurrent Hindi words are included and explained in the Glossary and therefore not italicised in the narrative, while those appearing only once, as well as phrases and poems, are italicised and translated where they occur.

The Bibliography contains translations of titles of Hindi books and articles. In some cases the English renditions are neither exact nor literal but instead convey the essence of the content.

The names of the four central protagonists of this book have been spelt differently in various archives and publications. I have standardised them and omitted the final "a" (Santram, not Santrama; Satyadev, not Satyadeva). Santram adopted the surname BA, and most of his writings show his name as "Santram BA". At some places he simply signed as "Santram". In some government files his name is recorded as "Sant Ram". I have used "Santram" throughout, except when directly quoting from sources.

Yashoda Devi is occasionally mentioned in documents as "Jasoda Debi" or "Yasoda Devi". I consistently refer to her as "Yashoda".

Swami Satyadev Parivrajak's early writings bear the name "Satyadev". In government files and English newspaper reports he appears as "Satya Deva" or "Sat Deo". In his later writings he used "Satyadev Parivrajak". I have used "Satyadev" throughout.

In government reports and English newspapers Satyabhakt is frequently referenced as "Satya Bhakta" or "Satya Bhakte", though in his Hindi writings he wrote his name as a single word. I have employed "Satyabhakt".

Acknowledgements

WHEN EMBARKING on this research journey, my focus shifted from my usual exploration of broad social histories to a more intimate examination of the lives of four remarkable individuals. Over the past eight years, these individuals not only became the subjects of my inquiry but also seamlessly integrated themselves into the fabric of my daily life. Their stories became a part of our household, woven into our everyday conversations.

As this book materialises, it bears the indelible imprints of numerous people, institutions, friends, and family who have sustained and nourished me in countless ways.

The research support and grants extended over the course of these eight years by the Institution of Eminence, Delhi University, and the Department of History have been instrumental in facilitating this research. I am particularly indebted to my two diligent research assistants, Aakhya Isha and Samran Ahmad, who helped prepare the manuscript meticulously. Within the department I am grateful to my colleagues, including Parul Pandya Dhar, Aparna Balachandran, Seema Bawa, Raziuddin Aquil, Shalini Shah, Prabhu Mohapatra, Sanghamitra Mishra, Rahul Govind, Shalin Jain, Santosh Rai, and many others. The friendly environment in the department has been a constant source of encouragement, even during challenging times.

During my three-month deputation as a Visiting Professor and ICCR Chair at the Institute of South Asian, Tibetan, and Buddhist Studies, University of Vienna, I had the privilege of dedicating my time to writing Chapter 5, focusing on Satyadev and his travels. I am grateful to Martin Gaenszle, and especially Alaka Chudal, for their gracious hospitality. Alaka, who was also delving into writings of the self in Hindi, engaged in fruitful conversations with me that enriched my research.

In 2022, while a Visiting Fellow at the Neubauer Collegium for Culture and Society at the University of Chicago, I was delighted by the opportunity to engage with distinguished scholars and friends, including Dipesh Chakrabarty, Rochona Majumdar, Andrew Ollett, Ulrike Stark, Tyler Williams, and Anand Venkatkrishnan. These insightful discussions added depth to my research on Santram and Satyabhakt in particular.

Various collaborative projects have been a source of personal and academic growth. Partnering with S. Shankar from the University of Hawaii for a special issue of the journal *Biography* on "Caste and Life Narratives", which was also published as a book, was a deeply fulfilling experience. I also thank Cynthia Franklin and John Zuern of *Biography* for hosting an enriching workshop at the university. Many participants, including Tapan Basu, Bindu Menon, Y.S. Alone, Mukul Sharma, and Sumit Baudh, engaged in thought-provoking debates, which helped me foreground caste and life narratives as reciprocally generative sites of serious study. Subsequent collaborations with S. Shankar and K. Satyanarayan on "Critical Caste Studies" further broadened my perspective.

I also had the pleasure of working with Laura Brueck, Hans Harder, and Shobna Nijhawan on a project titled "Literary Sentiments in the Vernacular", which culminated in a special issue of the journal *South Asia* and a book. I also thank Shobna for providing occasional articles from *Sudha*.

My heartfelt gratitude to the numerous libraries and archives that have aided me in unearthing rare and invaluable sources. Among these sanctuaries, the Hindi Sahitya Sammelan in Allahabad stands out as a veritable treasure trove, and I thank Ravinder Yadav-ji for his assistance there. In Allahabad, Swatantra Pandey at the Bharti Bhavan Library also helped in providing some crucial materials on ayurveda.

I wish to warmly acknowledge Abhijit, Rajarshi, and Gopal of the Centre for Studies in Social Sciences, Kolkata, for sharing select files of Hindi magazines that had been digitised through the Centre's collaboration with the British Library. Bhairav Dutt and B.D. Sharma of the Marwari Pustakalaya in Chandni Chowk helped in locating some of the older books. Sabhanarayan Mishra at the Nagari Pracharini

Sabha library in Banaras offered significant assistance. Vijay Jha's help was instrumental in locating elusive articles from *Chand*.

The British Library has always been a delightful place for research. Within its hallowed halls I stumbled upon a rare correspondence between Santram and Marie Stopes, unearthed Satyadev's passport, and discovered a trove of books. My deep appreciation to Tom Derrick and Graham Jevon for digitising quarterly lists of Indian books and periodicals.

The Prime Ministers' Museum and Library at Teen Murti has become a second home to me, consistently astounding me with its extensive collection. Similarly, the National Archives of India, particularly its proscribed materials, files pertaining to the 1930 census, and individual collections proved useful. I thank Surendra Kumar, H. Manglem, and Ved Swami from the Archives of Contemporary History at Jawaharlal Nehru University, for providing assistance in my search for materials on Satyabhakt.

Laura A. Ring, the Southern Asian Studies Librarian at the University of Chicago Library, provided access to various materials and tracts within the library's collection. I owe a debt of gratitude to Srikant for making available an essential file on Satyadev from the Patna State Archives.

Interviews conducted and insights shared generously by friends and scholars, who are experts in specific genres and fields, have been invaluable resources for this research. Satnam Singh and Shanti Swaroop Bauddh of Samyak Prakashan provided important inputs on the life of Santram. I extend my gratitude to Madhu Chaddha, the great-granddaughter of Santram, who generously shared information and photographs. My profound thanks to Mark Juergensmeyer for sharing his unpublished interview notes with Santram BA. My interactions with Mahesh Prajapati of the Santram BA Foundation have been inspirational.

Conducting an interview with Samir Sharma, the great-grandson of Yashoda Devi, and Rachna Sharma, Yashoda Devi's granddaughter-in-law, in the comfort of Yashoda Devi's beautiful home in Allahabad, was an absolute delight. They graciously shared with me some rare photographs of Yashoda Devi and regaled me with some fascinating anecdotes about her life. A telephonic conversation with another family member, Sudha Sharma, provided additional inputs. As always, my tremendous gratitude goes to Roopa and Suneet, my family in Allahabad, who not only assisted me in connecting with Samir-ji, but have consistently extended their warmth and hospitality during my numerous visits to Allahabad. Sabhajit Shukla, Additional Assistant Secretary of the Nagari Pracharini Sabha Library in Allahabad, offered useful information on Satyadev's connection with the Sabha. Sujata Mody provided helpful references on Satyadev. Prior to this research, my academic focus had never delved into the realm of communism. However, the guidance and wealth of information shared by Karmendu Shishir, who has an encyclopaedic knowledge of Hindi sources, was crucial in my exploration of Satyabhakt. Additionally, I thank Aditya Nigam for reviewing my drafts on Satyabhakt. I extend my appreciation to Jeremy Seabrook for his inputs. As always, I warmly thank Permanent Black and Rukun Advani, my esteemed publisher and dear friend, for the unwavering support and collaboration, a partnership that has been instrumental in bringing my monographs to fruition.

Parts of this work have been presented at various invited lectures, conferences, and workshops at the University of Chicago, University of Vienna, AAS Seattle Conference, Heidelberg University, Northwestern University, Queen's University, 25th Paris ECSAS, MLA 2020 Seattle Convention, 50th Annual Conference on South Asia at the University of Wisconsin-Madison, SOAS, Govind Ballabh Pant Institute in Allahabad, Ashoka University, Jawaharlal Nehru University, and Delhi University. I am grateful for the valuable feedback provided by friends, scholars, and participants at these presentations. In particular, I extend my appreciation to Ishita Pande, Anjali Arondekar, Rachel Berger, Douglas Haynes, V. Geetha, Durba Mitra, Ram Rawat, Mahesh Rangarajan, Aparna Vaidik, Madhavi Menon, Ravikant, Preetha Mani, Stephen Legg, Akshaya Mukul, Anand Swamy, and Kama Maclean.

Earlier versions of parts of the book have appeared in academic journals such as *Biography, Porn Studies, South Asia: Journal of South Asian Studies, The Indian Economic and Social History Review, Economic and Political Weekly*, *Asian Medicine*, and *Studies in History*. Valuable inputs provided by anonymous referees helped in facilitating multiple rounds of revisions.

I would like to thank a variety of individuals and organisations for the photos and illustrations used in this book. My grateful acknowledgement to them all – they are given as the sources after the captions in the list of figures which follows the table of contents above.

Finally, a big hug to my sisters – Ritu, Diksha, Roopa, Divya, Tanu, Sumedha, Priya, and Megha – who have been the anchors of my life. Their unwavering support, non-judgemental presence, and steadfast commitment have been my constant source of strength.

During this period, my son Ishaan embarked on his PhD in Hindu Religious Studies at UC Berkeley, offering me a different perspective that challenged my way of thinking. His innovative and out-of-the-box intellectual approach, even during our occasional disagreements, has been greatly stimulating.

I find myself always struggling to find the words to express my love and deep appreciation for Mukul, my soulmate, who has stood by me through thick and thin.

In the course of completing this book I lost my mother, Damyanti Gupta. I miss her every single day, and it is to her enduring legacy that I dedicate this work.

Introduction
Vernacular Freedoms and Life Narratives

LOCATED IN HISTORY and literature, this book is an attempt to write histories of the social – by which I mean society, the private-public sphere, and the worldviews of a populace – through individual actors, life narratives, genres, and subjects visible in the Hindi print culture of early-twentieth-century North India. Amidst the colonial adversities of their time, the four protagonists of this book envisaged utopian (and at times dystopian) dreams of vernacular freedoms – i.e. politically, socially, and culturally autonomous idioms and sensibilities of freedom – through their distinct vantage points of caste, ayurveda, travel, and communism. The book explores multiple linkages between vernacular literary nonfictional forms and genres, Hindi–Hindu identities, and conceptualisations of autonomy and freedom in modern India.

I first encountered Yashoda Devi (1890–1942), the leading woman ayurvedic chikitsak from Allahabad, in 1997 when I was studying Hindi didactic manuals for my first book, *Sexuality, Obscenity, Community* (2001). Similarly, I came to know Santram BA (1887–1988), the anticaste crusader, more closely while researching intercaste marriages for a later book, *The Gender of Caste* (2016). However, these writers featured only tangentially in those books, whereas they are central to the present one. My work has consistently revolved around certain key themes.

First, I have in much of my past work sought to show the reconstitution of Hindu patriarchies in early-twentieth-century North India, and second the gendered aspects of caste dynamics over the same period, arguing that these worked in tandem with the rise of an aggressive Hindu nationalism which attempted embracing Dalits within a hierarchical Hindu fold – which, in turn, harboured inherent contradictions. Third, my primary analytic lens for gendered readings of social histories of this time and region has been the relatively understudied Hindi *bhasha* (vernacular) archive of popular nonfictional writings, ranging from didactic manuals, pamphlets, books, magazines, and newspapers to advertising images and cartoons. And fourth, the thrust of my research has consistently revolved around broader collective and social histories of gender, caste, and religious identities. Individual stories have, until now, been peripheral to my writings.

In this book I attempt to write histories of the social through narratives of the self. In particular, what fascinates me are figures who, though not canonical authors, fell off the grid and were written out of the grand narratives of literature and history. This seems unwarranted: these marginalised and minoritised individuals had a ubiquitous presence within the early-twentieth-century Hindi print bazaar of North India and have continually surfaced in unexpected corners over my 35-year research journey. *Hindi Hindu Histories* therefore puts a spotlight on four individuals who were perennially "others", characters in the footnotes of literature and history. This is a fate they did not deserve because their writings, though now available only in a handful of libraries and archives, represent pioneering contributions in their respective fields.

In the nascent stages of this research I compiled a roster of eight authors who encompass a range of intellectual and thematic domains. This group included Gangaprasad Upadhyay, an important figure within the Arya Samaj movement, who made prolific contributions to its ideological tenets; Jyotirmayi Thakur of Kanpur, whose extensive writings delved into gender and domesticity; Haridas Manik, who specialised in crafting popular and mythical history books; and Krishnakant Malaviya, editor of the influential political weekly *Abhyudaya* and author of provocative treatises on matters connected with sexual relations. However, as the project expanded I soon realised that tackling an octet would be overly ambitious and consequently narrowed the focus to a more manageable quartet, albeit one connected with an expansive landscape of genres. Alongside Yashoda and Santram I focus here on Swami Satyadev Parivrajak (1879–1961), a maverick travel writer, and Satyabhakt (1896–1985), a leading communist journalist.

Santram and Satyadev hailed from the Hoshiarpur and Ludhiana districts of Punjab, respectively. Yashoda's early years were spent in Badaun and Bareilly, with a relocation to Allahabad following her marriage. Satyabhakt received his early education in Bharatpur, Rajasthan. Notably, these four belonged to the Shudra, Khatri (considered a synonym of Kshatriya by some), Brahmin, and Bania (Vaishya) varnas, respectively.[1] While each wrote on various subjects, the central analytic category for Santram was caste, for Yashoda gender, for Satyadev religion, and for Satyabhakt class. While venturing into a range of genres, each specialised in one, which then defined their legacy. Thus, Santram's work rose to prominence from his contributions to anticaste and sexology literature, and from his extensive translations into Hindi. Yashoda gained renown for her ayurvedic knowledge and health writings, instruction manuals, self-help books, household recipes, and cookbooks. Satyadev left his distinctive mark through travelogues, chronicling his experiences in the US and Europe, along with autobiographical works. Satyabhakt specialised in crafting popular communist pamphlets as well as producing apocalyptic and utopian texts.

So, why have I chosen within the same book to include authors from different regions, castes, and genres, each with distinct and dissimilar rhetorical purposes? What lies in between Santram's anticaste, intercaste marriage crusade and heterosexual sexological ethics; Yashoda's affinity with ayurveda, culinary-household recipes, and female bodies infused with moral-reformist values; Satyadev's quixotic travel narratives and obsession with a muscular ascetic Hindu self and Hindu sangathan; and Satyabhakt's endeavours to reconcile communism with Hinduism in pursuit of a communist utopia? As already noted, despite their extensive contributions, Santram,

---

[1] I thank Karmendu Shihir for information on Satyabhakt's caste.

Yashoda, Satyadev, and Satyabhakt have been minoritised in histories of caste, medicine, travel, and communism respectively. Although three of the four went on to live well beyond India's independence, their literary careers began in the early twentieth century. Their most active, prolific, and creative phase was between 1910 and 1950, during which they also subtly negotiated their own relationship with colonial authority and its dominant presence.

Located firmly in the Hindi print market of the early twentieth century, they were part of the publicists who made Hindi their primary tool of expression. While Santram was a polyglot, and the others had varying linguistic capabilities, they consciously chose to write in Hindi because the language was central to the world they identified with and understood the nuances of. Despite employing Khari Boli Hindi as their medium, each raconteur debunked in their own way a standardised, Sanskritised Hindi, and instead translated, vernacularised, and localised it, designing their prose in an eclectic, composite, and simple Hindi with a keen awareness of their readership. While carving their niche and honing their skills in particular genres and subjects, they focused primarily on nonfictional prose narratives, evident in their books and articles. Because they saw themselves as educators performing seva and service for the nation and the language, many of their writings included didactic elements. Concurrently, they actively engaged in a performance of the self, self-representation, and self-fashioning. Santram authored a comprehensive autobiographical memoir, while Satyadev penned two autobiographies. Although both were drawn to the Arya Samaj, their autobiographies represent two spectrums of the field because they put them to very different uses: one to present a trenchant critique of caste, the other to uphold the ideals of Hindu sangathan and a Hindu nation. Yashoda continually published letters in her praise from satisfied clients, stamping herself as an authority in the field of ayurveda, and Satyabhakt ensured the preservation of his selfhood as a prominent communist by depositing his papers in the National Archives and the Teen Murti Library.

While crafting selves in their chosen genres, these individuals were not merely authors; they were also activists and founders of organisations and institutions. Santram founded the Jat-Pat Torak Mandal (JPTM; the name translates as, roughly, "Organisation to Break Caste") in 1922, and remained its driving force, dedicated to combating caste discrimination and actively promoting intercaste marriages. Yashoda inaugurated her own Stri Aushadhalaya (Women's Dispensary) in Allahabad around 1908, possibly the first of its kind in India, which garnered a remarkable clientele. Despite being a firm individualist, Satyadev established the Satyagyan Niketan (literally, Home for the Knowledge of Truth), a platform through which he published his books and retained copyright. In 1936 he acquired substantial property for the Niketan in Jwalapur, Haridwar, ultimately bequeathing it to the Nagari Pracharini Sabha – a reputed organisation that had been set up to promote the Devanagari script – in 1943. The last of these four, Satyabhakt, was the founder of the Indian Communist Party and chief organiser of the first Indian Communist Conference at Kanpur in December 1925. Additionally, he opened a bookshop called the Socialist Bookshop, again perhaps the first of its kind in North India, and briefly started the Satyug Press.

Another central thread running through the book concerns the cultural and literary portrayal of sexualities and masculinities as analytical categories within the Hindi print realm. Three of the individuals in focus embodied these as critical tropes of social identity. Santram was a pioneering translator of Marie Stopes' sexology writings into Hindi. He also vehemently opposed brahmacharya, advocated birth control, and proposed a heterosexual ethics. Yashoda provided a piercing critique of masturbation and championed conjugal sexual restraint. Meanwhile, Satyadev ardently promoted ascetic masculinity and brahmacharya as essential life principles.

Crucially, while belonging to the broad spectrum of the middle class, all four were rooted in a Hindu orientation and placed themselves within a Hindu framework, implicitly or explicitly. Each selectively drew on their understanding of Hinduism to develop conceptual and theoretical tools for different ends, which signified their limitations but also certain creative possibilities. Finally, in their literary and aesthetic creations they frequently foregrounded vernacular dreams of utopian freedom and autonomy. Their ideals of freedom came from varied visions – a casteless society, disease-free families based on ayurvedic wisdom, a Hindu nation, and a communist Ram Rajya. They thus put forth ideologically different forms of vernacular freedom, unsettling the concept and reshaping its very meaning. Collectively, these effervescent narrators and communicators produced an extensive body of work, spanning prose, essays, autobiographies, translations, and didactic literature which collectively displays a remarkable diversity and ecumenical literary expression.

And yet all the writers I have chosen seem to lack internal coherence, a singular identity, or a permanent address. They simultaneously navigate contradictory terrains within themselves, and in opposition to each other. At various moments their views and actions can appear narrow and eclectic, inward and outward looking, conservative and progressive, observant and heedless. They have the dexterity to both reaffirm and break boundaries, to enslave and liberate, to reassemble and dismantle. Santram's anticaste politics and iconoclasm coexist with his faith in Hinduism; Yashoda's gender ideals work in tandem with her critique of men; Satyadev's anti-Muslim venom and Hindutva nationalist rhetoric comfortably coincide with a cosmopolitan celebration of transnationalism; and Satyabhakt's communism aligns seamlessly with his faith-based politics.

These writers occupy a liminal, enigmatic space: Santram between Gandhi and Ambedkar; Yashoda between traditional and modern medical methodologies; Satyadev between transnationalism and rabid Hindu nationalism; and Satyabhakt between communism and Hinduism. They also challenge the dichotomous binaries of theoretical vs empirical, English vs vernacular, and the West vs the rest. It is this multi-straddling that makes them fascinating characters – they defy easy labels and reflect the paradoxes of their times. My book thus seeks to capture the plurality of voices and concerns in public debates in the Hindi print sphere of colonial India. Although occasionally influenced by sectarianism and normative assumptions, the creative and innovative achievements of these authors need to be highlighted in the history of Hindi and North Indian Hinduism.

The book thus offers a vivid historical spectacle of Hindi and Hindu. Rooted in plural histories, it repudiates singular narratives, monolithic signposts, and totalising perspectives. It undermines the idea of a standardised, homogenised, and rigid categorisation of Hindi, Hindu, and History. In the sections of this introduction that follow I outline the broader contexts and discussions that emanate around some of the keywords of this work – vernacular as a methodology, the Hindi–Hindu public sphere and its manifold paradigms, writings of the self, and the meanings of freedom – all of which shaped the scripts of these authors. However, I do not touch on formulations of caste, ayurveda, travel, or communism – those are discussed in detail in various chapters.

Malleable Circuits of the Vernacular[2]

When I began my doctoral research in 1996, I was keen to explore the interface between Hindu nationalism, sexuality, and gender in early-twentieth-century North India. I soon realised that while the emergence of communalism had been done to death in the scholarly literature, there had been little work on its links with sexuality. As I explored the "conventional" official archives I drew almost a blank: most of the data on riots, cow-protection movements, and the issue of noisy music near mosques was in many ways blind to gendered politics. However, I stumbled on a rich repertoire of vernacular materials in the bylanes and small local libraries of Allahabad, Lucknow, Banaras, and Kanpur, and among the uncatalogued Hindi books at the British Library. These sources brimmed with potential for detailed discussion and analysis on the areas that interested me.[3] My passionate affair with the vernacular began then and has continued unabated since. In *The Gender of Caste* I again explored vernacular print as a critical tool to examine the representation of Dalits, and to argue that differentials of gender were critical

---

[2] This section draws from Gupta, "Malleability of the Vernacular". It is also informed by Gupta, Brueck, Harder, and Nijhawan, "Introduction". I thank Laura Brueck, Hans Harder, and Shobna Nijhawan as co-authors.

[3] Gupta, *Sexuality, Obscenity*.

in structuring patterns of domination and subordination. *Hindi Hindu Histories* too unsettles the logic of the archive: as a historian of modern India my constitutive rather than supplementary archive has become the under-read vernacular – in my case Hindi popular tracts, magazines, and cartoons.

There have been insightful critiques of the semantic connotations of the "vernacular" in India. Etymologically the word is based on the Latin term *vernaculus*, meaning native, homely, vulgar, belonging to slaves; for this reason Nirmal Selvamony, for example, dismisses the vernacular as a "homoarchic mode of existence".[4] And, pointing to the drawbacks of its terminology, Durba Mitra sees its use as a "systematic obfuscation and erasure of diverse forms of knowledge from inclusion in a formalised discipline."[5] Some choose to speak only of "Indian languages and literatures".[6] The scholar of Hindi Francesca Orsini, while not averse to the term "vernacular", prefers "multilingual" as it "recognizes that no language is an island, and no language alone is enough."[7] However, many others deploy the word for its varied flavours: the political theorist Partha Chatterjee sees the vernacular as a discursive space which is less alienated from the popular.[8] S. Shankar refers to the vernacular as a "point of vantage from which to counter the glare of the global", "a toolbox of critical theory",[9] whose perspectives "are no more worthy of automatic dismissal from theoretical discourse" than those of the transnational.[10] The authority on Kerala's literature, Udaya Kumar too perceives the vernacular as "marked by innovative transactions with local and cosmopolitan idioms and languages of earlier and newer epochs."[11]

The word thus invokes debates ranging from scepticism to investment: is a vernacular signifying practices narrow or capacious;

[4] Selvamony, "Vernacular as Homoarchic".
[5] Mitra, "Sexuality and the History", 1225.
[6] For example Kothari, *Uneasy Translations*.
[7] Orsini, "Vernacular", 205.
[8] Chatterjee, "Introduction", 21.
[9] Shankar, "The Vernacular", 191–2.
[10] Shankar, *Flesh and Fish*, 21.
[11] Kumar, *Writing the First*, 182.

a vehicle of hegemonic appropriation or a marker of dissent; a cementer or interrupter of normative scripts? The answer may simply be that it can be both since its meanings and uses are contingent on its contexts, and on the locations of its writers and readers. It is an expansive, polysemic, porous, and malleable mode. The practice and potential of employing a feminist and a Dalit vernacular, not just as an object of analysis but as a critical methodology of the marginalised, is a case in point. At the same time, many Dalit intellectuals have interpreted the acquisition of English as a subversion of power. Thus, English too, like the vernacular, can be both at different times: a means of neo-savarna oppression, deprivation, and disempowerment as well as a language of survival, decolonisation, liberation, and enfranchisement.[12]

Moreover, the vernacular is not just a substitute or shorthand for widely spoken and understood Indian languages, as opposed to "elite" ones, particularly Sanskrit, Persian, and English. Preetha Mani, for example, argues that "colonial era vernacularization positioned English as *the* paradigmatic vernacular."[13] There are also, for instance, many Hindis within Hindi. Nor is the vernacular only a marker of subordination to higher linguistic codes and more powerful knowledge systems. Santram, a Shudra in the caste hierarchy of Punjab, through his translations of Marie Stopes and Sanskrit sex classics utilised Hindi as an effective vernacular tool for subverting both English and Sanskrit, and to write back to both the Empire and the colonised elites. The relationship between English, Sanskrit, and a vernacular Hindi appeared in his work as one of transactions and negotiations rather than impositions.

The vernacular is also not an antithesis of cosmopolitan or modern, as all languages are, or can be, vernacular, cosmopolitan, and modern: Satyadev and Santram vernacularised English and cosmopolitanised Hindi. Nor is the vernacular simply interchangeable with traditional, indigenous, folk, local, or regional. The location of the vernacular for Yashoda was contemporary and modern, even as she regularly drew from mythological indigenous traditions and

---

[12] Uma, Rani, and Manohar, "Introduction".
[13] Mani, *The Idea*, 7.

pasts. All the raconteurs under discussion simultaneously deployed local, Indian, and Western writers and idioms to carve their knowledge systems in the vernacular, providing a bridge between the global and the local, universal utopias and grounded realities, Western and indigenous knowledges.

Nor is the vernacular just a linguistic category or a lexical device. It of course encompasses *bhasha sahitya* (literature in the vernacular), and can be a synonym for one's *matribhasha* (mother tongue), which questions language hegemony of any kind. But it has also been deployed generically for imaginations, emotions, longings, tongues, and varied forms of knowledge, and its meanings have crossed art, music, sports, crafts, sexology, and science.[14] A vernacular architecture, landscape, and aesthetics, for example, may involve the use of resources that respond to local climates.[15] It thus signifies a way of thinking and a specific sensibility.

Nor is the vernacular simply synonymous with the colonised, the enslaved, or the "inferior". Missionaries, for example, effectively deployed the vernacular to propagate Christianity in colonial India. Moreover, the non-vernacular archive, more often than not, largely records the extraordinary, the cataclysmic, and the official, while the vernacular is a tactic and practice of the everyday, a language for the expression of lived thought and mundane material conditions.

While the vernacular may intersect with the lingual, it is also a political site. Its focus is seen to lie in the realm of fiction. Carrying a subaltern tinge, it is usually not regarded as a "serious" or an "authentic" archival source.[16] Scholarship in the vernacular is often not taken into account beyond its respective regions, with attitudes to it oscillating between anecdotal recognition and neglect. It is perceived as lacking capacity in relation to social science expositions, which continue to rely for their methodological underpinnings on the West.

What happens if we revise this provincialisation and empiricalisation of the vernacular? It has been noted that settled ways of divid-

[14] Pande, "Introduction", 1098–1101.
[15] Suartika and Nichols, *Reframing the Vernacular*.
[16] For a critique: Chatterjee, "Introduction".

ing up the human sciences need to be thoroughly questioned.[17] Describing a "cosmopolitan vernacular" in premodern and early modern India, the Sanskrit authority Sheldon Pollock goes on to show that well into the twentieth century vernacular intellectuals produced works of enormous learning, demonstrating mastery of the entire histories of their traditions.[18] The political theorist Sudipta Kaviraj argues that in some ways "vernacular critical thought" was "more original and more intransigent towards Western reasoning than what appeared in English."[19] And the reputed Tamil scholar A.R. Venkatachalapathy notes that in the early twentieth century "while history writing in English was almost exclusively concerned with dynastic history and obsessed with chronology, a major strand of Tamil historiography turned towards cultural history and literary historiography."[20] The cultural critic Rashmi Sadana underlines that two leading "Indian novelists who write in English – Amitav Ghosh and Arundhati Roy – affirm their loyalty to 'bhasha worlds' as a way to assert their own politics" and "loyalty to particular causes, people, or ideas."[21]

In certain ways the protagonists of this book reversed this process. Writing in popular Hindi, they selectively and flexibly appropriated English and Western ideas while also using the vernacular as a mode of resistance against unwanted intrusions. A vernacularisation of the political universals of race by Santram, biomedicine by Yashoda, communism by Satyabhakt, and freedom by Satyadev helped forge strategic provincialities and recognise what Homi Bhabha refers to as historically contingent alternatives that acknowledged different and plural ways of knowing and thinking.[22] Bhasha archives are thus critical for writing histories of colonial India.

Resonances of colonialism are palpable in the formation of the vernacular. While the British often deployed the vernacular to belittle

---

[17] Spivak, "Teaching Literature".
[18] Pollock, "Cosmopolitan and Vernacular in History".
[19] Kaviraj, *The Trajectories*, 63.
[20] Venkatachalapathy, *In Those Days*, 4.
[21] Sadana, *English Heart*, 152, 169.
[22] Bhabha, "Unsatisfied", 193, 205.

Indian languages, the vibrant vernaculars, rather than English, were what significantly contributed to expanding and commercialising the print market and, from the late nineteenth century, making the written word available as a mass commodity at a relatively low cost in urban India. Despite wavering colonial support, vernacular publications thrived and were sustained on the one hand by public institutions, libraries, publishing houses, presses, and the laws of the market, and on the other a substantial growth in urbanisation, the middle classes, literacy levels, solitary reading practices, and distinct vernacular publics.[23] Providing a panoptic view of the growth of vernaculars in different regions, the historian of modern India Sumit Sarkar points out that vernacular materials sometimes received colonial patronage, or faced state censorship, but were also often outside its gaze and grasp.[24] For example, sexual issues in the vernacular were often disliked for their perceived vulgarities by a section of puritanical British officials, but creativity in the use of certain idioms often allowed Indian writers to get away with what was branded as "obscene". The registers of vernacularisation in late colonial India were varied, as they had a stake in politics and changing social mores which contributed significantly in reproducing, transforming, and contesting gender, caste, class, and religious identities. The vernacular print sphere also marginalised Sanskrit and Persian, and paved the way for the standardisation, modernisation, and democratisation of languages and literatures. There was an explosion of vernacular prose in periodicals, newspapers, tracts, novels, travel accounts, and autobiographies.

Thus, while steering clear of essentialisations of the vernacular as the most natural medium of expression or as an identitary trope, I still adopt vernacularity as a critical mode of reading and writing, and for new theoretical methodologies.[25] Vanja Hamzic, while study-

---

[23] Ghosh, *Power in Print*; Venkatachalapathy, *The Province*. For print cultures in UP: Orsini, *The Hindi Public*; Gupta, *Sexuality, Obscenity*, 30–4; Nijhawan, *Women and Girls*; Stark, *An Empire of Books*, 1–28; Mody, *The Making*.

[24] Sarkar, *Modern Times*, 309, 326–72.

[25] Gupta, *et al.*, "Introduction", 811–12.

ing discourses on sexual and gender diversity in the Muslim world, builds a strong case for "insurrectionary vernacular knowledge" as a prerogative of any critical project. Vernacular taxonomies and epistemologies provide potentialities for crafting new, noisy, and robust knowledges not dependent on, and even challenging, dominant and mainstream discursive social practices.[26] All the key players of this book deployed in their different ways parables available in the vernacular, not only within narrow political and nationalist frames, and not only against colonialism and Western hegemony, but also for plural discursive insurrections that provide tools and methods for destabilising social histories of caste, medicine, travel, and communism. And, even as Satyadev also made the vernacular a site of power, control, and exclusion, while Yashoda used it to uphold normative codes for high-caste Hindu women, a vernacular vocabulary became simultaneously a way of giving words to delegitimised people and subjects, and to create meanings of resistance. A vocabulary of the Hindu vernacular and popular knowledge helped Satyabhakt in providing an ethical edge to communist utopian desires. Similarly, Santram mobilised protest against caste and endogamy by camouflaging some of his radical ideas in idioms of the shastric and the vaigyanik which were legible only through rationalities specific to the vernacular. Precisely because of its malleability, fluidity, and innovative transactions, the vernacular held out a productive promise to all these writers.

Translation is intrinsic to the vernacular, and to this book. Prathama Banerjee says the history of any intellectual tradition is also a history of translation.[27] Translation is a process through which individuals, languages, and cultures meet, interact, contend with one another, and transfer meaning from one semiotic system to another, thus problematising all assumptions about authorship as solitary. Writing in English but being based largely within the Hindi archives, I am automatically invested in a project of translation since I attempt to offer critical access and renewed attention to margin-

[26] Hamzic, *Sexual and Gender*, 9, 143, 194.
[27] Banerjee, *Elementary Aspects*, 215.

alised vernacular voices.[28] Beyond this, the four central figures in this book were also frequent translators. Rendering English, French, Russian, Persian, and Sanskrit texts into Hindi and vernacularising them, translation became for them a political, ethical, and aesthetic act for anticaste praxis, for vernacular sexology, for proclaiming the relevance of communism, and for manoeuvring their marginality into authority. As has been argued, "manipulation" is integral to translation as one transmits, adapts, and transforms texts to suit one's purpose. Thus, "a translator *creates* but *copies* (or *rewrites*), reproduces *faithfully* but has scope for *intervention*, aims at *equivalence* but ends up producing *difference*."[29] The translations by the protagonists of this book nuance arguments about colonial-era translation politics and practices being central to the project of imperialism, and being based on asymmetrical relations of power that erase indigenous narratives. Translations are more than a two-way process, signalling not only a rendition from a regional, local, or vernacular language into English, but also the other way round. While the colonisers produced "strategies of containment", and reinforced "hegemonic versions of the colonised" through translation,[30] the colonised utilised it for creative transactions in everyday life, to articulate subaltern and subordinated discourses, and to voice varied desires and freedoms in the vernacular. Given, for example, his location in the social hierarchy, Santram, by translating "taboo" texts, used it as a statement of strength and protest.

The vernacular, while pervasive, is also often positioned as marginal. While adopting vernacularity, the historical and literary journey of this book centres on "those that slip through official sources", "the popular and unpopular, marginalised and condemned."[31] Talking of margins is not only productive for the retrieval of voices and visions, it also shows such writings as a vibrant part of the underbelly and subcultures of anticolonial Indian life. All the protagonists of

---

[28] For indispensability of translation for the vernacular: Venuti, *The Translation*; Shankar, *Flesh and Fish,* 103–42; Kothari, *Uneasy Translations*; Niranjana, *Siting Translation*.

[29] Santaemilia, *Gender, Sex and Translation*, 1.

[30] Niranjana, *Siting Translation*, 3.

[31] Blackburn and Dalmia, "Introduction", 21.

my stories were on the margins of the political left, right, and centre. While starting an organisation, a clinic, or a party, they were dismissed from institutional structures. Satyadev, while an admirer of the Arya Samaj, remained on its periphery; Santram was reduced to a footnote in Ambedkar's anticaste history; Yashoda was never recognised by the ayurvedic mahamandals or its established bodies; and Satyabhakt was thrown out of the Communist Party. None of them was an official member of the Congress, the Hindu Mahasabha, or the Communist Party. Nonetheless, all of them had extensive reach; they left their footprint not only in the Hindi print arena but also on the shaping of modern mentalities.

Writing histories of a caste-oppressed devadasi collective, Anjali Arondekar argues that the provenance of the Gomantak Maratha Samaj represents an intersection of "archival abundance and historical minoritisation: it is both removed from the archival mandates that govern minoritised histories and, at the same time, intimately acquainted with them and their most subtle efforts on history-writing."[32] Outside centres of power, democratisation and the portability of print enabled subordinate castes, women, and communists to express their opinions, beliefs, and ideas, and their constant presence in books and other media of their time defies marginality. In foregrounding these writers as generative locations for theorising literature and history, my book proposes a radical heterogeneity within these fields. Caste, gender, religion, and class were made political questions by those at the margins of authority. Thus, Devi and Santram redeployed the language of classic, scientific, and medical authority to make claims of sexual autonomy and anticaste egalitarianism.

Hindi and Hindu: Negotiating Language, Literature, and Religion

The commercialisation of print led to a steady growth of presses and publishing houses, resulting in a concomitant proliferation of vernacular language publications. For instance, the number of printing presses in UP rose from 177 in 1878–9 to 568 in 1901–2 and

---

[32] Arondekar, *Abundance*, 17.

743 in 1925–6. By 1925–6 UP had surpassed Bengal in the production of vernacular books.³³ Amidst contentious debates and divides between Hindi and Urdu, which also often got mapped onto Hindu and Muslim religious identities, by 1925 publications in the Devanagari script far exceeded and surpassed those in the Nastaliq.³⁴ As Hindi became the dominant print language of a large section of the middle classes, reformers, and writers, a robust Hindi public sphere came to flourish in the heartland of the Gangetic plains. Several researchers have commented on diverse aspects of this rise of the Hindi language and literature in North India from the late nineteenth century.³⁵ Certain features stand out in this scholarship.

Firstly, the work of this group has ranged from studying the lives, writings, and contributions of pioneering authors and publishers such as Bharatendu Harischandra, Mahadevi Varma, Mahavir Prasad Dwivedi, Dularelal Bhargava, Hanuman Prasad Poddar, and Agyeya,³⁶ to the role of publishing houses like the Naval Kishore Press, the Ganga Pustak Mala, and the Gita Press,³⁷ in the promotion and consolidation of Hindi as a language of public discourse in the late nineteenth and early twentieth century. Alongside, two influential organisations that played a central role in advancing Hindi were the Nagari Pracharini Sabha, founded in Banaras in 1893, and the Hindi Sahitya Sammelan, established in 1910 in Allahabad. *Hindi Hindu Histories* extends this scholarship by focusing on overlooked

---

³³ Gupta, *Sexuality, Obscenity*, 50.
³⁴ *Report on the Administration of UP, 1923–24*, 91.
³⁵ Dalmia, *The Nationalization*; Gupta, *Sexuality, Obscenity*; King, *One Language*; Mani, *The Idea*; Mody, *The Making*; Mukul, *Gita Press*; idem, *Writer, Rebel, Soldier*; Nijhawan, *Hindi Publishing*; idem, *Women and Girls*; Orsini, *The Hindi Public*; Rai, *Hindi Nationalism*; Stark, *An Empire*. Also see Basu, *Hindi Dalit*; Dimitrova, *Hinduism and Hindi Theatre*; Govind, *Between Love*; Savary, *Evolution*; Schomer, *Mahadevi Varma*.
³⁶ For these writers see, respectively, Dalmia, *The Nationalization*; Schomer, *Mahadevi Varma*; Mody, *The Making*; Nijhawan, *Hindi Publishing*; Mukul, *Gita Press*; Mukul, *Writer, Rebel, Soldier*.
³⁷ For these presses see, respectively, Stark, *An Empire of Books*; Nijhawan, *Hindi Publishing*; Mukul, *Gita Press*.

individuals and organisations that substantially extended the world of Hindi, who advertised themselves aggressively, and who founded institutions as well as publishing houses: many of Santram's books, for example, were published by the JPTM, the organisation he founded. Yashoda had her own publishing house, the Devi Pustakalaya, and a printing press owned by her husband Sri Ram Sharma, the Banita Hitaishi Press, which together published almost all her books. Very early on, Satyadev decided to retain copyright over his books and published many of them in a series entitled Satya Granth Mala through his organisation called Satyagyan Niketan. Satyabhakt, as mentioned, started an enterprise in the shape of the Socialist Bookshop which also sold his books; he too tried his hand at publishing and printing through his own press, called the Satyug Press. Yashoda and Satyadev amassed considerable wealth through their Hindi writings and were among the leading commercial sensations of their times.

A second thread of scholarship surrounding the growing Hindi public sphere in our period has discussed distinct genres, i.e. short stories, plays, novels, women's periodicals, and popular pamphlets, which created new possibilities of imagining realism, literary modernity, sexuality, and nationalism.[38] Fiction, taking diverse shapes in novels, stories, poetry, and plays, has often been regarded as central to literary articulations in the colonial period. The canonical Hindi writers of these times, from Bharatendu to Premchand, are best known for their fictional narratives. Preetha Mani eloquently questions the central and superior status accorded to the novel as a symbol of modernity, vernacularity, and national assertion. She brings the short story to the fore, pointing out that the "operating literary distinction that colonial-era vernacularization processes established was between prose and poetry – not the novel and the short story."[39]

---

[38] For short stories, Mani, *The Idea*; for plays, Dimitrova, *Hinduism and Hindi Theatre*; for novels, Dalmia, *Fiction as History*, and Govind, *Between Love*; for periodicals, Nijhawan, *Hindi Publishing*, idem, *Women and Girls*, and Mody, *The Making of Modern*; for popular pamphlets, Gupta, *Sexuality, Obscenity*.

[39] Mani, *The Idea*, 24.

Prose thus became the dominant form of expression for familial and political matters; however, it was not just centred on the novel or the short story. In fact, the political and cultural moment was conducive to the growth of nonfictional and non-literary prose and genres in novel ways, which exploded through newspapers, periodicals, essays, pamphlets, travel accounts, and autobiographies.[40] The pre-eminence of nonfiction in modern times has been acknowledged: "Hybrid, innovative, and unconventional, creative nonfiction is the preeminent expression of our times . . . There's a special intimacy that comes from recognizing the voice of an essay or memoir as the author's, from listening to that author think and wonder, reminisce, confess, reflect."[41]

My protagonists, who in the main wrote specialised yet compelling nonfictional prose, fit this description. In relation to their favoured genres, I would agree with Derrida who famously said that "every text participates in one or several genres, there is no genreless text."[42] Genres, moreover, as has been argued, are "not fixed categories with clear-cut boundaries but constellations of rhetorical modes and formal structures grounded in varying degrees of fact . . . They are also shape-shifters, in a continual state of flux."[43] Guided by commercial and symbolic economies, my quartet seems to have seen genres as being not rule-bound, but rather dynamic, heterogeneous, flexible, and porous. Their nonfictional prose, indeed, puts a question mark on the centrality of fiction.

A third thread running through the scholarship on Hindi is the focus on linguistic divides and conflicts, particularly between Urdu and Hindi.[44] A characteristic of this linguistic warfare was an attempt to regulate and "purify" Hindi and purge it of Persian, Arabic, and Urdu flavours, to insist on a standardised grammar, syntax, and dialect, and to assert the supremacy of a manufactured Sanskritised Khari Boli. This transformed Hindi from conveying collective

---

[40] Gupta, *Sexuality, Obscenity*, 304; Nijhawan, *Women and Girls*; idem, *Hindi Publishing*; Orsini, *The Hindi Public*.

[41] Singer and Walker, "Introduction", 1.

[42] Derrida, "The Law of Genre", 65.

[43] Singer and Walker, "Introduction", 3.

[44] King, *One Language*.

imagination and liveliness into a purveyor of narrow sectarianism and regional chauvinism.⁴⁵ Hindi's linguistic nationalism and homogenising-hegemonic ambitions were deeply problematic for other Indian languages and regions, and for the forging of a larger unity.⁴⁶

Yet, such impositions from above found many dissenters within the larger heterogeneous and eclectic world of Hindi. As a lived language, with a wide variety of authors littered through its rich history, Hindi also reflected considerable flexibility and openness. Its wide reach was facilitated by its decentralised production, distribution, and consumption, while this also connected localities with regional, national, and global spheres. As a dynamic arbiter of modernity, Hindi print became a space for aesthetic experimentation. Articulating diverse forms, many writers drew from dialects like Awadhi, Bhojpuri, and Braj on the one hand, and classic, "elite" languages like Sanskrit and Persian on the other. Equally, they borrowed their ideas from other literatures, regions, and countries – from Bengal and Punjab to West Europe and the Soviet Union. The likes of Premchand, Rahul Sankrityayan, and the Chhayavadi poets reflect the varied nature of Hindi writing. Many women and subordinate castes debunked the use of chaste Hindi in their works and instead cast their writings in a popular and accessible version of the language. Shobna Nijhawan has shown how many women's journals of the early twentieth century maintained a balance between an "erudite" and a composite Hindi. They promoted various *boli*s (speech forms) and resisted the transformation of Hindi into a hypothetically purified and elevated form.⁴⁷ Geetanjali Shree says "Hindi is my heritage. It is my mother-tongue and richly eclectic. Through it, I imbibe variegated cultures, philosophies, histories, religions, endless ways of seeing, being, expressing and questioning. It connects me to myself and shapes my past, present and future, in a dynamic and not static way. My home and my hearth. And, in a metaphorical twist, I may say my Om and my Earth!"⁴⁸

⁴⁵ Rai, *Hindi Nationalism*.
⁴⁶ Kumar, *Political Agenda*, 125–7; Orsini, *The Hindi Public*.
⁴⁷ Nijhawan, *Women and Girls*, 224.
⁴⁸ Shree, "Hindi Against Hindi".

The anticaste erudite activist, political sanyasi, vaid, and journalist who are my four raconteurs espoused this democratic way of thinking about language by writing an accessible, eclectic Hindi in order to reach a larger cosmopolitan urban readership. Within a vibrant Hindi landscape they skilfully blurred the lines that separated "high" and "low" literary expression. While many of them were multilingual – with Santram for instance being proficient in Persian, English, Urdu, Hindi, and Sanskrit, and Satyadev well versed in English, Sanskrit, and Hindi – they consciously chose everyday Hindi as their medium of literary expression. It was their use of Hindi that granted these authors polemical vigour, combined with immediacy of access to the lifeworlds they wanted to narrate. While Santram learnt Hindi very late in life, having earlier been more at ease with Persian and Urdu, in the process of switching to Hindi he vernacularised and democratised the language. Debunking the use of Sanskritised and chaste Hindi, Satyabhakt assimilated Urdu words into his prose, thus carving out his own idea of literary democracy. Notably, all four borrowed extensively from writers in other Indian languages and those of the West – from Vatsyayan to Marie Stopes, from Ambedkar to Marx.

Finally, scholars of Hindi have highlighted a growing nexus through this period between the growth of the language, the construction of a chauvinist community identity, and the firming up of a distinct Hindu nationalist modernity in which the reins were firmly in the hands of a middle-class, upper-caste literati.[49] Despite a heterogeneous and fragmented Hindi print milieu, till as late as the 1920s it was still largely controlled by the Hindi elite who belonged to the Brahmin, Bhumihar, Kayastha, Agrawal, Khatri, and Thakur castes.[50] These were largely the hegemons retailing dominant and normative ideals of gender, family, caste, community, and nation. Hindi magazines and newspapers like *Saraswati*, *Chand*, *Madhuri*, *Hindu Panch*, and *Abhyudaya* were routinely the arbiters of "print Hinduism" in this period. Many of the owners of Hindi newspapers and magazines were closely aligned to the Hindu Mahasabha

[49] King, *One Language*; Kumar, *Political Agenda*; Orsini, *The Hindi Public*; Rai, *Hindi Nationalism*; Bapu, *Hindu Mahasabha*, 121–8.

[50] Orsini, *The Hindi Public*, 4.

and/or the Arya Samaj.⁵¹ In short, the idea of Hindi literature was often also the idea of a middle-class literature, an upper-caste literature, and a Hindu literature.

And yet a fuller Hindi history of the period shows a diversified and fragmented picture from within because of a simultaneous democratisation of languages and subjects through popular texts and genres, journalism and literature, all these collectively stimulating new expressions of feminist, Dalit, and revolutionary consciousness.⁵² Many of Hindi's strands display an amorphous elasticity enabling new constituencies to take shape within a diversified print-public sphere. Many stalwarts of Hindi literature – Radhamohan Gokul, Premchand, Ganesh Shankar Vidyarthi, Rambriksh Benipuri, Jainendra Kumar, Mahadevi Verma, Sahajanand Saraswati, Rahul Sankrityayan, Pandey Bechan Sharma "Ugra", Agyeya, to name some of the very prominent – contest an exclusionary Hinduisation of Hindi. Dissent and protest, and egalitarian dreams through resistance became part of their robust literary interventions. Even as some linguistic arenas came to be tied up with religious identities, the micro politics of Hindi facilitated grassroots expressions from marginalised groups and a hybrid environment. This is evident from the emergence in the late colonial period of a flourishing Hindi Dalit print culture which creatively deployed the expanding technologies of print and circulation. Much before Marathi literature, says Tapan Basu, Hindi print was reaching out among growing numbers of literate Dalits, with Swami Acchutanand, Chandrika Prasad Jigyasu, and Bhikshu Bodhanand of the Adi Hindu movement pioneering the rise of Hindi Dalit literature over the 1910s–1930s.⁵³ The impact of the Russian Revolution and communism was vividly felt at this time and, as I show later, the anticaste and communist writings of Santram and Satyabhakt are very much a part of this polysemic Hindi world.

The growing antagonism and sectarian conflicts between Hindus and Muslims in the UP of the 1920s and 1930s have been much studied, as have the emergence of a martial Hindu nationalism and increased display of Hindu religious overtones in Congress propa-

---

⁵¹ Bapu, *Hindu Mahasabha.*
⁵² Blackburn, *Print, Folklore,* 10–11.
⁵³ Basu, *Hindi Dalit,* 5–10.

ganda.[54] My own work has reiterated the building of a coherent, modern, and aggressive Hindu formation during this time, with distinct gendered overtones.[55] Likewise, others have cogently argued a decisive shift among the Hindu middle-class Bengali intelligentsia from an earlier liberal reformism to a Hindu cultural indigenism, revivalism, and nationalism from the late nineteenth century.[56] Alongside, and in line with the world of Hindi, the project of "saffronisation" in early-twentieth-century North India was internally fraught because for various castes and classes, women and men, the ideas of being a Hindu were deeply heterogenous. A substantial section of the Hindu middle classes from diverse constituencies and professions, while not negating their religious identity, interpreted and represented Hinduism in an array of ways, with varied readings. Their opinions were open-ended and relational rather than univocal. The divisions between revivalists-nationalists and liberal reformers were often untenable, and there could at different times be opposed discursive positions within the same individual. Simultaneously, different standpoints could converge or diverge in debates on inclusion-exclusion, especially on questions of lower castes, women, and Muslims.

Explicitly Hindu in terms of religious identity, the quartet in this book nevertheless reflected these divergent strands within Hinduism, coining anew its emotive and affective power through a range of registers. Thus, Santram creatively drew on the *Mahabharat* to justify sex before marriage, and emphasise the transient and fluid nature of marriages cutting across caste boundaries. His writings reveal complex and contingent processes as he attempts to craft a modern, liberal, anticaste space through a trenchant critique of caste stigma and endogamy, outlining a transgressive intercaste love which can coexist with a language of shuddhi. Functioning within the paradigm of a Sanatani ethos, Yashoda highlights affinities of ancient ayurvedic knowledge with modern health concerns. In her persona we see on the one hand a reiteration of normative-dominant Hindu

[54] Freitag, *Collective Action*; Pandey, *The Construction*; Zavos, *The Emergence of Hindu*; Gould, *Hindu Nationalism*.
[55] Gupta, *Sexuality, Obscenity*, 222–320.
[56] For example Sarkar, *Hindu Wife*, 1–22.

conjugal values within a conservative ethos, and on the other an upholding of women's consent. Satyadev deploys Hindu ascetic traditions to endorse brahmacharya and project a virulently anti-Muslim Hindutva rhetoric. And, symbolising the Hindu Left, Satyabhakt relies on popular forms of Hinduism, egalitarian principles of sharing and equality in the Puranas, and Hindu beliefs of destruction and rebirth, to pitch for a communist utopian Ram Rajya.

While both Santram and Satyadev were influenced by the Arya Samaj's reformist rhetoric, they utilised it for contrasting purposes and ends. The erotic, domestic, and ascetic aspects of Hinduism rubbed shoulders in Santram, Yashoda, and Satyadev. Except Satyadev, none of the others focused on Hindu–Muslim relations. Rather, Hindu vocabularies offered an internal dialogue over a range that includes caste, sex, marriage, medicine, health, food, recipes, travel, utopia, and communism. The absence of any clear Hindu rule book and the presence, contrarily, of multifarious traditions and sacred texts made it easier for them to interpret and argue its varied tenets for their own ends. Hindu myths were thus selectively re-forged and recast to advocate anticaste positions, critique hegemonic bio-medical discourses, mould communism to indigenous utopian desires, and procure fodder for aggressive anti-Muslim positions. This is a melange signifying some of the internal fault lines within Hinduism. While the strand represented by Satyadev has come to dominate our present political-public spaces – a militant, chest-thumping and singular Hindutva model which now stamps down the multiplicity of Hinduism – the scenario a century ago provides a much more lively and contentious field with both Hindi and Hindu able to mean different things to different people.

Self-Writing, Life Histories, and Sexual Embodiments

The present book adds to a growing body of work that writes histories of the social and the political in colonial India through ideas and articulations of the self.[57] This variety of writing is perhaps a

---

[57] For example Kumar, *Writing the First*; Arnold and Blackburn, *Telling Lives*; Majeed, *Autobiography, Travel*; Kaviraj, *The Invention*; Karlekar, *Voices from*

precondition for identity, since memories of what we once were and have now become involve the cognitive, emotional, imaginative, and aesthetic abilities that constitute selfhood within the particularities of a context.[58] Gramsci speaks of knowing and expressing the self: "The starting-point of critical elaboration is the consciousness of what one really is, and is 'knowing thyself' as a product of the historical process to date which has deposited in you an infinity of traces, without leaving an inventory."[59]

Autobiography attempts to compile such an inventory, an "orderly guide" of experiences with self, family, and society which have been shaped by and give shape to history. In their pioneering work, Sidonie Smith and Julia Watson say autobiography is a constituent source for the historical fashioning of a being, an archive of memory and a performance of the self in a time period. Autobiography is written to justify one's perception, uphold one's reputation, dispute the accounts of others, settle scores, chronicle events, convey political-cultural information, reveal the mentalities of an era, enshrine a community, invent desirable futures, and in a sense to make history.[60] In dialogue with their immediate readers and putative audiences, the four subjects of this book actively frame the self for all these designs.

There has been considerable excitement and buzz around various modes of autobiographical writing in India. Studies have analysed life writings in various languages such as Urdu, Malayalam, and Bengali, gendered performances of the self, life narratives by and for Dalits, theatre autobiographies, religious biographies, and autobiographies of leading political figures.[61] While some commentators

---

Within; Kumar, *Dalit Personal Narratives*; Sarkar, *Words to Win*; Malhotra and Lambert-Hurley, *Speaking of the Self*; Ramaswamy and Sharma, *Biography as History*.

[58] Ender, *Architexts of Memory*, 230.

[59] Gramsci, *Selections*, 324.

[60] Smith and Watson, *Reading Autobiography*, 10, 14.

[61] Urdu: Naim, *Zikr-i Mir*; Malayalam: Kumar, *Writing the First*; Bengali: Kaviraj, *The Invention*; gendered performances: Malhotra and Lambert-Hurley, *Speaking of the Self*; Sarkar, *Words to Win*; Karlekar, *Voices from Within*;

have argued that a definition of the self is essentially a European construct and a legacy of colonialism, others have disputed the normative model of autobiography as an exclusive creation of the modern West or colonial rule and shown that self-reflexive writing in the autobiographical mode has long been a part of Indian literary traditions – and that there is a "long and discontinuous history" of life writing as a form which has provided "idioms for self-fashioning".[62] Nonetheless, colonialism and nationalism do provide an important context for the centrality of autobiography. Javed Majeed shows "how nationalism can be grounded in notions of individual personhood, how the idea of collective life is drawn from a vision of the individual self, and how the writing of autobiography can play a key role in formulating that complex tie between nation and subject, which allows nationalism to work as a key defining identity."[63] With colonial modernity, educational reforms, the proliferation of mass print cultures, and the establishment of prose as the dominant modern literary form, autobiography flourished from the late nineteenth century as a systematic and distinct genre, particularly in the vernacular. This was a pioneering time for the development of vernacular texts in India and the genre became in various regional languages an important form for many women and men – "for the writing of histories outside the professional or academic domain" since many dimensions of social, political, spiritual, domestic, and individual life which did "not find much room in scholarly histories of the period, managed ample space in these personal narratives."[64]

Compared to the genre's growth in other modern Indian vernaculars, autobiography developed late in the Hindi landscape. This

---

Dalits: Hunt, *Hindi Dalit*, 176–208; Kumar, *Dalit Personal Narratives*, 157–256; Pandey, *A History of Prejudice*, 131–93; Rege, *Against the Madness*, 9–92; idem, *Writing Caste,* 9–92; Shankar and Gupta, *Caste and Life Narratives*; Theatre: Hansen, *Stages of Life*; religious figures: Granoff, *Monks and Magicians*; political figures: Majeed, *Autobiography, Travel*.

[62] Kumar, "Writing the Life", 56; see also, variously, Pascal, *Design and Truth,* 22; Venkatachalapathy, *In Those Days,* 163–84; Ramaswamy, "Introduction", 1.

[63] Majeed, *Autobiography, Travel,* 2–3.

[64] Kumar, *Writing the First*, 2.

may have been due to the late standardisation of Khari Boli as representative of modern literary articulation in Hindi.[65] Making up for lost time, from the early twentieth century a substantial number of autobiographies got written in the language.[66] In 1932, recognising and firmly establishing autobiography as a serious, distinct, and flourishing literary genre, *Hans*, the famous monthly Hindi magazine whose editor was the celebrated Premchand, published in January–February its *Atmakatha Ank*, a special issue on autobiographies.[67] This carried fifty-two brief auto-sketches by both young and old, new and leading Hindi writers of the time, including Premchand, Jaishankar Prasad, Ramchandra Shukl, Shivpujan Sahai, Bhai Parmanand, Dhaniram "Prem", Shivrani Devi, Mahavir Prasad Dwivedi, and Gangaprasad Upadhyay – and Santram too was part of this collection.[68] At the same time, by comparison with many other vernaculars, scholarly and serious academic works on Hindi autobiographies have been few and far between.[69] Most such work has largely centred on two subjects – the seventeenth-century Jain merchant Banarsidas who wrote *Ardhakathanak*, regarded as one of the first Hindi autobiographies, and which signalled a new "vernacular aesthetics";[70] and Hindi Dalit autobiographies.[71]

While there have been rich debates on the meanings of terminologies – autobiography, self-writing, life narrative, biography[72] – I see life histories as hybrid and elastic narratives and deploy them in three

[65] For details Mody, *The Making*, 2–4, 13–15.
[66] For an overview of autobiographies in Hindi, Zamindar, "Modern Hindi".
[67] "Atmakatha Ank".
[68] Santram, "Vidhi ka Vidhaan".
[69] Some Hindi books on the subject: Singh, *Hindi Atmakatha*; Chaturvedi, *Atmakatha ki Sanskriti*.
[70] Snell, "Confessions", 79; for the narrow focus in this area: Snell, "Confessions"; Vanina, "The *Ardhakathanaka*".
[71] Dalit autobiographies aside, studies on other Hindi autobiographies can be counted on the fingers of one hand: Singh, "'A Question of Life'", 452–67; Snell, "A Hindi Poet"; Chudal, "A Life of the 'Other'". For some wonderful translations of Hindi autobiographies: Pradhan, *The Struggle*; Bachchan, *In the Afternoon of Time*.
[72] For an overview, Smith and Watson, *Reading Autobiography*, 1–20.

ways. First, the actors here wrote stories about selves through a kaleidoscope of genres, forms, and institutions – autobiography, travelogues, letters, social prose, translations, recipes, publishing houses, archives – which were tied up with their social, political, and cultural milieus, agendas, and interests in the public domain. Second, they wrote biographies and biofictions of other historical figures that buttressed the crafting of their own selves.[73] It has been argued, for example, that many Arya Samajis used "biographies of great figures, including mythological figures like Ram and Krishna, and the hagiographies of Swami Dayanand as models" for writing narratives about themselves.[74] The four subjects of this book wrote a range of biographical sketches, ranging from those on Bhishma to Buddha, and great Rajput women to Marx. In their biographies a crafted portrayal of others' lives became a guise for autobiography, the biographical often weaving an autobiographical subtext into its narrative.

Finally, I deploy life narratives instrumentally, as a significant tool with which to historicise and interpret caste, ayurveda, sexology, travel, and communism. First-person enunciations, being socially contingent and rooted in specific historical contexts, have for long been part of the methodological toolkit of historians. Richard Eaton, for example, deploys the genre of life narratives to enumerate a social history of the Deccan over four centuries.[75] In *The Audacious Raconteur* Leela Prasad picks up four subjects from South India, active between 1857 and 1931, who despite their remarkable talents did not gain wide renown but whose everyday acts of audacity and "Indian ways of knowing, creating, remembering and being" take us to "the unsubjugable person – whose sovereignty over the territory of self, culture, and art is unassailable."[76] And of course, as earlier discussed, some recent monographs have deployed the biographies of stalwarts of Hindi for social and cultural histories of Hindi and Hindu India.

The new modes of self-articulation by the actors in this book

---

[73] For details, Lackey, *Biofiction*.
[74] Singh, "'A Question of Life'", 455.
[75] Eaton, *A Social History*.
[76] Prasad, *The Audacious Raconteur*, 8.

strengthen or nuance some of the arguments made about self-writing. The process of performing the self initially begins with naming, and the protagonists of this book named themselves anew. The practices and politics of naming and renaming have been central to challenging stigmatised pasts.[77] After acquiring his BA degree, Santram dropped all caste nomenclature and proudly displayed his educational qualification and degree as his surname, signature, and distinct identity – Santram BA – which became an integral part of his name and writing. Named Sukh Dayal at birth, Satyadev took the name "Satyadev Parivrajak" when he was twenty years old, connoting a spiritual traveller seeking the Truth. The name also indicated a conscious line of thinking as it borrowed from ancient Hindu and Buddhist texts as well as the Arya Samaj, which often sent parivrajaks as preachers across India and overseas. Born as Chakan Lal, Satyabhakt too changed his name to one literally meaning "worshipper of truth". His press and the magazine that he edited for a short while were also called "Satyug", thus also reflecting his communist affinities with Hindu beliefs. Yashoda did not use "Sharma", her husband's surname, but suffixed her own first name with Devi, literally meaning "goddess"; Devi is commonly used by women in India, and letters addressed to Yashoda only as "Devi" reached her regularly. She also often appended her name with "*sab behnon ki aarogyakaankshi*" (wisher of health to all sisters).

The modes of self-fashioning and the personal lives of my subjects were also relational, embedded in practices of literary production, shaped by the social dynamics of power, and imbricated in public collectives. The French philosopher Jacques Rancière says an individual life narrative "is not a choice of method within an alternative that would set the particular against the general, the individual against the collective, the short-term against the long-term, the small-scale against the large-scale, or the cultural against the economic . . . It is a way of putting the alternative . . . Its principle is to bring out the general in the particular, the century in the moment, the world

---

[77] Paik, "Mahar–Dalit–Buddhist", 217–18; Pandey, *A History of Prejudice*, 207–10; Rao, *The Caste Question*, 205–13; Kumar, *Writing the First*, 6.

in a bedroom."⁷⁸ In the Indian context, Udaya Kumar argues that autobiographies are often public utterances rather than just expressions of pre-existing private selves.⁷⁹ Sudipta Kaviraj states that, like history, the autobiography is also "subtly, subliminally, and ineradicably political."⁸⁰ David Arnold and Stuart Blackburn stress that life histories in India reveal "a formation of self-in-society that is more complex and subtle than a mutually exclusive opposition between an all-subsuming collectivity on the one hand, and a rampant individuality on the other", and that self-narratives often define "themselves in relation to larger frames of reference, especially those of family, kin, caste, religion and gender."⁸¹ Santram thus clearly positioned his autobiography as an optic of an individual caste memory of pain and a collective of anticaste history; Yashoda, for women free of disease and ill health; Satyabhakt, for a vision of an indigenous communism; and Satyadev, for a lament on the "unmanly and weak" Hindu race, a nation "free of Muslims", and to describe momentous political changes and people, including Gandhi and Nehru. They thus wove themselves and their everyday lives into social histories.

It has also been argued that women's autobiographies are more domestic and personal rather than public or political, and often characterised by understatement.⁸² However, Yashoda selectively deployed the autobiographical mode – letters written by others in her praise, repeatedly emphasising her long familial experience in ayurveda and narrating stories of performing miraculous remedies on other bodies. This she did to celebrate her achievements and authority, and to make herself commercially viable. Unlike many other women's self-writings, her public performance of the self vis-à-vis other women shows her methodically amplifying her personal accomplishments and taking great pride in her skills.

---

[78] Rancière, *The Politics*, 171, 176–7.
[79] Kumar, *Writing the First*, 12–23.
[80] Kaviraj, *The Invention*, 7.
[81] Arnold and Blackburn, "Introduction", 19.
[82] For such debates, Malhotra and Lambert-Hurley, *Speaking of the Self*, 9–10.

Alongside, it has been argued that most Indian first-person narratives begin with an apologetic and modest tone, and that Indian first-person literature is particularly reticent in relation to writing about one's self.[83] Udaya Kumar says that the Indian self-narratives of men "rarely speak of private interiorities" and that "the distinctiveness of the individual life" is not their focal point.[84] Sudipta Kaviraj suggests that an autobiography is usually "unheroic".[85] M.S.S. Pandian argues that many Dalit texts "accentuate and underscore the self-conscious ordinariness of the lives narrated."[86]

Santram's autobiography is such an articulation, for he starts by undermining himself. By contrast Satyadev reinforces the assertion that an autobiography is a classic symbol and the quintessential ego-document.[87] For him, self-praise became a mechanism to evade or counter criticism, sell his books, and exercise control over the reception of his deeds in history, while also mirroring the urge to control his sexual desires. Moreover, in tune with Gandhi's autobiography,[88] but in contrasting ways, Santram and Satyadev brought intimate personal experiences and desires centre stage. Satyabhakt was fascinated by questions of death and rebirth and Yashoda described matters of the body through the experiences of others.

The representation of the self in these writers was not consistent or singular. It was reinvented, with selective concealing and revealing, and variable tellings. Thus, while narrating the self in his travelogues, Satyadev often fabricated himself as a global citizen who embraced diverse cultures, was remarkably cosmopolitan, and had a supple mindset. His two autobiographies, however, more usually crafted him as a staunch votary of an exclusive and singular Hindu rashtra. Underplaying the "troubling" aspects of his other writings and literary activities, Satyabhakt presented an alternative folk narrative and an oppositional autobiography to counter marginalisation

---

[83] Arnold and Blackburn, *Telling Lives*, 14–16, 54–5.
[84] Kumar, *Writing the First*, 13–14.
[85] Kaviraj, *The Invention*, 5.
[86] Pandian, "Writing Ordinary", 35.
[87] Dekker, "Introduction".
[88] On Gandhi's autobiography, Majeed, *Autobiography, Travel*, 211–68.

and record himself as an active and conscious subject of communist genealogy and history in India.

The relationship between self-identity, representation, body, and sexuality in colonial India has been the subject of interesting studies. The protagonists of this book too fashioned their selves through tropes of sexuality, such as brahmacharya, ascetic masculinity, sexology, masturbation, sexual desire, conjugality, intercaste marriages, heterosexuality, and unbridled sexuality: these inhabited their encounters and accounts amidst a proliferation of material on sex in the vernacular. This did not necessarily signify a transgressive moment, as it often reproduced dominant moralities. For example, the Hindu political sanyasi – the celibate monk – became a compelling and potent figure for the assertion of political power by the Hindu national body-politic.[89] It was this body of an exemplary Hindu masculine and ascetic self that sculpted the nation in Satyadev's autobiography. Yet, at other moments, bodily desires and matters of sex could challenge normative codes of conduct, producing cracks in orthodox mandates and disciplinary power regimes.[90] Durba Mitra cogently shows that philologists, Indologists, and sexologists in colonial India, while tracing the origins of modern sexual sciences in Sanskrit erotic scriptures, used them to articulate the "social fact" of female sexual deviance. She underscores how these "new fixed structures of knowledge" were "guides for masculinity and patriarchal power" and showcased "control of female sexuality as the primary index for stages of civilisation."[91] While partially convinced by her arguments, my explorations of Santram and Yashoda also reveal that such translations were not so homogeneous and sometimes paved the way for transgressive sexual registers, unruly appropriations, and dissonant texts of pleasure. Yashoda and Santram, as subaltern vernacular sexologists, redeployed the language of sexual science to make claims different from those in medical authority, moving instead in a realm of sexual autonomy and caste politics. The writings

---

[89] Chakraborty, *Masculinity, Asceticism*; Banerjee, *Make Me a Man*.
[90] Gupta, *Sexuality, Obscenity*, 49–84.
[91] Mitra, *Indian Sex Life*, 26, 27, 61.

of Santram, Yashoda, and Satyadev also reveal the oppressive vigilance of male sexuality through discourses on brahmacharya and masturbation. And Satyabhakt published a series of pamphlets on bodily care and cure. Such embodiments became significant in the crafting of selves and others. Finally, all the subjects of this book engaged with dreams of freedom, often mediated not through political institutions but subjective embodiments.

Utopian Desires of Freedom

Hindi Hindu Histories is also partially a social history of utopian dreams of freedom, aspirations, and ideas. Searching for a liberal definition of freedom, T.H. Green defines it as self-perfection, individual self-realisation, non-interference, and freedom from politics.[92] Searching for a republican alternative, Philip Pettit views freedom as non-domination, a condition in which individuals are not subject to the arbitrary power of others.[93] In contrast, Hannah Arendt proposes an existentially grounded, radical, agonistic, and subversive idea of freedom that is disruptive of an institutionalised normative order, and which signals collective participation and political action.[94]

However, while theorising the political, Prathama Banerjee displaces Western European philosophical readings that often turn "empirical historical events into universal philosophical archetypes." Challenging the political as being universal, stable, and self-evident, she instead asserts the historical specificity of modern political thought and its intersections with diverse traditions of theory and practice, arguing further that "what is political becomes so and does not remain so forever."[95] Her argument can well apply to freedom, as any singular, universal, or Western idea of it may often be limited. Discussing perceptions of freedom by seven stellar Indian male visionaries – Vivekananda, Aurobindo, Gandhi, Tagore, Ambedkar,

[92] Green, *Lectures on the Principles*.
[93] Pettit, *Republicanism*.
[94] Arendt, *The Human Condition*.
[95] Banerjee, *Elementary Aspects*, 5, 8.

M.N. Roy, and Jayaprakash Narayan – Dennis Dalton brilliantly highlights the concept's distinctive enunciation, signifying new theoretical territories of political thought on freedom. Anything but derivative of Western discourse, these "journey theorists" were engaged in a dialogic spirit of the reciprocal elucidation of freedom, while drawing from Indian intellectual traditions. Finding threads of connectedness in their conceptualisations of freedom, Dalton argues that all of them went beyond paradigms of national independence and an "outer" political freedom from colonialism. Their quest for freedom signified an internal ethical conduct, a deeply personal-spiritual search for self-transformation. They cohered on the priority of means over ends, nonviolence as the right model, and ethics as integral to politics and public life. Unlike popular Western notions of a binary opposition between positive and negative liberty, these external and internal forms of freedom were seen as deeply connected and complementary qualities.[96]

Nevertheless, despite this shared idea of freedom – encompassing Vivekananda's pragmatic Vedanta, Aurobindo's spiritual mysticism, Gandhi's principles of swaraj and satyagraha, Tagore's poetic universalism and critique of nationalism, Ambedkar's turn towards Buddhism, M.N. Roy's radical humanism, and Jayaprakash Narayan's communitarian democracy – the spiritual and the political, the inner and the outer expressions of freedom could take on fluid meanings for people in varying contexts, locations, and situations. Besides these pioneers, within the dystopian world of colonial-imperial onslaught of that time freedom emerged as a constitutive ideal for many Indian women and men – for Hindus and Muslims, intellectuals and activists. Leela Prasad shows raconteurs "in the public square . . . audaciously challenging the ideological bulwark of colonialism" and articulating an "epistemic sovereignty".[97] While informed by readings of a nation coming into being, writers, activists, and social reformers had diverse aspirations of freedom that went beyond the national and signified its more prosaic representa-

[96] Dalton, *Indian Ideas of Freedom*.
[97] Prasad, *The Audacious Raconteur,* 7, 140.

tions. Imaginations of freedom were also enmeshed with as many utopias which signified "histories of the present",[98] and were "one of the ways that nations create themselves."[99] It has been argued that "all utopias are, by definition, fictions; unlike say historical writing, they deal with possible, not actual worlds. To this extent they are like all forms of imaginative literature."[100] Not just in terms of words – swaraj, satyagraha, azadi, swatantrata, *swadhinta* (independence) – freedom became a mobile thought that could perform differing functions for different authors and their respective constituencies. Its articulation was not universal or absolute, but situational, conditional, and contingent, based on cultural and intellectual autonomies conceived ingeniously.

The protagonists of my book were not political theorists, philosophers, thinkers, or scholars. Yet the terminologies and aesthetics of utopian freedom were infused in their writings. Grappling with linguistic, cultural, and political challenges, they evolved innovative indigenous-vernacular meanings to express it, rendering freedom to their readers through varied modes. Each of them drew on Hindu religious thought, traditional resources, indigenous symbols, and their everyday experiences to set out culturally grounded ideas of freedom and autonomy. Yet they also adapted to the challenges of the modern world. Autonomy and sovereignty came to be perceived not just from colonial rule and its "distorted" impulses, but also from domestic tyrannies. Thus, as for Ambedkar, political freedom for Santram was a non-starter unless its telling illustrated a subversive anticaste stance. Moreover, freedom for Santram meant not only emancipation from the oppressive burdens of caste but also the enactment of an intercaste ethical heterosexuality. For Yashoda, freedom meant an eschewing of bio-medical agendas and hegemonies, an end to the dystopian maladies of modernity, and restraining the excessive demands of husbands. Such autonomy could be achieved through an ethic of ayurvedic healing and household remedies, a

[98] Gordin, Tilley, and Prakash, "Introduction", 1.
[99] Sargent, "The Necessity", 2.
[100] Kumar, "Aspects of the Western", 23.

moralist-disciplinary control over their bodies by women and men, and the creation of an ideal conjugal family. Satyadev's perception of freedom was counterintuitive, as in its very espousal he posed its counter-history – dispensing with the idea of equality. Creating a fantasised free world of foreign travel, he dreamt simultaneously of a sectarian freedom that excluded Muslims. Satyabhakt envisaged freedom not only from capitalist and colonial exploitation but also from the hegemony of the Comintern, and from a dry atheism and secularism. His recipe of freedom rested on certain ethical principles of Hinduism, and a utopian communist conclave of a future satyug achieved post-apocalypse. Through such improvised mappings, these authors often evaded censorship. Their allegories of utopian freedom were thus embedded contingently in the production of anticaste statements, gendered ayurvedic readings, communist Ram Rajya, and ironically and paradoxically even in anti-Muslim sentiment, thus revealing the possibilities and limits of freedom.

Trajectory of Chapters

Containing eight chapters, this book has each actor in chapter pairs. The first two chapters focus on Santram. Through his life-writings the first chapter unveils a social history of caste in North India. Despite lingering on the fringes of scholarly attention, Santram's narratives crafted diverse interpretations of anticaste dynamics, where on the one hand he emerged as a fervent champion of intercaste marriages, and on the other embodied a discourse of caste reform and respectability within the paradigm of Hinduism – with ambiguous implications. He also wrote extensively on sex and birth control, and translated Mary Stopes. The second chapter contextualises his writings on sexology amidst a burgeoning print culture, facilitating the widespread dissemination of what was often labelled obscene material as a commodity. The chapter shows Santram navigating diverse landscapes by drawing inspiration from classical works on kamashastra, while also embracing insights from Western sexologists, emphasising pleasure and desire as integral aspects of modern sexual life.

The first of the next two chapters, on Yashoda Devi, one of the most commercially successful and famous women ayurvedic practitioners of her day, positions her at the heart of colonial Indian health and medical histories by delving into her extensive writings on ayurveda, disease, and gender relations. Challenging male dominance in medicine, Yashoda proposed native cures to regulate the bodies of Hindu women and men within the domestic and national spheres, occasionally unsettling gender hierarchies. Selectively incorporating Western methodologies, Yashoda's project transformed disease, illness, and healing into arenas shaping socio-cultural identities. Chapter 4 explores the entanglements between histories of food, home remedies, vernacular health, medical knowledge, and gender in Hindu middle-class urban households. Focusing on Hindi cookbooks and healing remedies, the chapter conceptualises recipes as a distinct genre predominantly authored by educated middle-class women, and serving as a platform for their voices to be heard. Yashoda, in particular, puts a spotlight on women kitchen pharmacists who preserved, consumed, authored, and transmitted local food and health practices.

Chapters 5 and 6, on Satyadev Parivrajak, explore his travel writings on America and Europe, emphasising his role as a pioneer in this genre. I argue that Satyadev's travelogues were part of a decolonising effort by a subjugated nation to reclaim a realm of freedom. As performative political acts, his narratives carved "perfect masculine bodies", symbolising beauty and pleasure, with a dialogue between East and West, slavery and freedom. I go on to his autobiographical writings, which show a modern-day worldly political ascetic whose writing rests on three pillars: an exemplary celibate Hindu masculinity, a segmented freedom unencumbered by Muslims, and a profound antagonism towards Gandhi. Collectively, these writings contribute to the intellectual history and genealogy of sectarian Hindi–Hindu literature, while showcasing the cultivated antecedents of a modern, monolithic, and militant Hindu nation.

Satyabhakt – outstanding Hindi journalist and organiser of the first Indian Communist Conference in 1925 – is the subject of the last two chapters. His engagements with communist politics,

Hindi public sphere, and workers' movements in the Gangetic region intertwined caste, gender, and nationalism with indigenous communism. While marginalised in the annals of Indian communist history, he shows the rekindling of suppressed strands of Left dissent, reviving debates between internationalism and nationalism, materialism and spiritualism, and class and caste. I examine some of his writings to explore the intricate relationship between religion and communism as a lens to understand the Left in North India at this time. Early anti-colonial communist intellectuals saw no contradiction in integrating religion, ethical traditions, and morality into their quest for dignity, equality, a just polity, and social liberation.

I
SANTRAM BA
(1887–1988)

1

Reading Self, Resisting Caste, Reimagining Marriage

Fig. 1.1: Santram BA.

SANTRAM BA, WHO LIVED for 101 years (1887–1988; Fig.1.1), was a veteran Hindi writer and radical Shudra caste social reformer from Punjab. He started writing actively in 1912 and specialised in publishing anticaste literature, especially in support of intercaste marriages, with more than a hundred books/booklets and three hundred articles in leading magazines to his credit, including his autobiography, *Mere Jeevan ke Anubhav* (Experiences of My Life; hereafter *MJKA*; 1963; Fig. 1.2).[1] A member of the Arya Samaj for a considerable time, he founded the Jat-Pat Torak Mandal (JPTM) in 1922. In spite of his vast written repertoire, Santram has been marginalised and his claim to fame has largely been that he invited Ambedkar to deliver the keynote address at the 15 May 1936 annual conference of the JPTM.[2] The invitation was cancelled because of internal opposition, which was convinced that Ambedkar's

[1] *MJKA*.
[2] Some works on Santram include Dharmvir, *Dalit Chintan ka Vikas*, 170–89; Bharti, "Santram BA".

Fig. 1.2: Jacket front, *MJKA*, 1974 edn.

views would be unacceptable and controversial. Ambedkar went on to publish the cancelled lecture as a long essay which became the classic *Annihilation of Caste*.[3]

The covers of Santram's autobiography and his other anticaste writings require close scrutiny for several reasons. Applauding Santram, an article in *The Indian Rationalist* stated in 1954:

> He waged a major war against the caste system, all on his own, and he succeeded in giving the old demon a bad shake. It is no discredit to him that he attempted the impossible and that the demon is still very much alive and kicking. If the great Buddha failed to destroy caste,

---

[3] Ambedkar, *Annihilation of Caste*, i–viii. For a fine account of Ambedkar's *Annihilation of Caste*, its origins, and context, see Sayeed, *Understanding*.

where is the chance for another to succeed? But to Sant Ram belongs the credit of repeating the performance of Buddha in recent history. His life deserves close study by every rationalist.[4]

Santram, though a member of the Shudra caste, stood apart from other prominent anticaste radicals such as Ambedkar and Periyar. While they challenged caste by distancing themselves from Hinduism, Santram provided a trenchant critique of caste and advocated caste reform within the paradigm of Hinduism, which accounts both for his limitations and possibilities. His life narrative is significant not only because of its dominant strand of caste suffering, but also because of the other layers discernible, as he takes the middle ground between Gandhi and Ambedkar, bourgeois and subaltern, Arya Samaj and Ad Dharm, and love-hate for Hinduism. It is from this in-between space that Santram produces his anticaste rhetoric, quoting selectively from past texts to forge a contemporary polemic which shows him simultaneously as publicist, activist, and social reformer.

Falling between the definable grids, he operates on the margins, which is also in part because of his historical and geographical location. Though from Punjab, he refrained from both Sikh politics and Gurumukhi: most of his writings are in Hindi. The allure of Santram for me lies precisely in his *trishanku* (middle ground) status. Studying his writings one passes through crossroads and bylanes littered with caste, reminding us of the routes traversed and those not taken, of the impossibility of decisively classifying and pigeonholing him. This in-between space perhaps exemplifies many anticaste thinkers of the period. While Santram may appear dated next to other caste radicals, his quests are pertinent in having left a legacy, a memory of something that stirs the oppressed while baffling us by its seeming constraints.

When Santram wrote his autobiography in the 1960s he had already mapped out his life in distinct phases which he painted in broad brushstrokes. Vivid and playful, *MJKA* is also a piece of propaganda challenging caste. Various episodes in the autobiography

---

[4] Thruvengadam, "Sant Ram", 65. I am grateful to Akshaya Mukul for this reference.

are slanted to fit larger scripts, the personal narrative being informed by such elements as his Shudra status, the Arya Samaj, Ambedkar, and the JPTM. He starts by underlining his ordinariness, while emphasising caste as central to his identity:

> I thought that writing one's autobiography was like flaunting one's greatness ... I am no extraordinary person ... For my whole life I have only struggled against caste and served the Hindi language ... My friends said caste is the biggest enemy of India. To remove it would be the biggest service to the nation ... Your autobiography will in a way be a history of fighting against caste in modern India and of the diffusion of Hindi in Punjab ... Thus I decided to write this book ... When a man engages in social reform to eliminate caste, then, not just strangers but even his own family and relatives oppose him. His photos are not published in the papers. No statue is made of him. All his life he must burn on a pyre.[5]

Rancière's view – that "ordinary life has to be recognised not only as a possible subject for a poem but as a poetic subject par excellence"[6] – suits Santram's autobiography, which is the poignant framing of an ordinary life with caste as its constant focus.

Through Santram's life and anticaste writings this chapter attempts to illuminate and rethink caste in early-twentieth-century North India. It examines Santram's accounts of the caste-modulated self, social reform and the nation, the stories he told others about himself, and his anticaste thought. Santram shows up everyday caste taboos around roti-beti, the constraints of Gandhian and Arya Samaj politics, and the flaws in Sanatani Hindu orthodoxy. He moves between private and public, personal and political, self and nation, individual and community, his perspective suggesting how embroiled reformers were within the contradictory currents of colonial India. He produces multiple meanings and mutable positions on caste, where on the one hand he is a staunch advocate of intercaste marriages, and on the other ambiguous about caste reform and respectability. Modernity sits uneasily in his work because when

[5] *MJKA*, 3–6.
[6] Rancière, *The Politics of Literature*, 175.

attacking caste he relies on reason on the one hand and devotion on the other. This duality alongside his cocktail of ideas makes his life narrative a politicised form of resistance and critique of caste, but equally an account of accepted caste models and messages. His life seems to suggest the possibility of enabling and transforming caste in practically the same breath.

I also focus on Santram's critique of caste, which he expresses through various forms of intimacies, such as love, food, and marriage. Santram particularly subverts endogamy and upends conformity by promoting intercaste marriages. Here, several ideas are contextually relevant. Anthony Giddens observes that "the possibility of intimacy means the promise of democracy."[7] And Alex Lubin says "intimate matters" are inextricably related to "civil rights activism in the public sphere."[8] Intimacy is experienced in love and pleasure, and also expressed through relationships and representations, associations and exclusions. Santram too explores intimacy to delve into the emotional and physical aspects of caste-and-gender entanglements, and their divergent receptions in public life. By challenging endogamy and caste hierarchies, he folds caste into histories of intimacy, love, and marriage to draw out the inextricable connections between caste and gender. This shapes his counter-narrative of caste in the JPTM.

Life History and Caste: Self and Collective Identities

Individual caste memory and collective caste history fuse in Santram's writings, particularly in his autobiography. In the words of one of his admirers, "His life-story of ninety-seven years is not just a story; in many ways it is a history of caste-annihilation in modern India, and promotion of Hindi in Punjab."[9] Autobiographies have repeatedly worked as a tool of the downtrodden, subalterns, and Dalits.[10] In such writings pain, suffering, and quotidian caste

[7] Giddens, *The Transformation*, 188.
[8] Lubin, *Romance and Rights*, xi.
[9] Vidyarthi, "Jat-Pat ke Khilaf", 142.
[10] Pandey, *A History of Prejudice*, 131–2.

violence, combined with a language of personhood and collective rights, have often seemed like cultural capital.¹¹ Laura Brueck argues that the Hindi Dalit literary sphere signifies a "counterpublic", a distinct political and aesthetic movement;¹² Toral Gajarawala emphasises that "Dalit literature is the space where realism now lives";¹³ Tapan Basu has traced the emergence of a Hindi Dalit print culture during the 1920s and 1930s through the writings of the anticaste intellectuals Acchutanand and Jigyasu.¹⁴ In his classic work, Paul Gilroy emphasises that Black autobiography is "an act or process of simultaneous self-creation and self-emancipation."¹⁵ In similar vein M.S.S. Pandian says: "Not bound by the evidentiary rules of social science, the privileged notion of teleological time, and claims to objectivity and authorial neutrality, these [Dalit] narrative forms can produce enabling re-descriptions of life-worlds and facilitate the re-imagination of the political."¹⁶

As in many Dalit life narratives, caste provides the overarching framework of Santram's autobiography as he imagines, constructs, and scripts memories of his subalternity within a landscape where suffering, contestation, and self-liberation are most apparent. When read in conjunction with *Hamara Samaj*, his most important book,¹⁷ his autobiography shows the centrality of caste alongside the ambiguities involved in thinking about the methods of obliterating it.

Both books have gone into several editions and are being published, even now, not by the Arya Samaj but by Dalit publishing houses. Many of Santram's other books and booklets on caste have also found a fertile ground in Dalit publishing.¹⁸ Significantly, Satnam

---

[11] Hunt, *Hindi Dalit*, 176–208; Kumar, *Dalit Personal Narratives*, 157–256; Pandey, *A History of Prejudice*, 131–93.

[12] Brueck, *Writing Resistance*, 50.

[13] Gajarawala, *Untouchable Fictions*, 3.

[14] Basu, *Hindi Dalit*.

[15] Gilroy, *The Black Atlantic*, 69.

[16] Pandian, "Writing Ordinary Lives", 35.

[17] The book was translated in various languages, including Telugu: Thruvengadam, "Sant Ram", 67.

[18] Besides *MJKA* and *Hamara Samaj*, Samyak Prakashan has republished many of Santram's booklets against caste.

Singh, a leading Hindi Dalit writer, and Samyak Prakashan, a prominent Dalit publishing house, interpreted and published parts of *MJKA* in 2008 and proclaimed the book was the "first autobiography of Dalit literature" (*dalit sahitya ki pehli sva-jeevani*; Fig. 1.3).[19]

Lamenting that Santram's life and philosophy have been "lying in the darkness of history" (*itihaas ke andhere konon mein bikhra pada hai*), Satnam Singh says:

Fig. 1.3: Jacket front of Satnam Singh's version of *MJKA*.

Dalit literary writers have not been able to decide till date which should be considered the first autobiography of Dalit literature in Hindi, even though Dalit literature came into focus largely through autobiographies . . . In the January–February 1932 autobiographical special issue of *Hans* magazine . . . Santram BA had already written his [brief] life-narrative. It can be said with certainty that this is the first published self-narrative by any Dalit writer (in modern times) . . . In the July 1955 monthly issue of *Aajkal*, Santram wrote another self-narrative . . . Giving a detailed shape to these, in 1963, he published his autobiography titled *MJKA*. Thus, this is the first autobiography of Dalit literature in Hindi . . . Even on the basis of the main characteristics of Dalit literature, we should have no hesitation in considering him as its first autobiographer in Hindi . . . for it contains experiences of caste humiliation and the fight against caste oppression.[20]

[19] Singh, *Santram BA*, cover.
[20] See Singh, *Santram BA*, 3, 6–12. In the *Hans* referred to, Santram was perhaps the only low-caste author included: Santram, "Vidhi ka Vidhaan", 42–4.

Satnam Singh also hails Santram as the first Hindi Dalit journalist – as the first newsman to write fearlessly in prominent newspapers and magazine of his time.[21] While Singh's claim may be disputable, it underscores the significance of Santram's autobiography, which in its formulation overlaps with Dalit life testimonies. It is equally significant that Santram's name features in many Dalit anthologies and encyclopaedias.[22] Samyak Prakashan and many Dalit-Bahujan organisations regularly observe Santram's birthday (Fig. 1.4), and he is particularly memorialised by the Prajapati Kumhar caste.[23] Some of its members have established a Santram BA Foundation in Shahjahanpur, UP, which hosts a commemoration ceremony every year.[24] The centenary of the formation of the JPTM in 2022 was much celebrated by them.

Fig. 1.4: Poster celebrating Santram's birthday.

When republishing Santram's *Hamara Samaj*, Shanti Swaroop Bauddh, the publisher of Samyak Prakashan, said this of the author: "Though born in a potter caste, [he was] the one who challenged the biggest Brahmin

[21] Singh, *Santram BA*, 107–12.

[22] For example: Paswan and Jaideva, *Encyclopaedia of Dalits*, 189–90; Kshirsagar, *Dalit Movement*, 323–4.

[23] A Kumhar "is sometimes termed, honorifically ... Prajapati, after the Vedic Prajapatis, who were lords and creators of the universe, because they make things of the earth." Once, runs the legend, Brahma divided some sugarcane among his sons, and each of them ate his piece, except the Kumhar – who put his into a pitcher full of earth and water in which it struck root. When the god, some days later, asked his sons for the cane, they had none to give him, but the Kumhar offered his to the god and received from him the title of Parjapat or "Glory of the World": Rose, *Glossary of Tribes*, 562–3.

[24] Prajapati, *Santram BA*.

scholars and defeated them on the strength of his intellect in no time – this honourable Santram BA is indeed the pride of our society."[25] This kind of celebration of Santram underlines the profound heterogeneity of Dalit politics. There has been a subversive drive among Dalits whereby they have attempted to create long genealogies of Dalit literary history. This has sometimes entailed claiming a wider terrain of the oppressed by pushing the boundaries of Dalit discourse. In *Why I Am Not a Hindu* Kancha Ilaiah shapes the word Dalit-bahujan to mean that in spite of contradictions "there are cultural and economic commonalities as well as commonalities of productive knowledge which mesh them [Other|Backward Classes and Dalits] together like threads in a cloth."[26] Similarly, Dalit Panthers cast their net wide and use the term Dalit in a generic and inclusive sense.[27] These taxonomic redefinitions account for the acceptance of Santram in Dalit anthologies.

Familial and Social Roots: Caste Discrimination, the Arya Samaj, and Hindi

Santram was born on 14 February 1887 in Purani Bassi, a small village in the Hoshiarpur district of Punjab. His father, Ramdas Gohil, was a Central Asian trader with business interests in Yarkand and Ladakh. His mother was called Malini Devi and Santram was the fourth of the couple's seven sons and one daughter.[28] While his family had done well financially, their social roots were humble, their caste being that of the Prajapati Shilpkar Kumhars, which lay way down in the caste hierarchy and had a Shudra status in Punjab. H.A. Rose draws on Denzil Ibbetson, the colonial ethnographer par excellence of Punjab, to identify the Kumhar as

> the potter and brick-burner of the country . . . He is a true village menial, receiving customary dues, in exchange for which he supplies

[25] Santram, *Hamara Samaj*, 3rd edn, Shanti Swaroop Bauddh, 3.
[26] Ilaiah, *Why I Am Not a Hindu*, ix.
[27] Murugkar, *Dalit Panther*, 237; Shankar, *Flesh and Fish*, 67–74.
[28] *MJKA*, 5–6; Santram, "Taunted and Scoffed", 2; Gopal, "A Hundred Years", 8.

all earthen vessels needed for household use . . . He also, alone of all Punjab castes, keeps donkeys . . . He is the petty carrier of the villages and towns . . . His social standing is very low, far below that of the Lohar and not very much above that of the Chamar; for his hereditary association with that impure beast the donkey, the animal sacred to Sitala, the small-pox goddess, pollutes him; as also his readiness to carry manure and sweepings.[29]

It was noted in the *Gazetteer of the Hoshiarpur District, 1883–84*, that "Donkeys are kept by the potters (Kumhar), who do a good deal of the carrying trade between Palampur and Hoshiarpur."[30] Many degrading caste sayings pertain to Kumhars in order to mark their Shudra status:

kumhar ki gadhi, ghar-ghar ladi

[The potter's donkey is used by the whole village][31]

Other sayings reveal the poverty of the Kumhar:

kumhar ke ghar baasan ka kaal!
kumhar ke ghar chukke ka dukh!

[A scarcity of pots in the potter's house!
A want of saucers in the potter's house!][32]

And:

dheel dhoti baniya, ulta moonchh subir,
bainda pair kumhar, ke teenu ke pehchaan

[The trader wears his dhoti loose, the brave turns his moustaches up,
A potter is bare-footed – this is how to identify all three][33]

Santram himself had this to say about the Kumhar caste: "These people do not make pottery. The label of Kumhar has been imposed on them because of their birth-caste. Many of them do commerce

[29] Rose, *Glossary of Tribes*, 562.
[30] *Gazetteer of the Hoshiarpur District*, 107.
[31] Singh, *Santram BA*, 13.
[32] Fallon, *Hindustani–English Dictionary*, 144.
[33] Singh, *Santram BA*, 14.

and business in the country and abroad. Many have mules, on which they carry goods and sell them in hilly places."[34]

Given this background, Santram realised the importance of education very early. It has been pointed out that while in colonial India untouchability and caste hierarchies were reproduced through educational institutions, the first generation of Dalit intellectuals nonetheless saw education, knowledge, language, and print as central for social assertion.[35] Print journalism helped nurture a Hindi Dalit counterpublic, the boundaries of which were "located squarely in the interpretive framework of caste."[36] Santram epitomises the subaltern's effort at self-refashioning through education: with his pen and his writing he literally remade himself. Like many Dalits he viewed education and publishing as critical tools for claiming upward mobility and dignity.[37]

He was educated in Bajwara, Ambala, Jullundur, and Lahore, acquiring his BA degree in 1909 and activating his writing career in 1912.[38] From this time his writings appeared without any caste nomenclature – he proudly adopted his degree as his signature, signing his books and articles "Santram BA".[39] The subordinated often wrote their names suffixed with a defiant flaunting of their degrees to show their acquisition of an education and suggest they neither were nor felt humble. This was a discursive means of challenging historical injustices through a transformative process of linguistic self-determination. Naming and renaming, sometimes by the addition of a suffixed abbreviation or honorific, was a form of resistance.[40]

It has been noted that Dalit autobiographies constantly recount experiences of humiliation, thereby making a "public claim regard-

---

[34] *MJKA*, 4.

[35] Auxiliary Committee, *Review of the Growth*, 217–28; Constable, "Sitting on the Verandah", 385.

[36] Brueck, *Writing Resistance*, 50.

[37] Santram celebrated the spread of education, particularly in Hindi, in Punjab: "Jullundur Kanya"; "Punjab Kaumi Vidyapeeth"; "Rashtriya Shiksha".

[38] *MJKA*, 9; Singh, *Santram BA*, 13.

[39] Gopal, "A Hundred Years".

[40] Paik, "Mahar–Dalit–Buddhist", 217–18; Pandey, *A History of Prejudice*, 207–10; Rao, *The Caste Question*, 205–13; Kumar, *Writing the First*, 6.

ing the norms that govern the treatment of each other in society."[41] Santram's autobiography is infused with memories of caste prejudice and records his attempts to carve out a life of dignity. He tells us repeatedly how harshly and constantly he was reminded of his Shudra status over humiliating and bitter encounters in school and college, and these are a vital part of how he represents himself in *MJKA*:

> When I was admitted in class four in Ambala, my caste was also mentioned in the register . . . My co-students constantly harassed me, calling me by my caste name Kumhar. And why would they have not done so when even a saint and poet like Tulsidas ridiculed *kumhara* . . . I took the students' taunts quietly and painfully . . . In my [college] boarding house, the kitchen in which I had food was orthodox . . . One day a few fellow students . . . quarrelled with me and kept a chit on my seat stating that since I belonged to a low caste, I should have my food outside the kitchen, or else they would take the matter to the principal . . . I angrily declared that they could forget the principal, for even if they took the matter to the governor, I would have my food nowhere but inside the kitchen.[42]

From everyday caste humiliation we move to a world of myths about food and skin colour, and then to a critique of caste intellectuals and scriptural Hindu texts, through all of which he shapes his critique of caste.

Within the contentious and casteist atmosphere of Punjab, the teachings of Dayanand Saraswati and the spread in the province of the Arya Samaj – which at least theoretically distanced itself from casteism[43] – came to acquire a special attraction for Santram.[44] Many Dalits and "low castes" became followers of the Arya Samaj, thus critically contributing to the creation of the first generation of Dalit intellectuals in Punjab.[45] Many of the region's Ad Dharm activists,

---

[41] Kumar, *Writing the First*, 17.
[42] *MJKA*, 16, 17–18. See also Santram, *Jat-Pat ke Sambandh*, 6–8.
[43] Jones, *Arya Dharm*, 204.
[44] Santram's early writings reveal a deep attraction for the Arya Samaj: *Dayanand*; *Arya Samaj aur Varna*.
[45] Juergensmeyer, *Religious Rebels*, 72; Jones, *Arya Dharm*, 309–10; Adcock, *The Limits*, 128.

too, were initially associated with the Arya Samaj.[46] While in 1901 the Arya Samaj membership consisted overwhelmingly of Hindu upper castes, by 1911 its Punjab membership had quadrupled through the entry into it of other castes.[47] The 1921 census estimated that as many as two-thirds of the Arya Samajists of the region were of the lowest castes.[48] Hoshiarpur, particularly, proved fertile ground as it included a large number of "untouchables", approximately 23 per cent of the population.[49] Both Santram and Mangoo Ram – the latter being the dynamic leader of the Ad Dharm movement – hailed from Hoshiarpur. Mark Juergensmeyer points out that the Arya Samaj's ideology became particularly popular among urban Hindus of the mercantile castes.[50] Santram covered this middle ground by belonging socially to the Shudra caste while being economically associated with the urban mercantile class. His attraction for the relatively progressive ideology and egalitarian principles of the Arya Samaj has to be understood in this educational, urban, and social context – which also ultimately proved inhibiting and a drawback. At the same time, like many other "low castes", Santram selectively appropriated or rejected the ideological underpinnings of the Arya Samaj to suit his objectives of social status and equality.[51]

He was a supporter of vegetarianism, shuddhi, sangathan,[52] and brahmacharya, the last of which he came to reject totally. The Arya Samaj's ambiguity regarding caste when it came to the crunch was a source of certain inconsistencies within Santram, even when he was in conflict with his Arya Samaj "upper-caste" fellows and lamenting the various hurdles in his way.[53]

---

[46] Juergensmeyer, *Religious Rebels*, 27, 35–7; Adcock, *The Limits*, 128.
[47] *Census of India*, 1911, *Punjab, XIV (I)*, 137.
[48] *Census of India*, 1921, *Punjab, XV (I)*, 181.
[49] Juergensmeyer, *Religious Rebels*, 72.
[50] Ibid., 38.
[51] Rawat, *Reconsidering Untouchability*, 136–44; Adcock, *The Limits*, 159.
[52] Santram, "Hindu Sangathan".
[53] For example, Santram's "Chaturvarna Ved-Moolak Nahin"; "Jati-Panti ke Dushparinam"; "Jati-Panti ya Mritu?"; "Varna Vyavastha ka Vastavik Swaroop"; "Varna Vyavastha".

His love of Hindi developed in conjunction with the headway that the Arya Samaj was making in Punjab:

> Hindi was taught in none of the schools of Punjab . . . I did not know any of the Nagari script till the third year of my college. In my adolescence I considered Persian to be the sweetest language, Iran to be the best paradise on earth, and Saadi, Omar Khayam and Firdausi the greatest poets . . . However, Lahore and the Arya Samaj changed my views dramatically . . . In those days the *Saddharma Pracharak*, the mouthpiece of the Arya Samaj was published in Urdu. I used to read it with great enthusiasm. Its editor . . . Swami Shraddhanand announced a date from which the paper would switch over to Hindi . . . To read the paper I started learning the Nagari script . . . I left my love for Persian in favour of Hindi.[54]

Santram was fluent in English and Urdu. While a few of his writings were in Urdu,[55] and even in Marathi and Gujarati, the bulk of his work was in Hindi and he pitched himself as its promoter. He acknowledged his debt to Mahavir Prasad Dwivedi, the editor of *Saraswati*, "for his valuable guidance in improving" his writing; "it was due to his encouragement" that he "made Hindi writing his profession and source of livelihood."[56] He now created a name for himself in the print-public Hindi world and was most influential via his publications against caste and in support of intercaste marriages.[57]

---

[54] *MJKA*, 133–4.
[55] F. 3, 8–10 and 12–18, II: "Speeches and Writings by Him", "Individual Collections: Papers of Santram BA, List 430" (hereafter List 430), PMML.
[56] "Report from Judges in Regard to Prizes to be awarded on Best Hindi Books", 6–1/1953, Ministry of Education, NAI. Santram also wrote a moving obituary of Chintamani Ghosh, owner of the Indian Press (which published many of Santram's books) and publisher of *Saraswati*: "Swargiya Babu Chintamani". While not believing that Hindi could be the national language of all, Santram passionately promoted it in Punjab and UP, often opposing Hindustani: "Hindi aur Hindu", 73–4; "Hindi ka Swaroop", 193–5; "Hindi Mein Striyon"; "Isse Anek Logon Ne Hindi Likhna Seekha"; "Punjab Mein Bhasha"; "Punjab Mein Hindi"; "Sanyukt Prant ki Hindi"; Hindi *Gadya Vatika; Sahitya Sudha*.
[57] For example *Hamara Samaj; MJKA; Agar Kashti Dubi; Antarjatiya*

He began writing in Hindi periodicals like *Panchal Pandita* of Jullundur and the weekly *Saddharma Pracharak* of the Gurukul Kangri as early as 1910, and went on to contribute around three hundred articles in leading Hindi magazines, including *Chand, Madhuri, Prabha, Saraswati, Sudha, Hans, Saptahik Aaj, Naya Samaj* and *Nayi Dhara*.[58] To spread the message of the JPTM, he also edited two monthly magazines, one in Urdu called *Kranti* and the other in Hindi, *Yugantar*, which began publication in January 1932 and continued for four years (Fig. 1.5). Both of them ceased publication before too long due to a want of funds. Post-independence, Santram was associated with *Vishwajyoti*, published from Hoshiarpur.[59] Even as he was promoting linguistic nationalism, Santram was wresting Hindi from its exclusive clasp by the literate, the casteist, and the dominant. In his hands Hindi was vernacularised and democratised, as well as made a mobile site for contestations of caste and for addressing a more heterogeneous audience.

On the personal front there were two tragic calamities: the death of his first wife Ganga Devi in June 1924,[60] and then of his fourteen-year-old son Vedvratt in May 1928.[61] Both painfully affected Santram's transition into early adulthood. After some years his friend in

---

Vivah hi Kyun; Arya Samaj aur Varna Vyavastha; Hindu aur Jat-Pat; Hindutva jo Hinduon; Jativaad ka Janaza; Jat-Pat ke Sambandh; Jati-Bhed Prashnotri; Pakistan ki Sthapna; Rashtriya Ekta aur Jatibhed; Vinaash ka Marg; "Achhuton ko Kya Karna Chahiye?"; "Antarjatiya Vivah Pratha"; "Antarjatiya Vivah"; "Chaturvarna Ved-Moolak Nahin"; "Hindu Manovritti ke Kuch Namune"; "Hindu Manovritti"; "Hindu Vinash ke Marg Par"; "Jat-Pat Torak Mandal ka Sandesh"; "Jati-Panti ke Dushparinam"; "Jati-Panti ya Mritu?"; "Kranti ki Lehar"; "Lahore ka Jat-Pat Torak Mandal"; "Varna Vyavastha ka Vastavik Swaroop"; "Varna Vyavastha".

[58] *MJKA*, 32–3, 70; Santram, "Taunted and Scoffed", 2.

[59] *MJKA*, 136.

[60] Santram married Ganga Devi in 1899, when he was just twelve years old. Her loss affected him deeply. Later, when he most tragically lost his only son, he was unable to work for many months: *MJKA*, 73, 93–8, 99–112.

[61] Vedvratt was born in 1911 and died of pneumonia in 1928. He was taught Hindi by Santram, and even wrote a few stories in *Balsakha*, the famous

Fig. 1.5: An issue of *Yugantar*.

the JPTM, Bhumanand, persuaded Santram to remarry across his caste, and with this Santram began a new phase of his life. He had a daughter Gargi – named so by his friend Rahul Sankrityayan[62] – his only surviving child, to whom he was extremely close.[63] Though Santram's extended family was well-off, he spoke constantly of his poverty and financial difficulties since he was uncompromising on his principles and never had a permanent job, nor was he ever satisfied with any of the jobs he did have.[64]

In what follows, I draw from Santram's autobiography and his other anticaste publications, parts of which are also a history of the JPTM, to underline how and why Santram attempted to create a hybrid liberal domain, a middle ground between Gandhi and Ambedkar, the Arya Samaj and the Ad Dharm. His contradictory uses of modernity in his critiques of caste, and his explorations of intimacy and intercaste marriages show an insider-outsider perspective allowing him to sometimes swim within the boundaries of Hinduism but more often go against its mainstream.

---

children's monthly magazine. An obituary was published in the magazine: Shukl, "Ek Phool". While Santram had quite a progressive stance regarding the upbringing of children, and wrote several books and articles on the subject, the theme is not part of this book. His *Hamare Bachhe* also promoted anticaste thought among children (218–22). Many other subjects on which Santram wrote, for example travel and biography, are also not discussed here.

[62] Sankrityayan, *Jinka Main Kritagya*, 111.
[63] Interview with Madhu Chaddha.
[64] *MJKA*, 19, 32–3, 44–6.

A History of the JPTM and Anticaste Thought

Deeply impressed by a fiery speech delivered by Parmanand in Lahore in November 1922, Santram and a group of his friends formed the JPTM, which was given its name by Santram.[65] Eighteen people were initially associated with the organisation, including two women.[66] Representing the more militant anticaste wing of the Arya Samaj, unlike other radical regional caste movements, the JPTM was largely an urban-based movement among literates.[67] It soon had more than five hundred members from the various provinces of India,[68] including businessmen, government servants, barristers, professors, engineers, and doctors, all from diverse caste backgrounds – including Dalit, Khatri, Brahmin, Bania, Jat, Arora, and Kayastha. The JPTM also opened its branches in Ajmer, Meerut, Kashi, and Agra.[69]

Parmanand was initially the JPTM's president, but as its secretary Santram was its driving force. Articles were published on the JPTM in leading newspapers and magazines. The editor of *Chand* extended a hearty welcome to the organisation when it was formed.[70] The organisation itself launched monthly journals – *Jat-Pat Torak*, *Kranti*, and *Yugantar* – with Santram as editor. It published booklets against caste and distributed them free of cost, this being noted by the government.[71] JPTM members also attended Arya Samaj meetings and festivals to preach against caste.[72] The JPTM's first priorities

[65] Santram, "Lahore ka Jat-Pat". Also: "Jat-Pat Torak Mandal ka Sandesh".
[66] *MJKA*, 184–5; General Review, *The Jat-Pat*, 1.
[67] For more details, Graham, "The Arya Samaj", 536–44.
[68] Santram, "Jat-Pat", 550.
[69] Santram, "Lahore ka Jat-Pat", 190–1.
[70] Editor, "Jati-Pati Torak".
[71] "Fortnightly Report on the Internal Political Situation in India for the Month of May 1933", 18/6/1933, Home Poll, NAI.
[72] General Review, *The Jat-Pat*, 2–3; Santram, *Caste Must Go*, 1–2. The JPTM was strongest in the period from 1922 to 1947: Interview with Santram by Juergensmeyer. I am grateful to Mark Juergensmeyer for sharing his unpublished interview notes with me.

were to break the birth-based caste system and promote intercaste marriages – focal points to which I will return later.

In colonial India caste became a protean category for colonial capitalism, social reform, and Hindu nationalism, with the decennial census playing a central role in, on the one hand, strengthening the politicisation of the Hindu religion, and on the other "secularising" and challenging configurations of caste.[73] In his *MJKA* Santram entwines one part of his life narrative with the JPTM's movement in 1931 to remove the caste-based column from the census and from forms at colleges and universities. The JPTM gave a petition to the government to this effect as well,[74] and the *Tribune* took the matter up, publishing articles in support of the JPTM view.[75] Achieving some success, this campaign made the JPTM famous and accelerated its mobilisation, with people from all the big cities of India starting to join it.[76] It was noted in the 1931 Census of Punjab that "At the same time a tendency was noticeable for persons of low castes, well placed in life, to return no caste, and there had been a propaganda in this connection, particularly by the *Jat-Pat Torak Mandal* ... Instructions ... issued ... were that 'no caste return' should be recorded in cases in which the person enumerated had a genuine objection to the caste entry, having ceased to observe caste in his marital and inter-dining relations."[77] Interestingly, Juergensmeyer con-

[73] Bayly, *Caste, Society, and Politics*, 1–96, 144–86; Dirks, *Castes of Mind*, 3–18.

[74] 45/46/1930, Home Public, NAI. Also: 45/72/1930, Home Public, NAI; 2/3/1931, Home Public, NAI. Petitions were again submitted by the JPTM before the 1941 census: 1/1/1939, Home Public, NAI.

[75] "Petition from the Jat-Pat Torak Mandal for dispensation of caste during the ensuing census", 45/46/1930, Home Public, NAI. Letters were submitted by orthodox bodies against this petition.

[76] *MJKA*, 187–8; General Review, *The Jat-Pat*, 4–5; Santram, *Caste Must Go*, 2; "Caste and the Census", *Indian Social Reformer*, 61 (25), 21 February 1931, 395–6; "Anticaste Census Campaign", *Indian Social Reformer*, 61 (3), 20 September 1930, 44.

[77] *Census of India, 1931, Punjab, XVII (I)*, 325. The impact of the campaign of the JPTM was felt in many regions of India, and was noted in the census reports of 1931. For example *Census of India, 1931, Bengal & Sikkim, V (I)*,

siders the 1931 census and the campaign of the Ad Dharm around it as its "crowning moment", when "everything came together" because the movement was successful in listing Ad Dharmis as a religious community, separate from Sikhs, Muslims, and Hindus.[78] Moreover, the movement exacerbated tensions between the Ad Dharm and the Arya Samaj. Santram's move in the 1931 census acquires significance within this background.

It is in his anticaste thoughts that one sees Santram as an absorbed rationalist thinker who often assimilated and synthesised diverse viewpoints to offer a trenchant critique of caste. He says in an article of 1927:

> The Hindu attitude (*manobhav*) is so polluted that trying to change it is futile. Only a social revolution can remove the accumulated social filth of thousands of years . . . Since infancy, Hindus imbibe a lesson of hatred for Chamar, Bhangi and Sansi . . . Abundant effort has been made to reform this vile ethos and selfishness . . . of Hindus, but "like the dog's tail, it has remained the same."[79]

In tune with Ambedkar's perspective on the village, Santram regards it as a critical site of caste oppression.[80] His critique is a cry for rights and equality.[81] "Caste has made the Untouchable and the Touchable Shudras the slaves of *savarna* Hindus, who have maimed their soul, crushed their spirit and made them lose that human dignity which makes life worthwhile. There can be no friendship between a slave and his master."[82]

424; *Census of India, 1931, UP, XVIII (I)*, 545; *Census of India, 1931, Jammu & Kashmir State, XXIV (I)*, 312.

[78] Juergensmeyer, *Religious Rebels*, 72–80.

[79] Santram, "Kranti ki Lehar", 1032.

[80] Santram, "Letters to the Editor: Hereditary Lambardars", *Tribune*, 13 February 1951, in F. 6, II: "Speeches and Writings by Him", List 430, PMML. Also, "Achhuton ko Kya Karna Chahiye?", 190. For Ambedkar's views on the village, Sharma, *Caste and Nature*, 123–30.

[81] "Memorandum Presented to the British Cabinet Mission by Shri Santram, President Jat-Pat Torak Mandal, 1946", in F. 5, "Speeches and Writings by Him", List 430, PMML. Santram's critique of upper-caste Hindus is biting: "Hindu Manovritti ke Kuch Namune"; "Hindu Manovritti", 425.

[82] Santram, "The Real Cause of Pakistan".

And yet the framework of Santram's critique remains a Hindu ethos. At one place he thus argues that the Chuhras, a sweeper caste, have two different religious traditions. One, under Muslim influence, has taken Lal Beg as its icon of worship, and the other recognises Maharishi Valmiki as the teacher of the Balmikis; the former needs to be forgotten actively while the latter has to be championed.[83] We also hear of a case brought in 1915 against *Arya Musafir*, an Arya Samaj Urdu journal published from Punjab, allegedly for publishing articles that gave offence to Muslims while Santram was its editor.[84] Ironically, this did nothing to dispose either Hindu orthodoxy or the Arya Samaj in his favour, because Santram's Shudra background, radical stance against varnavyavastha, and robust support for intercaste marriages were anathema to them. A vicious article attacking Santram and the JPTM included this: "The extinction of Caste by the efforts of the Lahore [Jat-Pat Torak] Mandal would mean the destruction of Varna-Asrama-Dharma . . . Mr Santram is making the Veda false, if he says that food and marriage are not essential factors in settling the purity of a person . . . May the Jat-Pat Mandal see through the false Game and save themselves and the land of their birth from effacement by their own efforts!"[85] Another writer believed Santram's writings reflected "the snarl of a donkey, and [that he] could not hide his potter caste."[86] Even the iconic Hindi writer Suryakant Tripathi "Nirala" revealed his Brahmanical leanings in opposing Santram. In a long article titled "Varnashram-Dharma ki Vartman Sthiti" he expressed deep regret at Santram's creation of the JPTM. He was scathing too about both intercaste marriage and inter-dining, attacking Santram for favouring roti-beti ties between achhuts and Brahmins:

> Among various sins (*dosh*), that of touch too is considered a sin . . . Coming in contact with, and due to the touch of, low-castes, the essence of one's dvija caste (*dvijatiyatva*) is destroyed, misconduct (*duracharan*) becomes widespread, there is a degradation of society, and

[83] Santram, *Hamara Samaj*, 124, 189–90; idem, "Hindu Sangathan"; Prashad, *Untouchable Freedom*, 98–9; Interview with Santram by Juergensmeyer.
[84] *MJKA*, 37.
[85] "The Caste in the Kali Yuga", *The Dharmarajya* (Delhi), 6 July 1939, 3.
[86] *MJKA*, 225.

varnashramdharma is debased . . . I might have considered JPTM meaningful, to some extent, if it were a "Jati-Pati Yojak Mandal" [Society to Organise Caste] . . . It is nothing but a myth to believe that by having roti-beti ties with achhuts one can integrate them in society, or that by not doing so a vast majority is left out of Hindu nationalism. The equanimity of two hearts, which is the foundation of marriage and the basis of love, will be completely absent in such a marriage. And the marriage practices of Europe, which Santram so approvingly supports, too show inequality. No poor labourer has ever been married to a girl from a lord's family . . . If just by passing their BA the low castes start teaching Brahmins, they will look as ridiculous as Santram.[87]

Further, the JPTM and Santram, while close to the ideology of the Arya Samaj, also had tensions and were ambivalent both about it and the Ad Dharm movement. Santram lamented religious conversions, supported shuddhi, and advocated vegetarianism. He framed his critique of caste by embracing the "lower castes" within a Hindu fold and attempted to "improve" some of the perceived practices of the "lower castes". Yet even in these arenas he did not just replicate the teachings of the Arya Samaj but often radically reinterpreted them, chastising the continuity within them of caste prejudices. For Santram shuddhi did not so much symbolise a militant Hindu nationalism as provide a way of assertion by the "lower castes" for radical caste reform.[88] As has been argued, "Sometimes conventionality is a defense against norms too, a way to induce proximity without assimilation . . . and sometimes it's a way of creating another, counter conventional, space."[89] For example, transgressing normative discourses on caste, a cartoon in *Yugantar* shows a concupiscent Brahmin male ogling a sweeper woman and, even while expressing his lust for her, categorically denying the possibility of her ever being "purified" via shuddhi (Fig. 1.6).

Taking on board the Arya Samaj propaganda regarding the alleged abduction of Hindu women by Muslim men, Santram expres-

[87] Nirala, "Varnashram-Dharma", 836–42.

[88] For Santram, the success of shuddhi and sangathan rested solely on the promotion of intercaste marriages: "Hindu Sangathan", 276–7.

[89] Berlant and Prosser, "Life Writing", 181.

Fig. 1.6: Cartoon entitled "Ponga Pandit" in *Yugantar*, October 1933, 6. The verse below it says: "You are sensuous, titillating, and intoxicating, look at me with a smile! But even if I embrace you carnally, I will still always be a Brahmin, while no purification can be conducted for you, dear: you will forever remain a sweeper woman."

sed anxieties over the conversion by women to Islam on account of romance and marriage, and lamented this variety of Muslim "aggression".[90] However, unlike many of the writings by Arya Samajis, Santram acknowledged the broad-mindedness of Muslims in accepting such marriages within their fold, disparaged the narrow-mindedness of Hindus, and was open to the idea of amity and marriage ties between Hindus and Muslims.[91] This is in line with his attitude to missionaries and Christianity, which too is ambiguous. He drew selectively from various religious idioms and identities to build his arguments against caste: "Islam recognises the equality of all Muslims, rich or poor. Similarly, Christianity does not recognise any difference between a cobbler and a clergyman. But the very foundation of the caste system is laid on the present-day Hindu Dharma,

[90] Santram, "Hindu Striyon ke Apharan"; "Hindu Striyon mein Islam".
[91] *MJKA*, 48–53; Santram, "Hindi aur Hindu", 74.

which sanctions the superiority of Brahman over Shudra."[92] Elsewhere he says: "If I had been an untouchable, then to get rid of this slavery, I would have become a Muslim . . . If I were a Muslim, I would have opposed the Hindu rule more than Jinnah . . . The dominance of the Brahmin spells the subordination of the Shudra and the Muslim . . . I consider the morbid mentality of Hindus to be the root cause of anti-Hindu sentiment among the Indian Muslims and the untouchables."[93] For every dream, movement, and problem – independence, freedom from the British, communalism, Hindu-Muslim unity, and the formation of Pakistan – the central solution for Santram was an anticaste stance and support for intercaste marriages.[94] Freedom was for him nothing but freedom from caste. A magazine critical of his views put it this way: "On reading Santram's articles, if his name is hidden, it appears that you are not reading a Hindu lover but a supporter of Miss [Katherine] Mayo."[95]

Santram's contradictory position in relation to the Arya Samaj is clear from the fact of his radical anticaste views bringing him in direct conflict with its leading ideologues; he himself remained socially marginal to the organisation and was excluded from its established hierarchies of power. He narrates this incident from a time when he was an agriculturist in Patti in 1914–16:

> Something occurred that created a huge furore against me in society. I ordered many texts from the agricultural departments of countries like Australia, America, France, and England to improve my yield . . . It came to my mind to manure my fields with the bones of dead cattle that were lying around. I collected a huge heap on my land when my friend, the famous story writer Sudershan, came to visit me. He was at the time the editor of *Arya Gazette*, and when he chanced on the heap of bones he was extremely angry with me, saying that in spite of being an Arya Samajist I was mired in this sin. I argued with him . . . that these

[92] Santram, "Abolish Castes to Be Free". Also "Memorandum Presented to the British Cabinet Mission", F. 5, "Speeches and Writings by Him", List 430, PMML; Santram, "The Real Cause of Pakistan".
[93] *MJKA*, 206–13.
[94] Santram, "Hamari Swatantrata", 507; idem, "Sampradayik Ekta".
[95] *Hindu*, 6 October 1943, 2. Also *MJKA*, 212.

bones were of dead animals . . . and a rich source of manure . . . But he would not listen . . . He wrote a stinging statement against me in *Arya Gazette* . . . the Hindu press condemned me in strong terms . . . threatening to drag me to court . . . A deputation of residents of Patti questioned me . . . I argued that if they had no objection to keeping their match boxes, which were prepared from phosphorous, the essence of bones, inside their sacred kitchen, they should not oppose me providing manure to my lands.[96]

Many such incidents occupy the pages of *MJKA*; in them Santram makes it clear that while the JPTM is categorically against varnavyavastha, it is a sacred doctrine for the Arya Samaj.[97] He often mocks the difference in terms of rhetoric and action in the positions of the Arya Samaj. There were spats between him and Lajpat Rai, particularly on the issue of untouchability.[98] And he offers this critique of Bhai Parmanand: "After some time, he [Parmanand] became lukewarm . . . Through him Seth Jugal Kishore Birla offered us a donation of ten thousand rupees if we agreed to change the name of the society from JPTM to Hindu Samya Vad Mandal. But despite Bhaiji's great influence and persuasion we refused Seth Ji's offer and did not change the name of the association."[99]

The demand for a change of name, from "Jat-Pat Torak", i.e. Breaking or Annihilation of Caste, to "Hindu Samya Vad", i.e. Hindu Harmony, was something to which Santram said a categorical "no". By 1924 serious tensions had emerged between him and the Arya Samaj, on which he says: "By beating the broken drum of this merit-deeds-nature (*gun-karm-svabhaav*)-based caste system, Arya Samajis are unwittingly only strengthening birth-based caste dis-

---

[96] *MJKA*, 38–41.

[97] Santram, "Taunted and Scoffed", 2.

[98] Lajpat Rai wrote against Santram in *Vande Mataram* in 1926, and Santram refuted him in the same paper: Interview with Santram by Juergensmeyer. Also Thruvengadam, "Sant Ram", 66.

[99] Santram, "Taunted and Scoffed", 2. Bhai Parmanand, Gokul Chand Narang, and Mahatma Hansraj, all staunch Hindus and members of the JPTM initially, were against Ambedkar and separated from the JPTM.

crimination ... Naming it as the Vedic caste system, they are actually protecting the very same caste system."[100] Moreover, "All our energy is getting used in the work of Arya Samaj, and we are unable to propagate our own work. Thus, we ourselves have left this futile work [of the Arya Samaj]." It appears that he was also disturbed by the opposition of certain dogmatic Arya Samajis from within the JPTM to Ambedkar's likely arrival at the annual conference, after which he was greatly disillusioned by the Arya Samaj.[101] Their constant negotiations and estrangements reached a breaking point, so that Santram finally dissociated himself from the Arya Samaj.[102] He was thereafter, it appears, drawn to Buddhist ascetic traditions.[103]

Santram's relationship with Dalit organisations and leaders appears equally troubled: he did not fit easily into the Dalit movements of the time. While often invoking narratives associated with Dalit movements he could not – unlike Mangoo Ram or Ambedkar – become a leading champion of the Dalit cause. He rarely acknowledged the existence of the vibrant Ad Dharm movement, though, as noted earlier, both he and Mangoo Ram hailed from Hoshiarpur. Juergensmeyer says the JPTM "was not a model for the Ad Dharm, since its urban, reform Hindu, intercaste composition was quite different from what the Ad Dharm would embrace."[104] It can also be argued that the JPTM, like the Arya Samaj, was worried about the increasing assertiveness of the Ad Dharm movement and hoped to blunt its edge by absorbing Dalits into its fold and into a pan-Hindu identity. Both Mangoo Ram and Santram drew some of their inspiration from the Arya Samaj, but both found its ideology restricting; both rebelled against it in different ways – Santram from within, Mangoo Ram from without. In Santram's autobiography, where his tensions with the Arya Samaj are stressed while erasing and silencing the Ad Dharm, his mid position is made clear. And yet Santram led a strike of sweepers in Jullundur in 1938.[105] While

[100] Santram, "Chaturvarna Ved-Moolak Nahin", 103–4.
[101] Prajapati, *Santram BA*; Interview with Satnam Singh.
[102] Juergensmeyer, *Religious Rebels*, 38–9.
[103] Singh, *Santram BA*, 3.
[104] Juergensmeyer, *Religious Rebels*, 39.
[105] Kshirsagar, *Dalit Movement*, 323.

stating that he was never a part of the Ad Dharm movement, he also claimed at one point that his friend Mangoo Ram was a member of the JPTM.[106] It is also noteworthy that Santram wrote a long article, "Kranti ki Lehar" (Wave of Revolution), in 1927, in the famous magazine *Saraswati*, in which, besides being ardently in favour of intercaste marriages, he voiced support for the Adi Hindu movement and its dynamic leader in UP, Swami Acchutanand. He went on to say:

> Now a new spirit has awakened among the Dalit brothers. This feeling is of self-respect (*atm-samman*) and self-reliance (*svavalamban*) ... They say that "we are the original inhabitants of India. We are Ad-Dharmis. We are not Hindus ... The whole history of Hindus is a history of unspeakable atrocities on Shudras" ... The Hindus will try to suppress this revolution that has taken place in the thought of Dalit brothers ... Is the demand of Dalits not true? Haven't Hindus been oppressing them since time immemorial? ... Hindus, you cannot stop this new wave, this revolution rising among the Dalits ... If the worm of purity of blood (*lahu ki pavitrata ka keeda*) does not let you rest in peace ... then why do you stop the untouchables from demanding their separate rights?[107]

In a rebuttal, one Mangaldev Sharma, twisting the title of Santram's article, published another named "Bhranti ki Lehar" (Wave of Fallacy) in the October 1927 issue of the Hindi magazine *Madhuri*, in which he was scathing about Santram:

> The words in which he [Santram] has introduced his sentiments in his [article] "Kranti ki Lehar" ... can never be regarded as respectable ... As per our understanding, his revolutionary clothing (*vidrohi ka jama*) is such that instead of creating the havoc of a revolution, it will sink its very purpose ... It seems that his movement has nothing to do with Hindu sangathan and national reform. For him, Hindus can go to hell and the nation in a state of abyss, but he will definitely flow his river of waves (*lehar ka dariya avashya bahayenge*).[108]

[106] Santram, "Lahore ka Jat-Pat", 190; Interview with Santram by Juergensmeyer.
[107] Santram, "Kranti ki Lehar", 1032–5.
[108] Sharma, "Bhranti ki Lehar", 415–16.

The vicious attacks on Santram and the JPTM by both the Hindu orthodoxy and the Arya Samaj signify that his position was uncomfortable, in fact unacceptable, to both. Equally, Santram walked the line between Gandhi and Ambedkar by not fully opposing the "disturbing faults" of Gandhi, particularly his leanings toward Sanatani Hinduism, nor fully supporting the "superior merits" of Ambedkar, particularly regarding conversion. Santram's telling of his life not only contributes to the Gandhi–Ambedkar debate on caste but, by falling between their grids, signifies a third stance. Though he was uncomfortable with both these political figures, he appears closer to Ambedkar, not least because he had some sharp exchanges with Gandhi. In this context he narrates an interesting incident:

> I led a deputation of the JPTM to Gandhi at Lahore and requested him to help our movement. But the Mahatma said that caste was a good thing as it eliminated hard competition in the choice of profession . . . At this I replied – "Mahatmaji, it is a good thing for a Brahmin, or Kshatriya, or Vaishya boy to follow the profession of his father, but how can it be in the interest of a sweeper boy to continue to remove night soil and clean latrines for generations? Mahatmaji, you are a Bania by caste; your hereditary profession was to sell salt, oil and flour. Why don't you go and earn your living by selling those commodities? Why have you come here to preach politics and ethics?" At this there was laughter in which his wife and Seth Lal Bajaj also joined.[109]

And here is Santram in a letter:

> According to the Shastras, there are only four castes or varnas and the untouchables are out-castes, i.e. out of the fold of Chaturvarna. Now some of our social reformers, including Mahatma Gandhi, are in favour of removing untouchability, but hesitate to destroy its root cause, the four castes. Therefore, the question naturally arises, what will be the position of the Harijans among the caste Hindus after their untouchability has been removed? Will they be satisfied if they are converted from untouchable out-castes to "touchable caste" Shudras? I do not think so, for what they demand is social equality and not mere removal of untouchability.[110]

[109] Interview with Santram by Manchanda, 18–19.
[110] Santram, "Place of Harijans".

Santram was in dialogue with, and an admirer of, both Periyar and Ambedkar, finding affinities with them. He published an article on Periyar in *Viduthalai*, the leading Tamil daily, in June 1953.[111] He appears to have been even closer to Ambedkar, of whom he often expressed great admiration rather than any overt criticism. And yet he was troubled by him too, as is reflected in the notorious withdrawal of the invitation to Ambedkar for the 1936 JPTM conference.[112] Many members of the JPTM, on reading the text of Ambedkar's speech, found it too hot to handle, especially his direct and scathing attack on Hinduism and support of conversion. Though he never directly says so, Santram seems to be in implicit agreement with some of the objections, though he continued to remain Ambedkar's friend,[113] and both exchanged a series of letters, often sharing anticaste thoughts, writings, and anecdotes. Ambedkar often requested Santram for inputs from the Hindi belt on some of the articles published on caste in Hindi, and his opinion on certain other publications. For example, Ambedkar asked Santram for his views on his draft of *What Hindus Have Done to Us* in a letter dated 11 June 1942; thanked him for sending a cutting of his article published in *Sansar* in a letter dated 20 July 1945; and apologised for not sending his opinion on Santram's *Hamara Samaj* quickly in a missive of 4 September 1949.[114] In another letter to Santram, Ambedkar wrote: "I admire your efforts for breaking up the caste system. But allow me to say that I do not agree with the way you are attacking the problem. I do not see how you can break up caste without annihilating the religious notions on which the caste system is founded. I cannot develop the argument now ... In the meantime, I must leave it to you to deal with the question in the way you like."[115] And, most significantly, it was Santram

---

[111] List 430, PMML; Interview with Santram by Manchanda, 6. Santram often acknowledged Periyar's support and friendship: Interview with Santram by Juergensmeyer.

[112] For a good discussion on the whole context of the invitation and its withdrawal, see Sayeed, *Understanding*, 111–13ff.

[113] Santram, "Taunted and Scoffed", 7.

[114] Letters written by Ambedkar to Santram. I am grateful to Shanti Swaroop Bauddh for sharing copies of these letters.

[115] "Religious Notions on Which Caste System Is Based Should be De-

who went on to translate *Annihilation of Caste* into Hindi for the first time, and published it under the banner of the JPTM.[116] He then also published it in Urdu in his journal.[117]

The persistent problem with Santram remained his reliance on Hindu idioms and "upper castes" even in the realm of intercaste marriages. Yet today Santram's writings find greater acceptance among Dalits than liberal Arya Samajis, even when his larger history is almost forgotten. He was no Mangoo Ram or Ambedkar, yet he signifies the liberal vision of a middle-ground ethos, at times hamstrung by his context and at others ahead of his times. His stance on intercaste marriage is his most lasting legacy for anticaste politics.

Transgressive Intimacies: Championing Intercaste Marriages

prem na dekhe jat-kujat.
bhookh na dekhe jutha bhaat.

[Love sees no caste boundaries.
Hunger is indifferent to food taboos.]

– quoted by Santram in support of
intercaste marriage[118]

With this quote Santram brings together two critical taboos of roti-beti in order to challenge them.[119] Roti-beti taboos have been

---

stroyed", Dr Ambedkar's Letter to Jat-Pat Torak Mandal, *Tribune*, 11 December 1935, 5.

[116] Santram, *Jatibhed*. Also Interview with Santram by Manchanda.

[117] Kshirsagar, *Dalit Movement*, 323. Bhagwan Das, the famous Dalit writer, noted that the JPTM was the only organisation working against caste discrimination, and its *Kranti* was the only Urdu magazine that published Balasaheb's speeches in Urdu translation. Das developed a friendship with Santram. He further stated that Babasaheb deeply valued Santram's dedication to the anticaste struggle and his impeccable character, and used to send copies of his new books to Santram for comments: Das, *In Pursuit of Ambedkar*.

[118] Santram, *Antarjatiya Vivah hi Kyun*, 31.

[119] In a sense Santram is also equating love with hunger, while translating love also in terms of sex, and seeing both as a drive.

central to the caste practice of spatial and bodily exclusions. Endogamy, a cornerstone of caste, also reveals the pervasive imprint of caste on women's bodies. Even while operating within heteronormative paradigms, intercaste marriages have produced daily policing and everyday violence, along what Foucault calls the alliance model of sexuality where, through the arrangement of marriages, relations and boundaries of caste and religion are policed.[120] Increasing anxieties and fears around Dalit conversions forced the Arya Samaj and the Hindu Mahasabha into a rhetoric of support to intercaste marriages, but on the ground there were fraught debates and unease on the question as most reformers underwrote an exclusive grammar of difference in sexual regimes.[121] Ambedkar argued that intercaste marriage was a hallmark of Dalit progress and an important solution for annihilating caste, since it challenged the relationship between the maintenance of caste purity and the control of women's sexuality.[122] Santram made a categorical intervention in this arena by bringing together caste, gender, sexuality, and desire in his discourse on intercaste marriages, making it a major vehicle of his anticaste articulations.

Before I venture into details, I should add that Santram also often broke food norms by inter-dining, not only with Dalits, but also with Muslims, his autobiography being littered with such examples. For instance, his wife Ganga Devi, who did not believe in pollution taboos, engaged a Muslim woman as a cook when Santram was working at Patti in 1917. This displeased the Sikh peasants of the neighbouring villages, who threatened to boycott not only Santram but all those associated with him.[123] In 1930 Santram invited two of his Dalit friends, Ishwar Das and Harnam Das, for dinner. Santram served them food inside his kitchen and they drank water from his well. This created mayhem in his village: his house was boycotted.[124]

[120] Foucault, *The History of Sexuality*, 106–11.
[121] Gupta, *The Gender of Caste*, 77–84.
[122] Ambedkar, *Annihilation of Caste*, 59–64; Rao, *The Caste Question*, 232–33; Rege, *Against the Madness*, 59–64.
[123] Santram, "Taunted and Scoffed", 7. Also *MJKA*, 39.
[124] *MJKA*, 47–8.

The panchayat ordered that he be seen as an outcaste and stopped his hookah-pani. Santram's reply was defiant: "I do not smoke hookah, and there is water in my home."[125] In 1931 at a marriage in Purani Bassi among the Pathans, Santram's friend Sher Khan secretly brought a sweet rice dish for him. Santram said he would eat it not in hiding but openly in front of everyone, which created an outcry in the village.[126] Yet another incident is told to show his view:

> At Dehra Doon I went to the shop of a Muslim confectioner and asked him to give me sweets worth two annas. He looked at me from the head to toe for five minutes and then said – "I am a Muslim." I replied, "What then? I have not asked your religion. I can take your sweets if you are not a poisonous snake." He replied, "I am not a poisonous snake." With these words he ordered his servant to go while he himself rose and brought a good deal of sweets for me. I told him that I requested sweets worth two annas only. At this the confectioner said, "Please do not talk of price. Take the sweets. It is first time that I have come across a broad-minded Hindu like you, who does not differentiate between a Hindu and a Muslim in the matter."[127]

Through this kind of social behaviour, and unorthodox cooking and eating practices, Santram challenged Hindu food taboos and rules of commensality, thus posing emancipatory possibilities within the politics of food. While hailing the arrival of the JPTM under the leadership of Santram, the editor of *Indian Social Reformer* highlighted the limitations of reform movements like the Brahmo Samaj and the Arya Samaj: "But very little has been done by the Arya Samaj and other bodies to break the citadel of caste system by the arrangement of intercaste-dinners, intercaste-marriages . . . These movements, instead of coming forward boldly and frankly to champion the cause of social reforms, have become part and parcel of the orthodox retrogressive Hinduism . . . It is with this object of infusing a new spirit that JPTM has been started recently."[128]

---

[125] Chaddha, "Unki Yaden", 30.
[126] Santram, "Taunted and Scoffed", 7.
[127] Ibid. Also *MJKA*, 68.
[128] "League to Abolish Caste System", *Indian Social Reformer*, 33 (20), 13 January 1923, 320. This view was endorsed by Har Bhagwan, assistant

Coming back to the question of marriage, the first and foremost rule of the JPTM was to break the birth-based caste system and promote intercaste marriages. The JPTM's rules stated that the only Hindus who could join the organisation were those who pledged not to marry within their caste, and if already married promised the same for their children. There was a separate department in the JPTM to promote intercaste marriages: it maintained "a register in which all eligible candidates for intercaste marriages" were entered.[129] A list of such marriages was published in the JPTM's booklet *Madhur Veena* and in its 1929 directory.[130] A review of the activities of the Mandal in 1939 stated that "at the least computation such marriages must be 500 in number."[131] Though the JPTM had a limited and largely urban membership and following, it cut across regions and had intercaste marriages as its central goal. In his writings, including his autobiography, Santram gives many examples of intercaste marriages that he and the JPTM promoted and facilitated without the intervention of any priests or the performance of religious ceremonies and rituals (Fig. 1.7).

Fig. 1.7: Intercaste marriage performed by the JPTM: Vijay Kumar MA (Vaishya) and Chand Rani BA (Brahmin), with Santram and Sunder Bai.

---

secretary of the JPTM, in an interview with James Reid Graham in December 1938 in Lahore: Graham, "The Arya Samaj", 537–8.

[129] General Review, *The Jat-Pat*, 4; Santram, *Caste Must Go*, 2.

[130] *MJKA*, 188; "Jat-Pat Torak Mandal, Lahore", *Indian Social Reformer*, 36 (35), 1 May 1926, 550.

[131] General Review, *The Jat-Pat*, 4.

However, it appears that most of these intercaste marriages pertained to the top three varnas, the dvija castes. Rather than vertical, it was horizontal alliances between the top three varnas that were more often encouraged in the name of intercaste marriages. Santram describes an incident in 1914: "I had two friends Parmanand and Bhumanand. Parmanand was Arora by caste and Bhumanand a Brahmin . . . Parmanand requested me to persuade Bhumanand to marry his younger sister . . . Bhumanand agreed . . . His father, family and friends opposed it and no one came for the wedding . . . It was a brave act to break caste taboos at that time."[132] Santram often faced threats for facilitating such marriages.[133] In his article "Bhranti ki Lehar", Mangaldev Sharma says: "Even in dire circumstances, Kshatriya-Brahmin girls will never be married to Chamars."[134] All the same, due to Santram's efforts intercaste marriages became a symbol of progressive urban modernity, even if operating mainly through the JPTM within a small circle of elites.[135]

After the death of his first wife, Santram himself remarried a Maharashtrian Brahmin widow, Sunder Bai Pradhan in December 1929 (Fig. 1.8). This was the variety of intercaste pratilom marriage most attacked by the orthodox – between a Shudra man and a Brahmin widow, similar to Ambedkar's second marriage. Santram's friend Bhumanand put it thus : "This marriage breaks caste ties, promotes widow remarriage, and also breaks regional differences."[136] The central focus of intercaste marriages allowed Santram to emphasise the permeation of caste within intimate spaces, and to show that it was in such arenas that caste really needed to be challenged.[137]

[132] *MJKA*, 36; Interview with Santram by Manchanda, 4.
[133] *MJKA*, 56–9.
[134] Sharma, "Bhranti ki Lehar", 419.
[135] It was, for example, noted by one Rai L. Chranji Lal Sah, a magistrate at Almora, that "a majority of hight caste young educated Brahmins of Kumaon of their own free will . . . are joining the JPTM. And are, also voluntarily inter-dining with so-called depressed class people . . . It is possible that they may willingly inter-marry with the above-named caste people in the course of a very short time": 50–16/1933, Home Poll, NAI, 801.
[136] Santram, "Vidhi ka Vidhaan", 43.
[137] Santram wrote a long article in *Sudha* in support of Vithalbhai Patel's Hindu Intercaste Marriage Bill, proposed in 1918, which validated mar-

Fig. 1.8: Santram (centre) with his second wife, Sunder Bai, 18 February 1954.

Considering caste a disease, Santram said it rested on the four taboos of touch, occupation, food, and marriage.[138] Relentlessly questioning Manu and endorsing Ambedkar, he passionately promoted intercaste, interregional, and interreligious marriages as central to the eradication of caste.[139] He offered multi-pronged arguments to disrupt the logic of endogamy, resorting to sacred, religious, devotional, moral, and scriptural discourses on the one hand, and relying on social, secular, modern, scientific, economic, and rationalist arguments on the other; together, these brought different castes into new modes of relationality. Both these registers were supported by extensive documentation and arguments. Selectively

---

riage between Hindus of different castes. It faced stiff opposition from the orthodoxy and was finally dropped: Santram, "Antarjatiya Vivah". The article referred to those opposing the bill as cowardly, parochial, fearful, and short-sighted, and adopted a question–answer format to critique all the objections raised against. For details on the bill, Mitta, *Caste Pride*. Santram continued to support the intercaste marriage bill, regarding it as "the first step towards freedom": Santram, "Hindu aur Swarajya", 8–9.

[138] Santram, *Hamara Samaj*, 3.

[139] Once, while critiquing Manu, Santram was asked by a learned scholar if he was more knowledgeable than Manu. At this Santram replied, "Yes! Manu did not know what is meant by 'telepathy', what is a 'telescope', how did a rail run, while I know about all these things. If Manu was something, he may have been in his times. At present our knowledge is much greater": Interview with Santram by Manchanda, 8.

quoting from the ancient texts, Santram served up past examples of *anulom* (homogamy) and pratilom intercaste marriages. For example, Pramatta, a Brahmin woman, married a barber and gave birth to Matang, the great rishi. Arundhati, a Kshatriya, was married to Vashishth Rishi, the son of a prostitute. Their son Shakti married Adrishyanti, a Chandal girl. Shakti's son, Parashar, the great rishi, married Satyavati, a fisherman's daughter, and was the father of Vyas, author of the *Mahabharat*. Bhim married the demoness Hidamba, and Ghatotkatch was their child.[140] Santram included in his list leading personalities like Gandhi, Parmanand, Nehru, Gokul Chand, and Raja Narendra Nath, all of whom had intercaste/interregional marriages, and arguing that none of them could be excommunicated from Hindu society.[141]

From here he easily moved to modern, scientific, and "secular" arguments, layering them with the ideas of equality and justice. Paul Gilroy speaks of the African American autobiographer Frederick Douglass, who brought "the illumination of reason to the ethical darkness of slavery."[142] Nearer home Periyar passionately invoked radical empiricism and a verifiable view of science for his anticaste mission.[143] The historian of caste Anupama Rao challenges the association of Dalits with non-modernity, tradition, "pasts", and community.[144] For Santram, it is clear that enlightened discourses and rationality were valuable aids for emancipatory politics. He wondered "Why such Hindu kings like Ramchandra, Harishchandra, Krishna, Shivaji and Pratap did not think of . . . providing education and full citizenship rights to untouchables and Shudras?" And elsewhere: "Attempting to take help of shastras in finding solutions to eradicate caste and untouchability is like washing dirt with more dirt."[145]

He adapted a Western liberal model to a distinctly Indian register to mould a new anticaste selfhood. He often resorted to quoting

[140] Santram, *Hamara Samaj*, 11–14.
[141] Santram, "Hindu Rishis and the Caste".
[142] Gilroy, *The Black Atlantic*, 59.
[143] Geetha and Rajadurai, *Towards a Non-Brahmin*, 514.
[144] Rao, *The Caste Question*.
[145] *MJKA*, 222.

scholars such as the German-American anthropologist Franz Boas, a prominent opponent of ideologies of scientific racism, to support his arguments.[146] Resembling the pattern in some Dalit narratives, Santram selectively praises British rule: "For many untouchables and Shudras, the British rule is an unmatched God's gift . . . Untouchables will be very foolish to prefer a Hindu dominated state over British rule."[147] He also often recalled the fact that George V's daughter had married a commoner, proving that marriage rules were much more flexible in the West.[148] Opposing a pro-caste article written by one Mukhopadhyay in *Sudha*, Santram argued that in no country other than India was marriage decided on the basis of birth. While class distinctions could shift over time, caste enforced endogamy, and "no Chamar, however learned he may be, could socialise with the Brahmins." The clearest way to overcome this, he argued, was inter-caste marriages, based on compatibility determined on the basis of virtue, deeds, and nature instead of birth-based caste.[149]

Replete with discussions of "difference" and "sameness" and its varied connotations, Santram interrogated notions of homogeneity, oneness, self-sufficiency, self-knowledge, singular identity, and binarity, and stressed the advantages of what he called "cross-breeding", which, he argued, led to the birth of a stronger and more creative third:

> It is a universal principle of science that the mixing and coming together of two different products leads to a better and nicer third. Thus, oxygen and hydrogen, when combined, produce the best and the purest product of water . . . When horses and donkeys cross-breed, the *khachchar* (mule) is born, more powerful and stronger than the two . . . Similarly, intercaste marriages lead to better relationships, a more equitable society, and stronger nation.[150]

[146] Santram, *Hamara Samaj*, 124. Having read widely, Santram also wrote articles vehemently critiquing the Ku-Klux-Klan and Nazi Germany for its inherent racism: "Ku-Klux-Klan"; "Naziyon ke".
[147] *MJKA*, 208. Also Santram, "30 June 1948", 49.
[148] Santram, "Antarjatiya Vivah", 601.
[149] Santram, "Jati–Panti ke Dushparinam", 219–22.
[150] Santram, *Antarjatiya Vivah hi Kyun*, 1–2. Also Santram, "Antarjatiya Vivah Pratha".

Endogamous unions, he argued, were an inferior form of marriage and could even be equated with incest – i.e. to a marriage between brothers and sisters. The coming together of the intellect and brain of the Brahmin and the physical strength of the Kshatriya would, he believed, lead to better progeny.

Within Santram's arguments lay their limitations, domestications, and occlusions, given that he sometimes reiterated the stereotypical and essentialist perceptions of the "characteristics" of the various varnas. He appropriated select ideas around national growth, development, progress, masculinity, and particularly eugenics to push for intercaste marriages – with double-edged implications. Lack of masculine power, weakness, lower levels of intelligence, the constant defeat of Hindus in past wars, unhealthy progeny, and a weak nation were all depicted as among the evils of endogamy. Intercaste marriages, conversely, ensured stronger, healthier, and brighter children; diversified occupational categories; increased masculinity. In short, this was the solution for Hindu progress.[151] Visions of selfhood, autonomy, equality, progress, freedom, modernity, and rationality were imparted in Santram's narrative in conjunction with traditional Hindu and ritualistic paradigms, revealing an argumentative pendulum that swung between the spiritual and the material.

This undercutting of caste through his arguments deploying stereotypes was more or less constant. Once, at the annual conference of the Arya Samaj in Lahore, there was a debate between Santram and Ramdev, a teacher at Gurukul Kangri, on *varnavyavastha*, with the latter supporting it and Santram vehemently opposing it. On this occastion Santram stated in a lighter vein:

> You say that people should be branded with their varna label, and men-women with same label should marry . . . Now suppose the husband and wife are of the same varna, and have similar characteristics: both get easily angry, and tend to fight. Their qualities are the same. In such a home, there will be constant arguments and fights. As opposed to this, suppose one of them is calm and quiet, then there are much fewer

[131] Santram, *Antarjatiya Vivah hi Kyun*, 5–15.

chances of their family life breaking ... Similarly, marriage within the same varna is not good.[152]

This vocabulary disparaging binaries and boundaries implicitly reinstates them.

At the same time, Santram challenges not only caste hierarchies but also patriarchal hegemonies. Because of endogamy, he says, in jatis where women outnumber men, there has been a phenomenal growth in the practice of dowry; whereas when this was the reverse and men outnumbered women, the latter were sold as commodities and the sex trade proliferated.[153] He thus urged women to attack the "disease" of caste vigorously, since the endogamous marriage could in no way be regarded as more positive, stable, or better than intercaste marriage.

Lauren Berlant argues that "Central to the development of narratives that link personal life to larger histories, and to practices and institutions of intimacy, desire also measures fields of difference and distance. It both constructs and collapses distinctions between public and private: it reorganizes worlds."[154] Santram in this sense seems to occupy paradoxical social sites – appropriating caste as a sign of privilege in some cases while disparaging it in others. The various modes of articulation result in ambiguous implications. On the one hand he opposes the essentialised characteristics of the different varnas and of women, and on the other his ideas about healthy progeny, powerful nation, etc. implicitly reinstate caste and patriarchy.

Woven into these views was his belief that children of intercaste unions not only inherited the qualities of both parents but also did not belong to one or the other of the constructed caste categories, and instead occupied a third, liminal space. While gendering intercaste marriages, he upheld ideologies of productive and reproductive labour, but inherent in his arguments was also a plea to refigure relationships between women and men. Herein lay Santram's paradox:

[152] *MJKA*, 199–201.
[153] Santram, *Antarjatiya Vivah hi Kyun*, 17. Also "Bhartiya Jeevan", 794.
[154] Berlant, *Desire*, 13–14.

he used a version of the poison as its own remedy. At the same time, the disruption of endogamous marriages signified a challenge to caste difference and intimate desire. When read in conjunction with Santram's equally vast sexology literature, the subject of the next chapter, his discourse on intercaste marriages opens up further radical possibilities.

Santram's autobiography and other writings are not merely literary ornaments, they are communicative acts through which he evolves his own anticaste idioms, codes, and practices. While caste suffering forms an axis of his writings, it is not central to it; rather, it is the forms of resistance to caste that are critical. Santram's narrative offers a richly textured account of his private life and public commitments, whereby his anticaste tropes endeavour to reach a hybrid, liberal ground, straddling the middle ground between Gandhi and Ambedkar, and between the Arya Samaj and the Ad Dharm. He cannot be easily slotted as he rides on uncertainties with a deep hankering to get rid of caste without letting go of Hinduism. In spite of his deep frustration with the Arya Samaj, he attempts to amalgamate Arya Samaji and anticaste ideas. Giving caste an urban flavour, he deploys social reform through largely city-based, educated, "anticaste" people, and creates a counter-archive of caste. Recalcitrant histories of caste may be gleaned by studying Santram's life narrative, and his story is open to subversive appropriations and emancipatory practices of caste dissent. It is perhaps for this reason that Dalit writers and intellectuals have claimed Santram more than have members of the Arya Samaj. His dual identification as a Shudra and a Dalit, and as within and outside the Arya Samaj, gives a radical tinge to his life. Similar to Phule, Periyar, and Ambedkar, his trenchant critique of endogamy provides the intersection between anticaste thought and gender, challenging connections between sexual regulation and caste reproduction. Santram's erudite enunciations in support of intercaste marriages call upon ideas of caste intimacy as a way to get at the terribly material, embodied character of caste-gender dynamics, and as a way of breaking the shackles of the varna-jati complex.

2

Cast(e)ing and Translating Sex
Vernacular Sexology from the Margins

Probably, like Kunti, the mother of the Pandavas, no one can regard an unmarried mother and her child as bad and dirty . . . Social stigmas attached to pre-marital sex will gradually diminish and eventually disappear . . . There will be much more parity between women and men . . . It is quite natural for both women and men not to be monogamous . . . Intelligent and thinking human beings will refuse to be tied in a lifelong miserable relationship . . . It will be easier for a woman to live with many men and for a man to live with many women . . . There are many women and men who feel the need and desire multiple partners . . . The woman will not have to state the fatherhood of her child . . . There are many amazing women who want to have sexual relations, want to have a child but do not wish to have a permanent husband or marry. They will have a right to do so . . . The main purpose of intercourse is the fulfilment of sexual desires . . . Every big city will have a school of sexual science.[1]

THIS POTENTIALLY radical passage by Santram reflects a heterosexual ethics that gives women a greater place in the governance of their sexual life. Santram celebrates a utopian sexual future of man–woman relationships, as well as a better familial and social order which supports the free choice of multiple partners and sex before marriage. This chapter focuses on Santram's

---

[1] Santram, "Vivah ka Bhavishya", 303–7.

vernacular writings on sex, conjugality, and sexology, including his translations of several books by Marie Stopes into Hindi for the first time.

In early-twentieth-century India sexology largely operated along gendered and casteist lines. Its discourse was overwhelmingly constructed as an elite, bourgeois project dominated by upper-caste, middle-class male intellectuals who gave it power and authority.[2] The lower castes and women, disempowered social actors, were excluded from the science of sex. By bringing a Shudra to the centre of our understandings of vernacular histories of sexology, this chapter views the "spatiality of the margin as a place of possibility" which can "open up new configurations and assemblages" and destabilise the sexual.[3] Further, to rephrase Dipesh Chakrabarty, the sexology writings of Western writers and male upper-caste Hindu sexologists are "at once both indispensable and inadequate in helping us to think through" the articulations of vernacular sexology in late colonial North India. This is a subject that needs also to be studied from the margins, even if it often reiterates the dominant viewpoints, the margins being as "plural and diverse as the centers".[4]

Santram's name has been obscured vis-à-vis the canon of sexology and omitted by pedagogic authority. Also, while most of Santram's admirers, Dalit scholars, and printing presses continue to publish his anticaste literature, they have marginalised other facets of his identity. In particular, his huge repertoire of publications on matters of sex has been erased from memory and is hardly available in India.[5] He appears to have been the only low-caste sexology writer in a field dominated by high-caste authors. Through the figure of Sant-

[2] Sexologists – such as A.P. Pillay, Sitaram Phadke, and R.D. Karve – exemplify the upper-caste, male-centric bias of the field. On Pillay: Ahluwalia, "Tyranny of Orgasm". On Karve: Botre and Haynes, "Sexual Knowledge"; idem, "Understanding R.D. Karve".

[3] Nirta, *Marginal Bodies*, 27–8.

[4] Chakrabarty, *Provincializing Europe*, 16.

[5] For example, my search for Santram's *Rati Vigyan* in India's libraries yielded no results. Finally, I located it at the TUFS Library, Japan, which was generous enough to send me a copy.

ram I aim to retrieve a lost archive and resuscitate the voice of a Shudra sexologist, while showing that the denial of epistemic credibility to Santram contrasts sharply with his remarkable productivity and considerable corpus on the subject. Santram was a self-styled sexologist who, with no formal sexology education or professional title, operated outside institutional settings. He promoted himself as a public intellectual on matters of sex and caste. His textual engagements with sexology present an "inauthentic" voice, and yet this putative amateur produced sexual knowledge which had a wide reach and appeal.

I wish to ask, further: what happens when an anticaste theorist ventures into the domain of sexology?[6] Can his sexology be also implicitly anticaste and anti-masculinist? Can anticaste work think intimate desires? In other words, I am interested in examining how Santram's anticaste rhetoric was intertwined with translation and the vernacular in the formation and transmission of sexology, and a sustained theorisation of sex. I argue that Santram's pioneering work against caste and in support of intercaste marriages cannot be separated from his equally copious writings on sex and sexuality, as in different ways both were attempts to question dominant assumptions of power and to undermine hegemonies, patriarchies, and ideals of purity. If the dominant form of sexology – as captured by Pillay and Phadke – upheld a conjugal imperative that was conducive to, and strengthened, gender and caste hierarchies, Santram's sexology is the opposition. It subverts endogamy by promoting intercaste marriages in his anticaste writings, and opposes norms of chastity as well as castigations against non-procreative, non-conjugal female sexuality in his sexology.

Santram's writings stand at a crossroads, revealing intersections between anticaste thought, intercaste marriages, sexology, science, Sanskrit sex classics, translation, and the vernacular. His mediations on these subjects are all the more significant because he took on the languages of power – Sanskrit and English – defying the upper-caste and Western monopoly over knowledge, including sexual knowledge.

---

[6] I am inspired here by Holland, *The Erotic Life of Racism*, 3.

He translated and vernacularised them to challenge monogamous procreation, restrictions on female sexuality, and caste-based power. His subversiveness was also implicitly an attempt to include Shudras in the Sanskrit intellectual tradition and English scholarly modernity.[7] Immersed in the world of Hindi, his writings not only contribute to creating a counter-archive and a cultural resource for the study of sexual sciences in India, they also help in addressing the vernacular and translation as a significant, if ambivalent, site for the reproduction, transformation, and contestations on matters of sex. Utilising repertoires of representation and circuits of production, I argue that Santram straddled multiple terrains, drawing from classical works on kamashastra on the one hand, and on the other relying on Western sexologists to underline pleasure and desire as important facets of modern sexual life. His insightful narratives on marriage, sex, and pleasure created intimate spaces, conjoining the private–public and opening up ancillary terrains such as touch, sex and sexuality; intercaste love, desire and intimacy; and transgressive sexual norms. Sexuality for Santram was a cover story for various kinds of dissonances because he laid claim to authority by questioning savarna morality and carving out a space to think about the body beyond the parameters imagined by the burgeoning middle-class and upper-caste world. Through Santram I thus attempt to speak to different sets of scholarly writings – historical works on caste and Dalits from a gender-sensitive perspective; translation studies that have creatively examined its meanings in the context of gender and sexuality; the vernacular as a site of contestation; and studies on sex and sexual sciences in late colonial India.[8]

---

[7] For debates, Anand, "Sanskrit, English and Dalits"; Dasgupta, "Sanskrit, English and Dalits".

[8] On caste and gender: Chakravarti, *Gendering Caste*, 107–11; Chowdhry, *Contentious Marriages*; Gupta, *The Gender of Caste*; Rao, *Gender and Caste*; Rege, *Writing Caste*; idem, *Against the Madness*, 13–56. On translation studies: Bauer, *English Literary Sexology*; Larkosh, *Re-Engendering Translation*; Santaemilia, *Gender, Sex and Translation*. On the vernacular: Chatterjee, "Introduction", 1–24; Kumar, *Writing the First*; Shankar, *Flesh and Fish*. On sexuality and sexual science: Ahluwalia, *Reproductive Restraints*; Berger, *Ayurveda Made Modern*; Botre and Haynes, "Sexual Knowledge"; Hodges, *Contraception,*

The first section of the chapter maps print cultures and the development of sexology in Hindi in the late colonial period, and what writing in the vernacular implied for the eminence of classical erotica like the *Kamasutra*. It also examines some contentious debates on copyright issues around sexology publications. The second section explores how Santram "legitimised" his writings and established his mastery in vernacular sexology, in the process turning his unequal and seemingly negative caste identity into a positive claim of authority. Towards this end he moulded translation to offer a hybrid sexology that interwove the shastric and the vaigyanik by translating Sanskrit sex classics as well as Marie Stopes into Hindi. The final section examines how Santram critiqued male sexual behaviour and addressed women as active recipients of and participants in sexology. He thus articulated heterosexual ethics to disseminate an understanding of sex that would nourish the modern conjugal couple. Alongside, he opposed brahmacharya and supported birth control through empathy with a woman's perspective.

As a whole, the chapter widens the landscape of vernacular sexology by showing the problems and possibilities of reinscribing it from the margins. It shows a world of epistemic possibilities that could at times collude and at others defy the imperium of mainstream sexology.

Vernacular Print Cultures and Sexology in Hindi

A substantial growth in vernacular publications on sex provides a compelling context for Santram's output on the subject. The interwar period, in particular, was a time of increasing experimentation and intellectual interest in sexology globally.[9] In urban India, issues around sex came to be appropriated in discussions on ayurveda, eugenics, prostitution, child marriage, birth control, and brah-

---

Colonialism; Pande, *Sex, Law*; Savary, *Evolution*; Mitra, *Indian Sex Life*; Arondekar, *For the Record*.

[9] Fuechtner, *et al.*, *A Global History*; Bauer, *English Literary Sexology*; Leng, *Sexual Politics*; Chiang, *Sexuality in China*; Schaffner, *Modernism and Perversion*.

macharya.[10] New questions proliferated through transnational discourses on sexual hygiene, public health, juridical regulation of sexuality, age of consent, and venereal disease, along with shifts in gender relations and conjugal narratives. Simultaneously, a dynamic print capitalism facilitated the widespread production of so-called ashlil material as a commodity, and vernacular erotic consumerism became a critical part of the publishing boom.[11]

The language of sexual science often needs a corporeal presence and the nearness of lived experience that the vernacular can offer. Print indexed sex as an object, and Hindi became central to histories and texts of sex and pleasure. The commoditisation of what Ishita Pande calls "global/Hindu sexology" literature in Hindi included Santram's writings.[12]

Alongside, given the British colonial presence, debates around obscenity intensified. There were serious attempts at the moral regulation of society by controlling what were perceived as obscene publications. Most of the British reports disliked the sexual vernacular and were repulsed by many of its depictions of sex, describing them as "bazaar trash" and "grossly indecent".[13] It was reported in 1909–10 that poetical works had mushroomed and that the subjects were largely erotic and immoral.[14] It was also recorded that many of these books were semi-pornographic.[15] A section of the colonised elite implicitly agreed, with their attempts to control obscenity overlapping with those of the colonials, though for different reasons. A section of Hindu reformers and the Hindi literati also trenchantly critiqued such publications.[16]

---

[10] On these various subjects, see respectively Berger, *Ayurveda Made Modern*; Savary, *Evolution*; Mitra, *Indian Sex Life*; Pande, *Sex, Law*; Ahluwalia, *Reproductive Restraints*; Hodges, *Contraception, Colonialism*; and Haynes, "Gandhi, Brahmacharya".

[11] Gupta, *Sexuality, Obscenity*, 39–49.

[12] Pande, "Time for Sex", 279–301; Botre and Haynes, "Sexual Knowledge", 999.

[13] Danton, "Book Production", 246.

[14] *Report on the Administration of UP, 1909–1910*, 51.

[15] *Report on the Administration of UP, 1924–25*, 112.

[16] Gupta, *Sexuality, Obscenity*.

However, it was not easy to make sexual pleasure the focus of a moral panic since attempts to fashion moral subjects were constantly fractured and reimagined. Many popular writers, along with everyday reading tastes and practices, were indifferent to what the moral police considered taboo. A section of the vernacular print world managed to escape the colonial gaze as it was not dependent on its patronage; moreover, sex literature was often hidden and consumed in private. Thus, even amidst various contentions, there was an efflorescence of printed sex literature in Hindi, particularly of erotic sex manuals. Some of them used a highly Sanskritised register, usually catering to an elite audience. Simultaneously, there were several popular versions and multiple editions written in colloquial Hindi.[17] The textual politics of sexology in Hindi, while fracturing the hegemonic claims of English and Sanskrit in the field, spread from elite medical circles and Sanskrit scholars to Hindi-speaking publics, where a diverse constituency of educated middle-class, upper-caste men were the main actors and authors. Sexology in the vernaculars often drew its prowess from Indian erotica and/or modern sexology texts, liberally reinterpreting them to suit specific needs. However, the offerings of vernacular sexology were not often neatly translatable as Western sexology. There was a lack of fixity in the meanings served up by the local variety, which encompassed a spectrum of ideological rubrics and texts, including eugenics, conjugality, marriage, home science, sexual health issues, birth control manuals, erotic, "obscene" and pornographic material, sex advisory literature, and popular writings on sex.[18] There were also various words like kama shastra, koka-shastra, riti shastra, and *rati kriya* (the art of love-making) in the Hindi vernacular that could all work as replacements of "scientific sexology". The word kama, for example, meant "sex", "pleasure", "desire", and "erotic love". At least thirty Hindi titles of this time contained the words kama, koka, riti, and rati.[19]

Scholars such as Jyoti Puri argue that classic Sanskrit erotic texts,

[17] Ibid., 49–66.
[18] Baishya and Mini, "Translating Porn Studies", 2–12.
[19] For example, Gupt, *Gupt Prachin*; Sharma, *Kok Shastra*; Zamindar, *Kok Shastra*.

especially the *Kamasutra*,[20] were largely unknown in colonial and postcolonial India, remaining more visible in the West, or in the "popular consciousness of the English-speaking elites", and most importantly in "academic debates on sexuality".[21] Similarly, Wendy Doniger says that "The *Kamasutra* plays almost no role at all in the sexual consciousness of contemporary Indians."[22] The contention is that with the coming of colonialism, and a simultaneous flowering of Hindu prudery, texts like the *Kamasutra* vanished from the Indian print-public sphere. However, this view elides the plural afterlife and efflorescence of the *Kamasutra* in vernacular print cultures. A casual glance at the buzzing industry of popular Hindi sex treatises shows numerous references to the text. The profound influence of the *Kamasutra* in these works differs from the citation and translation politics of its use in European texts. While printing led to the standardisation of the *Kamasutra* as a text, it also opened it for mass production, creative transmission, democratisation, (mis)quotation, and selective translation, making the reconstitution of erotic desires a subject of the vernacular that cut across age, caste, class, and gender. Commenting on Richard Burton's translation of the *Kamasutra*, Anjali Arondekar notes that the "assumed cultural and political differences between sexology as a discourse in which matters of 'illegitimate sexualities' are legitimately studied and pornography as a discourse in which the same matter takes shape more furtively, collapse in their shared relationship to empire."[23]

Revelling in Hinduism's erotic past, many authors used the language of scientific sexology for their claim to textual authority, which they equated with Vedic knowledge by arguing that the Sanskrit erotica comprised timeless and foundational texts of sexology, the reason being that "India's ancient texts had *always* been attuned to modern sexual rhythms."[24] Many such books, including Santram's, went into multiple printings, underlining the insatiable appetite of

[20] For a lucid overview of *Kamasutra*, see Roy, "Unravelling the *Kamasutra*".
[21] Puri, "Concerning 'Kamasutras'", 605.
[22] Doniger, "From Kama to Karma", 63.
[23] Arondekar, *For the Record*, 106.
[24] Pande, "Time for Sex", 280. Also Pande, *Sex, Law*, 169–206.

Indians for the erotic, even as reformers and nationalists were disparaging it. They were so popular that though they often copied each other, authors and publishers claimed exclusive rights, with cases in court over copyright infringements. For example, Babu Piare Lal Zamindar of Aligarh was the author and copyright owner of *Kok Shastra*, which, initially published in 1900, had by 1905 been reprinted seven times, each reprint running to 2000 copies. Written in a relatively simple Hindi, the book had sections like "Jawani Diwani" (Crazy Youthfulness) and was reported to have been particularly popular among young boys.[25] Zamindar filed a case against Hakim Ram Kishen of Lahore for printing and selling his book under the same title, and the district judge of Aligarh ordered Kishen to either deliver all copies of the book to Zamindar or pay him Rs 600 as damages.[26] In another case Jagannath Prasad, publisher of the book *Sachitra Bara Kok Shastra* (1928), reprinted four times by 1932, went to court against Gopal Das for copying large parts of the book in his *Asli Sachitra Kok Shastra*. Prasad argued that Das' book was a "colourable imitation" in which "no less than nine chapters dealing with nine different subjects have been copied." Das maintained that there were "common sources from which both the books have been compiled and common ideas dealt with in them." At various stages he stated "that he had prepared his book from the manuscript of an old *Kok Shastra*", and for its various chapters he had taken the matter from old and contemporary books like *Kok Vigyan, Kamasutra, Koksar Vigyan, Kama Vigyan aur Sachitra Kok Shastra, Adarsh Patni*, and *Shahanshahi Kok Shastra*. Finally, he lost in the High Court as well and had to pay Jagannath Prasad Rs 2275.[27]

The case underscores the absurdity of claims of copyright infringements and of distinctions between originals and copies, particularly in relation to Hindi sexology books. Chapters like *stri ya purush mein kama cheshta kab jagrit hoti hai* (When does sexual

[25] Zamindar, *Kok Shastra*.
[26] *Hakim Ram Kishen vs Babu Piare Lal*, 7 Ind Cas 101, 21 June 1910. http://indiankanoon.org/doc/1839213/, accessed 15 January 2019.
[27] *Gopal Das vs Jagannath Prasad and Anr*, AIR 1938 All 266, 10 January 1938. http://indiankanoon.org/doc/426845/, accessed 15 January 2019.

desire kindle in a woman or man), or *sanyog kis samay karna chahiye* (At what time should one have sexual intercourse) cut across many Hindi sexology books of the time. Moreover, both parties upheld the primary source and legacy of Sanskrit erotica, with the "offender" stating that these were in the public domain and beyond the claims of violation. However, since the reproduction and sale of these books were tied to substantial profits, assertions of originality were nevertheless made because victory in court held the potential for a decent harvest.

These debates highlight a flourishing sexology literature. People like Santram firmly believed that the intricacies of sex and the erotic life of conjugality needed to be discussed explicitly because sexual pleasure was an important facet of modern married life. Like many others, Santram creatively deployed mass print technology, literary diversity, and the commercial press to his advantage, bringing sex from the elites to the masses. Embracing the hugely commercial trajectory of the eroticised spectacle, his writings often blurred the lines between sexual science, erotic art, and obscenity. His books were widely publicised through magazines and advertisements in books, and were available through the post as well as in the newly emerging book markets, local kiosks, and railway stations. Furthermore, through the vernacularisation and translation of Marie Stopes' most important books on the one hand and Sanskrit sex classics on the other, Santram made claims of authority and offered a hybrid sexology that managed to combine classical ideas on sex, sexual notions circulating in the market, Western sexologists' viewpoints, and emerging notions of conjugality and love.

Translating Marginality into Authority: Marie Stopes and the Sanskrit Sex Classics

Though Santram wrote mostly in Hindi, he was a polyglot fluent in Persian, Urdu, Hindi, Sanskrit, and English who later picked up Marathi and Gujarati from his second wife, Sunder Bai.[28] Translations

[28] *MJKA*, 109.

were an important component of his publications, many of which were commissioned. There have been fascinating debates on translation as original or derivative, primary or secondary, and scholars have also asserted that there is often an inherent transgression in the act of translation.[29] These deliberations aside, Santram, as earlier noted, was the first to translate Ambedkar's *Annihilation of Caste* into Hindi.[30] Between 1926 and 1928 he translated Alberuni's famous *Tarikh-al-Hind* (The History of India) in three volumes, and I-Tsing's record of the Buddhist religion as practised in India. Some of the other important works he translated into Hindi were Louis Jacolliot's *The Bible in India* in two parts, O. Hashnu Hara's books, Robert Dodsley's *The Economy of Human Life*, and Dale Carnegie's *How to Win Friends*, which went into several impressions.[31] Through these translations Santram sought the epistemic credibility he needed to join the canon:

> In our Hindi world, a translator is looked down with contempt and considered worthless, a trivial creature (*naganya praani*) who is seen as surviving on leftovers (*jhoothan khanewala*) . . . But he creates a bridge between the past and the present, between a foreign land and its own people . . . Just as honey bees carry pollen from one flower to another, in the modern age, translators have a critical role in the flowering of a culture, as they are its highly educated messengers.[32]

[29] Venuti, *The Translation Studies*.
[30] Santram, *Jatibhed*.
[31] For Alberuni: Santram, *Alberuni ka Bharat*, 3 vols; for I-Tsing: Santram, *Itsing ki Bharat Yatra*; for Jacolliot: Santram BA, *Bharat mein Bible*, 2 vols, with a foreword by Bhai Parmanand. Louis Jacolliot (1837–1890) was a French scholar and author who for a period became chief justice in the court of Chandernagore. In his sensationalist book, *The Bible in India: Hindoo Origin of Hebrew and Christian Revelation*, first written in French in 1869, he celebrated Vedic culture and stated that the Bible borrowed considerably from it. The translation of the book in two parts by Santram was commissioned by Dularelal Bhargava, the editor of *Sudha* and proprietor of the Ganga Pustak Mala Press, and was extensively advertised in the pages of *Sudha*; for Hashnu Hara: Santram, *Ekagrata aur Divyashakti*; idem, *Karmyog*; for Dodsley: Santram, *Manav Jeevan ka Vidhaan*; for Carnegie: Santram, *Lok Vyavhaar*.
[32] Santram, "Sahitya Sansaar", 257.

Deeply influenced by Dr Marie Stopes, and seeing the popularity of her books in Europe and America, Santram was the first translator (in the 1920s–30s) of her most celebrated books into Hindi, including *Married Love*, *Contraception* (which was interestingly translated by Santram as *Santan Sankhya ka Seema Bandhan arthat Dampati Mitra*, lit.: "Limiting the Number of Children, i.e. A Friend of the Couple"), and *Enduring Passion*.[33] This amounted to a project laying new claims to authority as by this method he "espoused a universality of knowledge production by vindicating the translatability of discrepant systems of knowledge."[34]

Santram also wrote his own books on sexology, which were a combination of select translations from Sanskrit sex classics like Vatsyayan's *Kamasutra*, Koka Pandit's (popularly known as Kokkok) *Rati Rahasya*, Padmashri's *Naagar Sarvasva*, excerpts from Freud and Stopes, and his own thoughts on the subject.[35] These included *Rati Vigyan*, a book which was not only instructive but also titillating;[36] *Kama Kunj*, a sex manual for women and men published by the prestigious Naval Kishore Press of Lucknow;[37] *Adarsh Patni*, a book advising women on various matters, including love and sex;[38] and *Adarsh Pati*, a book on similar lines for men. Rajpal, the owner of Rajpal & Sons, a publishing house based in Lahore, published many of Santram's books (Fig. 2.1).[39]

Finally, Santram wrote articles in *Madhuri* and *Sudha*, leading women's magazines of the time, in support of the "true" publications

---

[33] Santram, *Vivahit Prem* (*Married Love*); idem, *Santan Sankhya* (*Contraception*); idem, *Rati Vilas* (*Enduring Passion*).

[34] I draw this observation from a different context in Chiang, *After Eunuchs*, 11.

[35] *Rati Rahasya*: A medieval Indian sex manual, composed in the eleventh or twelfth century CE; *Naagar Sarvasva*: an erotic treatise written probably around 1000 CE by a Buddhist scholar, Padmashri. For details, Ali, "Padmasri's 'Nagarasarvasva'", 41–62.

[36] Tandon, *Hindi Sevi*, 307.

[37] For details on the press, Stark, *An Empire of Books*.

[38] The book saw more than nineteen impressions.

[39] Jigyasu, *Dharma ki Balivedi*.

of sexual science, which also worked as publicity material for his sex manuals.[40] He often said he received hundreds of letters on the subject.[41]

Like his anticaste writings, Santram's sexology works were attacked. Articles were published in magazines; for example, one titled "Patan ki Or" in *Sudha* defamed him and Dhaniram Prem as *durachari* (debauched), and condemned them for their writings on kama vigyan, which reflected kama vasna and bestial proclivities (*pashvik pravritti*).[42] Banarsidas Chaturvedi too critiqued Santram for his work in this terrain.[43] Declaring himself a champion against obscenity, and lamenting that all Hindi readers – who according to him included traders, lawyers, government servants, and college students – were *kaamuk* (lascivious) and *vyabhichari* (adulterous), he said they wanted to consume only this type of literature.[44] When Santram's article "Vivah ka Bhavishya" was published, Arya Samajis and Sanatan Dharmis were up in arms and called him a moral anarchist.

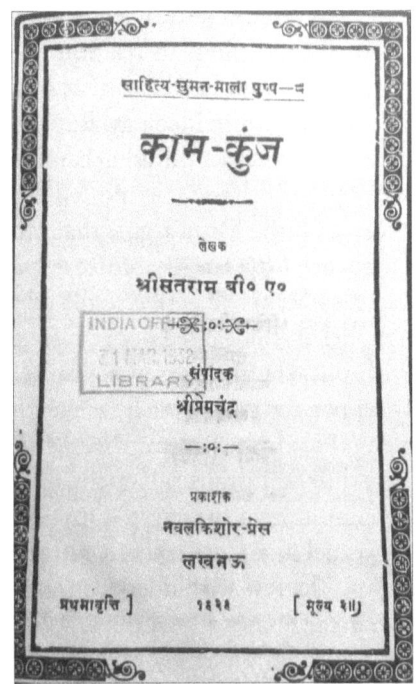

Fig. 2.1: One of Santram's many books on sexology.

At the same time, this kind of conjunction of English and Sans-

---

[40] For example, Santram: "Naagar-Sarvasvam", 396–9; "Sanskrit Sahitya"; "Rati Rahasya"; "Vivah ka Bhavishya"; "Kamashastra aur Dharmik Pakshpat".
[41] Santram, *Kama Kunj*, 168.
[42] The charges were strongly refuted: Prem, "Guptendriya Ang".
[43] Dutt, *Banarsidas Chaturvedi*.
[44] Singh, "Kya Hindi-Pathak".

krit by a Shudra anticaste ideologue could carry potentially revolutionary meanings in relation to both sexual morality and caste norms. Santram saw himself as mainly an anticaste activist steeped in a non-Brahmin ideology. But since he also saw himself as an educator, his anticaste thinking cannot be separated from his sexology writings as both were permeated with the questioning of savarna authority. Durba Mitra argues that modern social scientists utilised the language of science to obfuscate questions of caste power by claiming caste as an objective result of social evolution, and to uphold a model of an idealised upper-caste monogamous conjugality. In line with this, she shows how sexual science literature in Bengal largely supported caste hierarchy as a textual fact and an ethnological necessity.[45] However, Santram seems to be redeploying sexology for a very different project. Lamenting the Brahmanical monopoly over ancient erotica, he says: "Our Sanskrit literature has many texts on sexual love . . . Of these, only seven [or] eight have been printed . . . The rest are hidden from the world, lying in ancient libraries and in the homes of Brahmins."[46] In wresting such texts from the privacy of the dominant and placing them in the public domain for general consumption, Santram democratises sexology and emphasises that those who do not know Sanskrit or English will be greatly benefited by his writings on the subject.[47] He also sometimes uses the sex classics in creative ways within his anticaste literature. For example, during a heated argument on the caste system with Pandit Hemraj Vaidya of the Arya Samaj, the latter harangued Santram for not believing in the Hindu shastras, upon which Santram asked Vaidya: "Do you believe in all shastras?" Vaidya replied: "Yes I believe in all of them." Santram retorted: "Then you should definitely also believe in kokashastra." It was the perfect *coup de grâce*: Vaidya was deeply embarrassed.[48]

Santram was a firm believer in the need for an uninhibited acknowledgement of sexual pleasure. In an interview he announced that he had a great fondness for books on sex and was an avid reader of

[45] Mitra, *Indian Sex Life*, 15–16, 155–6.
[46] Santram, "Naagar-Sarvasvam", 397.
[47] Ibid., 399; Santram, "Rati Rahasya", 601.
[48] *MJKA*, 202.

Sanskrit classics on the subject; moreover, "Lala Lajpat Rai's son Amrit Rai was a friend of mine. I found many good books related to sex in the library of Lala Lajpat Rai."[49] On another occasion he declared: "Sex is the thing without which the life of a person is monotonous . . . Without which the songs of the poets are prosaic, the articles of the writers are dull and the attitude of the world is arid."[50]

He imagined sexual freedom in the literary domain at a time when it was tenuous in actual practice. A substantial number of social reformers, nationalists, and British officials regarded the subject from a Victorian lens, through which it was either altogether taboo or disgusting, and charges of obscenity therefore commonplace. The prefaces, translator's notes, and inserted footnotes become significant when reading Santram's translations.

Taken as a whole, certain features stand out in these writings by Santram. Like other writers of his time, he stresses inspiration from shastric and scientific literature on kamashastra and sexology, quoting extensively from them to authenticate his work, while simultaneously attacking other works on the subject as fake and pseudo. In an article he says:

> From the letters that I have received, it is clear that there exists a great desire to gain knowledge on the subject of sexual sciences in the public. People are unable to find the true texts of such scriptures, so they want to quench their thirst for knowledge by purchasing fake texts . . . which are bad translations of English books . . . They contain colourful pictures of naked men and women, and are sold in the name of authentic pictorial kokashastra . . . However, scholars who invented the works of sexual sciences were men of high character . . . Their texts are very useful for students of human procreation and ethics. For the information of scholars and thinkers, here is a brief introduction to the work of the great Pandit Kokkok on the subject so that readers identify the fake from the real.[51]

Santram's translations are selective; he cannibalises the earlier textual sources: "With the help of ancient texts such as *Kamasutra*,

[49] Interview with Santram by Manchanda, 29.
[50] Santram, *Rati Vigyan*, 3.
[51] Santram, "Rati Rahasya", 601–2.

Rati Rahasya and *Naagar Sarvasvam*, I have prepared a book named *Kama Kala*. Leaving aside the useless, all the useful things in these texts have been written in such a scientific way that the advantages of sexual science are visible to all."[52] He claimed these writings by him were prescriptive, essential for sexual compatibility and fulfilment. He stressed their credibility by drawing liberally from key Western authors, often citing Havelock Ellis, Marie Stopes, Sigmund Freud, and Richard Schmidt. As has been argued, Western sexual knowledge functioned as a legitimising source in vernacular texts.[53] Santram's case is confirmation of this assertion: "Pandit Kokkok's real book is called *Rati Rahasya* . . . It has not been translated and printed into Hindi or in any other native language so far . . . Mr [Richard] Schmidt, the teacher of Sanskrit in Germany's Munster University, has translated it into English . . . But due to the fear of government reporters, it has not yet been published . . . The book is like a lamp on sexual art."[54]

The fear of being banned on charges of obscenity was constantly referred to, and, like many other authors of this genre, Santram regularly stressed in all his articles and introductions that his writings were not ashlil. An advertisement of his book *Kama Kunj* in the leading Hindi magazine *Madhuri* promoted it as a critical book for the modern conjugal couple (Fig. 2.2).[55]

Santram's *Rati Vigyan* had a chapter exclusively on this subject titled "Kya Kamashastra ka Vishay Ashlil Hai?" (Is the Subject of Sexual Sciences Obscene?)[56] Categorically denying it was so, he went on to differentiate between *bhava* (sentiment) and *buddhi* (intellect), and *deshachar* (pragmatism) and vigyan:

> On hearing just the word kamashastra, many people begin to vilify it to uphold their false religiosity and supposed purity . . . But even if a minuscule of thought is given to the subject, it will be clear that, in

[52] Ibid., 605.
[53] Savary, "Vernacular Eugenics?"
[54] Santram, "Rati Rahasya", 602–3.
[55] *Kama Kunj* was continuously advertised in *Madhuri*: *Madhuri*, February, March, and April 1930.
[56] Santram, *Rati Vigyan*, 28–45.

branding any book of sexology as obscene, only irrational sentiments are at work, rather than any rationality or intelligence . . ."[57]

. . . A thing that is accepted by reason cannot be obscene. Pragmatism may temporarily declare sexology to be obscene, but in facing science prudence faces death. A thing that is declared essential by the intellect and science cannot be declared repugnant.[58]

The language of vigyan at Santram's disposal often made it possible for him to speak of the unspeakable. He went on to quote Sir James Stephen's *Digest of the Criminal Law* and E.H. Starling (Professor of Physiology at the University of London) to justify the necessity of books on kamashastra.[59] In his preface to *Vivahit Prem* he says: "Those who consider kamashastra as obscene must read this book. After studying it, they will be convinced that kamashastra is a definitive science meant for public benefit."[60]

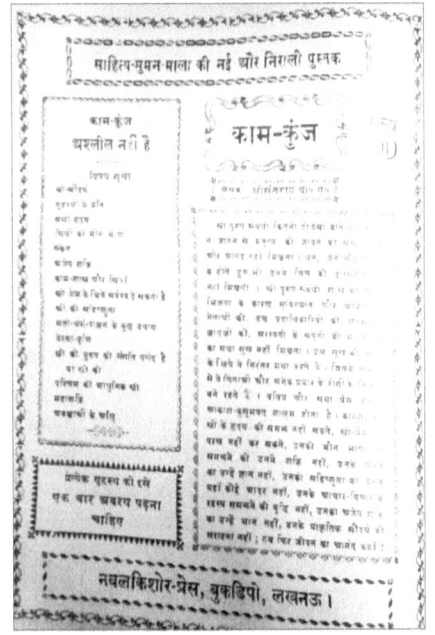

Fig. 2.2: The advertisment for *Kama Kunj* in *Madhuri*.

Heike Bauer argues that "Translation can . . . usefully be described as a process of trans- and cross-cultural negotiation and re-formulation of ideas, governed by socio-historical circumstance."[61] Santram's mediations on sex through multiple means and diverse texts

---

[57] Ibid., 28.
[58] Ibid., 31.
[59] Santram, *Rati Vigyan*, 35, 40–1.
[60] Santram, *Vivahit Prem*, Preface, iii.
[61] Bauer, "Not a Translation", 381, 383.

bear out this observation. His "two-way translations" between classical erotic arts and modern sexology's canonical concepts, with modifications and a creative synthesis, illuminate his intellectual claims and recontextualise the sexology code in the vernacular to suit the different social terrain of colonial North India. What Purnima Mankekar states for late-twentieth-century India can well apply to Santram's writings:

> Diverse genealogies of the erotic have always coexisted in Indian public culture(s) . . . Recent years have also seen the flowering of heterogenous print media . . . These media use a range of aesthetic codes to represent the erotic, and many juxtapose transnational discourses with more familiar "Indian" ones; for instance, a copy of the Indianized *Cosmopolitan* might include excerpts from the *Kamasutra* alongside articles on safe sex and dating . . . We might consider how local cultural forms are produced in articulation with the translocal and also how the transnational itself is reconfigured as it intersects with the local or indeed the national.[62]

While translating and interpreting Stopes, Santram repeatedly complimented and provided credence to her views by comparing them with the *Kamasutra* and *Rati Rahasya*. He began his preface of *Vivahit Prem* by entwining Stopes with Kokkok under the heading "Anuvadak ka Nivedan" (Translator's Submission).[63] He then quoted liberally from the Sanskrit classics in the footnotes of the book.[64] For example: "In our scriptures on sexual sciences, too, there are descriptions of how we should behave on the first night with our new bride . . . Because men and women do not have enough knowledge of each other's nature, they are unable to get the true fulfilment of pleasure."[65]

Through this "vernacularisation" and "unruly appropriation" of Stopes and Vatsyayan, the sexual sciences offered a discursive space for thinking and argumentation.[66] It was by this process of selectively

---

[62] Mankekar, "Dangerous Desires", 406–7.
[63] Santram, *Vivahit Prem*, Preface.
[64] Ibid., 27, 32–3, 97.
[65] Ibid., footnote on 27.
[66] For the idea of "unruly appropriation", see Fuechtner, Haynes, and Jones, "Introduction", 3.

weaving together traditional-indigenous and classical-Hindu with modern-Western (Christian) notions of sex, eroticism, and science that new discourses on these subjects were formulated in our period. The translations were, moreover, made widely accessible to a Hindi-reading public by being priced relatively cheap.

Santram was a great admirer of Stopes, referring to her as "the greatest teacher of sexual science" who had "not only studied sex texts of Sanskrit, but also of many other languages of the world."[67] He did not believe that ancient Hindu erotica encompassed the field's entire range and insisted it was insufficient to meet the demands of the modern conjugal couple: "An old thing naturally looks dearer. But this does not mean that all old things are good and new things are all bad."[68] Therefore it seemed to him that knowledge of Western sexologists, including Havelock Ellis, Magnus Hirschfeld, Edward Carpenter, Richard Schmidt, E.H. Starling, Margaret Sanger, and above all Marie Stopes, was critical: "We Indians tend to bask only in the glory and knowledge of our ancestors [on the sexual sciences] . . . Whereas people in the Western world, who have progressed in other scriptures, have also increased their knowledge of the sexual sciences. Many of their discoveries are truly amazing and valuable. No nation or country can claim a copyright on [sexual] knowledge."[69] In his preface to *Vivahit Prem* he says the eighth chapter of Stopes' book, which deals with "the correct way of intercourse", goes far beyond any classical works on kamashastra as these works were not always adaptable to modern sexual yearnings. Complementarily, modernity was not a curse but held the promise of liberation: unlike many other Hindi sexology writers, Santram questioned the "bald claim of having always been modern",[70] and instead celebrated the liberation of love in modern times: "Where earlier love was considered a malady, it has now become a *dhanwantri vaid* [god of therapy]. Love sickness is now becoming the science of "lovepathy" [*sic*]. In the present age, clever and qualified doctors

[67] Santram, *Rati Vilas*, Preface.
[68] Santram, *Sahitya Sudha*, Preface.
[69] Santram, *Rati Vigyan*, 205.
[70] Pande, "Time for Sex", 284.

cure the complexities of love and heal a number of diseases. The medicine for many a disease is said to be love and pleasure."[71]

It could be argued that Stopes' writings away from their cultural contexts could seem perplexing. But this is not so if one thinks of the translation of sex texts as "a choreography from which one might commence, rather than a conversation that occludes or wraps up its trajectories."[72] Santram reframes Stopes in vernacular idioms and contexts to make his translations viable. Translating transnational sexual norms into local practices, his writings are a "folklorisation"; he translates Stopes so as to make her texts seem a narrative of "us" rather than a translation of the "other". At times he takes pains to explain cultural difference in a footnote, as happens in his version of the second chapter of *Married Love*, titled "The Broken Joy".[73] Santram poetically translates this as "Rang mein Bhang" and inserts this footnote: "The author [Marie Stopes] has written this book keeping in mind the English community. That is why these things are more applicable to them. Here we are married in the manner of a 'lottery'. Here men and women are not given the chance to know and love each other before marriage."[74]

It seems clear that his unauthorised translations of Stopes were a serious bid to translate sex without becoming complicit with its analytical regimes. While claiming that his translations were "true" and "authentic" renderings of the original text, he often resorted to creative rewriting and mediation. Switching codes, he inserted footnotes and perspectives, indigenising Stopes according to the local worlds of conjugal relationship.

He also used his translations of Stopes' books to publicise his own. For example, when speaking of Stopes' views on birth control in *Vivahit Prem*, he wrote in various footnotes that he had translated all the important aspects of her book *Contraception* in another book.[75] His book *Rati Vigyan* was repeatedly mentioned in the footnotes

[71] Santram, "Prem ka Satya", 183.
[72] Arondekar and Patel, "Area Impossible", 154.
[73] Stopes, *Married Love*, 7–13.
[74] Santram, *Vivahit Prem*, footnote on 23.
[75] Ibid., footnotes on 11, 140, 158, 165–6.

of *Vivahit Prem*.[76] Moreover, his books on subjects other than sex extensively advertised his books on sex: *Sukhi Parivar* (Happy Family) had a full-page advertisement for *Rati Vigyan* on the back cover, stating it was a distinctive book on sex meant for private study which discussed issues of sexual compatibility and adjustment by using the works of Vatsyayan, Freud, and Stopes.[77] He referred to the book as *kamashastra ka sundar gutka* (the beautiful chemistry of the sexual sciences).

Santram added his own voice and views, and a tone all his own, to the translated texts. All his translations had creative prefaces that simultaneously reified and destabilised the sexual. This process shows Santram formulating something new through his own inputs, remoulding a range of writings on sexual sciences to present times and Indian contexts. It has been underlined that writing and translating texts of sex is a political act, with rhetorical and ideological implications which are also indicative of the translator's attitude towards moral norms, gender identities, and sexual behaviours.[78] I have tried to show that by weaving together sexual ethics, knowledge, and politics, Santram did indeed destabilise and question certain dominant and normative sexual norms. I now turn to this theme using examples of conjugality, brahmacharya, and birth control.

A Heterosexual Ethics: Conjugal Desires, Brahmacharya, and Birth Control

Santram was often ahead of his time on questions of sex and gender. He was, for instance, a firm believer in sexual pleasure for *both* women and men; he was against brahmacharya and in favour of birth control. Scholars like Durba Ghosh, Tanika Sarkar, and Mytheli Sreenivas, among others, have shown how and why gender relations were undergoing significant changes in colonial India, whereby women and men were negotiating complex subjectivities and reformers

---

[76] Ibid., footnotes on 46, 52, 94, 96, 97, 126, 207.
[77] Santram, *Sukhi Parivar*, back cover.
[78] Santaemilia, *Gender, Sex and Translation*.

were reformulating conjugal relations.[79] Substantial work has recently emerged on the intersections between sexual sciences, modern conjugality, and vernacular literature in late colonial India.[80] Santram's writings provide another critical chapter in this tradition of work.

Being a keen observer of women and men,[81] several ideals of conjugal sexuality interested him. He presented the sensuous and the sexual within the conventions of a heteronormative ethics and was ardently in favour of sex education, arguing that human bodies were different from those of animals as the former had to be taught the art of sexual pleasure and knowledge, including sexual positions, passionate intercourse, and the importance of arousing the woman.[82]

> Every heart desires a partner . . . The aim of kamashastra is to increase pleasure in marriage . . . It is indeed ironic that the sexual act itself is not considered obscene, and yet its description branded so! Embraces, kisses, and postures are all essential for sexual intercourse. Those who are married perform all these actions because God has decreed this "obscene" method for the origin of human beings. So, should we also prosecute God as per Section 292 and 293 of the Indian Penal Code?[83]

Addressing both male anxieties and female desires, he critiqued men for their ignorance on sexual matters while simultaneously advocating the recognition of women as active partners. He deployed sexology subversively to interrogate gender relations, divorcing sex from the reproductive or procreative imperative. His book *Kama Kunj*, while stressing the need for sexual affinity between the married couple, also reflected on the weakness and incompetence of Indian men in providing erotic fulfilment to women: "In the name of religion

---

[79] Ghosh, *Sex and the Family*; Sarkar, *Hindu Wife*; Sreenivas, *Wives, Widows and Concubines*.

[80] Savary, "Vernacular Eugenics?"; Botre and Haynes, "Sexual Knowledge".

[81] Many of Santram's writings focus on them: for example "Aajkal ki Sundriyan"; "Purushon ke Anand"; "Stri ke Saath"; "Subharya"; "Supati"; *Adarsh Pati*; *Adarsh Patni*; *Sukhi Parivar*.

[82] Santram, *Rati Vigyan*, 44–5.

[83] Santram, *Kama Kunj*, 166–7.

and politics, and given the ignorance of the sexual sciences, the extent of crime spreading in our country is not hidden from our readers. With no true knowledge of women's sexual languages, qualities, desires, and gestures, men construct opposed meanings of women's creativity and ethics."[84] And elsewhere: "A man is often foolish about the sexual sciences and does not understand diverse elements of the art of sex . . . Even when he has access to a youthful woman, he is forever deprived of sexual pleasures."[85] Attacking ignorant and selfish husbands who either forced themselves on women or were oblivious of women's desires, he says: "A clever man should excite the woman on the first night by undressing her softly, embracing and kissing her, in order to arouse her. Only when the libido inside her is fully excited and aroused, only then should intercourse take place. Men who are totally obsessed with sex and just jump on top of women are completely stupid."[86]

He often urges husbands to do the household work: "If the husband gives help to the wife in household work – fetches the water, washes the vegetables, lights the fire, lifts the child, then what is there to be insulted?"[87] To give credence to his views he approvingly quotes Mary Wollstonecraft, the famous advocate of women's rights;[88] and in the same book he says: "In terms of evolution, it is the woman's body which is the most developed in the world. Female attributes are sharper and her senses much more pronounced in comparison with that of a man . . . The final destiny of a man is to become a woman."[89]

Recognising women's bodily desires, Santram perceived women as active sexual partners and consumers of sexual knowledge. Female sexuality was often seen as having been rampant and ferocious in ancient India, but in the colonial period, with new middle-class ethics and the evolution of normative ideals of virtuous womanhood,

[84] Ibid., 1.
[85] Santram, *Vivahit Prem*, Preface, i.
[86] Ibid., footnote on 33.
[87] Santram, *Kama Kunj*, 37.
[88] Ibid., 171.
[89] Ibid., 152.

an idea of the disciplined, passionless, and chaste woman gained currency. The female body was seen as primarily meant for reproduction and maternal in nature. In the dominant sexology literature, too, it was the male body and the man's sexual anxieties that occupied centre stage. As against this, Santram argued for a heterosexual ethics grounded in love, female sexual gratification, women's rights, and humanist principles. In his language of female sexuality, foreplay and orgasm were advised.[90] He urged women to read books of kamashastra.[91] "Kamashastra has been much denigrated nowadays . . . Even knowing this, I have dared to pen my thoughts on the subject in a magazine, which is also extensively read by women. The reason is that I do not consider sex to be obscene."[92]

His anticaste literature too includes the advocacy of women's pleasure. He attacked the policing of women's desires. Women seen as laughing loudly or going out at night were not, in his view, suspicious. He blamed upper-caste scriptures and the *Ramayan* for preaching false notions of women's purity.[93] Unlike reformers, including the Arya Samajis, who were attacking the singing of galis and marriage songs by women, and calling them ashlil,[94] Santram was all for the fun and entertainment in them: "The joy that comes from all the women singing together is never achieved by beating the broken drum of a bhajan. Secondly, unlike women's songs, the bhajans are often so meaningless and lifeless."[95]

[90] Santram, "Vivahit Prem", 75.
[91] Santram, "Hindi Mein Striyon ke Liye", 442.
[92] Santram, *Kama Kunj*, 160–1.
[93] Santram, *Hamara*, 97–100.
[94] For details: Gupta, *Sexuality, Obscenity*.
[95] Santram, "Byah Shaadi mein Nritya-Gaan", 172. Again, in a two-part article on "prostitutes", Santram's perspective was different from that of many social reformers. He did not criminalise them or treat them as "home breakers", and did not link the growth of prostitution to modernity and urbanisation. Instead, he recognised how many "low-caste" and rural women, often due to extreme poverty, entered the profession. He also "ungendered" prostitution by talking of male sex workers: "A prostitute is a person whose business is to satisfy the sexual desires of a diverse range of people of the opposite sex or of the same sex": Santram, "Veshyavritti", 111; idem, "Veshya Samajik Paheli".

Romantic love, of course, emerged repeatedly as a powerful metaphor in Santram's anticaste work and sexology: "Love does not ask for anything. It imposes no rules and restrictions. It flows freely from one heart to another."[96] This notion of love was different from *pavitra prem*, i.e. spiritual love, as expressed for example in novels like *Saraswatichandra*.[97] Rather, Santram saw love and sex as being on the same page. Sexual relations also became in his work an arena for challenging caste hierarchies, though conversely his anticaste discourse was not expressed explicitly in his writings on sex. All the same, creatively translating the meaning of endogamy and savarna marriage, he wrote in *Rati Vigyan*:

> In order to lead a happy life, it is necessary to have a savarna marriage. By this, I do not mean that a Vaishya boy should be married to a Vaishya girl ... Caste divisions ... are artificial and meaningless. They are ... a big hurdle in the progress of our society. We should not consider the caste of a person by birth ... By savarna marriage, I mean a marriage between any man and any woman whose nature, virtues, values and heart are compatible, as that is absolutely necessary for the attainment of marital happiness.[98]

In light of Santram's comprehensive endorsement of intercaste marriages, his anti-puritanical stance on sexual matters can also be seen as a way to challenge kinship and subvert Brahmanical caste "purity". Moreover, from a phenomenological point of view his sexology writings make sense as he was implicitly taking on questions of untouchability and touch, and arguing for consensual sex irrespective of caste and class. Even while working within heteronormative paradigms his books, including his anticaste writings, were trying to make marriages more capacious and mobile, and providing the possibility for people to live differently gendered lives.

I move now to Santram's views on brahmacharya, believed to be one of the core doctrines of Hindu dharma, with the preservation

---

[96] Santram, "Prem ka Satya Swaroop", 186.
[97] An epic Gujarati novel, set in late-nineteenth-century India, written by Govardhanram Tripathi.
[98] Santram, *Rati Vigyan*, 63–5.

of semen seen as an aspect of male power. In the colonial period brahmacharya acquired new connotations and was transformed into a whole modern discourse which was then entangled in discussions around masculinity, national upliftment, the freedom movement, eugenics, healthy offspring, physical fitness, and social service. From Sanatan Dharmists to Arya Samajists, from Dayanand to Vivekananda and Gandhi – people waxed enthusiastic about brahmacharya for diverse reasons.[99] The market was flooded with prescriptions and books around it which in many ways reinforced Brahmanism.[100] Many Indian sexologists also supported brahmacharya. Ishita Pande argues that the shift in "reproductive temporality" introduced by disallowing marriages between children – following the passage of the Child Marriage Restraint Act, 1929 – enabled upper-caste "global/Hindu" sexologists to recast brahmacharya as a kind of adolescence and thereby render it timeless and universal. This then provided an opportunity for "the surveillance of infantile sexuality, the management of masturbation, and the pedagogization of sex."[101]

In this climate, influenced by the founder of the Arya Samaj, Dayanand Saraswati, Santram was initially a supporter of brahmacharya. However, he soon gave up on the idea and went on to assault it passionately, arguing it had proved to be greatly damaging for him:

> Due to the influence of the Arya Samaj on me, I gave huge importance to brahmacharya. Therefore, I did not keep my wife by me and even ran away from her shadow. My wife was greatly saddened by my attitude . . . But this supposed brahmacharya caused me more harm than benefit. My belief in brahmacharya was completely wrong. Later, when I read Mary Stopes' *Enduring Passion*, it greatly helped me . . . I decided to keep my wife with me and she was ecstatic for this reason.[102]

Subsequently, when away from his wife, he wrote her passionate letters. He even exchanged letters with Stopes, describing some intimate details of his life and seeking her advice:

---

[99] Alter, *Gandhi's Body*; Chakraborty, *Masculinity, Asceticism*; Mills and Sen, *Confronting the Body*; Haynes, "Gandhi, Brahmacharya".
[100] Gupta, *Sexuality, Obscenity*, 66–83.
[101] Pande, *Sex, Law*, 197.
[102] *MJKA*, 84–5.

CAST(E)ING AND TRANSLATING SEX 105

Although I am not fortunate enough to have any personal acquaintance with your good self, yet I have read many of your books . . . I have been convinced that you are one of the best authorities on venereal diseases . . . I am suffering from prostatic discharges after urinating since many years . . . After my marriage I tried to observe celibacy under the influence of false religious ideas. Although I and my wife lived together yet we had seldom coitus, after which I had to repent on my inability to keep continence . . . This condition went on for many years. Then I began to lead married life and got children. This relieved me of seminal ejaculations.[103]

This is reminiscent of the ideas of Karve.[104] Santram's ire too was directed against brahmacharya as a tool of sexual self-discipline, and he bolstered his critique by declaring it unnatural – as emotionally, physically, and medically pernicious. Within the widespread valorisation of brahmacharya, his is a voice of dissent pointing out that desires of the flesh are neither moral nor immoral but just natural and pleasurable:

Today, I want to write a few things on the subject of sexual science and to show that we have suffered a huge loss by sitting amidst old and outdated views and closing our eyes to the new discoveries of science . . . Our religious pandits continuously extol the glories of brahmacharya and build a picture of the terrible calamity facing young men around the evils of ejaculation and impotence. Such distorted views, rather than being of any benefit, have caused a huge loss. It is a complete myth that a person is weakened by sexual intercourse . . . The bulls that copulate every day are much stronger than the celibate bullocks that plough the land . . . The fact is that no celibate or unmarried man has ever lived longer than others . . . To sing the praises of celibacy and inculcate fear and insecurity among young men is wrong and baneful.[105]

Perhaps influenced by the second volume of Havelock Ellis' path-breaking *Studies in the Psychology of Sex* (1900), which stated that

---

[103] Letter addressed by Santram to Marie Stopes, dated 16 March 1930, in MSS no. ADD 58578, Stopes Papers, Department of Manuscripts, British Library.
[104] Botre and Haynes, "Understanding R.D. Karve".
[105] Santram, "Kamashastra aur Dharmik", 77.

moderate masturbation has no ill effect,[106] Santram argued that pandits were wrong-headed in their opposition to masturbation and nocturnal emissions.[107]

There was also a larger resistance to the brahmacharya ideal because, with the flooding of aphrodisiac advertisements in the market,[108] and the flourishing of erotic and romantic literature, a more attractive and easier ideal of modern manhood had become widely available. Santram's opposition to brahmacharya reveals that the discourse faced a considerable fissure from within.

Finally, birth control: this emerged as a prominent issue in debates around sexuality, with Gandhi and many others strongly opposing it, and anticaste ideologues like Periyar and sexologists like A.P. Pillay, N.S. Phadke, and R.D. Karve firmly supporting it.[109] In the Hindi print world many were opposed to birth control, which was tied to debates on obscenity on the one hand and anxieties about a supposed decline in Hindu numbers on the other.[110] When the leading Hindi journal *Chand* published an article on birth control titled "Santati Nigrah", many leading papers objected to it, calling it "obscene".[111] However, Santram was a fervent proponent of birth control, aligning with Stopes on the one hand and influenced by Periyar on the other. His translation of Stopes' *Contraception* was widely publicised as the first book on family planning in Hindi.[112] It was a book of 300 pages describing methods of birth control, and how to stop unwanted pregnancies with helpful illustrations of birth control devices.

While partially influenced by eugenic arguments, Santram's book *Santan Sankhya ka Seema Bandhan arthat Dampati Mitra* gave the

---

[106] Stengers and Neck, *Masturbation*, 133.
[107] Santram, "Kamashastra aur Dharmik", 77.
[108] Gupta, *Sexuality, Obscenity*, 66–83; Haynes, "Selling Masculinity".
[109] For the politics of birth control in colonial India, see Ahluwalia, *Reproductive Restraints*. On Periyar and birth control, Hodges, *Contraception, Colonialism and Commerce*; Anandhi, "Reproductive Bodies".
[110] Gupta, *Sexuality, Obscenity*.
[111] For a defence of *Chand* against such attacks, Prem, "Samaj Sudhar tatha *Chand*".
[112] *Naye Varsh ka Suchipatra*, 43.

right of birth control to women.[113] He dismissed assumptions that contraception would lead to *vyabhichar* (adultery) and increase kama vasna. In supporting birth control he argued as a modern feminist might – the woman's right over her body must lie with the woman alone: "A woman cannot make herself free for as long as she is not the owner of her own body. As long as the ideal conduct for a woman is determined by a man, there will only be man's rule in the world. Limiting the number of offspring – creating one, two or more children according to your wishes – is the first step that a woman can take for her independence."[114] The book created a huge controversy and many, including members of the Arya Samaj, called it "immoral" and "obscene" and threatened Santram with a court case. But some thanked him for publishing it.[115] Santram's parting thrust against the opposition was a rubbing of salt into their wound: "The publisher of the book and my friend Rajpal told me that those conservative Arya Samajis who criticise you for this book and threaten that they will drag you to the court, their wives too have secretly bought the book and read it with great enthusiasm."[116]

In the Hindi journal *Yugantar*, which he edited, Santram often published articles in support of birth control. An article titled "Santiti Nirodh aur Bharat" made the delightful point that brahmacharya was totally impractical for the purpose because it could be practised either by a *mahapurush* (great man) or by those who were impotent![117] Birth control was the clear way forward.

In another article, which was entitled "Kamashastra aur Dharmik Pakshpat", Santram interrogated certain Hindu religious claims in relation to sex, and decoupled sex from reproduction. While many Hindi-Hindu sex crusaders were bogged down in futile meditations on the question of the "ideal" time for sex, its duration and frequency,[118] Santram appears far more sensible in considering this kind of cogitation irrelevant. He pointed to the innate

[113] Santram, *Santan Sankhya*. Also *MJKA*, 161–2.
[114] Santram, *Santan Sankhya*, 4.
[115] *MJKA*, 161–2; Jigyasu, *Dharma ki Balivedi*, 53.
[116] *MJKA*, 132.
[117] Vanchu, "Santati Nirodh".
[118] For details, Pande, *Sex, Law*.

sexual rhythms of women that cut across barriers of age and the reproductive body:

> Our religious pandits and clerics claim that the sole purpose of marriage is to give birth to a child . . . They consider sexual intercourse for any other reason a grave sin. But the current social sciences do not accept this idea at all . . . How many times should one have sex? The answer to this is also given by religious pandits – not more than once in 28 days . . . However, erotic desire is a natural tide. Just as hunger and thirst are not the same among all . . . so is it with sexual desire . . . It is wrong to bind everyone by the same rope . . . Once a woman reaches menopause, it is often believed she no longer wants sex, which is also perceived as being against the purpose of producing a child. This is totally ludicrous. Sexual desire very certainly continues in women after menopause.[119]

In brief, Santram's writings on the sexual sciences, when read in conjunction with his views on intercaste marriages, provide a vocabulary of sexual passion alongside recalcitrant love and intimacy, and overall a prescient reconceptualisation of gender relations. In a sense, he was capitalising on the scientising of sexuality to theorise the possibilities of social, gender, and caste mixing. While the eugenic thrust of sexology was based on racial purity, Santram deployed it creatively for social mobility. He brought to centre stage desires which were "radically unthinkable",[120] and which had the potential to provide "new narratives of possibility".[121]

I began this chapter with a quote from Santram's article (in two parts), "Vivah ka Bhavishya". Undergirded by a physiological account of sexual pleasure resting on a liberal and egalitarian utopianism, the article dismissed valorisations of virginity and lauded non-reproductive pleasure, birth control, and even polyandry.[122] It urged a change in man–woman relationships: "In consonance with the times

[119] Santram, "Kamashastra aur Dharmik", 77–9.
[120] Butler, *Bodies that Matter*, 59.
[121] Berlant, *Desire*, 43.
[122] "Vivah ka Bhavishya" also talked of a fatherless child, thus making implicit questions of collective ownership. The article reminds one of Sankrityayan's *Volga se Ganga*, a collection of historical fiction short stories: in both cases, selective aspects of ancient human history are invoked to argue for freedom.

and circumstances, people's moral and social standards must change . . . The number of happy couples in the world is very small . . . The main reason for this misery is sexual unhappiness. To overcome this unrest, there is a need to change the relationship between men and women . . . The main purpose of marriage is sexual pleasure."[123]

It has been argued that "Utopian literature serves as a site for experimentation with alternative ideas of community, government, nation state, kinship, status, notions of home, family and property, gender and sexuality – in short, a complex political and social agenda."[124] Santram offers us an ethical and utopian narrative of sexual relations in which human bodies and their relationships allow for different conceptions of desire and aesthetics. He articulates ideas of hope and a liberal political terrain, envisaging a utopian future that holds the promise of sexual freedom. By appropriating the ideal of intercaste alliances and incorporating it within his writings on the sexual sciences, Santram makes caste more fluid, enacts a lower-caste poetics of sexuality, and upholds equality in caste and sex. He conceives a better way of organising society, particularly male–female relations, and a future in which sexual–familial power equations are less skewed in favour of men, tradition, and patriarchy. His sexological writings, as much as his anticaste ideas, are worth recalling because both were progressive and far-sighted, and because they need to be remembered in any thorough record of lower-caste resistance to Brahminic chauvinism, indigenist xenophobia, and patriarchal authoritarianism. My effort in this chapter has been to at least try exhuming him out of the obscurity within which he has for so long and so unfairly been buried.

---

[123] Santram, "Vivah ka Bhavishya", 302.
[124] Pohl, *Women, Space and Utopia*, 10.

II
YASHODA DEVI
(1890–1942)

3

Procreation and Pleasure
Women, Men, and Ayurveda

MODERN WESTERN BIOMEDICAL knowledge has been seen as a critical tool for the assertion of disciplinary authority and power over the body of the colonised by the colonial Indian state, which displaced indigenous knowledge systems.[1] Simultaneously, scholars have been sceptical about the actual impact of Western medicine on many indigenous populations and have questioned the efficacy of its disciplinary power.[2] A study of perceptions, practices, and self-identities of the Indian people – who were in any case differentiated by gender, region, language, caste, class, community, and religion – fractures claims about the marginalisation of indigenous medical practices, while also questioning the hegemony of Western medicine.[3] Early British attitudes to traditional Indian medical practices – ayurvedic, unani, and folk – were often tolerant and even appreciative, though seldom without qualification.[4] By the late nineteenth century, however, Western medical practitioners in India came to regard indigenous medicine as necessarily inferior and became hostile to ayurveda. The loss of British support and the erosion of royal

---

[1] Arnold, *Colonizing the Body*; idem, *Science, Technology*; Kumar, *Science and Empire*.
[2] Harrison, *Public Health*, 1.
[3] Pati and Harrison, *Health, Medicine*.
[4] Arnold, *Science, Technology*, 66.

patronage put ayurvedic practitioners in a precarious position. They reacted both defensively and assertively, reviving and reconstituting the ayurvedic tradition on the one hand, and promoting it on a nationalist platform on the other.[5]

Gendered social histories of health and medicine in colonial India, and the role and relationship of women to both Western and indigenous medical practices, have not escaped the attention of feminist historians. An important realm of study has centred on the role of white Western women medical missionaries and doctors who came to India. They were guided by a complex combination of concerns and ideals: missionary zeal, philanthropy, the desire to "save" Indian women from the "unhygienic" zenana, inspiration from a larger women's movement, the possibility of a promising field of employment, and a search for professional status and power often denied to them within their own country.[6] Some have delved into the lives and contributions of the first generation of professional Indian women doctors, such as Rukhmabai and Kadambini Ganguli, as well as the role of nurses, and care in hospitals by and for women.[7] A third focus has been the medical profession's assertion of authority over indigenous women's bodies. Exploring links between soldiers, venereal disease, brothels, and Indian prostitutes, scholars emphasise that sex workers faced heightened surveillance because they were perceived as carriers of venereal disease, leading to the establishment of "lock hospitals" and the Indian Contagious Diseases Act of 1868.[8] Concurrently, Western science and medicine, combined with social reform, targeted midwives and indigenous reproductive technologies. The marginalisation of the traditional dai by the British and Indian middle classes helped in shaping a new

---

[5] Panikkar, "Indigenous Medicine"; Gupta, "Indigenous Medicine"; Brass, "Politics of Ayurvedic"; Sivaramakrishnan, *Old Potions*. Something similar was happening in unani: Alavi, *Islam and Healing*.

[6] Burton, *Burdens of History*; Balfour and Young, *Work of Medical Women*; Lal, "The Politics of Gender"; Singh, *Gender, Religion*.

[7] Mukherjee, *Gender, Medicine*; Karlekar, *Voices from Within*, 173–8.

[8] Levine, *Prostitution, Race*; Whitehead, "Bodies Clean"; Sarkar, *Religion and Women*, 205–9.

biomedical regime, institutionalised midwifery, and fostered a high-caste, middle-class identity.[9]

Many of these studies tell us a story familiar to feminist scholars – of tensions between male-dominated medical authority, a female sphere of healthcare, and the inscription of gender differences on the female body. While insightful, I wish to complicate some of these images by exploring the arena between modern Western male/female doctors of the time and the indigenous dai. I do so by concentrating on a high-caste, middle-class woman practitioner of indigenous medicine, and her understanding of and relationship to Western medicine, households, women, men, and the nation. By studying the extensive writings of Yashoda Devi (hereafter Yashoda),[10] one of the most commercially successful and famous women ayurvedic practitioners at the beginning of the twentieth century in UP, this chapter explores the links between Western and indigenous medical practices on the one hand, and between health and body, medicine and gender, and sexuality and nation on the other.

A Brahmin by caste, Yashoda was the daughter of Pandit Dalchand Mishra, an ayurvedic vaid based in the town of Dataganj in the Badaun district of UP,[11] who at some point moved to Bareilly. Yashoda received her training in ayurveda from her father, underscoring the family's role in producing ayurvedic medical knowledge. After her marriage in 1906 to Pandit Sri Ram Sharma – a disciple of her father who continued teaching her – Yashoda moved to Allahabad in 1908. At the young age of sixteen she began an active practice, soon becoming a leading ayurvedic practitioner. She established her own Stri Aushadhalaya in Allahabad around 1908 and went on to open a Female Ayurvedic Pharmacy.[12] Subsequently, her dispensaries were established in many other towns of Bihar and UP, for instance in

[9] Guha, *Colonial Modernities*; Gupta, *The Gender of Caste*, 43–51.

[10] I am grateful to Samir Sharma, greatgrandson of Yashoda Devi, for granting me an interview, and providing me invaluable information on, and rare photographs of, Yashoda, including her birth and death dates.

[11] Mentioned on the cover of Yashoda's journal *Stri Dharma Shikshak*, 15 July 1909.

[12] Yashoda, *Dampati Arogyata*, 1–4; idem, *Nari Sharir*, 48.

Patna, Agra, and Banaras. Her contribution to her family's income was the most substantial. A huge number of women came to her with their personal and physical problems, and she received innumerable letters from all over India. She was so popular that letters reached her even if just addressed to "Devi, Allahabad".[13] She received a sack full of letters daily;[14] in fact, she had to take a post box at her post office because their inflow was so voluminous.[15] (See Fig. 3.2.)

Yashoda was a prolific writer with over a hundred books to her credit, each running from anywhere between twenty and a thousand pages. Largely addressed to women, but not limited to them, they covered a broad range, including intricate questions related to marriage, sex, man–woman relations, women's health and sexology, popular ayurvedic home remedies, food recipes, and health guides. The texts were produced for use as household advice manuals, as medical and food recipe books, as social-prescriptive texts, as ayurvedic remedies (particularly for women's sexual health), as advertisements for the products and aushadhis she manufactured, as case studies of her patients, and as collections of letters of praise that she received. Yashoda had her own publishing house, Devi Pustakalaya, and a printing press called Banita Hitaishi Press, owned by her husband Sri Ram Sharma, which published all her books.[16] She advertised these and her other products extensively in her publications and in leading journals of the time.[17]

In UP, Allahabad became the heartland of Hindi publishing,[18]

---

[13] Yashoda, *Nari Dharmashastra*, last page.

[14] Interview with Rachna Sharma.

[15] Yashoda's various books mention this address as Stri Aushadhalaya, Post Box No. 4, Colonelganj, Prayag.

[16] Interview with Samir Sharma. After Sri Ram Sharma's first wife passed away, he married Yashoda. There was a twenty-year age gap between the two. Yashoda was initially taught ayurveda by her father, and then Sri Ram Sharma continued to teach her, though he did not practise much himself. Sri Ram Sharma realised that there was a great demand for a woman ayurvedic chikitsak, and supported Yashoda at every step in the endeavour: interview with Rachna Sharma.

[17] Yashoda, *Nari Sharir*, 48–50; idem, *Kanya Kartavya*, back page.

[18] *Report on the Administration of UP, 1907–8*, 52.

a place that pioneered women's journalism and where women's education blossomed.[19] Yashoda operated within this vibrant women's print world, using Hindi and adopting its writing styles and metaphors. Many of her books went into several editions and impressions, revealing their popularity and reach. An examination of the catalogue of Hindi books published in UP between 1900 and 1940 shows that no woman was writing as much as Yashoda, and in such detail, on the range that encompassed women, ayurveda, and sexology. She probably wrote and sold more books than any other woman writer and was arguably one of the most widely read woman authors of her time. I first came across and wrote on Yashoda way back in 2005,[20] and subsequently some work on her has emerged.[21] This and the next chapter place her centrally in colonial India's health and medicine history.

Fig. 3.1-i: Yashoda Devi *and* Fig. 3.1-ii: Sri Ram Sharma (both in 1921).

[19] Nijhawan, *Women and Girls*; Orsini, *Hindi Public Sphere*.
[20] Gupta, "Procreation and Pleasure".
[21] Gupta, "Vernacular Sexology"; Berger, *Ayurveda Made Modern*, 95–9; Rai, "Gendering Late Colonial".

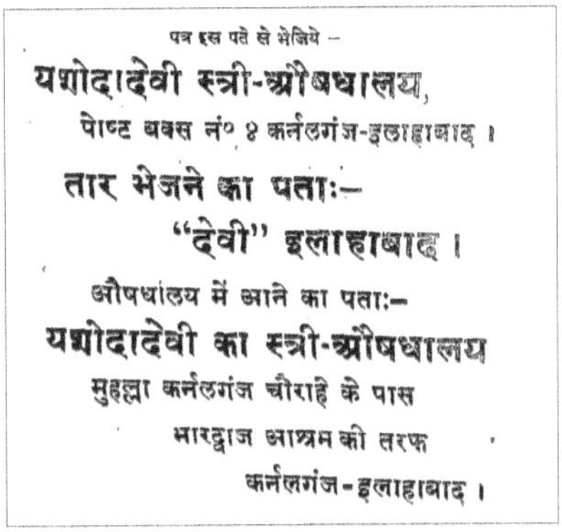

PROCREATION AND PLEASURE 117

> पत्र इस पते से भेजिये –
> यशोदादेवी स्त्री-औषधालय,
> पोष्ट बक्स नं० ४ कर्नेलगंज-इलाहाबाद ।
> तार भेजने का पता:–
> "देवी" इलाहाबाद ।
> औषधालय में आने का पता:–
> यशोदादेवी का स्त्री-औषधालय
> मुहल्ला कर्नेलगंज चौराहे के पास
> भारद्वाज आश्रम की तरफ
> कर्नेलगंज - इलाहाबाद ।

Fig. 3.2: Post Box address for letters: Yashoda Devi.

While specialising in ayurveda, the range of Yashoda's practice and publications was so wide that through them she managed to penetrate the everyday lives of women and men, shaping their medical, sex-related, and health questions, and, to an extent, their nationalist identities. Similar concerns were expressed in other books written at this time; thus, while I focus on Yashoda, her writings resonate with the norms and interests of her age. What was the character of medical knowledge upheld in these writings, and what role did they play in expressing new modes of identity formation? Did they celebrate ayurveda and indigeneity and critique Western medicine unequivocally? How were women, men, and their marital sex lives viewed by Yashoda? Were women overwhelmingly represented as victims, patients, and ideal housewives, or also as actors and healers? Was patriarchy questioned or gender stereotypes reconstituted? In attempting to study these questions, the chapter interrogates neat dichotomies – between subaltern and hegemonic, feminine and masculine – often made while examining the interrelationship between traditional indigenous medical practices in colonial societies and the impact of modern Western biomedical systems on them. It also indicates the critical role that middle-class women can play in challenging or consolidating dominant patterns. Finally, it highlights the multifaceted linkages between gender, sexology, nationalism, indigenous medicine, and health reform in colonial India.

The chapter is divided into three sections. Providing a context, the first section briefly explores the Hindi print industry's role in promoting health literature, and the impact of biomedicine on ayurveda. The other two sections move to gendered readings, focusing on Yashoda's writings. They attempt to reveal two parallel trajectories within her writings – one that sought to discipline bodies, household, and family life; and the other that offered equivocal readings of man–woman relations, sexology, sexuality, and pleasure.

Popular Health Literature, Biomedicine, and Ayurveda

Catering to an increasing demand for healthcare information, a considerable popular literature in Hindi came to promote a diversified medical landscape. Dispensing knowledge in simple language, print democratised medical information and transformed disease into a public matter. Sections of the educated middle classes took on the role of medical pedagogues, disseminating knowledge on health, disease, and the body to families, women, men, and boys. The UP Public Health Department published popular Hindi medical tracts, promoting norms for cleanliness and hygiene, allopathic treatment, and vaccinations. Simultaneously, the Nagari Pracharini Sabha and prominent commercial publishing houses in UP began giving considerable space to matters of health and disease.[22] Numerous publications emerged on common everyday diseases, epidemics, sexual sciences, reproduction, childcare, and brahmacharya.

Ayurvedic discourse too came to use print extensively. The oral tradition of ayurveda adapted itself to the new commercial form. In the late eighteenth and early nineteenth centuries many British Orientalist scholars showed an interest in ayurveda and wrote treatises and *materia medica*s on it.[23] However, with the decline of British support a new genre of ayurvedic literature was generated. Written predominantly by ayurvedic practitioners, it used a language of moral self-improvement. Many of these texts lamented, for example, that the old ayurvedic system was on the verge of extinction and emphasised the urgent need to restore it to its former glory.[24] The language of self-enhancement gradually merged with a vocabulary of

[22] Sharma, *Indigenous and Western*.
[23] Ainslie, *Materia Indica*; Wise, *Commentary on the Hindu*; Muthu, *Short Account*. The book described ayurvedic medicine from the Rig Veda to the Buddhist period to Ashoka.
[24] Ballabh, *Marnonmukhi Arya Chikitsa*; Lal, *Vaidyak Sar*.

self-assertion and identity politics. By the early twentieth century most indigenous writers on ayurveda in colonial UP chose Hindi, not English or Urdu, as their primary language. This also fed into linguistic politics, Hindu community identity, and urban middle-class discourse.[25] There was an implicit association of ayurveda with the ancient glory of the Hindus, which was extended to the use of Hindi (with an overdose of Sanskrit) as the language of publication. The ancient Hindu past came to be seen as an age of resplendence for ayurveda, and the present was blamed for its declining status.[26]

By the early twentieth century Hindi publications on ayurveda came to thrive – journals, advertisements, conference volumes, popular books and pamphlets, cookery books, home remedies for everyday ailments, instruction manuals, and dialogues with Western medicine. In 1934–5, for example, at least twelve Hindi journals on ayurveda were appearing from UP alone.[27] There was *Stri Chikitsak*, a Hindi monthly journal devoted to the ayurvedic treatment of women's diseases brought out by Yashoda, with a circulation figure of 5000 copies per month.[28] She also published other journals, such as *Stri Dharma Shikshak* and *Kanya Sarvasva*, which regularly carried columns on women's health, home remedies, and culinary recipes. Hindi books on ayurveda far outnumbered the journals.[29] Many of the books used a highly Sanskritised language and were voluminous. At the same time, there were popular, thin, cheap books on ayurveda in colloquial Hindi, popularising its methods, and glorifying its ancient lineage. Many claimed inspiration from ancient ayurvedic texts, particularly the *Charaka Samhita*, the *Susruta Samhita*, and the *Ashtanga Samagraha*. The writers of such books not only codified ayurveda as a medical science with ancient roots but

[25] Sharma, *Indigenous and Western*; Berger, *Ayurveda Made Modern*; Rai, "Invoking 'Hindu' Ayurveda".

[26] Shukl, *Ayurveda ka Mahatv*.

[27] *Statement of Newspapers and Periodicals*, 82–9, 96–7, 100–1, 108–9, 140–1, 160–1.

[28] Ibid., 152–3.

[29] For example Lal, *Vaidyak Sar*; Shukl, *Ayurveda ka Mahatv*; Vaidya, *Chikitsa Chandrodya*; Ghanekar, *Aupsargik Rog*.

also used pictures and advertisements extensively to popularise their medical practice and prescriptions, with Yashoda acquiring mastery in this art.

This literature facilitated the emergence of a new type of ayurveda, a new brand of vaids, and a new discourse. Till the early nineteenth century, ayurvedic training had relied on *guru–shishya* (master–disciple) apprenticeship outside hospitals. From the early twentieth century the decline in patronage and British support slowly gave way to the emergence of ayurvedic colleges, professional associations, and hospitals, leading to a standardisation and professionalisation of ayurveda.[30] However, oral transmission via family lineages also continued.[31] Historians have viewed ayurveda as a form of resistance to colonial medicine, while also showing that indigenous practitioners continually reinvented ayurveda, braiding it with select strands of Western medicine and science, even while constantly arguing for their own superiority.[32] In riding the wave of Indian nationalism, ayurveda was caught in a central paradox of the nationalist project – the promotion of a distinct cultural identity by introducing institutions and practices modelled on an international norm. Projit Mukharji thus shows that in the early twentieth century a new ayurvedic body of knowledge emerged, distinct from both biomedical and classical ayurvedic perspectives.[33]

A significant book, *Ayurveda Mahatv*, written by Saligram Shastri and published in 1926 by the prestigious Naval Kishore Press, questioned the ideological underpinnings and therapeutic implications of allopathy. Running into 267 pages, it offered an elaborate and vociferous defence of ayurveda, maintaining it was the best of all systems of medicine.[34] It ended with a plea for a boycott of all foreign medicines to drive away the Western system from "this sacred land", and to reinstate ayurveda to its former supremacy and glory.[35] Besides

---

[30] Brass, "Politics of Ayurvedic".

[31] This was also the case with unani: Alavi, *Islam and Healing*.

[32] Mukharji, *Doctoring Traditions*; Sharma, *Indigenous and Western*; Berger, *Ayurveda Made Modern*.

[33] Mukharji, *Doctoring Traditions*; idem, *Nationalizing the Body*, 129–33.

[34] Shastri, *Ayurveda Mahatv*.

[35] Ibid., 8–150.

such purists, however, there were syncretists and integrationists;[36] they argued for a partial synthesis of the principles of biomedicine with ayurveda and tried to establish connections between the two.[37] One ayurvedic doctor of Kashi University said science and knowledge knew no bounds of country, time, religion, or caste; regardless of origin, it was pure, respectable, and worth learning.[38]

At the same time, ayurveda was defended as an embodiment of certain eternal truths. Various Orientalist scholars and some Western doctors were frequently quoted to prove the efficacy of this ancient medical system.[39] *The Materia Medica of the Hindus*, a book published in 1870, recorded its indebtedness to Dr T.A. Wise for his masterly way of placing the merits of "Hindu medicine" before the eyes of the Western world.[40] Others – various ayurvedic doctors deploying the terms vigyan and shastra – traced the ancient sacred roots of ayurveda and simultaneously claimed it was a timeless science.[41] Yashoda too suffixed these words to many of the titles of her books.

It has been argued that the mutual enrichment brought about by a "creative synthesis" between Hindu ayurveda and unani tibb, and the apparent absence of rivalry between its practitioners, the vaids and the hakims, exemplifies the continuing vitality and fruitful intermingling of scientific traditions in India well into the eighteenth century.[42] However, there was another strand visible by the early twentieth century. Some of the ayurvedic writings incorporated the Hindu nationalist rhetoric that was gaining strength.[43] The Arya Samaj showed keen interest in promoting the cause of ayurveda, publishing several treatises in its praise.[44] Many writings bemoaned the supposed loss of the golden Hindu past of ayurveda;[45] articulating it

[36] Leslie, "Interpretations of Illness", 179.
[37] Ramakrishnaiya, *Ayurveda and Its Merits*, 1.
[38] Ghanekar, *Aupsargik Rog*, 1–2.
[39] Sharma, *Bhartiya Vanaspatiyon*; Ramakrishnaiya, *Ayurveda and Its Merits*, 1.
[40] Dutt, *The Materia Medica*. Also Sharma, *The System*, 280–99.
[41] For example: Chaudhari, *Ayurveda ka Vaigyanik Svarup*.
[42] Arnold, *Science, Technology*, 4.
[43] Jaffrelot, *The Hindu Nationalist*, 11–79.
[44] Chaudhari, *Ayurveda ka Vaigyanik Svarup*.
[45] "Ayurvedaunnati Kaise Ho", *Vaidyaraj*, 1 (1), 1911, 2.

in terms of a grave crisis, they traced a linear decline from the Muslim to the British period.[46] For example, Babu Haridas Vaidya, a leading ayurvedic doctor of Agra, published seven volumes on various aspects of ayurveda. Lamenting its present deplorable decline, he attributed it to "Muslim rule" when hakims were given importance and vaids were marginalised. *Dawakhane* (unani pharmacies) and *shafakhane* (Urdu for hospitals) replaced aushadhalayas.[47]

Thus, the ayurvedic discourse in colonial India was largely ambivalent, moving along a pendulum. It expressed itself in multifaceted ways – as self-criticism, as an assertion of self-identity, as the celebration of ancient heritage, as an upholder of Hindu nationalist identity, as a claim to "scientificity", and as a critique of modern medicine while partially endorsing some of its principles.

A Gendered Ayurvedic Authority on Domestic Health

Besides looking at works on ayurveda, while framing my arguments here I also draw on other structuring ideas within the scholarship on the history of medicine and gender in colonial India. There has, for example, been a discussion on public health/eugenics/birth control, on sexual discipline, and on the proliferation of a market for sexual material.[48] Most studies on ayurveda have pointed out that it was totally a male domain. Indeed, ayurvedic training was technically closed to women practitioners and was mainly in Sanskrit. While indigenous women medical practitioners were present in almost every household, their work was informal and the world of professional vaids was predominantly male. As a woman, Yashoda – commercially successful, practising ayurveda, and writing on matters of sex – was not even mentioned in the established professional circles of

[46] Shastri, *Ayurveda Mahatv*, 1; "Ayurveda ka Mahatva", *Vaidyaraj*, 1 (2), 1911, 13.

[47] Vaidya, *Chikitsa Chandrodaya*, 12–14.

[48] On public health etc.: Whitehead, "Bodies Clean"; Anandhi, "Reproductive Bodies"; on sexual discipline: Alter, *Wrestler's Body*; on sexology markets: Gupta, *Sexuality, Obscenity*.

vaids and there was widespread indifference, even hostility, towards her by ayurveda's normative authority. The Ayurvedic Mahamandal, for example, was as late as 1941 a completely male domain.[49] Some of these male vaids also filed a case against Yashoda, calling her remedies "inferior" and "inauthentic".[50]

However, even though Yashoda was on the margins and written out of the dominant Sanskrit discourses, her practice and writings attracted a huge following. The denial of epistemic authority to Yashoda was thus in sharp contrast to her popularity, her large clientele, and her high respect in society. She seems to have exerted considerable influence on medical health, particularly of women. Her fame spread to far-off places like Africa and Fiji. She claimed that all women, rich or poor, were her sisters and distributed medicines for free to poor women. She had a rest house where women from remote areas could come and stay for treatment, though bookings had to be done in advance.[51]

Moreover, since it was even more critical for her to establish her mastery in a male-centric domain, she deployed multiple tools to her advantage in innovative ways – establishing her dispensaries and clinics in many cities of North India; widely promoting her books and journals; combining her vast ayurvedic knowledge with select modern practices; using advertisements, visuals, letters, case studies, and questionnaires; deploying an easy language; and highlighting her gender identity. Her clients, their disorders, and the social organisation of her clinical work were distinctive. She wrote: "After studying ancient ayurvedic texts, those experiments which have been tested by me and discovered to be a ramban for curing sexual illnesses are included in this book."[52] She framed her authority by flagging her "eighteen years of experience" as a healer par excellence of *desi stri chikitsa* (indigenous female therapy);[53] and she stated that she combined "rati shastra with santati shastra." She promoted herself as

[49] Pratapsingh, *Ayurveda Mahamandal*.
[50] Interview with Sripat Sharma.
[51] Yashoda, *Dampati Arogyata*, 1–4, 7.
[52] Ibid., 328.
[53] Ibid., cover.

an expert who had translated the ancient indigenous medical art of ayurveda to make it a "scientific" tool, enabling her to diagnose and cure present-day sexual illnesses and the "perversions" of Indian society.[54]

To make her books commercially viable she used pictures and photographs in them. For example, her book *Dampatya Prem* had 158 visuals and images of conjugal romance.[55] Her manuals were precise and detailed, describing her various cases and their cures. Her book *Nari Sharir Vigyan* ran into 1144 pages. *Dampati Arogyata Jeevanshastra* and *Dampatya Prem aur Ratikriya ka Gupt Rahasya* comprised 728 and 520 pages, respectively. She started several magazines, such as *Kanya Sarvasva* and *Stridharma Shikshak*. An important journal she edited was *Stri Chikitsak*, catering solely to the ayurvedic treatment of women's diseases.[56] Like Santram, while interspersing her writings with Sanskrit, she often wrote in colloquial Hindi for a lay readership so that even women with basic reading skills could follow most of her writings.[57] Her work was mainly addressed to women readers: "For the convenience of women, I have made this book so simple that women who are not well educated can also easily understand it."[58]

Yashoda moved in a relatively new territory. There were hardly any dispensaries in India based on indigenous belief systems which catered exclusively to women.[59] For women in purdah it was difficult to leave home, and even more difficult to be examined by male medical practitioners.[60] Women's access to cash was limited and there was still a strong bias against Western medical systems. In any case, learned physicians, male or female, were scarce at this time. As a woman and a practitioner of an indigenous medical system,

[54] Ibid., inside cover.
[55] Yashoda, *Dampatya Prem*.
[56] *Statement of Newspapers and Periodicals*, 152–3.
[57] Yashoda, *Bharat ka Nari*, 5–6.
[58] Yashoda, *Dampati Arogyata*, 432.
[59] Yashoda, *Adarsh Pati–Patni*, 89–93.
[60] 266–67/1872, Public, A, Home Deptt, NAI; Balfour and Young, *Work of Medical*, 34–5.

Yashoda thus fulfilled two much-felt needs and so had no difficulty carving out a large space for herself. Her client base was also protected by the segregation in them of the sexes. Her dispensaries and writings became so popular that she warned her clients against fake copies of them:

> Extensive copying of my writings, remedies, and name is carrying on. Some people have thus named their shops Stri Aushadhalaya. They also eagerly search for any woman named "Yashoda Devi" whom they can employ as a servant in that dispensary so that notices can be taken out in her name. Some even think that if a girl is born to them they should name her Yashoda Devi so that they can run their dispensary in her name. Everyone should beware this rampant fake industry and dispensaries for women that are being run in my name.[61]

Like other ayurvedic practitioners of her time, Yashoda revived and reconstituted the indigenous medical tradition of ayurveda, and with greater success than many others.[62] She recognised the context of medical pluralism and, while critiquing Western medicine and doctors,[63] continued interacting with them to suit her needs by adapting some of their techniques. All the while, she maintained the distinctiveness and superiority of ayurvedic insights and methods. This amounted to providing a vision of an alternative modernity by the evasion of tidy epistemological frames. Professional in her dealings and running a well-organised network, she created a dialogical modernity, reshaping ayurveda as the bearer of modern technologies and print cultures that combined cultural beliefs and values suited to the needs of the middle-class urban household, with the housewife as its manager. One of the items in her agenda was worded thus: "I want that my new methods, extracted with the help of ancient methods, should be propagated throughout the country, and everyone, particularly women, should benefit from them."[64]

---

[61] Yashoda, *Dampati Arogyata*, 372.
[62] Panikkar, "Indigenous Medicine"; Gupta, "Indigenous Medicine".
[63] Yashoda, *Vivah Vigyan*, 195, 337.
[64] Yashoda, *Dampati Arogyata*, 464.

To argue for modern ayurveda as a counter-cultural medical system against "hegemonic" biomedicine may not have been Yashoda's explicit intent, but she did offer a clear defence of ayurveda, particularly its usefulness for women. Reflecting on the fact of ancient male founding fathers of ayurveda having paid little attention to women's health, she maintained that the basic precepts of ayurveda were, all the same, extremely useful for women.[65] She also accepted that some Western and unani medicine tenets could aid ayurvedic treatments for women.[66]

Given the skewed gender relations in her context, Yashoda made the most of being a woman: instead of downplaying her gender, she foregrounded it to enhance her popularity, achievements, and necessity as a *woman* practitioner. Male indigenous practitioners, having completely ignored women's health, were made worse by seeming intrusive and voyeuristic threats to a woman's most intimate spheres; in fact, she said, many of the wives of male vaids came to her for the treatment of their sexual problems.[67] Besides, modern medical methods too were inadequate in offering cures for women's ailments as they were not geared to investigate the root cause of woman-specific problems.[68] In such a scenario, only an Indian woman practitioner with access to spaces closed to male practitioners, and specialising in an indigenous medical system like ayurveda, could serve the purpose.[69] She equated her women's dispensary with the high court: "This Stri Aushadhalaya is like the high court for women where women patients can send their petition and draw the benefit of themselves being able to collect or order medicines to cure their diseases."[70]

Contesting male control over ayurveda, she enlarged the language of sisterhood.[71] Presenting herself as a caring female physician, a beloved wife, and every woman's friend, she projected herself as living

[65] Yashoda, *Nari Sharir*, 9–11; idem, *Dampatya Prem*, 337.
[66] Yashoda, *Nari Sharir*, 12–14.
[67] Ibid., 18–20.
[68] Yashoda, *Dampatya Prem*, 337.
[69] Yashoda, *Adarsh Pati–Patni*, 91.
[70] Yashoda, *Dampati Arogyata*, 2–3.
[71] Yashoda, *Nari Dharmashastra*.

proof of an epistemic investment in women's sexual problems and diseases.[72] She wrote: "My book will serve women as a clever midwife and a talented, knowledgeable friend – Yashoda Devi, wisher of health to all sisters."[73]

At one level, her concerns as representative of the Hindu middle class overlapped with Hindu reformist rhetoric, revivalist ayurvedic assertions, and conservative nationalism; at another they resonated with Western biomedical agendas; at yet another she implicitly challenged certain norms and ideals. Like many science and medical books of the time, her books placed family, gender, and sexuality at their centre.[74] Ayurvedic medicine in most such works is located in the context of middle-class social and domestic life, and shows how the language of the body as well as body processes constructed cultural and nationalist identity. This was because much of this literature was also prescriptive and didactic, targeting middle-class Hindu women, emphasising their social responsibility in maintaining the health of their families and the Hindu nation.[75] Propagating Hindu conservatism, Yashoda celebrated a mythical golden past of ideal women by writing biographies of virtuous and brave Rajput women.[76] Drawing from such imagined pasts and combining them with present needs, she sought to reorder household and conjugality with images of an ideal and obedient wife imbued with reformist endeavour, controlling and sexually disciplining her body and social movements.

The domestic space was meant to be regulated and organised by regimens of hygiene, sanitation, and cleanliness. Time was rationalised, and thrift, budgeting, providence, and temperance were emphasised.[77] Having imbibed the normative discourse of an ideal housewife, Yashoda offered detailed instructions over 134 points on household management. These included various subjects – for example, specifying when to take a bath, how to cook food, how to

---

[72] Yashoda, *Dampatya Prem*, 257, 337; idem, *Nari Sharir*, 218–21.
[73] Yashoda, *Dampati Arogyata*, 8.
[74] For example Thakur, *Gharelu Vigyan*; *Leader*, 5 January 1939, 5.
[75] Prakash, *Another Reason*, 148–9.
[76] Yashoda, *Bharat ka Nari*.
[77] Yashoda, *Kanya Kartavya*, 8–10, 52–4; idem, *Adarsh Pati-Patni*, 20–40.

maintain records, and how to ensure thrift in the care of the household.[78] *Kanya Sarvasva*, a journal for young girls edited by Yashoda, had regular columns called "Grh Svachata" for household cleanliness, "Sharirik Shastra" for bodily care, and "Pakshiksha" on culinary knowledge.[79] Cooking was an intrinsic part of the care of the body and medical treatment of the ill within the home. Modern and scientific methods of cooking were stressed, acknowledging that the British had contributed in teaching these values. However, these were moulded to contemporary indigenous needs in Yashoda's books, combining hygiene with a virtuous gendered morality and ethic.

Around this time, mothering and childcare gradually became an arena of "rationality" and constant advice for women. Many Hindi publications appeared on *sharir palan*, i.e. bodily health, of the family, particularly on *shishu palan* (care of the child, largely described as male). Addressed to the middle-class woman, these were intimately linked to the new models of domesticity.[80] Recommendations on "scientific" pregnancy, "correct" neonatal care, childbirth, care of the newborn, breastfeeding, and child-rearing filled many pages of the books written at this time, including those by Yashoda.[81] Her magazines carried regular columns on subjects such as a pregnant woman's lifestyle and children's education. It has been argued that pregnancy, breastfeeding, and early infant care are determined not only by culture but also by power.[82] In UP, too, the need to modernise maternity and discipline motherly love was highlighted to establish the class and caste status of Hindus. Middle-class women visiting

---

[78] Yashoda, *Nari Dharmashastra*, 60–70. Also Yashoda, *Nari–Niti*, 6–11; idem, *Vivah Vigyan*, 20–32.

[79] Yashoda, *Kanya Sarvasva*, 1 (2), 1913, 91–3; 1 (3), 1913, 113–14; 1 (4), 1913, 143–4; 3 (1), 1915, 89–92, 93–4. This was not unique to Yashoda. For example, the book *Stri Subodhini*, published by the Naval Kishore Press, had topics like protection of the womb, women's health and diseases, education of dais, medical care, and treatment of illnesses of household members: Girdavar, *Stri Subodhini*.

[80] Savary, *Evolution*.

[81] For example Dube, *A Guide to Mothers*; Kala, *Santan Palan*; Gaur, *Santan Shastra*; Yashoda, *Shishu Raksha*.

[82] Ram and Jolly, *Maternities and Modernities*, 1–2.

Yashoda actively discussed these subjects, helping regulate domestic practices and assert the power of the middle-class Hindu household.

A Moral Sexologist: Reproduction, Intercourse, and Masturbation

Yashoda was, above all, a woman ayurvedic (moral) sexologist and therapist. However, though in slightly different ways from Santram BA, she too was marginalised from mainstream sexology discourses. Foucault argues that sexology was an arena dominated by male medical experts.[83] In her study on women sexologists in Germany, Kristen Leng points out that "for many male sexologists, women were precisely objects to be studied, managed, and contained."[84] However, she argues that sexology was a contested terrain "not limited to a select few (male) authors and canonical texts," and that sexology as a field destabilised "our understandings of expertise and authority," allowing "for a fuller exploration of sexology's polyvalent political potential."[85] As shown previously, in early-twentieth-century India sexology primarily operated along gendered and casteist lines. Not only ayurvedic vaids but even established sexology literati deemed Yashoda's knowledge and writing as inferior – that is, in the rare instances they did not completely ignore her.

This did nothing to diminish Yashoda's activity, popularity, and fame. While a number of upper-caste, middle-class women had established themselves in the Hindi print-public sphere, with many writing on matters of health and conjugality and espousing a reformist-moralising discourse, rarely do we come across so many texts by a single ayurvedic woman practitioner which speak explicitly of sexual matters and attempt to reform sex life. In this sense, by the sheer volume of her work in this genre, Yashoda was unique. Her forté and specialisation lay in curing women's sexual problems – excessive menstrual bleeding, vaginal discharges, repeated miscarriages, and

---

[83] Foucault, *The History of Sexuality*, 72.
[84] Leng, *Sexual Politics*, 3.
[85] Ibid., 34.

infertility. In discussing her knowledge of cures for women's sexual diseases she says:

> This book contains causes, identification and simple cures to remove all *gupt rog* [secret sexual diseases] among women. It has been prepared by churning many texts of ancient ayurvedic knowledge over several years, spending considerable labour and money, and will significantly help all women. For women who do not disclose their gupt rog even to their families on account of a sense of shame, this book is a lifeline, a clever midwife that tells you about all diseases, and a clever doctor that teaches you knowledge worth millions for very little money.[86]

She also specialised in the treatment of infertility and claimed to have a cure for barrenness, publishing many letters by women who claimed to have had a child (almost always male!) after her treatment. She had various medical solutions and potions for miscarriages and menstrual pains.[87] There was an elaborate discourse on menstruation as a marker of female fertility, health, and generative power, and Yashoda's remedies for disorders in this area seem to have had a huge demand among women. She also dealt with vaginal discharges and infections (leukorrhea) and sexually transmitted diseases in women. Her treatments naturally attracted a lot of women because she claimed a success that never entailed surgical interventions or operations.[88] (See Figs 3.3.)

Drawing inspiration from biomedical sexology and a hedonistic consumer culture, she also incorporated graphic visuals of male and female reproductive anatomy in her description of sexual problems. In the manner of a professional physician, Yashoda prepared case histories of her women patients following upon long conversations with them and a detailed questionnaire they were asked to fill out.[89] Her clinical encounters and personal relationships with women patients show that the medical culture she was fostering took shape not only as books and manuals but also as knowledge-producing practices. She emphasised that she herself, with her own hands, conducted the

---

[86] Stated in an advertisement: Yashoda, *Stri Dharma Shikshak*, 7.
[87] Yashoda, *Nari Sharir*, 200–1; idem, *Dampatya Prem*, 359.
[88] Interview with Sudha Sharma.
[89] Yashoda, *Dampati Arogyata*, 8–11.

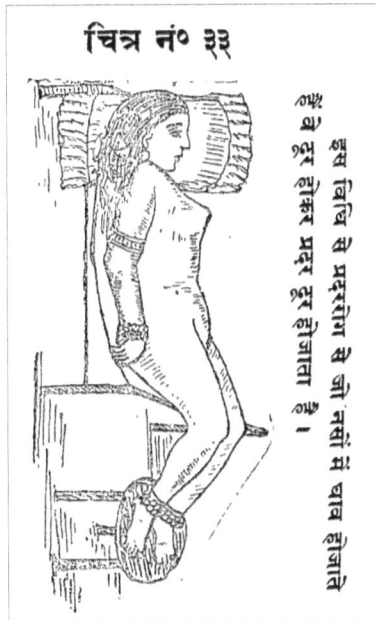 

Figs 3.3-i and 3.3-ii: Illustrations relating to the cure of leukorrhea and venereal disease.

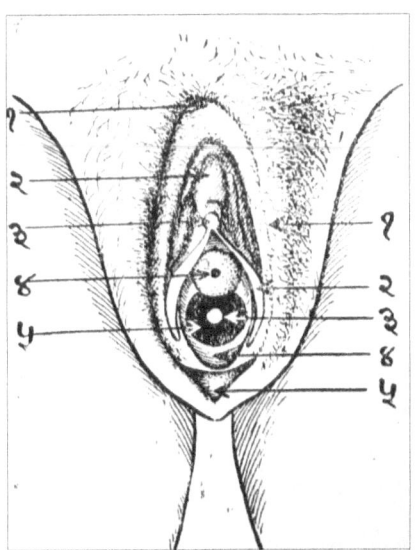 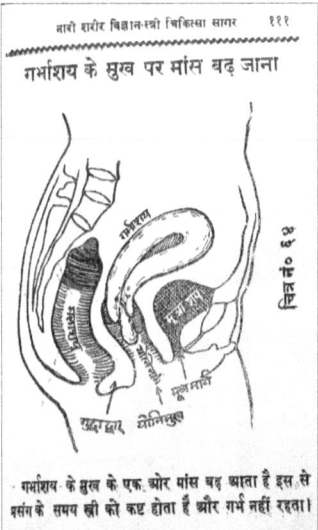

Figs 3.4-i and 3.4-ii: Illustrations of female genitalia.

Fig. 3.5: Yashoda with helpers – Ganga Dai is on Yashoda's left.

physical examination of all her women patients.[90] She proclaimed her debt to Dr Satyabhama Bai, a medical doctor (BA, MD) from Nepal who seems to have had a considerable impact on her earlier writings, and whose books she also published.[91] Also noteworthy is the fact that Yashoda derived help from the lower social orders, since she regularly used the knowledge of traditional women healers and midwives. A bevy of around forty helpers, many from the lower castes, lived in her home. Ganga Dai, a Kahar by caste, was Yashoda's trusted confidante who accompanied her in all her medical outings.

Ganga Dai, who had hands-on experience, was further trained by Yashoda and stayed for most of her life in Yashoda's home, even after Yashoda's death. In my interviews with the granddaughter and granddaughter-in-law of Yashoda, both stressed that Ganga Dai had been treated as a daughter: Yashoda had taught her and often slept on the same bed with her. Another low-caste woman, Jamini, also worked with this duo throughout.[92] Her husband apart, Ganga Dai was the hidden actor in Yashoda's success, though she was never formally acknowledged in her writings (possibly pointing to other layers of caste-class dynamics: see Fig. 3.5).

An interesting facet of Yashoda's more progressive views is that she did not believe in menstrual taboos or any form of "isolation" during

[90] Yashoda, *Nari Sharir*, 218–21; idem, *Dampatya Prem*, 257.
[91] Bai, *Jeevan Raksha*; idem, *Dhatri Vidya*.
[92] Interview with Sudha Sharma; Interview with Rachna Sharma.

that period, and women continued to work in her kitchen at such times. She also firmly opposed any *chhut-chhat* (pollution taboos).[93]

Sexuality engaged Yashoda's constant attention and was seen by her in scientific, medical, and moralistic terms. Her books constantly discussed her clients' sexual lives: *Dampatya Prem* was, for example, specifically devoted to it.

Her view was that sexual science and passionate intercourse were an intrinsic part of ayurveda.[94] Printed sex manuals were at this time flooding the Hindi market. In them the lines between sexual science, erotic art, and obscenity were often blurred.[95] Yashoda, however, clearly distanced herself from what she called the "dirty" works of kamashastra and the publishing of "obscene" pictures whose sole purpose was to titillate and which, she felt, led to an increase in disease among women and men.[96] Her books by contrast discussed issues such as sexual intercourse in accordance with the "scientific" principles of ayurveda.[97] In her discussions we see an excessive preoccupation with reproduction: she repeatedly stresses that sex is only meant for procreation.[98] The central purpose of marital love was reproduction.

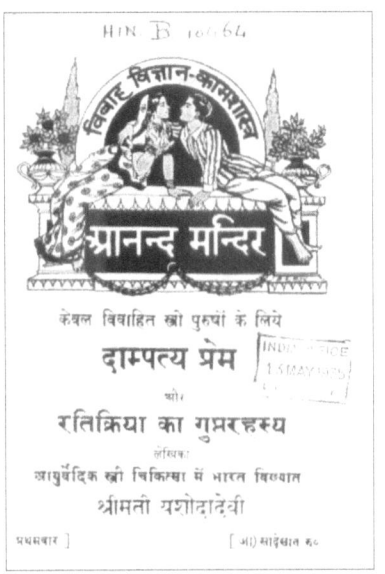

Fig. 3.6: "Vivah, Vigyan, Kamashastra: Anand Mandir" (Marriage, Science, Sex: Temple of Pleasure).

---

[93] Interview with Sudha Sharma.
[94] Yashoda, *Dampatya Prem*, 85–149.
[95] For details, ch. 2.
[96] Yashoda, *Dampatya Prem*, 11, 60, 181–3.
[97] Yashoda, *Vaidik Shastra*; idem, *Dampatya Prem*, 61–4; idem, *Dampati Arogyata*, 3.
[98] Yashoda, *Dampatya Prem*, 152, 223.

Fig. 3.7: The happy outcome of conjugal love.

This was the common emphasis of her time: a moral and uncontroversial approach to sex required seeing its function solely as biological reproduction.[99] Yashoda told women how to recognise "pure" semen, the ideal time to have sex, how many times to have sex, how to have a healthy child, and offered various prescriptions for proper sexual conduct.[100] In the bulk of ayurvedic, medical, and santati shastra literature there was a marked obsession with the male child.[101] Yashoda's preoccupation with healthy male progeny was also explicit.[102] On this she wrote: "Just as a good farm and fine seeds are needed for the production of exquisite fruits and superior food grains, so too to produce the best [male] offspring, there is a critical need for a combination of the good farm, like the *raj* (menstrual discharge) of the woman, and excellent seed, like the semen of the male."[103] There were social constraints on her of other kinds as well. As a woman sex reformer catering mainly to middle-class women,

[99] For example Dube, *Santan Vigyan*; Shastri, *Janan Vigyan*.
[100] Yashoda, *Dampati Arogyata*, 77; idem, *Dampatya Prem*, 149–87, 351–6.
[101] Savary, *Evolution*, 97–137.
[102] Yashoda, *Dampatya Prem*, 152, 223. Also see Rai, "Gendering Late Colonial".
[103] Yashoda, *Dampatya Prem*, 256.

Yashoda often imposed self-censorship and endorsed patriarchal stances to appear respectable and acceptable. Her heteronormative, monogamous ethic was based on moderation, self-control, and "legitimate sex":

> Women should not be considered only products for intercourse or machines for sexual pleasure.[104]
>
> Husbands and wives should love only each other and derive affection, happiness, and sexual enjoyment only from each other.[105]

Her years of interaction with female patients made her realise that she would be unable to cure many of them without addressing questions about male illnesses. This also suggests that, while recognising that her niche in the world of medical practice depended mainly on her female clientele, she wished to establish increasing respectability by extending her claims and cures to the other sex as well. So she prepared a list of more than forty questions for men, and asked her women clients to persuade husbands suffering from any kind of illness to answer them and mail the replies to her. She assured the women that all such letters would be treated as confidential.[106] Her advice and remedies were thus meant not only for women but often also for the married couple. I have argued elsewhere that

Fig. 3.8: Sample representation of monogamous conjugal blisss.

---

[104] Ibid., 50.
[105] Ibid., 510.
[106] Yashoda, *Grhini Kartavya Shastra*, last four pages.

one needs to problematise notions of Hindu male sexuality as well and the strains to which it was put, particularly in the colonial period. Though the fear of unregulated female sexuality was great, male sexuality too had to be controlled; sexual mores applied to men as well. The Hindu male too was, clearly, being inundated with moralising treatises on sexuality and medical questioning that tested his idea of manhood.[107]

Alter has emphasised that in the colonial period, particularly, there was an attempt to turn the power of sex away from the chaos of passion into disciplined masculine strength.[108] Vivekananda called for sexual abstinence to build a nation of heroes.[109] Gandhi too believed that stored-up semen was the source of splendid energy in the male body and a necessary prerequisite for the integrity of the nation.[110] Many Hindu publicists, Sanatan Dharmists, and Arya Samajists eulogised semen control. In their arguments and publications this was no longer just a moral doctrine of self-discipline. Their modernist discourse was intertwined with eugenics, childbirth, and a scientific "rationality". Healthy bodies ensured strong Hindu men who, in turn, were indispensable to a modern masculine nation. Semen control had grown into a building block for claims to social and political power, cultural identity, and a scientific way of life.

Yashoda's writings endorsed this discourse and urged restraints on male sexuality. In deeply problematic ways, she argued that male sexual pathology became manifest through four main "evils": loss of semen, excessive sexual intercourse, homosexuality and *vipreet maithun* (anal sex), and *hast maithun* (masturbation).[111] Masturbation became her central target of attack, being seen as the root cause of physical and mental illnesses and domestic tragedies. She warned against it on supposedly scientific and moralistic lines. Claiming to have received more than 100,000 letters from unwell men, she

[107] Gupta, *Sexuality, Obscenity*, 66–83.
[108] Alter, *Wrestler's Body*.
[109] Sengupta, *The Frail Hero*, 120–49.
[110] Parekh, *Colonialism, Tradition and Reform*, 172–206; Fox, *Gandhian Utopia*.
[111] Yashoda, *Dampatya Prem*, 248; idem, *Arogya Vidhan*, 25.

ascribed this to the idea that "those from men who masturbated were many more than letters combining all other types of diseases."[112] She found an excess of masturbation among male students and adolescents, some of them having begun self-pleasuring from as early as the age of eight or nine, and called it *dushkarm* (evil activity).[113] A variety of "male" problems were attributed to masturbation: "Masturbation results in the birth of grave male diseases and maladies ... These include malfunction of the senses, false excitement, physical debilitation, backaches, mental illnesses, semen loss, impure semen, weak eyesight, urinal infections, nocturnal emissions, night fall, wet dreams, impotency and infertility ... The woman does not get the full pleasures of sexual intercourse even for a day if her husband indulges in masturbation."[114]

To substantiate her claims Yashoda referred to illustrative instances, narrating vivid stories by women of men diseased by masturbation. An 18-year-old woman, whose husband wanted intercourse every day, said that during her absences from home as well as during her periods, her man masturbated to excess, which, Yashoda believed, led to the debilitating weakness he felt. This made him in her estimation not only a bad husband but also a bad citizen.[115] In wasting their energies thus, men ended up neither giving pleasure to their wives nor serving the nation.[116] She linked the addiction to masturbation and lustful thoughts to the modern "vices" that had brought in sources of racy entertainment such as the theatre, cinema, "dirty" books of kamashastra, sleazy romantic novels, and advertisements of aphrodisiacs which "made the heart and mind more fickle and volatile".[117] She also linked masturbation to madness – though

---

[112] Yashoda, *Nari Sharir*, 992; 707–17.

[113] Yashoda, *Dampatya Prem*, 224; idem, *Dampati Arogyata*, 9–10, 19; idem, *Dampati Arogyata*, 19–39.

[114] Yashoda, *Nari Sharir*, 707–22. Also Yashoda, *Arogya Vidhan*, 26–7; idem, *Dampatya Prem*, 224; idem, *Dampati Arogyata*, 9–10, 19.

[115] Yashoda, *Dampati Arogyata*, 16–25.

[116] Yashoda, *Nari Sharir*, 722.

[117] Yashoda, *Arogya Vidhan*, 1; idem, *Dampatya Prem*, 210, 221, 302; idem, *Dampati Arogyata*, 5.

only sometimes. In her discourse against masturbation she referred persistently to Western medical practices and quoted Western medical doctors – Dr Foot Saheb, Dr Desland, Dr Ilbert, Dr Saires, Dr Tissat and Dr Guiot – to support her claims.[118] She also acknowledged her debt to Dr Satyabhama and dedicated her book *Arogya Vidhan Vidyarthi Jeevan*, which was explicitly against masturbation and in favour of brahmacharya, to her.[119] Like other publicists of her time, her reflections on masturbation were framed within a nationalist discourse. Male self-pleasuring was seen as a prime cause of the degeneration of Indians and the crises of the nation.[120]

Excessive sexual intercourse with wives, according to Yashoda, was also a vice of the worst kind, leading to the waste in men of valuable energies, time, and health.[121] Men frequently wrote to her asking for medicines that would enable them to have sexual intercourse three or four times a day without leaving them feeling washed out.[122] Lamenting this constant demand, she complained that the newspapers were filled with advertisements for aphrodisiacs which made false and astounding claims. The marketing of such aphrodisiacs, she argued, was deleterious because, instead of helping preserve semen, its waste was ensured.[123] Simultaneously, she made a case for brahmacharya and the preservation of semen,[124] which she claimed was being wasted in huge quantities; this was because its "earning was less than its expenditure" (*amdani kam, kharcha zyada*).[125] She asked men to make love sparingly and contain their semen;[126] semen was power and power was life, the key to a healthy male body.[127]

The male "pervert", however, also shifted from being a sinner to

---

[118] Yashoda, *Arogya Vidhan*, 23–6, 29–30; idem, *Dampati Arogyata*, 26.
[119] Yashoda, *Arogya Vidhan*, 1, 5.
[120] Yashoda, *Dampatya Prem*, 210; Prakash, *Another Reason*, 152–4.
[121] Yashoda, *Dampati Arogyata*, 25; idem, *Dampatya Prem*, 210.
[122] Yashoda, *Dampatya Prem*, 217–18.
[123] Yashoda, *Arogya Vidhan*, 63; idem, *Dampatya Prem*, 151, 222–3.
[124] Yashoda, *Arogya Vidhan*, 43–52, 85, 134; idem, *Dampatya Prem*, 150–1; idem, *Vivah Vigyan*, 180, 313.
[125] Yashoda, *Dampatya Prem*, 16.
[126] Ibid., 150.
[127] Yashoda, *Dampatya Prem*, 225; idem, *Dampati Arogyata*, 3, 37.

a patient whom she could cure.[128] Her book *Dampati Arogyata* had an astonishing list of contents which ran into 24 pages and covered 623 topics, including "The Glory of Celibacy", "Problems Due to Loss of Semen", "The Harms of Masturbation", "Masculine Malnutrition Due to Semen Disorder", and "The Recognition of Pure Semen". It also contained compounds for "curing" hast maithun, *svapn dosh* (nocturnal emission), and gonorrhoea.[129]

Though commenting on the private space of the household's health, Yashoda's prescriptions had broader social, moral, and political implications. The private and the public, the inner and the outer, the interior and the exterior overlapped in her orderings on health and illness, their boundaries shifting with circumstances. In effect, they cut across the family and extended to the community: Yashoda's concern was also with the preservation of ethics and morality across the whole nation. No doubt this grandiose claim for national betterment was a discursive strategy to boost the sales of her potions. It worked. Such large endorsements were critical for Yashoda to promote sex reform at a micro level as well as to suggest methods of governing the collective sexual life of the nation.

Yashoda's achievements in the public domain, it can be safely surmised, were based on her empathy and ability to communicate a private sense of sharing and caring. With intimate conversations she seems to have established an instant rapport with her clients, implying both considerable power over and close relationships with the large number of women who came to her for help in a context where there was almost no one else to whom they could have turned. Without the art to communicate and win over her female patients' hearts and minds, she could not have been as successful as she was. She was the agony aunt for local women; unlike white women medical practitioners, she did not condemn the zenana quarters. She represented herself as a sympathetic listener whose background and world were those of the women who needed her: with them she shared a common vocabulary and body language. Her conversations were "empowering" for herself and the women who came to her. Her success

---

[128] Schaffner, *Modernism and Perversion*.
[129] Yashoda, *Dampati Arogyata*, 57–142.

story is also the story of women's networking as she provided a platform on which women could voice their intimate concerns and complaints away from household structures, safely removed from the world of their male partners.

While the question of women's reproductive capacities and fertility remained at the centre of Yashoda's concerns, she recognised the importance of women's bodily desires, sexual pleasures, and orgasms. Underlining the need for prolonged foreplay, she stressed the importance of hugs, kisses, and pillow talk to ensure the woman's sexual arousal and readiness for intercourse. Lovemaking was not to be hurried by the male and enjoyment for the woman was as important as for the man.[130]

She was not inhibited by the fear of confronting and interrogating masculine sexual privilege and male-centric beliefs about sex. She often urged her clients to have less sex, asked men to control their sexual urges, and recommended sex only for procreation. She voiced her strong protest against sex without the woman's consent, calling it a grave crime.[131] She referred to men who violated this norm by stating that their numbers were large and that such men had a misplaced sense of masculinity. And therefore such men, she did not hesitate to say, were worse than animals.[132]

> Even if the woman is in no mood and has no desire, the man tortures her sexually. In other countries, men cannot do anything [call for sex] without the woman's consent ... Many women who are ill come to me and say "What are we to do, our husbands just won't listen. Even if we say a firm 'no', they do not listen; even if we are ill they do not listen" ... Out of a hundred, ninety-nine men are such that as soon as they touch a woman or read a dirty book, their sperms start leaking out of them ... These sexually depraved and blind men who think that women are going to be thrilled if they want intercourse every day, and will give them a certificate of masculinity, and desire them even more, are really stupid.[133]

[130] Yashoda, *Dampatya Prem*, 259–63, 343, 500.
[131] Yashoda, *Nari Sharir*, 147; idem, *Dampatya Prem*, 218–20, 294.
[132] Yashoda, *Nari Sharir*, 738; idem, *Dampatya Prem*, 188.
[133] Yashoda, *Dampatya Prem*, 218–23.

It was boldly progressive and fearless of her to praise the sexual culture of the West, where the woman's consent was considered necessary and where men were more sensitive to women's sexual requirements. While emphasising the need for sex to be consensual, she had no inhibition in stressing the importance of sexual pleasure and sexual agency to her women patients. In the process, she provided an unusually scathing critique of Indian male habits and practices, recounting via generalities what various women had confided to her about the misdeeds of their husbands.[134] Men were also severely reprimanded for adultery and domestic violence and warned of its disastrous implications.

Yashoda's books narrated stories with titles that highlighted male brutality: for instance, "Blind lust and tyranny of the husband towards an ailing wife suffering from vaginal discharge".[135] Unlike, say, the writings in *The International Journal of Sexology*, where women were often blamed for their husband's sexual problems,[136] Yashoda directed her ire against men. In line with social-purity feminists, she blamed the excessive libidinal drive of husbands for an epidemic of venereal diseases, women's ill health, the alienation of wives, and miserable marriages. "Many husbands," she wrote, "behave worse than animals and torture their wives with sexual violence, destroying women's lives."[137] And again: "There is no shortage of men who force themselves on their wives ... In the past twenty-five years ... I have heard innumerable cases of such cruelty and of the brutality of husbands on their wives' bodies."[138] Most sex-related illnesses among her women clients were attributed to men, and she narrated innumerable sad stories by women who had suffered from venereal disease on account of the "misdeeds" of their husbands.[139]

She was prescient – and here she is reminiscent of Santram – in

[134] Yashoda, *Nari Sharir*, 409; idem, *Dampatya Prem*, 243; idem, *Dampati Arogyata*, 1–2.
[135] Yashoda, *Nari Sharir*, 654.
[136] Ahluwalia, "Scripting Pleasure", 30.
[137] Yashoda, *Nari Sharir*, 738.
[138] Yashoda, *Dampatya Prem*, 188.
[139] Ibid., 188, 226; Yashoda, *Dampati Arogyata*, 189–90.

व्यभिचार अर्थात् परस्त्रीगमन का परिणाम । पृ० १०४ (सर्वाधिकार सुरक्षित)

पर स्त्री गमन का फल । पृ० ५०८ (सर्वाधिकार सुरक्षित)

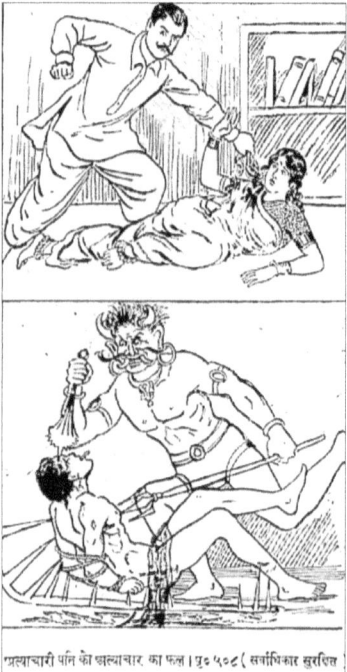

अत्याचारी पति के अत्याचार का फल । पृ० ५०८ (सर्वाधिकार सुरक्षित)

Figs 3.9-i, 3.9-ii, and 3.9-iii: The aftermath of male adultery and torture of a woman by a tyrannical husband.

demolishing myths that had come to be seen as common sense. One such was the belief that barrenness and infertility were due to some intrinsic defect in women; she argued that it was most often men who bore responsibility for these problems.[140] Infertility, she pointed out, could often not be cured without treating men as well, whereas in many such cases the men remarried and the wives suffered for no fault of theirs.[141] By and large men emerge in her writings as weak, useless, and stupid (*murkh*).[142] Her writings show a potential for subverting or inverting patriarchy, or at the very least the need to renegotiate social and family norms in the direction of equity for wives.

It is easy to dismiss the bulk of her writings because it is undeniable that they are an unrepentant upholding of conjugal norms and procreative impulses. However, her stress on female sexual dissatisfaction and dismay at the lack of consensual relations offers a different and perhaps novel alternative to the dominant perspectives on women's status and role in marriage. She negotiated and reinvented the terrain of man–woman relations, even if with contradictory and ambivalent implications. In the process of becoming, commercially, an exceptionally successful woman, she shows the possibilities and limits of traditional female physicians in a context hostile to such women.

While her middle-class status gave her some respectability, her methods appear to be socially more plebeian and culturally more popular. Her popularity and success in creating a genre of literature focusing on women's diseases inspired other women and men to write on issues of women, health, and medicine.[143] It appears that many small ayurvedic clinics, catering exclusively to women, came to be opened after her pioneering activities, even though they were never as successful as her's.

These texts perhaps tell us something other than the author's intentions. Even if partial and incomplete, they open up other avenues for studying gender and medicine in a colonial context. Yashoda's

[140] Yashoda, *Dampatya Prem*, 359–60, 475.
[141] Ibid., 439, 475.
[142] Ibid., 221–2.
[143] For example Agarwal, *Grhini Chikitsa*; Sharma, *Sukhi Grhini*.

texts embrace a range of standpoints that reify, construct, and question sexual conventions; even if patriarchal controls are reaffirmed in them, they are situated alongside a scathing critique of men. She moves at two parallel levels: her endorsements of procreation and the disciplining of bodies go hand in hand with readings of health, marriage, and sex from a woman's perspective. This points to a dense phenomenology of experience which allows us to hear women's voices through her many varied and unusual narratives.

Yashoda and possibly other women practitioners of ayurveda intervene in the domain of male practitioners to covertly contest both male control over the discipline and offer different arrangements from those available in male-dominant hospitals and dispensaries. As a moral sexologist, Yashoda moved within a nebulous territory, celebrating the indigenous medical system while offering only a constrained critique of Western medicine. She conformed to new modes of public health, hygiene, and medical science, successfully moulding modern values to Hindu systems and needs. Any study of health or medicine in a colonial society cannot rely on simple dichotomies: the boundaries between indigenous therapies and modern medical practices were often blurred, and sometimes overlapped. Binaries of tradition versus modernity mutually reinforce and totalise stereotypes of East–West difference in the discourse of colonialism. They are as problematic when they valorise ayurveda as when they condemn the backwardness of traditional medical systems. In Yashoda we see indigenous healing becoming another tool in constructing cultural identity and Indian nationalism. Her writings simultaneously reiterate and replicate gender hierarchies and provide occasions for questioning them. Finally, they allow us to examine the broader historical processes unleashed in colonial India. They reveal how middle-class formations, patriarchal practices, and nationalist identities were consolidated even as they were fractured from within.

In Chapter 2 I focused on the heterosexual ethics constructed by Santram. The vantage points of Yashoda were quite different. The divergent voices of advice in Santram and Yashoda show that the possibility of sexology from the margins, as those of anticaste reform, could cut both ways: they inhibited and emancipated at the same time. Usually upholding the sexual status quo, Yashoda restricted the meanings of sexuality by reifying the moral-sexual heteronormative-monogamous marital code. While Santram celebrated a utopian future, Yashoda constructed a dystopian present world of modernity. Her vernacularity was based on policing and prohibiting bodily functions and relied on the fears and dangers of unruly impulses, promiscuity, and illnesses. All of this also, perhaps, reflects the limits of a Brahmanical ayurvedic sexual discourse.

4

Kitchen Pharmacy
Culinary Recipes and Home Remedies

Preparing food not based on the principles of pak shastra . . . causes many diseases. This is the main reason why in every household women, men, elders, and children are falling sick . . . There is a saying that *ann hi maare, ann hi jilave* (food alone kills and food alone makes us live) . . . Only food ensures longevity, strength, and health, while not consuming it as per culinary recipes and temperaments not only makes one always sick but soon pushes one into the jaws of death. If women are masters of culinary knowledge, they can prepare perfect food in accordance with the disposition of their family members and the seasons. These foods are enough for women to protect themselves and their family from all kinds of illnesses on an everyday basis. However, until now there has been no such book [of recipes]. The present book has been prepared to remove the deficiency. – *Sab behnon ki aarogyakaankshi* (wisher of health to all sisters), Yashoda.[1]

Based on my experience of having treated lakhs of sick women, men, and children, in this book I offer nuskhe to cure many diseases. These recipes and their *vidhi* (methods) have been repeatedly tested and experimented upon, and I have discovered and learned them through a thorough churning of [ayurvedic] medical science . . . These recipes are a ramban for all illnesses. This book will prove very useful for all women

---

[1] Yashoda, *Grhini Kartavya*, Preface. This book's 2nd, 3rd and 5th editions appeared in 1915, 1924, and 1932, respectively, and it was a commercial hit. I have mostly used the first edition of 1913, unless otherwise stated.

in India . . . Women can carry these *prayog* (experiments) with their own hands, in their own homes, at a very low cost, thus deriving a huge benefit.[2]

THESE QUOTATIONS from two recipe books written in Hindi by Yashoda embody various messages and meanings. Claiming to be a master of recipes, and going beyond everyday knowledge, she sees the art of cooking and the preparation of gharelu nuskhe as a definitive science to be used to educate women systematically. Relying on ayurveda, vernacular knowledge, and tragic ailment narratives she reveals an elemental relationship between seasons, dispositions, food practices, illnesses, and health. Seeing food as a kind of medicine, she offers dietary therapies that connect cooking with healthy bodies. Justifying a gendered division of labour, she holds women exclusively responsible for the hard work required in kitchens for the health of their families. Thus, she issues a sort of summons to women, asking them to serve as the care-giving agents of her recommended regimen. In the process she also comes across as a commercial entrepreneur investing in the business of marketing her recipe books as the best in the field. Women are projected as both consumers and domestic doctors, ghar ka vaid and grh chikitsaks – people purposively engaged in the everyday practice of preventive medicine.

Yashoda perceives the medical economy of her recipes as superior to the available alternatives. She argues that her recipes offer self-diagnosis and self-treatment and also promote a non-invasive homespun technology that is cost effective. Instead of paying servants, women (and men), she says, are enabled by her books to prepare sound food and medicines even while sitting at home, and share them freely, simultaneously making them culturally relevant as the exchange of medical knowledge. Finally, while strengthening normative constructions of the "good wife", her recipe books rely on the activity of sharing between women and so attempt to create the bonds of sisterhood.

---

[2] Yashoda, *Dampati Arogyata*, 327–8.

These preoccupations in the writings of Yashoda reflect some of the central concerns of this chapter. Through the genre of popular printed recipes in Hindi I try here to conceptualise the entanglements of histories of food, health, and gender in Hindu middle-class urban households of early-twentieth-century UP. With the coming of print, recipes in the vernacular became one of the important ways of constructing an ideal Indian housewife; they also constituted an arena where educated middle-class women's voices came to be heard, recorded, and published. Women emerged not only as consumers but also as authors of recipes, personifying prosaic, gendered, authorial spaces and new ways of sharing quotidian knowledge. This chapter puts a spotlight on the nature of kitchen recipes – culinary guides (*pak vidhi*), cookbooks, and gharelu nuskhe – printed in Hindi. Since these recipes also denoted religious identities, caste hierarchies, and class status, the chapter reflects on their intrinsic Hindu, upper-caste, and middle-class character, which was tied up with political and nationalist alignments in the region.

In bringing these strings together I take the vibrant recipe world of Yashoda as my central lens, thereby studying women as culinary specialists, kitchen pharmacists, and home healers par excellence. The recipe books were a combination of Yashoda's vast ayurvedic knowledge, a personal narrative, a gendered pedagogical manual, a testimonial cum biography, and a culinary memoir.

I also expand the personal outwards into the public to look at the larger politics of Hindi cookbooks and recipes. The chapter is broadly divided into five interconnected arenas, with its first half concentrating on culinary cultures and its second on home remedies. The backdrop of the recipes burgeoning in the region was the politics of food in UP, which forms the first section. The next section conceptualises printed recipes as a distinct genre of Hindi print cultures. Projected as repositories of vernacular knowledge, and principally addressed to functionally educated and modern Hindu middle-class urban housewives, these recipes claimed authenticity and authority over the advice they dispensed on culinary and domestic remedies. The subsequent section considers class, religious, caste, and gender identities embedded in culinary texts, intermeshing them with

Yashoda's food writings. The last two sections examine domestic women healers as the bedrock of medicinal recipes, with particular attention given to Yashoda. They show women functioniong as kitchen pharmacists and domestic doctors. The last section looks at the political economy of this home pharmacy and the wider implications of women as domestic managers of everyday healing knowledge.

In brief, this chapter leads us into the home, which was the setting of most experiences of illness, gendered domestic skills of health and medicine, popular herbal remedies "from below", medical pluralisms, and a core arena of healing and medical decision-making.

The Politics of Food and Health in Colonial UP

Histories of food, showing its relationship to identity, power, subversion, urbanity, and global cultures, have emerged as an important field of studies in India.[3] Over the colonial period, food became an arena for the assertion of British superiority, the negotiation of nationalist politics, claims to autonomy, the display of notions of femininity and masculinity, and a means for strengthening middle-class, caste, gender, and religious identities.[4] The British articulated their difference and superiority through dietary manuals, even while negotiating their ambivalent craving for and loathing of Indian tastes and spices.[5] They pondered at length on their health and diet in an alien environment.[6] They brandished the dietary cultures of Indians to supplement their representations of manly and superior Englishmen cast among effeminate and misbegotten natives, particularly Bengalis – in the early days of colonialism.[7] At the other

[3] For example Burton, *The Raj at the Table*; Leong-Salobir, *Food Culture*; Ray, *Culinary Culture*; Ray and Srinivas, *Curried Cultures*; Khare, *The Eternal Food*.

[4] For an overview of food historiography in colonial India, Berger, "Alimentary Affairs"; Fischer-Tiné and Malhotra, "Introduction".

[5] Shahani, *Tasting Difference*.

[6] Arnold, *Colonizing the Body*, 36–43; Burton, *The Raj at the Table;* Mark Harrison, *Public Health*, 9–10, 14, 40–1.

[7] Sinha, *Colonial Masculinity*.

end of the spectrum they connected diets to their notion of "martial" Indian races.[8] They disparaged native kitchens and cooks as markers of filth and usually belittled a vegetarian diet.[9] Some Indians retorted to this construction of a gastronomic hierarchy by arguing for consumption of meat as a symbol of muscular nationalism.[10]

After 1857, food acquired more and more connotations for North India's Hindu middle classes.[11] The meteoric growth of the Hindu Mahasabha and the Arya Samaj sharpened the narrative of Hindu nationalism. Alongside the hardening of Hindi–Urdu linguistic identities, cow-protection movements between 1880 and 1920 contributed to cantankerous debates on vegetarianism and non-vegetarianism, with the former seeming to prove themselves ascendant. Vegetarianism became tied to brahmacharya, to the moral values of selflessness, and to notions of the purity and strength of the nation. Simultaneously the consumption of meat, particularly beef, became a way of vegetarian Hindus pinpointing their differences with the British, Muslims, and Dalits, all three being considered gluttonous, cruel, and impure, with the broader argument being that flesh-eating led to a propensity for sex, alcohol, and violence.[12] Clubbing meat-eating with alcohol consumption and smoking, Gangaprasad Upadhyay, a leading Arya Samajist of UP, offered a vociferous defence of vegetarianism. Selectively quoting scientists from the West, he posited a distinction between non-vegetarian food, which caused excitement of the senses (*uttejit karne valé*), and vegetarian food, which generated physical strength and energy (*shaktivardhak*).[13] Fasting and vegetarianism also, most famously, became part of the ensemble of ingredients with which Gandhi challenged colonialism, advo-

[8] Collingham, *Imperial Bodies*.
[9] Procida, "Feeding the Imperial Appetite"; Sengupta, "Nation on a Platter", 85–6.
[10] Roy, *Alimentary Tracts*.
[11] For an overview of the middle classes in colonial North India: Joshi, *Fractured Modernity*; Daechsel, *The Politics of Self-Expression*.
[12] Hauser, *A Taste for Purity*; Adcock, *The Limits*, 54–5, 169.
[13] Upadhyay, *Hum Kya Khaaven*, 101.

cated non-violence, and projected the body as a site in need of reform.[14]

Such debates were complemented by a nostalgic invocation of a supposedly "golden" Vedic past of strong men uncorrupted by Muslims and the British.[15] Discourses of food, medicine, and ayurveda deployed a similar rhetoric to project an ancient "national culture of hygiene" in which men were all strong and healthy people who ate wholesome food and lived virtually forever;[16] such men were naturally exempt from the afflictions of famine, cholera, and the plague.[17]

Food also became a marker of religious and caste hierarchies.[18] Connecting private bodily practices to social forces of caste supremacy, increasing altercations arose around inter-dining and purity–pollution taboos. The Arya Samaj made some half-hearted attempts to share food and water with "untouchable" castes, these efforts being often couched in a problematic language of caring correction and self-control. At the same time, countercurrents of Dalit food cosmologies began their articulation of a distinct culinary identity, challenging savarna domination.[19]

Comestibles also became a hot topic in the public life of the military, factories, railways, and bazaars, with worries over what might have touched what was to be eaten, who had cooked it, who had served it.[20] Modern developments such as the railways and restaurants

[14] Alter, *Gandhi's Body*; Roy, *Alimentary Tracts*, 75–115; Slate, *Gandhi's Search*.

[15] Gould, *Hindu Nationalism*, 135–9.

[16] Berger, *Ayurveda Made Modern*, 49; Mukharji, *Nationalizing the Body*, 142–3.

[17] *Abhyudaya*, 17 April 1908, *NNR*, 18 April 1908, 353; *Swarajya*, 16 November 1907, *NNR*, 30 November 1907, 1317; *Karmayogi*, 22 October 1909, *NNR*, 6 November 1909, 809; Vaidyaraj, *Aupsargik Sannipat*, 5–6, 17, 24.

[18] Alter, *Gandhi's Body;* Salobir, *Food Culture*; Ray and Srinivas, *Curried Cultures*.

[19] Gupta, *The Gender of Caste*, 159–61.

[20] Peers, "The Habitual Nobility of Being", 551–2; Joshi, *Lost Worlds*, 241–2, 253–4.

boosted public eating, making it difficult for the upper castes to maintain food taboos in terms of kaccha and pukka.[21] The demand by railway passengers for separate refreshment rooms for the high castes, and fresh food in line with dietary caste restrictions, encouraged a diverse food market for, of, and by Indians.[22] The 1931 census of UP noted that "No less than 73 per cent of workers in trade are concerned with food-stuffs, and if to these we add those employed in hotels, cafes, etc., and hawkers of drinks and foodstuffs the figure rises to 75 per cent."[23]

Some of the greatest worries over food and health arose among the Hindu middle classes. A mercantile culture had developed in many towns of UP, but there were growing economic insecurities and unemployment.[24] Bemoaning the loss of a hypothetical glorious past, kaliyug became a trope for the dystopian present, connoting unhealthy and weak bodies, the loss of manliness, an increase in illnesses and epidemics, contaminated food, adulterated ghee, and the rise in prices.[25] The problems of middle-class ill health were compounded by "bad" dietary habits. Markus Daechsel argues that in colonial North India "being middle class assumed the character of a medical condition that strangely replicated the pathological political situation this constituency found itself in."[26] The consumption of nutritious food became a way of overcoming the malaise. It came to be connected not only with taste but also with health, self-control,

---

[21] Kaccha is food cooked with water, or boiled; it is usually the everyday meal and must be consumed right away. Pukka is food cooked with ghee or milk, often fried, and can be stored for a longer time. According to Hindu caste commensality rules, the upper castes can accept uncooked and raw food items from the lower castes, and at times pukka food (as it is believed that ghee gives the food protection from spoiling and other forms of ritual pollution), but kaccha food is to be accepted only from one's own or equivalent or "superior" castes.

[22] Mukhopadhyay, *Imperial Technology*, 141–7.

[23] *Census of India, 1931, UP, XVIII (I)*, 402.

[24] Ibid., 24; *Report of the Unemployment Committee*, 19–20, 24–7, 33–7, 261–73, 391–4.

[25] Haynes, *The Emergence of Brand-Name*, 71–3, 182.

[26] Daechsel, *The Politics of Self-Expression*, 94.

hygiene, and a medicalisation of the family.[27] Food cravings, for example, were frowned upon and restrictions imposed on the widow, the brahmachari, and the *akhara* (gymnasium) wrestler – such people having been deemed most in need of countering sexual desires and the stresses of modern life. Middle-class nourishment came more and more to consist in a new domesticity where the ideal housewife was she who ensured scientific household management, healthy food, and indigenous medical remedies.[28]

In the household economies taking shape, food was the most significant component of middle-class expenditure.[29] A combination of price rise, financial hardship, low salaries, unemployment, and high cost of living brought about an insistence on thriftiness, frugality, efficiency, providence, and temperance.[30] Middle-class women were seen as responsible for the domestic economy; they were meant to keep an account of household purchases, be careful in their budgeting, be tight with their savings, and prevent waste. In one way or another, this went hand in hand with the preparation of food for the family.[31] There were, moreover, "serious hesitations of middle-class families to subject their digestive systems to industrial capitalism"; so they resisted mass-produced commodities and showed a distinct preference for fresh, unbranded items.[32] As against products like Horlicks and Ovaltine, ghee and milk continued to hold sway as the chief sources of good health.[33]

Denied an autonomous political existence, domesticity and conjugality, along with indigenous culinary and medical habits,

[27] Ibid., 99–106; Haynes, *The Emergence of Brand-Name*, 177–84; Prasad, *Cultural Politics*, 23–32.
[28] Gupta, *Sexuality, Obscenity*; Sreenivas, *Wives, Widows*; Walsh, *Domesticity*.
[29] Haynes, *The Emergence of Brand-Name*, 173.
[30] Gupta, *Sexuality, Obscenity*, 141.
[31] Joshi, *Fractured Modernity*, 71.
[32] Haynes, *The Emergence of Brand-Name*, 177–9.
[33] Berger, "Clarified Commodities"; Ray, *Culinary Culture*, 158–9. Many Hindi texts were full of praise for milk: for example Sharma, *Dugdh aur Dugdh*.

came to be expressed as a terrain of middle-class Indian sovereignty, even superiority, vis-à-vis the British. In this context printed recipes acquired importance in the battle to overcome a sense of loss and inadequacy, to uphold a professed ancient wisdom, to claim a degree of superiority, and to pitch for cheaper health solutions. With their restorative properties regularly reiterated, home-based curative recipes were understood as remedies not only for physical, mental, and psychological illnesses but also as a counter to the power imbalance of colonial rule.[34]

A Robust World of Cookbooks and Home Remedies

Recognising the demand for varied household recipes, prominent commercial publishing houses such as the Chand Karyalaya of Allahabad, and the Naval Kishore Press and the Ganga Pustak Mala based in Lucknow, took the lead with cookbooks, tracts on remedies for everyday ailments, and recipe columns in women's magazines like *Chand* and *Sudha*.[35] While there is a rich scholarship on cookbooks, relatively little work has theorised recipes as a distinct genre in colonial India.[36] However, studying early modern England, Elaine Leong places the production and circulation of varied recipes at the heart of household science, natural knowledge, and everyday home remedies.[37] Largely a modern genre, printed recipes in Hindi came into their own in the early twentieth century. While these were also often closely guarded family secrets, print brought oral transmissions into the public domain. Leong says gentlemen and gentlewomen were gripped by a recipe fever in early modern England,[38] and something similar can be seen among the middle classes in late colonial North India. Primarily to be read

[34] Langford, *Fluent Bodies*, 63–4.
[35] Nijhawan, *Hindi Publishing*, 182–4.
[36] Ray, *Culinary Culture*; Choudhury, "A Palatable Journey"; Gupta, "Culinary Codes"; Sengupta, "Nation on a Platter".
[37] Leong, *Recipes and Everyday*, 3–4.
[38] Ibid., 2.

and followed by the modern housewife, recipes were designed for and by women. While often part of vernacular didactic guides and home-science books, they were not perceived as layered with caste, religious, or moral connotations, but mostly seen instead as practical repositories of everyday knowledge. In middle-class domestic management they gained significance for their quantifiable, brief, precise, simple, user-friendly, and scientific character – discursive virtues to which every reader could easily relate. While Yashoda's writings sometimes included smatterings of Sanskrit, her recipes were written in a colloquial non-technical Hindi addressed to a lay readership of women: "for the convenience of women" she had written her recipes so simply that even those "who have little education can easily understand them."[39]

These recipes reinforced Hindu middle-class images of the ideal housewife while also allowing women to voice a specialist terrain of knowledge in print. Women contributors of recipes were named, giving them an authorial identity. Male publishers understood that women's long-standing knowledge as cooks and household healers was difficult to displace; they could profit by reproducing women's authority within the world of cooking and recipes.

Food Recipes and Cookbooks

Arjun Appadurai says there was an "informal, fragmentary, and minor" tradition of cookbooks in India because food was historically embedded in moral-medical Hindu beliefs and inscriptions.[40] However, with mass print technologies combining with the commerce around food, cookbooks came to be written in diverse ways – for example, in English for white memsahibs and in the vernacular for Bengali housewives. Rachel Berger examines the relationship between food, digestion, desire, and embodiment by studying Hindi cookbooks and guides to health in the early twentieth century. She shows these publications conceptualising an ideal Indian nation and sub-

---

[39] Yashoda, *Dampati Arogyata*, 432.
[40] Appadurai, "How to Make", 11–12.

Figs 4.1-i and 4.1-ii: Sample illustrations showing recipe columns.

ject through dietary choices.[41] Recipe columns started appearing in leading women's magazines. "Pak Shiksha" (Cookery Education) was often carried in the magazine *Chand*.[42] *Sudha* had a regular column called "Pak Shastra" (Culinary Science) from February 1930, which was later renamed "Bhojan" (Food).[43]

With cookbooks becoming marketable, a substantial number also came to be penned by men who projected themselves as culinary pedagogues. Some of the early ones were Bhakt Bhagwandas' *Ras Vyanjan Prakash*, Karthik Prasad's *Pakraj*, Ramlal's *Nutan Pak Prakash*, and Pandey Ramsharanlal Verma's *Pakprakash*.[44] The most popular were a series of culinary texts by two men. One was by Pandit Maniram Sharma, a resident of Daraganj, Allahabad, who wrote books like *Adarsh Parivar* and *Maharani* but became most famous for his cookbooks.[45] After Sharma's death Ramrakh Sehgal, the editor of

[41] Berger, "Between Digestion".

[42] For example, for the columns "Pak Shiksha": *Chand*, November 1922 to April 1923, 227, 314, 402, 519; November 1923 to April 1924, 105, 203, 306, 384, 470; May to October 1924, 94, 172, 274, 358; May to October 1925, 426, 516.

[43] For example, for the column "Pak Shastra" and "Bhojan": *Sudha*, August 1930 to January 1931, 125, 272, 409, 531, 701, 845; February to July 1931, 121, 261, 414, 533, 659, 760. For further details, Nijhawan, *Hindi Publishing*, 182–4.

[44] Bhagwandas, *Ras Vyanjan*; Prasad, *Pakraj*; Ramlal, *Nutan Pak*; Verma, *Pakprakash*. The translations of titles of all Hindi books are available in the Bibliography.

[45] Sharma, *Kanya Pakshastra*; Sharma, *Pak Vidya*. For a brief note on Maniram Sharma, Mitra, *The Indian Literary*, 85.

Chand, commissioned a compilation of his recipes: this was carried on by his wife Vidyawati Sehgal – she was also the manager of the publication house – as *Pak Chandrika*.⁴⁶ The book was extensively advertised in the pages of *Chand*, and Sharma's recipes became an integral part of the magazine's food column. The second was Mataprasad Gupt, a sweet vendor of the Vaishya caste from Pratapgarh. He opened a sweetshop in 1908 which expanded into three, all of them engaged in selling sweets and dry fruits, and coming to be regarded as among the best confectioners in the region.⁴⁷ The 1931 UP census recorded a remarkable increase in sweetmeat dealers.⁴⁸ Mataprasad Gupt was a member of the Arya Samaj, involved in caste reform, and acquired substantial wealth. He wrote at least two cookbooks, *Gud-Pak-Vigyan Mithai* and *Pakprakash aur Mithai*. These contained various food recipes with a special focus on sweets. *Pakprakash aur Mithai* was compiled by Ramakant Tripathi "Prakash" and published by the Naval Kishore Press.⁴⁹ Other culinary texts

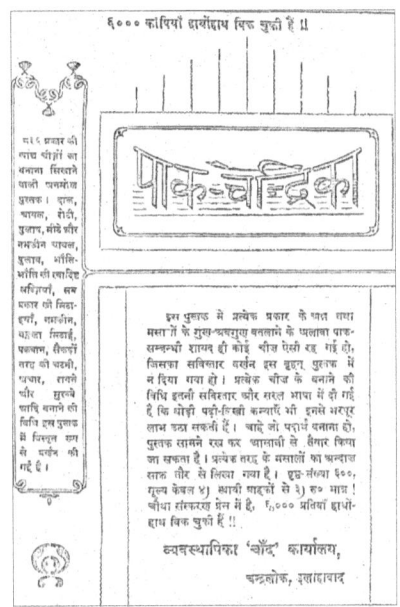

Fig. 4.2: Advertisement for *Pak Chandrika* in *Chand*.

⁴⁶ Sharma, *Pak Chandrika*. For a lucid analysis of *Pak Chandrika*, Gupta, "Culinary Codes".

⁴⁷ Sweetmeats emerged as a major profession. A magazine called *Halwai* was published quarterly from Allahabad by Raghunath Prasad Halwai in the 1940s: "Newspapers and Periodicals published in UP during 1940", F–53, 1, 41, KW, Part 7, 1941, NA, Home Poll I, NAI.

⁴⁸ *Census of India, 1931, UP, XVIII (I)*, 402.

⁴⁹ Gupt, *Pakprakash aur Mithai*; Gupt, *Gud-Pak-Vigyan Mithai*. For a brief sketch of Mataprasad Gupt, Gupt, *Pakprakash aur Mithai*, 1–6.

written by men in the 1930s and 1940s included Jagannath Sharma's *Pak Vigyan,* Hanumanprasad Sharma's *Aahaar Vigyan,* Mohanlal Bhargav's *Vyanjan Prakash,* Girish Chandra Joshi's *Adarsh Pak Vidhi,* Chotelal Trivedi's *Vyanjan Prakaar,* and Pandit Nrisinghram Shukl's *Vrihad Pak Vigyan* (a revised edition of which was published as *Adhunik Pak Vigyan*).[50]

Not to be outdone, women were busy writing cookbooks with a distinct flavour. One such early fun cookbook was Anant Devi's *Vyanjan Prakash,* which often resorted to the use of *dohas* (couplets) to narrate its recipes.[51] Then there was Shailkumari Chaturvedi's *Navin Pak-Shastra* and Rama Devi Tiwari's *Pak Prabhakar.*[52] Another prolific woman writer was Jyotirmayi Thakur of Kanpur who wrote many domestic manuals, including the cookbook *Gharelu Shiksha tatha Pakshastra.* And then of course there was Yashoda, whose big hits included *Grhini Kartavya Shastra arthat Pakshastra* (hereafter *Grhini Kartavya*),[53] which went into several editions and impressions.[54] Her journals *Stri Dharma Shikshak* and *Stri Chikitsak* regularly carried culinary recipes. Yashoda's forté, as we shall see, consisted in household ayurvedic medical recipes.

Recipes for Home Remedies

The Hindi print sphere was inundated with remedies for diverse ailments, and the normal boundary separating household recipes from the everyday health advice in vernacular medical literature was blurred. These medical recommendations also served as contestations over ideas of indigenous modernity and subaltern autonomy since they were touted as recipes for problems brought in by colonialism. Their authors were often quasi-genealogists invoking ancient ayurvedic principles to counter Western medicine and recommend a cultural identity not polluted by the West – a process well

[50] See Bibliography for details.
[51] Devi, *Vyanjan Prakash.*
[52] See Bibliography.
[53] Yashoda, *Grhini Kartavya.*
[54] Ibid. Also, Yashoda, *Achaar ki Kothri.*

described as "the nationalisation of the science of hygiene itself."[55] Rachel Berger shows that ayurvedic knowledge was a vital part of Hindu household life in colonial North India.[56] Shobna Nijhawan too argues that in home-remedy columns "ayurveda as a practice and therewith as useful information featured centrally."[57] The word functioned metonymically as a unifying banner for all kinds of non-Western medical practices by Hindus, as well as for non-allopathic popular medical writings in Hindi, including print recipes.[58] K.P. Girija remarks that many such recipe books were "looked down upon as non-scholastic by the practitioners of classical Ayurveda because of their wide popularity and everyday use," their writers being often "termed as quacks by the classical Ayurvedic tradition."[59] While referring to these home cures as "folk remedies", Projit Mukharji shows that recipes played an important role in "institutionalizing numerous marginalized medical ideas and practices."[60]

While they often sustained power hierarchies, as the repositories of women's domestic knowledge, recipes were part of the archives of family histories. They were often indifferent to allopathy and implicitly subverted male claims to medical knowledge. Unlike the overwhelmingly male-centric discourse in the professional, erudite, and authorial print literature of ayurveda, home remedies and healing practices, despite being perceived as a woman's domain, acquired a new respect and sense of authoritative worth by the very fact of appearing in print. Operating away from professional and syndicated networks, and differentiable from the work of purists, these writings invoked ayurveda in broad, general, and popular strokes. This enabled their receptivity within a plural and quotidian terrain of popular medicine strongly associated with traditional domestic wisdom. This was the benevolent and wise in-house wisdom of *dadi*s

---

[55] Mukharji, *Nationalizing the Body*, 143.
[56] Berger, *Ayurveda Made Modern*, 93.
[57] Nijhawan, *Hindi Publishing*, 187.
[58] Berger, *Ayurveda Made Modern*.
[59] Girija, *Mapping the History*, 45.
[60] Mukharji, *Nationalizing the Body*, 89, 172–6.

and *nani*s (paternal and maternal grannies), informal healing networks in neighbourhoods, and what might be termed a "knowledge commons" of exchange and sharing which the elite male domain of ayurveda had not managed to fence off and appropriate. This was an eclectic domain of and by women being made available to all – in part because it cast doubt on the world of high technology, patents, biomedicine and its adverse side effects, and the high price of allopathic treatment. Household recipes were touted as cheap and natural remedies with no side effects.

Chand and *Sudha* were ardent promoters of this new knowledge. *Chand* carried a regular column by the name of "Gharelu Dawaiyan" (Household Medicines), the editors of which in 1922–3 were Madan Mohan Chaturvedi and Shakuntala Devi Gupta.[61] These recipes were by both women and men, and had a variety of authors that included traditional ayurvedic male vaids as well as women like Shakuntala Devi Gupta, Mohini Devi Bhatnagar, Uttarakumari Vajpayee, and Champa Devi Srivastava. Another of *Chand*'s columns entitled "Grh Vigyan" (Home Science) carried similar imagery and contained home cures, besides other household tips. Occasional articles in *Chand* provided home cure recipes for fever, earache, cough, and constipation.[62] *Sudha* had a similar column named "Grh Chikitsa" (Home Remedies), which relied on indigenous science and ayurveda.[63] Shobna Nijhawan argues that the conglomeration of writers and authors contributing to the column on household remedies testifies to the fact of self-trained women and lay practitioners jostling with learned ayurvedic vaids, signifying new authorships that went beyond pandits and allopathic doctors.[64]

[61] For example, for the recipe column "Gharelu Dawaiyan" in *Chand*, November 1922 to April 1923, 316, 395, 516; November 1923 to April 1924, 79, 204, 308, 376, 448; May to October 1924, 273, 366, 464, 534; November 1924 to April 1925, 80, 212, 348, 434; May to Oct. 1925, 201, 299, 423, 523.

[62] Editor, "Daktari Dawaein".

[63] For example, for the recipe column "Grh Chikitsa" in *Sudha*: August 1930 to January 1931, 129, 276, 412, 529; February to July 1931, 124, 265, 415, 535, 641, 762. For further details on this column, Nijhawan, *Hindi Publishing*, 185–8.

[64] Nijhawan, *Hindi Publishing*, 188.

Fig. 4.3: Illustration accompanying column on home remedies: "Gharelu Dawaiyan".

Madhuri Sharma shows how words like "ramban" were often used metaphorically to proclaim the efficacy of certain recipes and products. Medicinal recipes were projected as the arrow of Ram which swept away all evil: they would cure every ailment.[65] The Chand Karyalaya brought out as a book a collection of home remedies entitled *Gharelu Chikitsa*, based on its column in *Chand*.[66] Its authors were said to be "Many Eminent Doctors and Wise Men and Women" (*Anek Suvikhyaat Doctor tatha Anubhavi Stri-Purush*).[67] The book contained several practical and easy-to-prepare remedies. It had separate sections on children which listed cures for indigestion, abdominal pain, cough, fever, diarrhoea, teething, etc.;[68] and on women which mainly covered gynaecology and reproduction, and included cures for menstruation troubles, labour pains, stillbirth, swelling of the breasts, leukorrhea, and insufficient breastmilk.[69] The largest section was on *vividh rog* (diverse diseases), which covered a wide range – from fever, cold, cough, itchy eyes, and sleeplessness, to malaria, plague, cholera, piles, epilepsy, and snakebite.[70] Self-help manuals and household recipes in the vernacular thus became important methods to record popular wisdom, quantify and textualise everyday medical traditions, and provide basic medical knowledge.

[65] Sharma, *Indigenous and Western*, 131.
[66] *Gharelu Chikitsa*.
[67] Ibid., Preface, 2.
[68] Ibid., 1–22.
[69] Ibid., 23–30.
[70] Ibid., 31–109.

Menu for a Hindu Nation and the Ingredients of Gendered Embodiments

In line with what Utsa Ray demonstrates in her work on culinary cultures in colonial Bengal,[71] the Hindi cookbooks of the early twentieth century embodied upper-caste, middle-class, and Hindu identities. These works often nostalgically glorified Hindu cooking traditions and claimed to draw their roots from ancient indigenous cuisines. The genealogies of a Hindu gastronomy were at times invented and at others appropriated and reinterpreted to cultivate a Hindu nationalism that was embedded in the kitchen. Yashoda's *Grhini Kartavya* constructed a golden culinary age when people were healthier and lived for an eternity: "People have abandoned their ancient greatness and forgotten their *shastrokt vidhaan* (scriptural statutes), because of which much effective advice is disappearing. Our ancestors took great measures to protect their bodies . . . They thus lived for thousands of years. For hundreds of years, no signs of old age were visible on their bodies."[72] In hypothesising a Hindu masculine ethos, *Pak Chandrika* viewed ancient food practices as the main contributor to the physical strength of Bhim, Bhishm, and other mythological rulers.[73] Tying this up with eugenics, another source stated: "Those who eat good food, their sons are healthy, strong and pious (*balishth, balvaan* and *pavitra*)."[74] Such authors often entwined their recipes with ayurveda.[75] Positing an organic connection between ayurveda and her cookbook, Yashoda blended information on the value of fruits, vegetables, pulses, and spices with ayurveda, arguing that the mix was wholesome as well as in tune with the Indian disposition.

Exaltations of the ancient were accompanied by laments over the present state of food knowledge and cooking abilities that were making men weak and lethargic. Maniram Sharma deplored what he noticed – that 90 out of 100 men were *ksheenkay* (emaciated).[76]

[71] Ray, *Culinary Culture*.
[72] Yashoda, *Grhini Kartavya*, 28–9.
[73] Sharma, *Pak Chandrika*, 3, 9–10.
[74] Verma, *Pakprakash*, 2.
[75] Sharma, *Aahaar Vigyan*, 21.
[76] Sharma, *Pak Chandrika*, 21.

He wrote: "In this land of Bhim and Arjun, these *pilpilé* (flabby), dry-mouthed, bony mass of three-and-a-half-foot men are certainly embodiments of our deplorable present condition . . . To remove this blight on the country and to show how to gain physical strength through food, I have compiled this book on account of a desire to see my countrymen wear a rosy visage (*gulabi chehra*)."[77] "Natural" and freshly prepared Indian food was praised, while alien, Western, and modern methods as well as canned foods were disparaged.[78] A case was made for home cooking as more economical, far-removed from the adulteration rampant in the market.[79] Mataprasad Gupt's *Gud-Pak-Vigyan* had its foreword written by Baba Ramchandra, a famous peasant leader from Awadh. Claiming a domain of autonomy for indigeneity, Ramchandran declared the book was unique in upholding the benefits of jaggery versus sugar, and in showing that sweetmeats prepared with the former were cheaper, *pavitra* (pure), swadeshi, and beneficial for the poor peasants of India.[80]

At the same time, even as many Hindus thoroughly enjoyed eating meat, most recipe books were refashioning the ideal Hindu upper-caste palate as synonymous with a vegetarian diet, thereby marking Dalits, Muslims, and the British as the "other" of this normative culinary nationalism.[81] Projecting vegetarianism as a mark of distinction of Hindu food, Sharma proclaimed that "All the methods in this book have been written considering religion and society. There is no custom of cooking meat here. It only has things of our Hindu religion (*Hindu dharm ki vastuen hain*)."[82] Announcing that food should be cooked in line with the nature and disposition of one's own Hindu nation, Yashoda too advocated vegetarianism.

Hanumanprasad Sharma's *Aahaar Vigyan* drew bodily distinctions between self and other, spiritual and material, to argue that the sole reason for the destruction of the life-force that made a man a man was meat-eating (*maansaahaar manushya ki jeevan shakti*

---

[77] Sharma, *Pak Vidya*, Introduction, 1–2.
[78] Sharma, *Aahaar Vigyan*, 6–8; Sharma, *Pak Chandrika*, 9–10.
[79] Tiwari, *Pak Prabhakar*; Sharma, *Pak Chandrika*, 27.
[80] Gupt, *Gud-Pak-Vigyan*, foreword by Baba Ramchandra, 1–3.
[81] For details Gupta, *Culinary Codes*, 180.
[82] Sharma, *Pak Vidya*, Introduction, 2.

ko nasht karne ka ekmatra upaay hai); the human teeth were never meant for meat-eating; and the consumption of meat had a direct correlation with heightened sexual arousal and alcoholism; in brief, therefore, forsaking meat would end communal and caste discord in India.[83] Sidelining the rich Mughlai and Awadhi cuisine of North India, these culinary texts were set within the limits of a specious Brahmanical ayurvedic discourse: this was Brahmanism disguising and enlarging itself as Hinduism by speaking of the best diets that needed to emanate from a supposedly "Hindu" kitchen.

While written in an avowedly straightforward manner, embedded in the politics of most cookbooks was a class and caste discourse couched in a vocabulary of cleanliness and purity: "The cook should not be dirty. He should be clean and pure, should not be ugly, should not have any infectious (contagious and airborne) diseases . . . Do not let an impure person serve food as it results in a recoil and guilt in the person eating it."[84] Borrowing from Western notions brought in by colonialism, this discourse of cleanliness, purity, hygiene, and organisation became a part of the domestic-science agenda in culinary texts.[85] Hindi cookbooks stressed four central modules – the space of the kitchen, the utensils to be used, the clothes to be worn while cooking, and the aesthetics of serving.[86] In her discussion of household-maintenance texts in Britain, Andrea Adolph says they combined household, medical, and culinary recipes to rhetorically indicate an equation of household goods with embodied inhabitants.[87] As the conveyances of a Hindu urban middle-class identity, recipes were meant to carry collective meanings that could be replicated in all kinds of middle-class households. The middle-class character of these recipe books is revealed in detailed contents lists

[83] Sharma, *Aahaar Vigyan*, 9–14.
[84] Bhargav, *Vyanjan Prakash*, 3–4. Also Sharma, *Pak Vidya*, 5; Sharma, *Aahaar Vigyan*, 17, 20, 28.
[85] Choudhury, "A Palatable Journey".
[86] Bhargav, *Vyanjan Prakash*, 3; Chaturvedi, *Navin Pak-Shastra*, 5; Devi, *Vyanjan Prakash*, 2; Sharma, *Pak Chandrika*, 29–30, 35–9; Thakur, *Gharelu Shiksha*, 52–4.
[87] Adolph, *Food and Femininity*, 52.

signalling aspirations of upward mobility. Yashoda's *Grhini Kartavya* showcased this character via outlining men working in courts, with women learning knitting, stitching, and handicrafts from home-schooling teachers, and servants employed for household work.⁸⁸ The kitchen interiors, utensils, foodstuffs, and goods described in these recipe books were markers of a middle-class lifestyle: neatly arranged kitchen contents, matching jars, and almirahs for storage.

These recipes were not meant only to result in delicious meals – a larger moral condiment was also inserted to make for wholesome indigenous food that would ensure a healthy family and a strong nation.⁸⁹ Limits came to be placed on various food desires and gorging in excess, while eating stodgy, oily, and spicy food was frowned upon.⁹⁰ Rachel Berger notes that Yashoda "introduced a logic behind food that wove together questions of embodiment, economy, and environment, and synthesising eating, cooking, and caring as stalwarts of efficient modern living".⁹¹ Yashoda herself wrote:

Fig. 4.4: The ideal kitchen.

> There is enormous ignorance regarding food and diet . . . on account of such illiteracy, thousands of people are nearly in the jaws of death or suffer as patients. Just as medicine prepared by an *anadi* (inept) ayurvedic

---

⁸⁸ Yashoda, *Grhini Kartavya*, 13, 34, 60–1.
⁸⁹ Sharma, *Pak Chandrika*, 15–16, 25; Joshi, *Adarsh Pak Vidhi*, 4.
⁹⁰ Yashoda, *Grhini Kartavya*, 27–8.
⁹¹ Berger, "Between Digestion and Desire", 1631.

doctor, without complete knowledge of its science, aggravates many diseases in the body, making it difficult to get rid of them, so does food prepared without knowledge of *pak shastra* generate various illnesses in our bodies.[92]

Each of Yashoda's recipes detailed its benefits and advantages, and when to avail of or avoid using them.[93]

The gendered nature of these cookbooks was central to their formulation. When women from the West first began coming into India, a spate of cookbooks and housekeeping management guides catering to their needs were published. These were geared to assist the white memsahib in running her household even as they suggested to their readers a culinary imperialism – an assertion of the superiority of the Western kitchen over the Indian.[94] Examining Bengali culinary texts and the space of the kitchen, Jayanta Sengupta argues that vernacular recipe books became vibrant sites of everyday resistance: they ridiculed the gastronomic excesses of gluttonous British officials and empowered Indian middle-class housewives through a politics of femininity, authenticity, and contradistinctions drawn with European cuisine. He sees this kitchen literature as a vehicle for the cultural politics of *bhadralok* (Bengali new class of "gentlefolk") nationalism.[95]

Hindi culinary texts were markedly gendered in nature too. Though several of them paid due obeisance to Maharaja Nala for writing the oldest known ayurvedic treatise on culinary science, it was clear to all that this ur-text did not associate the task of cooking with women.[96] By contrast, most Hindi cookbooks, especially those written by men, considered the kitchen a domain reserved for women. Bhargav's *Vyanjan Prakash* opened thus: "Cooking food is a woman's religious duty (*bhojan banana stri ka dharma hai*). It is excellent to place the burden of cooking exclusively on women's

---

[92] Yashoda, *Grhini Kartavya*, 27–8.
[93] Ibid., 144–6.
[94] Procida, "Feeding the Imperial".
[95] Sengupta, "Nation on a Platter".
[96] Nala, *Pakadarpanam*, 5.

shoulders as they stay at home all the time."⁹⁷ Equating the biological with the social, Maniram Sharma proclaimed: "Just like feeding breast milk to children is the prime duty of the female community, it is their main duty to prepare food and feed their family members."⁹⁸ Bhagwandas' *Ras Vyanjan Prakash*, Brahmanical in its orientation, carried a series of pictures depicting the kitchen as an exclusively female domain, with the place for eating being entirely peopled by males.⁹⁹ Women cooked, men ate; women served, men were satiated. In time this expanded into a decree. (See Figs 4.5.)

The golden Hindu culinary past would be replicated in the present if only women got it into their heads that they were not just born to be supportive handmaidens for their men, their highest destiny lay in being kitchen maidens perpetually stirring cauldrons and doling out dishes; when women chose not to be so, it showed in them the laziness, ignorance, and wastefulness to which their entire sex was genetically prone – their lack of care indicated most particularly in their reliance on cooks. This charming view of women and their abilities was pithily voiced by Sharma's complaint that "out of 100, 75 women are ignorant in cooking. And women are getting stupider by the day."¹⁰⁰

While not adopting Sharma's markedly condescending tone, Yashoda did follow the mythography that moulded women's role as cooks in the idealised ancient past: "Draupadi and Damayanti were both queens. They were very hardworking and intelligent. Thousands of maids were in their service, yet both would prepare food for their family members with their own hands, according to their disposition and the seasons . . . Women should devote themselves to all the household chores."¹⁰¹ Cooking as science and art had to be formally taught to women; therefore every home should have a cookbook. To inculcate gender-appropriate morals, cookery

---

[97] Bhargav, *Vyanjan Prakash*, 1.

[98] Sharma, *Pak Vidya*, 3.

[99] Bhagwandas, *Ras Vyanjan*. Also Gupt, *Pakprakash aur Mithai*, 3.

[100] Sharma, *Pak Vidya*, 4; also, Sharma, *Pak Chandrika*, 4–6; Bhargav, *Vyanjan Prakash*, 1–2.

[101] Yashoda, *Grhini Kartavya*, 65.

Figs 4.5-i, 4.5-ii, 4.5-iii, and 4.5-iv: A series showing women serving and men eating.

should be made compulsory for girls in schools for, like any other subject, it needed to be formally taught and practised.¹⁰² *Pakprakash aur Mithai* illustrated what was necessary by showing one woman reading and another cooking, making it clear that its audience comprised literate, middle-class women.

This was also very much Yashoda's view: she felt it was "imperative that women be imparted complete knowledge of culinary science from childhood."¹⁰³ Most cookbook writers disapproved of employing cooks and servants in the kitchen. While the Western memsahib relied on them, the Hindu middle-class housewife did not delegate labour to paid domestic workers; she cooked with her own hands and relished her work in the kitchen. One cookbook said: "The way Aryan women prepare food with innermost effort . . . can never be expected from a paid woman cook."¹⁰⁴ Weaving this into an idea of male happiness, another said that even if a paid cook were intelligent and expert in the art, she could never satisfy or bring joy to the husband who, after a whole day's hard work, badly needed to return home to a good meal made by the hands of a loving wife.¹⁰⁵

Fig. 4.6: Reading recipes, following recipes.

---

¹⁰² Gupt, *Pakprakash aur Mithai,* 3; Chaturvedi, *Navin Pak-Shastra,* 5; Verma, *Pakprakash,* 3; Sharma, *Pak Chandrika.*

¹⁰³ Yashoda, *Grhini Kartavya,* 27–8.

¹⁰⁴ Sharma, *Pak Chandrika,* 6.

¹⁰⁵ Shailkumari, *Navin Pakshastra,* 4–5.

As Haynes has noted, advertisers of food products in colonial India constantly adjusted their techniques to cater to various market segments: servants featured regularly in advertisements geared to Europeans but were invisible in those aimed at middle-class Indians.[106]

Needless to say, a celebration of women's unpaid domestic labour and inequality was built into these "Hindu" cookbooks. It is well recognised that the deification of women and valorisations of their contributions as sacred are patriarchal strategies in the creation of hegemonic notions that serve – completely contrary to what they assert – to subordinate women. These covert forms of coercion are clear from what underlies their rhetorical justifications of constant physical work as good for women's health.[107] The drudgery of daylong cooking, the endless and enormous tasks required of women enslaved in kitchens, the back-breaking physical labour involved in churning out several meals daily – none of this can be mentioned because all of it must metaphorically be swept under the kitchen carpet. Yashoda's typical and idealised middle-class kitchen has daughters and mothers cutting vegetables, grinding spices, lighting stoves, and cooking lentils.[108] There is no room here for the fundamental and inescapable material fact of sweat, fatigue, and lungs decayed by smoke.

Grhini Kartavya contained 613 recipes. Claiming gendered authority, this was a central text in making Yashoda a key populariser of ayurvedic-inspired cuisine.[109] This cookbook is distinct from the bulk of those written by men in showcasing women as agents, actors, and participants. The discursive technique by which this is achieved is the figure of the bhabhi. Popular histories of the bhabhi show her as both object and subject of erotic desire and sexual fantasies.[110] But another facet of the bhabhi figure that emerged, being embellished in part by the recipe book, was the idealised maternal,

[106] Haynes, *The Emergence of Brand-Name*, 49.
[107] Sharma, *Pak Chandrika*, 7; Bhargav, *Vyanjan Prakash*, 1–3.
[108] Yashoda, *Grhini Kartavya*, 10–11.
[109] Ibid., 5.
[110] Gupta, *Sexuality, Obscenity*, 151–61; Sreedhar and Baishya, "Transgressions in Toonland".

knowledgeable, and experienced woman friend: it is in this sense that Yashoda deployed the bhabhi figure – in fact this persona was modelled on, and came to embody, Yashoda herself. Through a married and mentoring bhabhi, recipes were imparted as female morality to a younger unmarried woman. The cookbook was designed as a kitchen conversation between these two women – a bhabhi, cleverly named Gyanvanti (lit. the knowledgeable woman), and Roopvati, the beautiful but inexperienced younger woman. Their conversations were sometimes formatted as questions and answers offering informed guidance and prescriptions. Interrogating the credentials of men in kitchen matters, Yashoda indicated her own superiority and authority over the medium through her own construction of the ideal bhabhi, whom she made the voice of expertise and sanity on food, cooking, and health issues.[111]

Another narrative method in this cookbook by Yashoda was her constant use of tragic narratives of illness and death, fictional or actual, to substantiate the value of her recipes. These food tragedies included everyday stories of and from family members, cases from next-door neighbours, and testimonies of intimate "known" people. All these cases were apparently witnessed by the bhabhi and her woman pupil "with their own eyes" (*ankhon dekhi baten*). The examples included food habits that had led to the death of a mother, a severe stomach ache in a brother-in-law, and near-incontinence of the bowels in a sister's son.[112] The narration of bodily ailments caused by the "wrong" food helped establish authorial intimacy and authority when giving advice.[113]

The cornerstones of Yashoda's recipes were the therapeutic qualities of food based on permitted and proscribed products, regimes of temperance and self-control, and a balanced diet. The cookbook was divided into two sections: the first part began with topics like *rogon ke karan* (reasons for diseases), *virudh bhojan se haani* (the harm done by inimical food), and *pratyek ritu aahaar vihaar* (seasonal

[111] The figure of the bhabhi as the informed woman was used as a trope by other women writers as well. For example Thakur, *Stri aur Saundarya*.
[112] Yashoda, *Grhini Kartavya*, 25, 30–45.
[113] Ibid., 74–7.

diet), each discussed through kitchen conversations followed by nutritive values, uses, and the medical benefits of different kinds of food, including vegetables, fruits, pulses, grains and spices.[114] The second part contained healthy food recipes for children, older people, and those suffering from various illnesses. The recipes moved seamlessly between food and ayurveda, each constantly adjusted according to disposition, nature, time, season, and place.

By Yashoda, perhaps more than any other writer of the time, the cookbook and the kitchen were enlarged into a woman's space, a domain of survival and sisterhood where women could sometimes practise and expound on their ideas of health, nutrition, and culinary knowledge. However, it was through her expertise in writing home remedies and recipes for curing illnesses that Yashoda acquired a cult status, and it is to this that I now turn.

The Educated Housewife as "Ghar ka Vaid"

Even as biomedical knowledge became for the British an important means to colonise Indian bodies, many of their subjects continued recalcitrantly with their faith in indigenous medical systems. In fact, the robust heterogeneity and plurality within medical traditions reveal hybrid, syncretic, and versatile interpretations, a coexistence of diverse medical systems and healing practices, with people accessing a range of treatments, sometimes simultaneously.[115] While there is rich work on the increasing professionalisation and state sponsorship of both Western and indigenous medical systems – including ayurveda – in colonial India, comparatively little attention has been paid to plural streams of folk and popular healing, particularly home remedies by women.[116] Studies have shown that folk healers and

[114] Ibid., 74–121, 142–3.
[115] Ernst, *Plural Medicine*, 6–9; Hardiman and Mukharji, *Medical Marginality*.
[116] For the changing contours of ayurveda in colonial UP: Berger, *Ayurveda Made Modern*; Sharma, *Indigenous and Western*. Some works on popular healing are Ernst, *Plural Medicine*; Hardiman and Mukharji, *Medical Marginality*;

subaltern therapeutics did not conform to the "correct" medical systems, creatively interacting with and resisting state-sanctioned elite forms of medical practices.[117] Lona Chamarin, the legendary witch goddess feared and revered in UP, was regarded as one of the powerful *siddha* (a traditional healing system) practitioners in the early middle ages.[118] She embodied the power and wisdom of Dhanvantari, the great physician of the gods, and was regarded as particularly skilful in curing diseases, especially snakebite.[119] Similarly, the curative skills and knowledge of wise midwives were often indispensable in times of birth, miscarriage, and abortion, and such women were frequently believed to possess extraordinary healing and supernatural powers.[120] While scholars have discussed itinerant peddlers of cures, travelling mendicants, compounders, faith healers, exorcists, and herbalists, they have missed the continuous invocation of folk and popular medicine in urban middle-class households where traditional knowledge of herbs, home remedies, and self-medication continued to be the first line of defence against disease, with women their chief dispensers. Here therefore I bring another layer between the hegemony of biomedicine and "legitimate" structures of ayurveda on the one hand, and subaltern therapeutics on the other, by focusing on popular medical printed recipes.

I concentrate on printed home-medicinal remedies for and by educated middle-class women who were often the chief household healers. Susan Brandt argues that "for elite women, healthcare practices satisfied their intellectual curiosity, enacted their religious devotion, and enhanced their social capital."[121] She shows that authors of household cures "encouraged female readers to imagine themselves as refined arbiters of healing acumen, natural philosophical

---

Hussain and Saha, *India's Indigenous*. Here too, however, the contribution of in-house remedies and written recipes in the vernacular has been marginalised.

[117] Hardiman and Mukharji, *Medical Marginality*.
[118] White, *The Alchemical Body*, 198, 505.
[119] Gupta, *The Gender of Caste*, 216–17.
[120] Ibid., 43–51.
[121] Brandt, *Women Healers*, 5.

expertise, and humanitarian benevolence."[122] Elaine Leong conceives the household as a key dynamic site of medical knowledge production, as a collective of everyday medical knowledge producers.[123] Preparing herbal remedies and medicines in-house, caring for the sick, and helping with childbirth were activities known to and practised by many Indian women, traditional medicine and medical care being a domestic skill, a craft considered humble enough to be largely dominated by females. One book on ayurveda proclaimed that women were extremely capable of curing everyday illnesses;[124] another asserted that if you wanted your women to be smart housewives, you had better ensure some knowledge in them of ayurveda and everyday home remedies.[125] A considerable number of the printed household recipes were becoming quasi conduct manuals too, showing what was normative and ideal to the educated middle-class Indian housewife.[126]

In fact, in this period there was a whole genre of women's popular medical writing. Jyotirmayi Thakur, a prolific writer of domestic manuals, wrote various books in Hindi that covered recipes relating to household management, medicine, and beauty in the 1930s and 1940s.[127] She began her book, *Gharelu Vigyan*, by lamenting the general ignorance of simple and practical things; her book would remedy this situation and come in handy over times of difficulty, specially when it came to curing various diseases.[128] The book contained home cures for eczema, herpes, eye pain, earache, dental diseases, headaches, malaria, diarrhoea, sores, dog bites, and fevers; cures for these maladies were supplemented with a wide range of beauty recipes.[129]

In 1929, paying tribute to the medical knowledge and wisdom of his grandmother, Kirankumar Mukhopadhyay described a visit

[122] Ibid., 37.
[123] Leong, *Recipes and Everyday*, 9.
[124] Vaidya, *Chikitsa Chandrodaya*, 16.
[125] Vaidya, *Arogyavidhan*, last page.
[126] Editor, "Daktari Dawaein", 64.
[127] Thakur, *Gharelu Vigyan*; idem, *Stri aur Saundarya*; idem, *Aahaar aur Aarogyata*.
[128] Thakur, *Gharelu Vigyan*, 1–3.
[129] Ibid., 79.

to her place when introducing his book entitled *Dadi ke Nuskhe arthat Ghar ka Doctor*:

> When I got up in the morning, I was amazed to see a huge crowd at the door. My grandmother was sitting on a small cot, calling each one to her and prescribing a medicine. These medicines were like sips of nectar (*amrit ke ghoont*). I have seen many leading doctors, vaids and hakims, who consider themselves an authority and claim to offer medicines like none other, which also wastes a lot of money (*dhan ka vyay*). However, in grandma's medicinal recipes there were none that were not available in every household all the time. Even if it proved necessary to buy an ingredient, it was not worth more than a penny and a half. After everyone left, I expressed the idea to my grandmother that she should collect her recipes and have them printed. She was delighted to hear this and got me to write them with great pleasure, but she did not get to see her prescriptions in print. She is no more, but her recipes still work. The only difference is that earlier she herself would tell people these recipes, whereas now she can only be present before all in the form of a book. Earlier, only people around her derived benefit; now these recipes will be used all over India.[130]

Yashoda, all the same, was the star in this field. She constituted a kitchen pharmacy that became a medical-cultural node for quotidian knowledge on home remedies. Claiming to revive forgotten oral recipes and moulding them to present needs – thus weaving the shastric with the vaigyanik – she developed into a masterly teacher and communicator. She wrote several such books and almost all of them included a section on her nuskhe, with detailed instructions on how to prepare them. Some of these works were voluminous – e.g. *Garbh Raksha Vidhan, Nari Svasthya Raksha, Vaidik Ratn Sangrah,* and *Dampati Arogyata* – and comprised popular ayurvedic recipes.[131] Others were pamphlets – e.g. *Ghar ka Vaid, Pradar Rog Chikitsa* and *Ritu Dosh*.[132] Various journals that she edited, such as *Stri Dharma Shikshak* and *Stri Chikitsak*, also regularly carried her recipes.

[130] Mukhopadhyay, *Dadi ke Nuskhe*, Introduction.
[131] Yashoda, *Garbh Raksha*; idem, *Nari Svasthya*; idem, *Vaidik Ratn*; idem, *Dampati Arogyata*.
[132] Yashoda, *Ghar ka Vaid*; idem, *Pradar Rog*; idem, *Ritu Dosh*.

Her *Dampati Arogyata* had an astounding list of contents which ran into 24 pages and covered 623 topics.[133] Its second part contained household recipes of aushadhis for "curing masturbation", nocturnal emissions, gonorrhoea, and other everyday illnesses.[134] It also listed the benefits of all kinds of milk, particularly cow's milk, and advice on how best to use it.[135] The book, as also others by her, were seen as gems of ayurvedic knowledge (*vaidratnas*), relying both on ancient vaidik knowledge and *vaigyanik vidhi* (the scientific method). Puerperal fever, colic, appendicitis, and fistula were shown as curable by decoctions; there were herbal cures for ear and nose infections, cough, wounds, burns, and sprains; body care and beauty products like hair shampoos, oils for luxurious hair, face creams, skin ointments, and soaps – all were shown; and there were remedies for menstrual pains, enhanced fertility, and infertility.[136] Her recipe for Sudarshan churna – a famous ayurvedic medicine for

Fig. 4.7: The cover of one of Yashoda Devi's books.

[133] Yashoda, *Dampati Arogyata*.
[134] Ibid., 57–142, 329–57.
[135] Ibid., 609–27.
[136] Yashoda, *Vaidik Ratn*; idem, *Dampati Arogyata*; idem, *Nari Dharmashastra*, last page.

curing all types of fever – was much advocated. Asking all householders to methodically prepare this powder and keep it in their homes, the recipe listed its benefits, preparation process, properties, and consumption method.[137] Over the course of her recipe for Sitopaladi churna, she said that vaids often kept their recipes secret, or used another name for it to earn profits.[138] By contrast, she was disclosing precisely how to make the same thing at home.

Food for Freedom: Political Economy of Home Remedies

Yashoda stated that ayurvedic shastra was like a huge ocean of nectar to keep the body healthy and that it suited Indian conditions. Herbal medicines rooted in the Indian soil and produced within the climate of the country were best as they cured the disease from its very root. Imported medicines were not suited to the Indian temperament.[139] She was simultaneously subversive of the syndicated and institutionalised ayurveda of Sanskritised Brahmin male vaids who were attempting to purge ayurveda from its folk and popular healing influences. Hers was thus a critique of Western women doctors on the one hand, and well-established males on the other: both, she said, had completely failed to understand and treat the diseases of native women.[140] There were others too who were advocating the use of cheap and popular indigenous medicines. An article in *Chand* entitled "Daktari Dawaein" (Doctor's Medicines) argued:

> If you look carefully, we eat a lot of medicines in the form of spices every day. Using them appropriately is the only way to avoid disease. Allopathic medicines are just gimmicks (*dhakosle*) and a major way of generating money by extracting ours. Once these allopathic drugs have entered your home, it is not only difficult but impossible to get them out. It has been observed that people are often ruined by falling into

---

[137] Yashoda, *Dampati Arogyata*, 329–30.
[138] Ibid., 335.
[139] Ibid., 4; Yashoda, *Nari Sharir*, 2.
[140] Yashoda, *Dampati Arogyata*; idem, *Nari Sharir*, 5–20.

the trap of Western medicines, but even then their body is not disease-free . . . We can assure you that there is nothing of substance in these allopathic drugs. It would not be inappropriate for such medicines to be called the "gimmicks of the rich" (*ameeron ke chonchle*).[141]

A Dr Baker was quoted as saying that more people died of allopathic medicine for fever than from the fever itself.[142] In the preface to *Gharelu Chikitsa* its publisher stated: "We present this collection of medicines that can be assembled at very low cost (*alp mulya*) . . . Several diseases of the body are not cured by expensive medicines (*mulyavaan dawaein*), but get cured immediately by medicines that are inexpensive (*dhele mulya ki dawaein*) . . . We hope that whether [you are] poor or rich, this collection will prove useful and beneficial to all.[143] Mukhopadhyay's *Dadi ke Nuskhe* similarly stated that such in-house medical recipes involved no expenditure.[144] Yashoda too said her nuskhe relied on local and easily available ingredients. She also garnered brownie points by making it known that she distributed her aushadhis free to poor women. In short, Yashoda projected her recipe knowledge as a celebration of indigeneity and tradition. It was non-invasive, cost effective, competent, and came as a blessing to every household economy.

But perhaps most providential of all, she construed the middle-class housewife as the decision maker, producer, disseminator and authority on medicinal remedies within the household. Sharing recipes between women across familial circuits signalled self-reliance, women-centred plural networks, and domestic female alliances that fostered bonds of sisterhood. As Yashoda said about her magazine: "With my *Stri Chikitsak*, women can understand their bodies and diseases, can prepare, and consume their own medicines with their own hands at home, learn the art of medicine by sitting in their own home and cure themselves, their family members and other women friends and sisters."[145]

[141] Editor, "Daktari Dawaein", 62–3.
[142] Ibid., 64.
[143] *Gharelu Chikitsa,* Preface, 1–2.
[144] Mukhopadhyay, *Dadi ke Nuskhe,* Introduction.
[145] Yashoda, *Nari Dharmashastra,* advertisement on 1st page.

Figs 4.8-i and 4.8-ii: Women sharing medical knowledge and preparing remedies.

It cannot be forgotten that Yashoda was in the end a commercial entrepreneur investing in a business within a context of enslavement and empire. To market her work she regularly stated that her sisters would have no need for books or reading literature on female healthcare other than those by her.[146] Retailing her recipes also entailed deploying letters of praise by women from far-flung places – Champaran, Munger, Banaras, Fatehgarh, Sitapur, Patna, Agra, Banda, Fiji, and Africa. Vouching for the magical effects (*jadu sa asar*) of her priceless (*amulya*) potions, letters were quoted from the royal women of Gopalpur estate, women from the Rehua estate in Bahraich, and the wife of a subedar major from East Africa.[147] As if this was not enough, Yashoda went on to publish a book with 10,000 such letters.[148] Amidst the emerging culture of medical consumerism, and through shrewd marketing, Yashoda was an

[146] Yashoda, *Stri Dharma*, 2.
[147] Yashoda, *Dampati Arogyata*, 686–713.
[148] Ibid., last page.

active participant in the surrounding vernacular capitalism and had a vibrant presence in the healthcare marketplace.

Yashoda's roaring practice in the 1920s–40s earned her a few thousand rupees each day.[149] She also acquired substantial wealth from selling her recipes, buying a huge bungalow on Lowther Road, Allahabad, and naming it Yashoda Bhawan. The compound here was large and allowed her enough space to grow various herbs. The medicines from these were prepared at home with the help of a retinue of helpers, servants, and midwives.[150] During the annual Magh Mela at Allahabad, she put up her stall of aushadhis and books for a whole month, during which time brisk sales were reported.[151]

Women's role in the kitchen has been much noted, but their significance in marketing their own products has not. Yashoda personified women as economic medical actors, offering consumers

Fig. 4.9: Yashoda Devi's house in Allahabad, 1930 (named after her).

[149] Interview with Rachna Sharma.

[150] Yashoda's descendants, great-grandson Samir Sharma, his wife, mother, and son continue to live in the same house. When I visited Yashoda's home in March 2023, the family proudly told me that they have continued to substantially retain its old structure.

[151] Interview with Sudha Sharma.

myriad choices. These women were shaping consumer practices and tastes while playing a new entrepreneurial role in the economy; this went beyond household production and became part of a flourishing urban food and medical commerce. We thus see, for example, advertisements of women cooking and preparing home medicines, and selling and trading in churnas and remedies. This activity of manufacturing and marketing indicated an unregulated and gendered market of medical knowledge outside the domain of formally acknowledged male physicians.

This chapter has tried to show that vernacular culinary-medical household printed recipes offer a perspective on the ways in which traditional knowledge and practices were given a modern tilt. It shows how they were adapted and transformed over time in response to and as the consequence of a flourishing print industry and changing socio-political contexts. A wealth of recipes combined the science of taste, nutrition, health, and medicine conceived as beneficial to the bodies of women and men. This Hindi print sphere of recipes assembled a counter-vernacular archive of cooking and cure, inspiration and incipient resistance. Recipes, we have seen, can collectively constitute a nation's culinary epic inasmuch as they glorify ancient food cultures and contribute to the imagination of a Hindu nation. This domain shows us a fusion of Hindu biological bodies with an assertively Hindu social, a world which stratified and mapped caste hierarchies, class status, and religious identities through food.

An intricate relationship has also been shown between food, illness, health, and remedies, whereby vernacular recipes were perceived as an answer to the various corruptions that were seen to have come with colonialism and westernisation, and modern urban lifestyles. While there was the indubitably destructive impact of the British on the economies of India, vernacular household recipes signified a pragmatic and robust heterogeneity in matters of food and medicine that were impervious to, and even subversive of, both Western biomedicine and syndicated ayurveda. Even while often strengthening the cosmology of domesticity and patriarchal inequality, recipes were also an arena in which Hindu middle-class women could claim a degree of creativity, credibility, superiority, autonomy, and even economic agency. And within this domain of womanly resistance Yashoda's spectacular public popularity and commercial success show us how gender dynamics shaped vernacular knowledge-making practices that could wriggle out of the grasp of colonialism.

III

SWAMI SATYADEV PARIVRAJAK
(1879–1961)

5

Fantasy, Fitness, Fascism
Masculine Vernacular Histories of Travel

Many a reader may wish to know what the specific reasons were for my visit to America? . . . There were three main reasons for this trip: (1) While living in America, I discovered that people there knew very little about the social, religious, and political life of India, and what little they did was gathered from the reports of clergymen and malicious writers against India. So, my first objective in this trip was to make the people of America aware of the current state of India. (2) There is a great difference between studying from books and practical experience. If a man wants to know the living conditions of people and their civilisation, it is necessary for him to meet all kinds of people and scrutinise everything in the country by walking across it. Therefore, my second objective was to know the true condition of America's social, political, and scientific progress. (3) I wish to serve the Hindi language. There is a need to increase its knowledge and scope. Therefore, my third objective was to collect material for the service of Hindi literature.[1]

The climate of Europe is robust and powerful . . . Man is the master of his destiny and he can make the impossible possible with his masculine self . . . A beautiful soul can only live in a beautiful body, and therefore the true citizen is only he whose body is fine and beautiful . . . In this book, we will describe those things of Europe, narrate those events,

[1] Satyadev, *Amrica Bhraman*, 3–4.

describe those scenes . . . whose sweet memories, with all their beauty, will provide immense pleasure, enlightenment, and happiness to the hearts of travel lovers, and will haunt them forever.[2]

THIS CHAPTER centres on the journeys and vernacular travel literature written in Hindi by Swami Satyadev Parivrajak (hereafter Satyadev).

It primarily highlights his voyages to and literary works about America and Europe. Satyadev travelled for almost forty years, beginning in 1905 with just Rs 15 in his pocket, and covered several thousand miles on foot. He was one of the first to systematically write travelogues in Hindi in the early twentieth century, inscribing more than 500,000 words on his travels. His name is largely lost within the academic historiography of English and the public archives despite continuing to be of some importance in Hindi literary circles. Yet his contribution in shaping the vernacular intellectual and literary history of the modern Hindu political imaginary, and in popularising Hindi travel writing, should not be ignored or forgotten. Through his travels he evolved a meta concept of the world which went beyond the narrow frames of territorial borders and national boundaries. From his perspective the nation took shape along the lines of the body of an exemplary Hindu masculine self. His imagination of the nation came to be written up as travel writings which, amidst competing imaginaries, exercised considerable influence in early-twentieth-century India. In fact, given the immense

Fig. 5.1: Satyadev in 1907.

[2] Satyadev, *Europe ki*, 3–5.

financial success and popularity he achieved through his writing, Satyadev has sometimes been thought of as the first star writer of the modern Hindi sphere of popular literature.[3]

Travel writing, a literary mode, has attracted scholars of literature and culture more than historians. The former have, for example, shown how the colonised world was geographically produced by the West.[4] Correspondingly, substantial work has emerged on travel accounts that saw the West through the eyes of Indians, and this focus has tried to define the analytical tools of travel writing from India.[5] In sum, the picture we have is of travel as a visible part of everyday life since ancient times.[6] Detailed accounts of Indo-Persian travels were produced in Mughal India.[7] Systematically, the travelogue as a genre was closely linked to colonial exposure and literary modernity.[8] It is clear that Bengalis, in particular, produced a rich corpus of travel writing and there is no doubt that the greatest Bengali writer, Rabindranath

Fig. 5.2: Satyadev in 1911.

---

[3] Dhingra, "Rajnaitik Sanyasi", 6.

[4] Pratt, *Imperial Eyes*; Winichakul, *Siam Mapped*; Dupee, *British Travel Writers*.

[5] Majchrowicz, *The World*; Bhattacharji, *Travel Writing*; Sen, *Travels to Europe*; Mohanty, *Travel Writing*; Mukhopadhyay, "Writing Home".

[6] Satchidanandan, "Travel Writing", 2.

[7] Alam and Subrahmanyam, *Indo-Persian Travels*; Fisher, *Counterflows to Colonialism*.

[8] Ray, "The Aesthetic", 122–9.

Tagore, was also the most widely travelled.[9] We have clear evidence that gender perspectives greatly enriched travel writing.[10] It has also been suggested that the bulk of these travel accounts are centred in discussions of nature and selfhood.[11] In a different vein, insightful studies on Indian masculinity have revealed colonial constructions of the body to show a dichotomy between the manly British and the effeminate colonial subject.[12] With the upsurge of right-wing Hindu political assertiveness, the connections between Hindutva, violence, and masculinity have become more and more obvious.[13]

While the underlying links have long been clear between movement and masculinity – given that travel has often been associated with male bravado[14] – in this chapter, by focusing on the writings of Satyadev, I try to show certain critical connections which have frequently been overlooked between travel and masculinity. Satyadev's vernacular travel chronicles encompassed a potpourri of purposes: to showcase exotic landscapes, beauty, and people; to provide a mirror to Hindu middle-class fantasies; to celebrate the West as a space of the fulfilment of desires; to fashion "perfectly fit" male bodies; to advertise a violent and muscular nationalism by extolling Nazism and Hitler; to craft and publicise a new Hindu self; to challenge colonialism; to promote Hindi as a language of unity; and to be commercially viable. I argue that within the frame of a colonised nation this combination of fantasy, fitness, fascism, and finance were attempts by Satyadev to reclaim a space of vernacular freedom, an indigenous notion of emancipation. This was a concept he crafted by upholding the value of "perfect masculine bodies" that embodied his

---

[9] Sen, *Travels to Europe*; Mukhopadhyay, "Writing Home".

[10] Smith, *Moving Lives*; Mills, *Discourses of Difference*; Ghose, *Memsahibs Abroad*; Lambert-Hurley, Majchrowicz, and Sharma, *Three Centuries of Travel*; Majchrowicz, *The World*, 157–87.

[11] Mohanty, *Travel Writing*, xiv.

[12] Nandy, *The Intimate Enemy*, 1–63; Sinha, *Colonial Masculinity*; Chakraborty, *Masculinity, Asceticism*.

[13] Banerjee, *Make Me a Man*; Alter, *The Wrestler's Body*; Chaturvedi, *Hindutva and Violence*.

[14] For a critique, Mills, *Discourses of Difference*, 111–13.

ideals of beauty and pleasure. In a context of serfdom and subjecthood, Satyadev's travel idioms and itineraries created a spectacle which sought to boost the morale of the cosmopolitan Hindu middle classes.

Even though he travelled extensively in the West, Satyadev wrote only in Hindi, communicating to the Hindi-Hindu reading public his idea of the biological – rather than the geological – bodies of nations. He idealised the West by showing up certain of its attributes – such as discipline, hard work, valour, beauty, self-reliance, and masculinity – interweaving this admiration with an aggressive Hindu nationalism. His travel writing was a performative political act that inscribed gendered landscapes of freedom. Underlying these pictures were his deeply personal perceptions of emasculation and effeminacy which helped him contextualise, apprehend, and offer up his view of the interface between East and West. For Satyadev the Hindu male's subalternised masculinity, and the larger degradation of India by the West, had to be overcome through a formula or compound that we might well see as an analogue of Yashoda Devi's recipes. Unlike her domestic remedies centred around women, Satyadev's remedial recipe comprised ingredients connected with the outdoors and an environment centred around men: the assertion of a masculinist ethos which supposedly characterised India's glorious Hindu past; an aping of the physical and work culture of male students in the West; an ideal of education as a process of showing the path towards "perfect bodies"; and, finally, this argument for physical perfection taking a logical step forward via admiration of Germany and Hitler as museums of masculinity. All of these were mingled into a new concoction which took shape as his travel writings.

A colourful and maverick figure, Satyadev wore many hats. A prolific Hindi writer, he was a political sanyasi, a Hindu nationalist, a philosopher, a fiction writer, an Arya Samajist, a virulent supporter of Hindu sangathan, a Hindi *pracharak* (propagandist) and *updeshak* (preacher), and above all a ghummakkad, *yayavar* (vagabond) travel writer. Among the Hindi writers who contributed to the genre of *yatra vritant*s (travelogues), pride of place has long been given to Rahul Sankrityayan – his eloquent work, *Ghummakkad Shastra*

(1948), having acquired cult status.[15] Sankrityayan believed in ghummakkad dharma, i.e. the virtue of wandering, as the greatest religion, and what he saw as basic qualifications for a ghummakkad were a basic education, the absence of romantic attachments, and a knowledge of languages.[16] Satyadev fitted this prescription to a tee – albeit retrospectively. Much before Sankrityayan (and the major Hindi poet "Agyeya"), he declared that movement and journeying was going to be the leitmotif of his life. Thus, very early on he took the surname "Parivrajak", which means a wandering sanyasi who constantly travels.

Satyadev wrote in various genres, including fiction, philosophy, grammar, and autobiography, but his forté was the travelogue. In one way or another, most of his other works were also the product of his travels. The influence of Satyadev's travel writing should not be underestimated: Harivansh Rai Bachchan, while affirming his roots in India, wrote in his autobiography that in his childhood he had dreamt of travelling to the places described in Swami Satyadev's *Travels in America*.[17] When Jayaprakash Narayan decided to go to America in 1922 he noted: "I had learnt from Swami Satyadev Parivrajak that one could learn while earning in America."[18] Jayaprakash Narayan also mentions the impact upon him of Satyadev's speeches, delivered in Patna, during which he narrated stories of his stay in America.[19]

Rambriksh Benipuri (1899–1968), a famous Hindi writer, said Satyadev's books on America were extremely popular among the youth of his day.[20] And yet there has been little scholarly work on Satyadev.[21] One exception is a book by Dinanath Sharma – a Hindi-language literary thesis that delves, somewhat expectedly,

---

[15] Chudal, *A Freethinking*; Srivastava, "Ghummakkads".
[16] Chudal, *A Freethinking*, 1, 54–6.
[17] Bachchan, *In the Afternoon*, 358.
[18] Singh and Sundaram, *Gandhi and the World Order*, 4.
[19] Interview with Jayaprakash Narayan by Sharma, 15. I am grateful to Akshay Mukul for this reference.
[20] Sharma, *Benipuri Granthavali–4*, 212.
[21] There are a handful of writings on Satyadev: Sharma, *Swami Satyadev*; Imam, "Satya Dev"; *Sri Swami Satya Dev*.

into Satyadev's writing style. Eulogising Satyadev, Sharma places him next to Hindi stalwarts like Mahavir Prasad Dwivedi and Purushottam Das Tandon.[22] Lauding his travel literature in particular, he says:

> Parivrajak-ji was the leading tourist author of the modern era. While travelling continuously for nearly forty years of his life, he visited many places at home and abroad . . . In fact, Parivrajak-ji had a firm belief in the basic principle of *charaiveti*, *charaiveti* (walking forever) and he followed this mantra with complete faith his entire life. Journeys to inaccessible territories and vulnerable regions represent Parivrajak-ji's indomitable courage and self-power. It would not be inappropriate to say that it was his travels that made Parivrajak-ji a writer.[23]

Satyadev himself constantly celebrated travel literature: "Travel is a major teacher. If a person is conscious and becomes aware of his senses, travel really does work as a divine boon. If a human being has the power to observe and enlighten his intellect, then nature opens up doors of knowledge. I have received great inspiration from my travels."[24] And elsewhere: "Travelling can be likened to an addiction. Just as a drunkard gets agitated without alcohol, and an exuberant elephant becomes restless during its moments of playfulness, similarly a traveller is compelled by an irresistible urge when seeking the pleasures of wandering around. It can also be viewed as the cyclical nature of the changing of seasons."[25] Declaring the genre of travel writing more pleasurable than fiction, he says:

> Those who have read my books on travel are familiar with my style. Based on the direct knowledge that I get from my personal experiences, I draw my travel descriptions. I have never believed in what I have merely heard, for it is my firm belief that truthful events are much more interesting and fruitful than fiction . . . I hope that, through this book of mine, millions of men and women in India will get the benefit of seeing Europe and that they will find plenty of material to improve themselves and the future of the country.[26]

[22] Sharma, *Swami Satyadev*, 260–1.
[23] Ibid., 116.
[24] Satyadev, *Germany Mein Mere*, 14.
[25] Satyadev, "Paris Mein Do Raaten".
[26] Satyadev, *Meri German Yatra*, note on 1st page.

Satyadev's numerous international journeys included a prolonged sojourn in America and five visits to Germany. His stay overseas was often for extended periods. His rich corpus of travel writings were centred mostly on his encounters with the West. His books on America, for example, included *Amrica Path Pradarshak* (1911), and perhaps the most famous of his works, *Amrica Digdarshan* (1912).[27] A bestseller was *Amrica ke Nirdhan Vidyarthiyon ke Parishram* (1912) on impoverished yet hard-working American students.[28] On Europe, he wrote books like *Meri German Yatra* (1924) and *Europe ki Sukhad Smritiyan* (1937). A practical travel guide appeared as *Yatri Mitra* (1936), which offered useful travelling tips. Most of the others, listed in the present book's Bibliography, were on his travels to the West, but one of his very popular travelogues, namely *Meri Kailash Yatra* (1916), was on his pilgrimage to Mount Kailash on the Tibetan side of the Himalaya.[29] Sold in their thousands, all these books were often rewritten and went into several editions, sometimes with slightly changed titles. Satyadev also wrote numerous articles on his travels in leading magazines of the time, particularly *Saraswati* and *Maryada*.

Satyadev's family background and the early landmarks of his life

---

[27] This most popular book on his travels to America was translated into English by A. Rama Iyer. Iyer was a lecturer in English at the National College, Trichinopoly, and a great admirer of Satyadev who noted: "These books have been sold in their thousands, and have done not a little to create the new spirit of nationalism in the Hindi-speaking provinces of India. None who reads his works can fail to be deeply impressed with his sanity, his rare courage and independence of conviction, his wide outlook, the singular purity and nobility of his character, and his fervent devotion to his motherland": Satyadev, *My Experiences in America,* Translator's Note, ii.

[28] The book was translated into Marathi, Urdu, and Gujarati. For example, Gunaji, *Americantil Garib*. Satyadev later published a revised edition: Satyadev, *Amrica ke Svavalambi*. Its first page stated: "Nearly one lakh copies of this book are being published in different languages of India, benefiting the children of the country." Explaining the change of title, Satyadev said that it was meant to inculcate a spirit of self-sufficiency and self-support among Indian students: Preface, iii.

[29] See the Bibliography for a full list of Satyadev's titles, their translations, and publication dates.

Fig. 5.3: The jacket of one of Satyadev's many travelogues.

can be traced from the initial chapters of his autobiography, government files, and some writings on him.³⁰ Born in 1879 in Ludhiana, Punjab, in a Sikh Punjabi Thapar Khatri family of moderate means, with mixed religious roots and leanings, Satyadev's birth name was Sukh Dayal. His great-grandfather was a Sikh but his grandfather had adopted Shaivism.³¹ Kenneth Jones says that Punjabi Hindus of the Khatri caste had a "questionable and flexible status" in the traditional caste hierarchy, were usually literate and urban based, and often acted as "traditional innovators" and "leaders into new worlds".³² Satyadev's father, "a bitter and angry man", was Master Kundanlal, and his mother Narayani Devi "a firm and quiet" woman. Satyadev's early education was at the Dayanand Anglo-Vedic College, Lahore, and here he was deeply impressed with the Arya Samaj's philosophy, which exercised a lifelong influence on him.³³ Very early in life he resolved on celibacy and the life of a brahmachari. At the age of twenty he became a sanyasi and spent time with a Dadu Panthi saint, Swami Mahanand, at his

---

³⁰ *SKM*; "Satya Dev Sanyasi", F. 139/1914, Confidential, Patna Archives (hereafter F. 139); Imam, "Satya Dev".

³¹ *SKM*, 9–10; F. 139.

³² Jones, *Arya Dharm*, 5.

³³ *SKM*, 9–18; F. 139, 18.

mutth (monastery) in Khandala, and took the name "Satyadev Parivrajak", signifying a spiritual traveller seeking truth.[34] His first name, Satyadev – a combination of truth and God – having mirrored a perhaps static engagement with the spiritual, was expanded to proclaim him as a voyager.

After this Satyadev spent four years in Kashi improving his Sanskrit while critiquing Brahmanical orthodoxy and preaching the principles of Arya Samaj over times of leisure. To fulfil a deep yearning to travel to the West – buttressed by the spiritually inclined travellers Swami Ram Tirth, Dharmpal, and Lat Swami, all of whom had returned from America – Satyadev embarked on his first journey to the USA in January 1905, when he was twenty-six, returning from there in June 1911 via France and Italy.[35] When advertising his 1957 book *Amrica Pravas ki Meri Adbhut Kahani*, Satyadev made it clear on the cover that he had started off for America with just Rs 15 in his pocket.[36] In the USA he studied for a year at the University of Chicago, for another year at the University of Oregon, and then travelled to many cities and states, including Seattle, Washington, California, Arizona, New Mexico, Texas, Oklahoma, Kansas, Indiana, Ohio, Pennsylvania, Pittsburgh, and New York. Remarkably, he seems to have covered over 2300 miles mostly on foot.[37] His 1913 book *Amrica Bhraman* was written like a daily diary with dates and times, providing detailed descriptions of the places he visited or where he stayed.[38] He says in it: "My book *Amrica Bhraman* is written in the true Robinson Crusoe style."[39] Here he also calls himself a "tramp" who has walked 2300 miles.[40] While spending considerable travel time in India as well, Europe atttracted him six times, the first of his journeys there being en route home from America.[41]

[34] *SKM*, 68–94.
[35] Satyadev, *Amrica Pravas*, 1.
[36] Ibid., cover page.
[37] Satyadev, *Amrica Bhraman*, 5; Satyadev, "Amrica Bhraman", 216–18; F. 139, 18.
[38] Satyadev, *Amrica Bhraman*.
[39] Satyadev, *Meri German*, 1.
[40] Satyadev, *Amrica Bhraman*, cover.
[41] Satyadev, *Germany Mein*, Introduction.

Travel Writing: A Passion for Hindi

Colonial modernity saw new technologies, including those that resulted in the expansion of better travel facilities, such as the railways and maritime networks, which in turn meant new opportunities for safer, cheaper, and more efficient mobility. Over the same period a proliferation of vernacular mass print cultures and the establishment of prose as the dominant literary form paved the way for travel literature to burgeon and led to enlarged conceptions of geography and traversable space. By the early twentieth century travel writing was firmly established as a component of India's print-public sphere in a range of regional languages. Bringing distant lands to one's homes, it encompassed traditional sacred topography and pilgrimage sites as well as secularised territories and unvisited arenas. As Daniel Majchrowicz says, this kind of writing signalled a textual encounter with a vaster world. Many of these "locally produced but globally sourced travel accounts" allowed writers and readers "to imagine the world in words" and helped reshape global pasts, presents, and futures.[42]

The travel writing genre developed a little late in Hindi.[43] It was first introduced in local periodicals by Bharatendu Harischandra (1850–1885). By the early twentieth century it had developed into a distinct genre, with prominent magazines and publishers investing in it and many articles and books appearing within its subject area.[44] A diverse spectrum of travel writers appeared – women and men, rich and middle class, of different castes and regions – all catering to diverse audiences. Among them were established literary figures, but a significant portion consisted of lay authors of middling literary rank driven by a passion for travel and writing. Satyadev was one of the earliest of these, the tallest and the most prolific. He established a variety of travel literature within which autobiographical fragments were entwined. He made this a popular genre that was taken seriously and seen as a part of the intellectual history of Hindi.

[42] Majchrowicz, *The World*, 3–4.
[43] For an overview of travel writing in Hindi, Tiwari, *Hindi ka Yatra*.
[44] For example Mishra, *Videsh ki Baat*; Shukl, *London–Paris ki Sair*; Sankrityayan, *Meri Tibbet Yatra*.

Satyadev began his writerly career in 1907, and in *Saraswati*, the most prominent Hindi journal of the early twentieth century. The journal had built a strong reputation for itself and flowered under the direction and editorship of Mahavir Prasad Dwivedi.[45] Established in 1900, it enthusiastically espoused the cause of travel literature. Satyadev became its leading face for popularising travelogues written overseas, which subtly expanded intellectual horizons, literary sensibilities, and nationalist articulations.[46] In his writings for *Saraswati* as well as in his other early writings he wrote under the name Satyadev, appending "Parivrajak" to his name only later. Between 1906 and 1911 he published more than forty articles, travelogues, news updates, and short stories in *Saraswati*, the vast majority of these relating to his travels and experiences in America.[47] In the course of just one year, 1907–8, he produced sixteen articles for the journal, often supplementing them with photographs of himself and of places he had seen in America. These were conspicuous displays of his authorship in American locations.

After his first return to India in 1911 Satyadev began publishing his books and travelogues under the "Satya Granth Mala" series through a small publishing house that he set up, called Satyagyan Niketan.[48] By now a full-time writer, he said he published his own books and held their copyright because he was "completely disillusioned with other publishers, who had ruined his books by publishing cheap versions."[49] This early entrepreneurial instance of self-publishing in

[45] Mody, *The Making of Modern*.

[46] For details, Mody, "Literature, Language", 200–20. Satyadev also wrote many articles in *Maryada* and *Abhyudaya*.

[47] A sample of Satyadev's articles in *Saraswati*: "Bijli ki Railgadi"; "Chicago Mein Meri Pratham"; "Chicago Vishwavidyalaya"; "Chicago ka Ravivaar"; "Nayi Duniya ke Samachar"; "Nayi Duniya ki Khabren"; "New York Nagri"; "Geneva Jheel"; "Amrica ki Striyan"; "Amrica ke Kheton"; "Amrica Mein Vidyarthi". Many of his fictional stories also revolved around his travels: "Ashcharyajanak Ghanti"; "Kirti Kalima"; *Ashcharyajanak Ghanti*. Some were also adapted from other languages: "Mala", from "La Parure" (The Necklace, 1884) by the French writer Guy de Maupassant.

[48] F. 139, 22–4.

[49] For example Satyadev, *Meri German*, note on 1st page.

combination with shrewd self-marketing proved rewarding for Satyadev as he amassed a considerable fortune by selling his books in unexpectedly high volumes. Aggressively promoting them as well, he heaped praise on himself, often with accompanying photographs, and advertised the benefits of buying his books.[50] His 1936 book entitled *Yatri Mitra* was hugely profitable and went into at least five editions. It offered the reader innumerable tips on travel and was touted as indispensable for the intending traveller. On its cover it said: "If you desire to make your travel truly worthwhile, virtuous, and really enjoyable; if you want to conquer the hardships of travelling to America and Europe; if you really wish to make your journey continually blissful – then make this book of mine your constant companion. You will find no friend truer on your entire journey."[51] Many of his other travelogues also went into several impressions and editions and made Satyadev a very wealthy man.

Antoinette Burton sees travel writings in English by Indian travellers to London as a space in which the "drama of the colonial citizen-subject was played out for the benefit of rulers and ruled alike."[52] Satyadev's vernacular narratives partly fit this mould, selectively complementing and contesting Eurocentric modes of representation. He framed Western cities and life as fundamentally different from those experienced in India, and as spaces for individual and social advancement and freedom. In congruence with conventional tropes and prefashioned ideas of travel literature, his writings contained certain stereotypes – vivid descriptions of places, people, leisure, knowledge, migration, and sea journeys – whereby the experiences he inscribed were "recognisable and repeatable".[53] At the same time he embellished his travelogues with dogmatic popular beliefs, a distinctly vernacular flavour, local epistemic references, an indigenous narrative style, and very specific predispositions that came to be recognisably his own. For example, while describing Paris, he stated:

[50] For example Satyadev, *Amrica Digdarshan*, carried advertisements for almost all his books in its second edition.
[51] Satyadev, *Yatri Mitra*, cover page.
[52] Burton, *At the Heart of the Empire*.
[53] Keck, "Picturesque Burma", 413.

Paris is the mother of the present era of independence; it is the father of innovation in Western civilisation . . . Paris is the *kamadhenu* (divine mother cow) of France, it is undoubtedly its *kalpavriksha* (wish-fulfilling divine tree) . . . Paris is the centre of beautiful women, filled with places for sexual pleasure . . . Obsessed with lust, thousands of wealthy young men, whose faces are like roses and whose bodies are beautifully shaped, come here and lose all that is theirs. From this perspective Paris is a terrible city . . . If, while you are walking on its streets or in its gardens, a woman whom you do not know smiles at you at night, consider her a deadly vampire and keep away from her.[54]

Drawing from what could be called the "treasure trope" of Hinduism, he deployed the brahmachari, the yogi, and the sanyasi – all unburdened by temptations of the flesh – as the figures especially suited for travel in the West. Implicitly of course this was part of his repertoire of self-promotion. As one of his admirers remarked of Satyadev: "In America, he was offered a number of temptations, but he refused and he observed celibacy, led the life of a brahmachari and maintained very good health."[55]

Witnessing, reporting on, and bringing the West home to India, Satyadev had a very clear notion of his audience and knew precisely who his readers were. He wrote mostly in a deliberately ponderous and pedagogical mode, and only in Hindi. The bait with which he lured readers to his work was the constant reiteration that his accounts were explorations of an "authentic" Western life: this was a reversal of the lens of authenticity that usually informed the Orientalist gaze, and by which Indians were habituated to receiving constructions of the West. Satyadev's accounts were based on showing his own self as keenly present in landscapes mostly untrodden by Indians. His delineations of first-hand, lived, everyday personal experiences of his own, freed of depictions of such locations by other writers, were key to his success.[56] He put it in a nutshell when he said: "God has created this beautiful world, but how many of us care

[54] Satyadev, *Meri German*, 165–6, 170–1.
[55] Interview with Raghubir Sahai by Sharma, 9.
[56] Satyadev, *Europe ki*, II.

to enjoy it? Indeed, this world is his who has seen it with his own eyes, heard its uplifting message with his own ears, and felt its inspiration through his own feelings."[57]

Assertions of experiential authenticity in this mode enabled a concomitant air of authority when he offered various practical tips to potential travellers for their trips to America and Europe. There were also inventories in his books on almost all aspects of travel – including luggage, porters, modes of travel, routes, clothes, currency, hotels, food, expenses, health suggestions, and places to see:

> Those who go to Europe should take very little stuff with them. It is advisable to take only two leather suitcases and a small hand leather box . . . Two pairs of suits, one warm and one cotton, should be made ready . . . Yes, a khaki-coloured coat and half-pants must be carried – they are very useful on the ship . . . One should take along only as much luggage as one can pick up oneself – so that one does not become a slave to porters.[58]

A clear proof of Satyadev's sharp eye for the market was that he wrote popular Khari Boli Hindi which kept a distance from the elevated idiom of Sanskrit. Simple Hindi, he argued, was necessary:

> [The] essential habit of a writer must be the use of uncomplicated language. The author should write in a manner that the common people can readily comprehend. The writing style should be such that the reader grasps the meaning effortlessly, without requiring the assistance of scholarly annotations. It is evident that the more arduous the language, the less its accessibility to humans . . . What purpose does it serve to write in a manner that eludes comprehension? Articles are not written to showcase scholarly prowess. One who harbours the passion that their voice and message reach the poorest of the poor and all their fellow brethren will certainly employ plain language. Conversely, one who uses difficult language signals to others a disregard, declaring "I do not care about your plight or well-being; my compulsion is paramount."[59]

[57] Satyadev, *Yatri Mitra*, 1.
[58] Satyadev, *Europe ki*, 25–6.
[59] Satyadev, "Hindi Sahitya", 462.

He supplemented his conversational language with a humble self-image, harping on the fact that his extensive travels involved very little money and were mostly done on foot. Often, he said, he financed them by working with his hands, doing hard physical labour on farms. By selling the chimera that virtually anyone could travel to the mighty West, he fuelled a desire for the global within the "native subalterns" who were the readers of his vernacular. Many young Hindu men were inspired by his writings to take to the road. Clearly, he provided them with a semblance of freedom that colonialism had failed to deliver.

While travel books about Europe, particularly England, had been written by Indians, Satyadev was probably the first to bring America to the Hindi public on such a large scale. These early travel writings gave him his initial star status as one who had come back not from England – the evil coloniser – but from America, formerly a British colony now ascendant and perceived as a symbol of freedom and modernity. His later travel accounts also made Germany rather than England their focal point of admiration, positing the former as the main challenger and staunch enemy of the latter. Inherently political, his choice of countries was carefully thought through and played a critical role in providing novel forms of validation to his travel writings.

Satyadev's travel writings were not just popular, they were eagerly awaited.[60] They transported readers away from the oppressions of the colonial present and the dullness of everyday existence into a sublime world of excitement in a global landscape. When writing from America his travel articles in *Saraswati* garnered such a volume of fan mail that he needed to establish a P.O. Box address.[61] Indeed the responses to Satyadev's contributions were so enthusiastic that Dwivedi went so far as to print the author's address in the US, explicitly urging readers of the journal to correspond directly with Satyadev.[62] Being unencumbered by any sense of modesty, Satyadev

---

[60] Essays in *Sri Swami Satya Dev* testify to this. Particularly Vidyalankar, "Swami Satyadev", 1–5.

[61] Satyadev, "Nivedan", 240.

[62] Editor, "Vividh Vishay" (Various Subjects), *Saraswati*, May 1911, 247.

himself amplified his popularity by arguing that the success of *Saraswati* over 1905–11 was largely due to his travel writings: "When I wrote in *Saraswati*, it was on account of my articles that *Saraswati*'s fame grew so substantially and its subscriber numbers started increasing so rapidly . . . I was the first Hindi writer to write educational and entertaining articles from America, and my travel-related articles greatly attracted male and female readers of Hindi. Like Chatak, readers eagerly awaited issues of *Saraswati* and crowds gathered in libraries to read my articles."[63] There is undoubtedly an element of truth in the swagger of this assertion, for *Maryada* and *Abhyudaya*, rival publications to *Saraswati*, invited Satyadev to contribute, which he did. Dwivedi perceived this as a betrayal and expressed his disapproval through sarcastic letters publicly denouncing Satyadev;[64] consequently, his work ceased to be published in *Saraswati* from October 1911 and was only resumed much later.[65]

In relation to Satyadev's affluence, Tekchand Dhingra reports a conversation after Satyadev's return from the US:

> Swami Shraddhanand-ji asked Swami-ji [i.e. Satyadev] what he would now do. When learning of Swami-ji's intention to write books in Hindi, Shraddhanand-ji responded sardonically: "Who will buy your Hindi books? You will die of hunger." There exists no comparable instance through the length and breadth of India of a young man with a degree from abroad daring to achieve financial success by writing books in Hindi. Swami Satyadev-ji Parivrajak stands as the sole exemplar [of such an enterprise], having achieved the distinction of a successful Hindi writer – and he has never had to ask money from anyone.[66]

---

[63] *SKM*, 134. Chatak means the sparrow that constantly opens her beak in expectation of monsoon rain.

[64] Editor, "*Maryada* ke 'Satyadev'" (*Maryada*'s Satyadev), *Saraswati*, September 1911, 448–9; Editor, "*Abhyudaya* aur *Maryada* ki Mehatta" (Greatness of *Abhyudaya* and *Maryada*), *Saraswati*, October 1911, 508; also see Mody, *The Making of Modern*, 267.

[65] Satyadev again began actively writing in *Saraswati* in the late 1920s. For example, just between January and June 1934 the journal carried four pictures of him and five of his articles.

[66] Dhingra, "Rajnaitik Sanyasi", 8.

Those who later went to America acknowledged the galvanising impact on them of Satyadev's writings. Krishnalal Shridharani (1911–1960), a famous poet and journalist who went to the US for further studies in 1934, had this to say: "I had read Swami Satyadev's book about America as a land of opportunity, and through it had learned that one could make a decent living in the United States by selling souvenirs or running an elevator, and that still one could have enough time to pursue one's studies. The book had fired the imagination of many ambitious Indian students; it paved the streets of New York with gold."[67]

Satyadev's championing of Hindi was expressed as a passion: "Beautiful language uplifts the fallen, revives the dead, imbues the timid with courage, and allows the soul to savour the essence of yoga."[68] He backed this up by expressing admiration for a German who refused to speak English to an Englishman: "We only examine the character of people through food habits and purity-pollution taboos! These Germans drink wine and listen to my lectures, while simultaneously carrying such pride for their language and their native land!"[69] He later composed a poem applauding the love Germans had for their own language, equating it with his love of Hindi:

> The essence of patriotism hidden in one's language . . .
> Fill your lotus-like heart with love for your language,
> The love of patriotism will thus shine in the inner recesses of our heart.[70]

On his return to India in 1911 Satyadev toured the country attempting to mould minds by delivering *updesha*s (sermons) that contrasted the educational systems of America and India. In these he argued the critical importance for Hindi to be made the Indian lingua franca.[71] With the blessings of Gandhi he spent a considerable

---

[67] Shridharani, *My India, My America*, 73. I thank Arun Venugopal for this reference.
[68] Satyadev, "Hindi Sahitya", 462.
[69] Satyadev, *Europe ki*, 195.
[70] Ibid., 195.
[71] F. 139, 12–14, 22–6.

period of time in Madras in 1918–19 promoting Hindi.⁷² This preference is elsewhere justified as necessary for the truly patriotic traveller: "Any boy who wishes to go abroad to study should not get his passport until he has learnt his 'national' language Hindi."⁷³ Satyadev had a long association with the Nagari Pracharini Sabha and willed all his wealth, library, and property to the Sabha.⁷⁴

Admiring the West: Beauty, Pleasure, and Physicality

> Readers, relish and taste the experiences of Europe,
> The melodious panoramic view that you will forever remember.
> You will always treasure Vienna, London, Berlin,
> The joys of cathedrals and gardens, and memories of majestic Zurich.
> People full of brawn and bravery, but materialist and greedy,
> I saw Paris and Prague, says "Dev" – Europe is stunning.⁷⁵

Europe ki Sukhad Smritiyan (1937), 340 pages long, begins with poetry which Satyadev composed under his *nom de plume*, "Dev", often deploying the medium to express an ineffable sense of awe and the achievement of immense aesthetic heights.⁷⁶ His discursive strategy was to capture the spectacle of daily life in the West by conveying the elements of wonder, discovery, and the exotic, and by liberal sprinklings of invention, parody, drama, poems, and stories. His articles and books on America carried colourful descriptions of his first night in Chicago, a fun-filled Sunday in the city, electric trains, the experience of working in fields, student life, cruising on Lake Geneva, interaction with a shopkeeper in Seattle, a visit to a kindergarten school, and the lives of American women. These were regularly supplemented with visual material.⁷⁷ Satyadev thus

⁷² Gandhi, *The Collected Works*, 17, 257, 277; Satyadev, *The Hindi Propaganda*. Also his *The First Hindi Reader* and *Hindi ka Sandesh*; Sharma, "Madras Mein Hindi-Prachaar".
⁷³ Satyadev, *Germany Mein*, 26.
⁷⁴ Lal and Tripathi, *Hirak Jayanti Granth*, 54.
⁷⁵ Satyadev, *Europe ki*, first page.
⁷⁶ Satyadev, *Europe ki*, 29; Satyadev, *Germany Mein*, 22–3.
⁷⁷ Satyadev, *Amrica Digdarshan*, 1–116, 132–57; idem, *Amrica Pravas*, 456–88.

directed attention to the everyday and commonplace aspects of American and European lives. Here is his account of Chicago:

> I saw the people . . . All were very clean and tidy, wearing new suits, their hair shining . . . All looked extremely happy and engaged in their work like honey-bee keepers. All were agile . . . Chicago has many places to celebrate and enjoy Sundays . . . Look at people's faces – "freedom" shines on their foreheads . . . Here is a museum, free for everyone on Sunday . . . Around Lake Michigan are many benches . . . The lake is smiling, you see expressions of love all around . . . There are many parks where pianos and other items for recreation are kept . . . In contrast, people in India spend their leisure time drinking cannabis, playing cards, flying kites, and indulging in futile chatter.[78]

The beauty of waterfalls, lakes, mountains, monuments, and buildings was exaggerated through images and tropes of this variety, and "authentic" descriptions. His article on Washington focuses on the Smithsonian Institution, the White House, and the Statue of Freedom on the Capitol dome; he provides their histories, describes their architecture, and offers information about their interiors. This is what he says on one part of the White House, and then about the Statue of Freedom:

> The decor of this hall is unique. See the golden work on these tables. The mirrors hanging on the front walls cost a lot. The beauty of the curtains from the windows is unique. The golden work on the ceiling is also commendable . . .
> The Statue of Freedom is real! All the achievements [of the US] are courtesy this goddess. She is the goddess of salvation (*moksha dayini Bhagwati*). The goddess has a sword in her right hand and a garland of flowers in her left hand. Upon seeing her, the pure and lofty feelings that arise in one's heart are indescribable.[79]

Topographic and ethnographic knowledge, romanticised descriptions of nature and places, historical sites, and geographical landscapes come interlaced with anecdotes about the customs, manners, and beliefs of people in the West. The incorporation of

[78] Satyadev, *Amrica Digdarshan*, 2–17.
[79] Satyadev, "United States of America ki Prasidh", 62.

visual elements in his writings and publications approximated the picture book format, converting everyday spaces into captivating landscapes and taking the reader on spectacular tours.[80]

Regardless of location, Satyadev's travel accounts contained vivid descriptions of unreachable places, and his tortuous negotiation of difficult journeys. His very popular account of travels through sacred Hindu-Himalayan geography, *Meri Kailash Yatra*, is particularly pertinent because of its great fame and popularity.[81] Applauding the book, Vidyalankar says:

> *Meri Kailash Yatra* . . . is a spunky and enlightening tale, and can be regarded as the first seminal text of travel in Hindi . . . Satyadev's journey to Kailash is the story of an unfettered man's exploration of an unknown path, gathered together by his conscious eyes and ears and understood by his sober mind . . . The picture given by Satyadev-ji is very interesting and eye-opening, as he describes the age-old relationship between India and the Kailash region . . . and the wonderfully spirited life of the Bhotias, residents of the northern end of Kumaon Garhwal.[82]

Avishek Ray argues that most travelogues by Indians of the late nineteenth and early twentieth centuries articulate an "elitist-exclusionary mindset that strived to showcase cultural proximity with the coloniser on the one hand, while distantiating the colonially un(der) exposed 'natives' on the other hand."[83] While claiming a genealogical closeness with the powerful West, Satyadev was attracted by much else in European society and provided a list:

(1) Open social life of Europe . . .
(2) Witnessing the Goddess of Freedom in reality . . .
(3) Wide spread of political education . . .
(4) Worship of personal freedom . . .
(5) A new criterion of truthfulness . . .
(6) Unity in clothes and food . . .

[80] For connections between visuals and travelogues, Osborne, *Travelling Light*.
[81] Satyadev, *Meri Kailash Yatra*.
[82] Vidyalankar, "Swami Satyadev", 3–4.
[83] Ray, "Aesthetic Gaze", 122.

(7) Cleanliness . . .
(8) Religious tolerance . . .
(9) Deep commitment and engagement with work.[84]

Clearly, he revelled in the social life of America and Europe, and felt very much at home there; in fact, given the choice, he says he would opt to be a part of European society.[85] "In European cities, coffee houses, hotels, and clubs are places where people from all walks of life eat, sit, drink and discuss all sorts of topics. Ordinary labourers easily intermingle with the biggest scholars and derive advantage from their scholarship . . . things you can never learn by reading fifty books you get to know very well through excursions."[86] What attracted him particularly was the West's culture of courage, strength, and hard physical labour: "Physical development is particularly emphasised in American universities. Each university has many special buildings for exercises, where special trainers are also present. Students exercise with great passion. Their arms and legs are strong, their bodies very tight and fit. Football and baseball are their main sports . . ."[87] An article on "Miss Parker's School" in America describes how children are taught patriotism and physical culture even in their kindergarten schools, which also requires them to learn and recite poems inspired by a martial spirit.[88] He celebrates the wide availability of gymnasiums for physical culture exclusively for girls and women – ". . . where there is such good arrangement for the health and physical improvement of girls, the country must be at the pinnacle of progress."[89] All this makes him advocate the strong case for Indian students to pursue higher education in the West; he is caustically critical of Hindu social taboos against crossing the seas.[90]

---

[84] Satyadev, *Meri German*, 176–84.
[85] Ibid., 187.
[86] Ibid., 174–5.
[87] Satyadev, *Amrica Pravas*, 86.
[88] Satyadev, "Miss Parker", 153–5.
[89] Satyadev, "Amrica ki Striyan".
[90] Satyadev, "Amrica ke Kheton par", 218–23.

A whole book written by him on the students of America went into several editions and translations.[91] This was a collection of stories of his experiences with poor, industrious, hard-working, and self-reliant American students whom he contrasts with students back home, urging the latter to learn from the former. In its introduction he is emphatic: "At this time, it is critical for our youth to understand the importance of the dignity of labour so that they can inculcate in themselves the positive values of industriousness, hard work and business."[92] The first story in the collection, "Samachar Patra Bechne Vala Chhah Varsh ka Balak" (A Six-Year-Old Boy Selling Newspapers), focuses on a boy who is proud of earning his own living and paying for his education. The moral of this tale is self-reliance;[93] Satyadev contrasts this with students at Kashi who beg to learn but, not having been taught the value of self-reliance, resemble the whole society of India in not being able to stand on their own feet. In his preface to the 1957 edition, Satyadev notes: "After reading this book, hundreds of Indian students went to America to study and my purpose of the book was fulfilled".[94] He also put out adverts in leading newspapers of the time encouraging strong men to go to America – and even to entire summer schools that revolved around his American experiences!

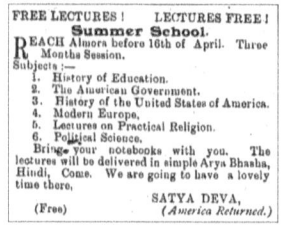

Figs 5.4-i and 5.4-ii: Two sample advertisements put out by Satyadev.

[91] Satyadev, *Amrica ke Nirdhan*; Satyadev, *Amrica ke Svavalambi*.
[92] Satyadev, *Amrica ke Nirdhan*, Introduction, 6.
[93] Satyadev, *Amrica ke Svavalambi*, 1–8.
[94] Ibid., Preface, iii.

The physically fit body was a key component within Satyadev's worldview, and he had much praise for this virtue in the American race: "It is an invariable principle of nature that only the fittest and the most capable have survived in the world. If you wish to exist, then become equal to your neighbours. Only that race can keep its name stable in the world, which follows this rule."[95] In fact, his understanding of cleanliness, beauty, and health is closely entwined with his idealisation of physical fitness, with "natural" being conflated with the beautiful and the moral.

A Dialogue Between East and West, Slavery and Freedom

As a sympathetic narrator of the West, Satyadev reveals a marked degree of cosmopolitanism and shows himself as an internationalist with an open and flexible mind. For such a man and intrepid traveller it was therefore particularly galling to find bureaucratic hurdles being constantly put in his path – his ordeals relate mostly to his passport and occupy many pages of his travel writing.[96] "In 1922, the Bombay passport department issued me a passport only for England . . . Unaware of the rule, I went to Germany, Austria, Sweden, France and Italy . . . Because of going to Germany, I was declared an offender and my passport was seized."[97]

Even the newspapers weighed in on the "strange case" of a refusal of passport to Satyadev.[98] In July 1924, and again in June 1926, he applied for a passport, giving ophthalmic treatment as his reason for travel, but it was curtly refused with this sentence: "There seems to be

[95] Satyadev, "Chicago ka Ravivaar", 240.

[96] These travel document ordeals sometimes appear as independent chapters in his books where they are entitled "Passport ka Jhagra" (Fights over Passport).

[97] Satyadev, *Europe ki*, 11–25. He went to Germany for ophthalmic treatment.

[98] "Refusal of Passport to Swami Satya Deva", *The Tribune*, 16 July 1922, 1.

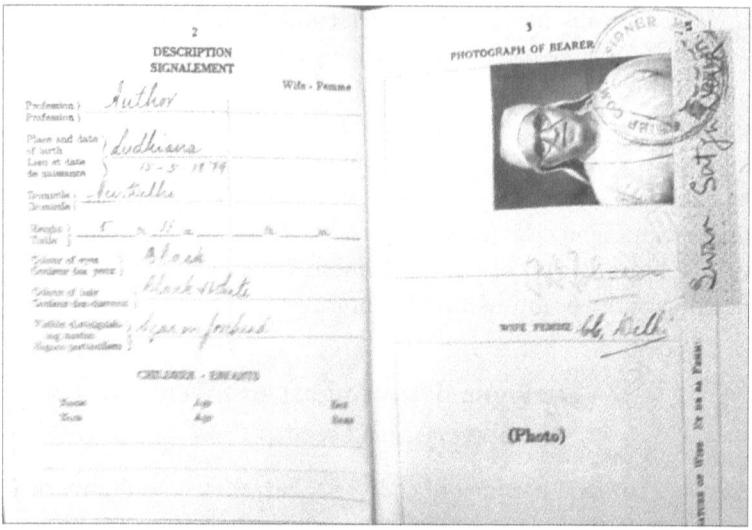

Fig. 5.5: Satyadev's passport.

a good case for refusing a passport on the strength of the Swami's previous record."[99] Eventually he was granted one in February 1927.[100] The denial of it was then repeated in 1933: "In any case since his record subsequent to the grant of the passport shows that he has been delivering objectionable speeches both on the Continent of Europe and in India, the Governor in Council . . . proposes to refuse the grant to him of a fresh passport and to cancel his previous one."[101] After much hard work and many rounds of applications he was issued a five-year passport on 9 March 1934 which was valid for the British Empire, Austria, Germany, France, Italy, Belgium, and Switzerland.[102]

[99] 10/XVI/1924, Home Poll, NAI.

[100] For more on Satyadev's passport ordeals in 1927, Satyadev, "Main Dubara Germany".

[101] "Refusal of Passport to Swami Satya Dev to Proceed to Europe", 28/3/1933, Home Poll, NAI.

[102] L/PJ/11/3/3121, IOR, BL. Also: 22/V/1923, Home Poll, NAI; 10/XVI/1924, Home Poll, NAI; 35/XII/1926, Home Poll, NAI; 10/XXIV/1927, Home Poll, NAI; 28/3/1933, Home Poll, NAI; 28/XI/1934, Home Poll, NAI.

The scholarly literature on international mobility has shown passports as essential to state monopolisation of the means of movement, as also to signal differential mobility and exercise control over migration based on a categorisation of racialised nationality.[103] Desirous of unfettered mobility, Satyadev longingly remembered his first journey to America when no passport had been needed. Lamenting travel restrictions and the need for separate permission letters for visits to each country, he says: "Now every civilised country has become almost like a prison cell. The freedom which was so celebrated is now flying out of the windows. Now that every country of Asia is being liberated, it appears that the civilised world has started to fear its independence."[104]

Satyadev's travel writings were never merely passive acts of collecting and archiving information, nor merely providing readers with knowledge of sites, landscapes, institutions, etc. He is interested in ideas deriving from his travels and so institutes a vibrant comparative dialogue between East and West, slavery and freedom, the individual and the collective, the personal and the political, the ideological and the practical. Travel writing, it has been shown, is often a political act with crucial connections to identity.[105] Tharakeshwar thus argues that travel writings by Indians during the colonial period translated colonial discourses in order to empower themselves, and to claim a nationalist rhetoric which often stood "at the crossroads of upper caste and male identities".[106] One strand of Satyadev's project does represent an identity-building project and a shaping of power dynamics: he attempts to recast a modern self which is westernised in some ways yet remains rooted in Indian tradition. His construal of the histories of other nations and of India is purposive: he is a staunch advocate for a reshaped Indian selfhood. In this direction he shows the zeal of a missionary, holding up

---

[103] For example Torpey, *The Invention*, 4; Mongia, *Indian Migration*, 112–39.

[104] Satyadev, *Germany Mein*, 12.

[105] For example: Schweizer, *Radicals*; Steves, *Travel as a Political Act*. An exhilarating recent addition to this corpus is Markovits, *A Passage to Europe*.

[106] Tharakeshwar, "Empire Writes Back?", 131.

a mirror to what is "good" or "bad" for Indians while shining a light on normative ideals and moral codes such as progress, intellectual growth, development, and education. Remembering his first experience of the US, Satyadev says:

> I found a significant contrast between the new world and the old world. In the old world, the spectre of inaction, laziness, laxity, and communalism (*akarmanyata, alasya, pramaad aur sampradayikta*) roamed without restraint ... People of the old world were averse to anything new, holding orthodox beliefs in high regard. I came from such an old world to this new country, where people respected novelty. Progress flowed through their veins, a strong work ethic was as innate as breathing, and a spirit of religious tolerance prevailed. I arrived among those who worshipped personal freedom and where an intense thirst for truth and knowledge was widespread.[107]

America and Europe stood in his mind for liberty and prosperity, India for slavery, misery, and oppression, and so he constantly expresses his desire to be free.[108] At other moments he suggests a sameness between East and West. In a poem, for example, he compares the majesty of the Rhine in Germany with the Ganga:

> In a Hindu heart, memories of Mother Ganga;
> A strong German finds echoes of his fatherland
>   in Rhine sounds ...
> Our song German, we are drunk with Germany;
> The Rhine embodies Germany, Germany remains its heart.[109]

He adopts an Orientalist idiom which is stereotypical in suggesting the West as intellectual and materialist, and the East as spiritual and religious. This determines his perception of some of the West's institutions: the efficiency of post offices, banks, educational institutions, railways, and the job market, as against the pathetic versions of these back home.[110] Modes of transport in particular – the road, the

[107] *SKM*, 115.
[108] F. 139, 28.
[109] Satyadev, "Germanon ki Pyari Rhine". Also Satyadev, *Europe ki*, 188.
[110] Satyadev, *Europe ki*, 196–8.

sea, trains, aeroplanes – being vital to his sense of well-being, make him juxtapose the beauty, the quality, and equalising tendency of railways, railway stations, and roads in the US with those in India:

> There are three or four classes of trains in the Indian Railways. There are no such double standards in America. There is no discrimination here. There is a chair for each passenger, on which he can sleep even at night. On one side of the car, in a small room, are two taps of cold and hot water. A bar of soap is positioned nearby ... Now look at the condition of our place. Like sheep and goats, men are herded into railway coaches. It becomes difficult for them even to breathe ... Despite these plights, Indians never think about how such problems can be remedied.[111]

Sujata Mody refers to Satyadev as a *desh hitaishi* (patriot) who was often based abroad and who, relying on his experiences there, provided useful instructions for refiguring national identities and boundaries. She argues that such writers and readers, based abroad and in India, "began to consider themselves as belonging to a larger collectivity of Indians with no geographical boundaries. They were all simply *desh hitaishi*s working together for the welfare of India."[112] In his article "Amrica ki Striyan" Satyadev thus lamented the present pathetic condition of women in India while praising the freedom, rights, liberty, health, and education for women in America. He praised the presence of diverse clubs in every city where women could gather for reading, donations, lectures, and jobs. Yet as a moralising Hindu patriarch he also critiqued the "excessive independence" of American women: their licentiousness had led to an "increase in immorality in big cities" and the culture of the "dancing ball". Overall, however, American women needed to be emulated by Indian women; social reforms were thus badly needed in India, particularly in the fields of physical health and education.[113]

---

[111] Satyadev, "Bijli ki Railgadi". Also Satyadev, "United States of America ki Prasidh", 2–3.

[112] Mody, "Literature, Language", 207.

[113] Satyadev, "Amrica ki Striyan", 132. Writing under the pen name "Banga Mahila" in *Saraswati*, Rajendrabala in an article "Nivedan" (A Plea) questioned Satyadev's flawed comparison of American and Indian women, also contending

It is clear from the above that Satyadev was not a blind devotee or uncritical admirer of every aspect of Western civilisation.[114] One of his stories, "Kirti Kalima", has as its central character Shivadatta, an ideal Indian immigrant student who also works as a labourer in a lumber mill to earn money. The story seems partially autobiographical: the character is fluent in English, does not drink, and boldly speaks his mind. It also critiques anti-Black and anti-Asian sentiment among white labourers, comparing this to the way high-caste Hindus treat "untouchables" back home. His critique of colour-based discrimination and unfair treatments of Blacks, marked by racial otherness, is unambiguous: "In civilised countries, where virtues should take precedence, it is astonishing to witness such partisanship towards a fair skin."[115]

Equally, Satyadev wants people in the West to be made aware of his home and nation. His stories often interpolate "bad" Christianity with "good" Hinduism. "In America, I have very well understood that Christian pastors are often very narrow minded," he says.[116] He challenges contrasting images of savage Indians and civilised Westerners while recommending the Hindu way of life to the rest of the world: "The custom of burning the dead is becoming very popular in Germany . . . It seems that in the next century, the common masses of Europe will start burning their dead and the malpractice of burying the dead will end forever."[117] Moreover: "We should guide Europe towards the right course by dressing up our noble and moral principles in a pragmatic manner. Unlike us, Europe lacks these virtuous ideals."[118] Such writings decentre Anglophone canons and associated sensibilities, even as they tend to foster chauvinistic Hindu histories.

---

that Indian women were often constrained by purdah norms. Banga Mahila was the most published woman author of *Saraswati* under Dwivedi's editorship: Mody, *The Making of Modern*, 214–19, 224–33; Pandey, *Banga Mahila*.

[114] Satyadev, "Amrica ki Striyan", 130.
[115] Satyadev, "Nayi Duniya ke Samachar", 250.
[116] Satyadev, *Amrica Bhraman*, 15.
[117] Satyadev, *Meri German*, 105.
[118] Satyadev, "Aakaash Mein", 538.

During his fifth and last journey to Germany he announced: "I undertook my first four journeys to Europe in Western attire, but this time it was my desire to travel in my hermit outfit and thus I did not have to undertake much preparation."[119] Most of the photographs in his books portray him in the attire of a Hindu swami, at times with a hat.

Satyadev was thus constantly negotiating and renegotiating the boundaries of nationalism and internationalism, and the spatial categories of nation/trans-nation, seeing no contradiction between the two. An interplay of the borderless world and the bounded nation produced his travel writing: on the one hand he is all for transnational mobility, flexible citizenship, and "contingent belonging";[120] on the other, as we shall see more clearly in the next chapter, he is firmly rooted in Indian habitations of a particular kind – a hegemonic and militant Hindu identity embedded in a pugnacious nationalism. His writings undoubtedly foreground a selective admiration of the "other", but the final destination for him always remains his own country. Travel is therefore a space for Satyadev to project his nationalist anxieties, which are refigured to suggest ways of governing the nation afresh. In his mind the nation is a biological rather than geographical construct and he reconstitutes space culturally to serve his ideal of the beautiful Hindu body. Except, in Satyadev, ideals of beauty and ideas of freedom were also tainted and pernicious: they were straightforwardly sexist in being focused on male physical perfection, and politically retrograde in their idolisations of Hitler and Nazism – the archetypes of masculinity to which I now turn.

"Perfect" Bodies: Masculinity and the Idolisation of Hitler

Laced with his ideas of beauty, physical perfection, and dreams of freedom, Satyadev's travel writing shows an obsession with masculinity

---

[119] Satyadev, *Germany Mein*, 3.
[120] Srivastava, "Ghummakkads".

as an imperative of citizenship. His descriptions of the nation as a body are imbued with idealised traits and attributes such as hard work, discipline, and masculinity; they serve as his clarion call to the Hindi-Hindu nation to embrace these ideals. The well-honed masculine body is in his conception an entity freed from weakness and imperfection. His explanations of the difference between the East and the West show a contempt for the weak and the infirm body that is India. He notes that while people in India consider fifty as old age, in Europe it is considered the beginning of youth:

> There is much juice of life in our thinking power. People here consider the right time of youth to be the age of fifty, and we consider old age to be our ideal. We sing songs about dying, we dream of the other world, we listen to the old and the dated – there is no novelty, no worship of spring . . . Hindus need the ideal of youth. All our false songs of mortification, memoirs reminding us of death, all our melancholy songs of pessimism should be burned. We need poetry and literature which provide a source of hope, energy, courage, youth, and ambition . . . Hindi poets and writers are immersed in Chhayavad . . . They are not concerned with singing songs of valiant masculinity that arouse courage among the people. They will either write songs of Radha-Krishna's flute, *nakh-shikh* (head to toe descriptions), gestures and glances, or will fly high . . . This flow of ideas about dirty old age has to end; instead we have to define and compose a new consciousness . . . so that the decrepit particles of our brains are released and replaced by the strong sperm of masculinity.[121]

Ironically, Satyadev's eyesight was extremely weak and in the 1920s he had almost grown blind. Some of his travels to Germany were, as noted earlier, explicitly for eye treatment.[122] This reinforced his preoccupation with physical fitness: it was quite obviously a necessary prerequisite for global travel. His discourse on brahmacharya was, similarly, part of his preoccupation with freedom, fitness, and masculinity. While celebrating travel as an act of rebellion to escape

---

[121] Satyadev, *Europe ki*, 194–6.

[122] Satyadev struggled with bad eyesight and suffered from myopia, often travelling to Germany for treatment: *SKM*, 251–62, 263–73, 560.

family and marriage, and championing his oath of celibacy as freedom, Satyadev linked it to the shaping of an immaculate male body (discussed in detail in the next chapter).[123] An ascetic and muscular body was seen analogously as the scaffolding for the new modern nation – a characteristic Indian response to the colonial charge of Indian effeminacy.

More problematically, Satyadev navigated the political contours of his travel writing through a glorification of Hitler's Germany, applauding the Führer and the country for its masculine ethos, to then build a case for an anti-imperial, aggressive, and violent Hindu nationalism in India.[124] His five trips to Germany were for extended periods of time over 1923–4, 1927–30, 1934–6, 1938–9, and finally in 1956 in part for the medical treatment of his eyes.[125] The first four visits were therefore almost precisely over the period of Hitler's ascendance and supremacy. The first chapter of *Europe ki Sukhad Smritiyan* starts with a short description of political relations between the different countries of Europe, revealing his clear bias in favour of Germany and dislike of Russia.[126] *Meri German Yatra* has some enchanting descriptions of Berlin and other parts of Germany, but there is alongside an overtly political flavour to the writing.[127] "Compared to England and France, Germany is more potent and masculine . . . There is amazing prowess in Germany."[128] And elsewhere in the same work: "It would be best if we sent our boys and girls to Germany instead of England, because this country is the centre of European culture at this time."[129]

Organicist ideas of the nation and self-purification emerged quite naturally out of these Wagnerian adorations of great heroes

[123] *SKM*, 46–9.
[124] It has been argued that the amoral worship of beauty and force, implicit in Nazi thinking, found new alliances with a strand of aggressive Hindu nationalism: Goodrick-Clark, *Hitler's Priestess*.
[125] Satyadev, *Germany Mein Mere*, Introduction.
[126] Satyadev, *Europe ki*, 3–9.
[127] Satyadev, *Meri German*, 95–106.
[128] Satyadev, *Europe ki*, 46.
[129] Ibid., 28.

leading the great nation into a great future. Describing a colourful and well-organised country fair in Weiden, a Bavarian village, he contrasts it with the pitiable state of villages in India and glorifies Hitler's regime:

> Weiden is a ... village ... having all the modern comforts – telephone, electric lights, flush and electric cars – with a bracing salubrious climate with moderate expenses ... The land lady informed me that the [Weiden country] fair would last continually for three days. She continued: "Every year, these soldiers of Hitler visit the village and teach nationalism to our children through popular performances" ... In India ... village society is deeply engrossed in illiteracy as well as in the mire of poverty ... When in the year 1934, I visited Germany for the third time, I realized the utility of these country fairs which had brought rich harvest to the great German dictator Adolf Hitler. His scheme of physical culture organization proved very successful. Pleasure-loving Germany had become the land of heroes. National socialism became the religion of the masses and no sacrifice was too great for them to defend the honour of their beloved country. Alas! There is no body to organize such village fairs in this unfortunate land of Hindustan.[130]

Historians have shown up a group of Hindu intellectuals influenced by the Nazi ideology, people who derived their worldview from a select fascist repertoire to create new languages of legitimation in a colonial context.[131] Satyadev is a variant on this tendency, deploying reverence for Hitler to convey instructions to his homeland. More or less contemporaneously with the originator of Hindutva, V.D. Savarkar, in whose philosophy violence and warfare were central religious tenets,[132] Satyadev too upheld war and violence as significant in defining a nationalist paradigm of freedom. There are repeated eulogies to Hitler's Germany in his work: "In 1928–29, no one knew that within six years Germany would be completely coloured in the Nazi colour and that the people of Germany would consider Hitler at par with Christ";[133] "The public is

---

[130] Satyadev, "A Country Fair", 357–9.
[131] Zachariah, "At the Fuzzy Edges".
[132] Outlined most cogently in Chaturvedi, *Hindutva and Violence*, passim.
[133] Satyadev, *Europe ki*, 61.

in love with Hitler";[134] "I am deeply impressed and delighted to see the management of the Nazi regime, including their good manners, impeccable organisation and competence."[135] And in an article on Hitler in *Saraswati*: "Hitler's young men are made of iron; when they rise, they make the impossible possible."[136] The crowning accolade which follows suggests that the origins of the Führer's greatness lie at least partly in his being a German sanyasi or brahmachari of sorts – he then even seeks to equate Hitler with Lord Ram: "Hitler did not marry, his needs are very few, he does not take part in frivolous events, he is passionate, deeply thoughtful, and a complete well-wisher of the German nation . . . Hitler has done no less work for Germany than what Lord Ram did for the Hindu community."[137]

These encomia continued on his return to India: Satyadev praised Hitler in various public meetings.[138] His autobiography, written in 1951, also contains an apologia for Hitler and Hitlerism: " felt deeply proud of the wisdom (*vivekni buddhi*) of Hitler the Great. For a man who can attain such a high position and make his heart so large and generous – for such a person why should his countrymen not give up their body, mind and wealth . . . Blessed are the mothers who give birth to such jewels. This is a symptom of being cultured (*susanskrit hone ka yahi lakshan hai*)."[139] These images strengthen and reaffirm Satyadev's own militant Hindu nationalism and give it vernacular meanings that could challenge colonialism. His cult of the body, encompassing his self-image as a yogic superman with the Nazi ideal of hyper-masculinity, includes fears and anxieties over racial "contamination". Projecting a race of people hypothesised

[134] Ibid., 303.
[135] Ibid., 298.
[136] Satyadev, "German Dictator", 182.
[137] Satyadev, *Europe ki*, 315–16.
[138] In a meeting in Kumaon on 20 August 1935, Satyadev made a speech filled with references to Hitler, arguing that he had saved Germany from the crippling war indemnity: *PAI*, 24 August 1932. In July 1939 he praised Hitler's Germany and stressed the need to introduce military education in schools: *PAI*, 29 July 1939. Also Satyadev, "German Dictator".
[139] *SKM*, 372–3.

as Aryan Hindus, he views them as the forerunners of a glorious heritage.[140] They seem to him a distinct and much "higher" species: he implies their hegemonic supremacy over all other varieties of people in India by reaffirming the Nazi ideas of racial hierarchy.[141]

Satyadev's vernacular travel writing extends and expands the existing frame of the travel writing genre. It becomes in his work a site for moral-ethical assertions as well as the propagation of cultural-religious processes of Hindi literary education, Hindu reform, and Indian radicalisation. It shows the possibility – via a new awareness of worlds outside India and beyond the conception of most Indians – of erecting dreams of success, masculine happiness, and a sense of freedom despite the fetters of colonial subjecthood. Satyadev worked with two kinds of indigenous masculinity: on the one hand he cited Western ideals and accomplishments, particularly those of America and Hitler's Germany, to push for an enhanced work culture among Hindus, and to make a strong case for certain social reforms; on the other he argued for an aggressive Hindu masculinity vis-à-vis the Muslims of India. Asking Hindus to emulate the West, he lamented the decline in their manliness and their descent into an effete, effeminate culture. His muscular asceticism draws inspiration from American, German, and Hindu traits in explicit contrast with the character of British colonisers on the one hand and Muslims on the other (discussed in detail in the next chapter).

Satyadev, it seems clear, was a vagabond afflicted with idealism and a genuine wanderlust. Travel writing emerged from his pen as a performance of the self in order to create and recommend new subjectivities to his countrymen. The vernacular is sharpened into a tool to critique bondage and slavery – not in opposition to a global cosmopolitanism but to supplement the articulation of an aggres-

---

[140] For intersections between Aryan theory and India, Trautmann, *Aryans and British India*; Goodrick-Clarke, *Hitler's Priestess*.

[141] Satyadev, *Europe ki*, 301–2.

sive Hindu politics. The peculiarity of his travel writings lies in his radical rejection of an Indian mentality alongside a wholehearted acceptance of Hindu spirituality. The nation was for him not so much a geographical body as a biological body to be shaped and formed through the gleanings of travel in alternative spheres of thought. His valorisation of a Hindu ethos alongside his critique of passports and territorial boundaries offers a contrast between the state of nature and the state of law, with the former perceived as pure, pristine, and eternal, and the latter as a modern perversion. Though sometimes mediocre and repetitive, his work attracted a wide readership because it provided imaginative escape and a promise of freedom from the routine and the mundane, beyond the drudgery of colonialism and bondage. Overlayered with a collage of fantasy, fitness, and freedom, Satyadev's homo-erotic travel writings captured the dreams of many Hindu middle-class men and provided solace via a modern, muscular vision.

However, as we will see in greater detail in the subsequent chapter, these travel writings also seriously caricatured and distorted beauty, physicality, and freedom in the process of advocating militant, violent, and aggressive Hindu nationalist sentiments. Muslims, Dalits, women, the differently abled, the peaceful, and the enfeebled were all implicitly made illegitimate members of this body politic and excluded from national citizenship. His anti-parochialism, multiculturalism, pan-Indianism, and cosmopolitanism coexist with a violently chauvinistic muscular nationalism. If Savarkar is, as Vinayak Chaturvedi suggests, the ghost father of the contemporary Indian nation, it may not be off the mark to suggest that Satyadev is the ghostly, lost, and unknown writer hidden behind the mainstream militant Hinduism in vogue today.

6

Fashioning a Hindu Political Sanyasi
Autobiography and Sectarian Freedom

Men have been divided into two categories – stay-at-home and explorers, conventional and the adventurous . . . The author of this book belongs to the latter variety . . . The Swami's life is in a sense the history of our national struggle . . . The Swami's story is a highly inspiring example of what tenacity, perseverance, and courage can do to overcome difficulties . . . The book gives many glimpses of the age when religious, social, and political movements were beginning to stir men into a new consciousness and when, in face of heavy odds, a new vision was gradually shaping the minds of men. – *The Sunday Tribune,* 17 February 1952.[1]

Swami Satyadeva is a well-known Hindi writer and public speaker . . . In this book he gives an account of life from childhood up to the year 1950 . . . It is a book for those who want to understand the logic of communalism. The author has expressed himself on all social, cultural, and political subjects very frankly . . . He hates Russia and communism and is a great admirer of Nazi Germany and Hitler . . . In autobiographies people do not touch controversial subjects, but in this book the author has trodden on delicate ground. His remarks about the partition of India and the assassination of Mahatma Gandhi, which he has strongly put, will hardly be appreciated by the people of this country . . . Swami Satyadeva thinks Bapu deserved to be murdered. – *National Herald,* 24 February 1952.[2]

[1] Anon., "Book Review of Swami".
[2] S.S., "A Book that Preached".

These two conflicting reviews of Satyadev's voluminous autobiography in Hindi – a work spread over 568 pages and 56 chapters, entitled *Swatantrata ki Khoj Mein arthat Meri Atm Katha* (In Search of Freedom, an Autobiography; hereafter *SKM*), and published in 1951 – reflect the diametrically opposed reactions that it provoked.³ It also created a stir in political circles, with the Nehru government issuing a press statement against it. What is perhaps unique about Satyadev's autobiography is that he followed it up with a sequel of 208 pages in 15 chapters the very next year – *Vichaar Swatantrya ke Prangan Mein: My Autobiography – Critics Answered* (hereafter *VSPM*) – in which he staunchly defended the autobiography to buttress his claims.⁴ Keeping these two texts at its centre, while also assessing his other writings on Hindu nationalism, I argue here that they provide a window to illuminate the political and social tensions that still divide modern India. Written with "shameless" honesty, Satyadev's autobiography is a foundational text showcasing the sophisticated precursors of aggressive Hindu nationalism and those implacably prejudiced against Muslims in contemporary India.

Placing himself at the centre of an evolving nation, Satyadev composed an autobiography vividly documenting political-public life – his own and that of the nation, between 1879 and 1950. His extensive travels, discussed in the previous chapter, and his everyday life were interwoven with frank views on relationships, people (especially Gandhi), events, and ideologies. The previous chapter having been on his travels, the present chapter focuses on these latter aspects.

Satyadev says in his autobiography: "My life story goes along with the history of the Indian nation, because I am part of it. I will have to describe the political leaders I have worked with . . . for the benefit of the future generation."⁵ The narration of his own life is quintessentially an ego-document, though the author himself

---

³ *SKM*. The English title was given on the cover of the book.

⁴ *VSPM*. This was largely a response to the trenchant criticisms of his autobiography.

⁵ *SKM*, 217.

equates his autobiography with a biography – his history of a colonised nation's attempt at freedom in which the self and the political are co-constitutive. Largely addressing a Hindi–Hindu reading public, his autobiography is also a chronicle of sexual constraint, ascetic masculinity, and sectarian freedom which found an audience receptive to the idea of a modern, militant Hindu nation uncontaminated by Muslims.

In the Weberian sense, Satyadev was a charismatic modern-day worldly ascetic, a political sanyasi, and a master narrator and orator with a huge fan following. In his persona there was no whiff of the stereotypical otherworldly, poor, and humble renunciant. Particularly in the 1920s and 1930s he became an important spokesperson of Hindu consolidation.[6] Cultivating the aura of a "foreign returned" wanderer retailing dreams of freedom and exotic travel, his eclectic mix of Western and Indian – indicated by his saffron apparel topped up with a conspicuously Western hat – suggested a figure whose authority derived equally from a venerated tradition of indigenous spirituality as well as the body of formidable ideas that had made the West such a powerhouse. This potent combination of continence, wealth, westernism, Hinduism, and violence made him stand out as unique and gave him his star appeal. Various contemporary bigwigs, including Motilal Nehru, Rajendra Prasad, Jayaprakash Narayan, Indra Vidyavachaspati, Harivansh Rai Bachchan, Rambriksh Benipuri, and Santram speak of the attractions and impact of Satyadev on them.[7] In its catalogue of publications – which has general headings like "novels", "plays", and "autobiographies" – the Nagari Pracharini Sabha continues to print a separate heading which shows "Books Written by Swami Satyadev Parivrajak": he is the only writer with an independent listing in the catalogue.[8] The Sabha also has a huge portrait of him within its premises.

---

[6] His book *Sangathan ka Bigul*, for example, saw mass runs and public readings, with a large number of gatherings. For details, Gupta, *Sexuality, Obscenity*, 233–4, 237.

[7] For example Bachchan, *In the Afternoon*, 358; Singh and Sundaram, *Gandhi*, 4; Sharma, *Benipuri Granthavali, Vol. 4*, 212; Vidyavachaspati, "Sri Swami", 10–11; Santram, "Swami ji".

[8] *Prakashan Suchi*, 14; Interview with Sabhajit Shukla. Satyadev had a long

There is, as noted, very little writing on Satyadev, and the little there is merely celebrates him uncritically.[9] Ignoring the controversies that erupted around his autobiography, his anti-Muslim tirades, and the rabidly right-wing tenor of his view of Gandhi's assassination, Dinanath Sharma, for example, has this to say: "The autobiography of Parivrajak-ji is the story of a person who is varied, multifaceted, and awe-inspiring. He negates the boundaries of bondage throughout. He is a vagabond . . . The great man of *In Search of Freedom* carries within himself a flow of dynamic collective consciousness whose vastness and beauty cannot but overwhelm the reader."[10]

In 1911, after his return from America, Satyadev was for a short period appointed headmaster of the DAV School in Dehradun. An article in a commemorative volume on him states: "In the year 1911, Shri Satyadev appeared like a shining star. He had just returned from America after a six-year stay there . . . His language had simplicity, freshness, and force, his thoughts smelt of freedom and humanity . . . I consider his rousing speeches between 1911 and 1920 as his gift to the nation."[11] Another article in the same volume notes: "This young sanyasi, who had returned from America, used to sing bhajans and give lectures fearlessly, and hardly any city in Uttar Pradesh and Bihar will have been spared his lion's roar."[12]

By the time of his autobiography in 1951 his celebrated travel writings had made him very famous. The autobiography itself, very much part of a genre taken seriously in the world of Hindi literature, needs to be placed within Hindi–Hindu right-wing writings that were widely read across North India, particularly from the 1920s.[13]

---

association with the Sabha and, as mentioned in the previous chapter, willed a considerable part of his property to it – which he also later regretted: *SKM*, 437–55. Also Lal and Tripathi, *Hirak Jayanti Granth*, 54–7.

[9] Sharma, *Swami Satyadev*; Imam, "Satya Dev"; *Sri Swami Satya Dev*.
[10] Sharma, *Swami Satyadev*, 175–6.
[11] Vidyalankar, "Swami Satyadev", 2.
[12] *Sri Swami Satya Dev*, 25.
[13] Mukul, *Gita Press*, 225–344; Gupta, *Sexuality, Obscenity*, 222–67; Gould, *Hindu Nationalism*, 31, 36, 72–3, 109.

Many of the motifs in this book show a commonality with ideologically similar nationalist authors of the time. The post-Independence turbulence over the coming into being of a new nation – which witnessed the upheavals and trauma involved in separating a largely Hindu India led by secular nationalists from Muslims led by Jinnah – was the broader context for the writing and reception of Satyadev's autobiography. Strains of authoritarian and Hindu-nationalist formations, socio-cultural conservatism, and "religio-nativist right-wing extremism" jostled with visions of secularism, pluralism, new civic identities, and liberal legal frameworks.[14] Gandhi's assassination on 30 January 1948, which shaped the most controversial section of Satyadev's autobiography, was a turning point in "tilting the scale against the votaries of Hindu nationalism";[15] it was, equally, a turning point "in the reception of state centric articulations of secularism."[16] There was over this time a push-and-pull between two strands of nationalism: secular pluralism and Hindu communalism. Satyadev's autobiography is symptomatic of the undercurrents of the latter tendency which, despite the ban on the Rashtriya Swayamsevak Sangh for its inspiration to Godse, simmered on in the underbelly of everyday Indian life until its metaphorical Second Coming in present times with the destruction of the Babri Masjid.[17] Satyadev's writings and politics were simultaneously symptomatic and atypical of their time – atypical in containing both a deep sense of anti-imperialism as well as a deep animosity for the great exemplar of anti-imperialism, Gandhi; symptomatic because they reflected some of the deepest prejudices of their day.

The autobiography was purported to be funded by a sum of Rs 2000 from the Bihar state given at the behest of President Rajendra Prasad – a claim denied by the central government – and the Arya Samaj branch of Aligarh. The life of Dayanand Saraswati had

[14] For extremism: Ahuja, "Authoritarian Shadows", 8, 13. For details on the scenario overall: Kudaisya, *India in the 1950s*; Guha, *India After Gandhi*.

[15] Kudaisya, *India in the 1950s*, 118.

[16] Khan, "Performing Peace", 63.

[17] On Hindu nationalism, Hansen, *The Saffron Wave*; Gould, *Hindu Nationalism*; Jaffrelot, *The Hindu Nationalist*; Zavos, *The Emergence of Hindu*.

left a deep impression on Satyadev and "touched his heart" (*usne mere hridya ko pakad liya*),[18] while the Arya Samaj had been a lifelong influence on him: their imprint on his autobiography is clear.[19] While travel remains a critical component of the autobiography, it is layered with his aggressive Hindu nationalism, and here I discuss the latter, focusing on three themes.[20] First, the performance of a political Hindu ascetic and the articulation of celibate masculinity which give impetus to the narcissistic and didactic tone of Satyadev's writings. Second, Satyadev's conceptualisation of a sectarian and conditional freedom which rests on Hindu domination and Muslim demonisation. And finally, Satyadev's relationship with Gandhi and defence of the assassination – underscoring his hatred of Gandhi's inclusive Hinduism – and the solidification of his career as a militant Hindu nationalist. I look in particular at Satyadev's construction of the Muslim in stereotypical and gendered terms as a sexual predator, which, in turn informs his view of Gandhi, whose religious pluralism and "effeminate" personality failed to conform to Satyadev's gendered norms. As a whole the chapter also reveals how, amid some shades of grey, Satyadev's autobiography enacts the process of Hinduising India which appears to have found its apotheosis seven decades or so after it was written.

Anatomy of a Hindu Ascetic: Sexual Constraint and Masculine Virility

If anyone asks me – "Swami Satyadev, what is the best recipe (*sarvashreshth nuskha*) you have found to remain fit all your life?," I will loudly proclaim – "Semen Retention" (*virya raksha*). If the same person asks me

---

[18] *SKM*, 32, 536. Satyadev attempts to follow a similar trajectory to Dayanand Saraswati: opposition to idol worship and superstitious Hindu practices, taking a new name, learning Sanskrit, becoming a virile sanyasi, and an assertive political and religious polemicist. However, he combined this with a model of wealth acquisition.

[19] *SKM*, 16–17.

[20] Of the fifty-six chapters, sixteen are devoted to his travel narratives, and a repeat of his travel writings, discussed previously. Almost all his writings – essays, stories, travel, autobiography – are largely cut from the same cloth.

the same question a second time and a third time, my answer will be the same – "Semen Retention". Whatever sharpness, brilliance and vigour (*tej, pratibha aur oj*) happens to be manifest in the body is due to the glory of semen . . . So never destroy this priceless treasure.[21]

From different vantage points, versions of asceticism were articulated by revivalists, Sanatan Dharmis, reformers, Arya Samajis, Bhagat Singh, Godse, Vivekananda, and Gandhi. For many, Hindu militant celibacy embodied opposition to colonial sexuality, a shunning of heterosexuality in favour of virile asexuality, a route to the promotion of physical culture, and everyday evidence of the materialisation of Hindu ascetic practices.[22] It has been argued that "in modernity, renunciation came to index political being, as opposed to . . . a timeless existential question."[23] The figures of the political sanyasi and the celibate monk became one of the most compelling figures for the assertion of political power by the Hindu national body.[24]

In this context Satyadev appeared as the avatar of a Hindu sanyasi who was also political, charismatic, articulate, and powerful because affluent. His combination of freedom, fitness, finance, and fantasy made him a model of Hindu ascetic manhood – here was a heroic figure as fit financially as he was physically, a yogi who was also a *bhogi* (materialist) who had travelled far and wide and was now bringing the West's best ideas home, while presumably having spread India's fame abroad.[25] Equipped with an ample grammar of

[21] *SKM*, 529.

[22] See, for these various positions, Alter, *The Wrestler's Body*, 237–55; Anand, *Hindu Nationalism*, 107; Mills and Sen, *Confronting the Body*; Scott, *Spiritual Despots*, 2.

[23] Banerjee, *Elementary Aspects*, 27–9.

[24] Banerjee, *Make Me a Man*; Chakraborty, *Masculinity, Asceticism*.

[25] The lone yogic man and the sanyasi is embodied in the figures of Narendra Modi and Yogi Adityanath in contemporary India. They are projected as the new poster boys of muscular Hindutva piety; they also exemplify a model of Hindu economy and commercial success, which is far removed from all kinship and family ties, making their personas morally edifying and faith-based: Visvanathan, "Narendra Modi's Symbolic". Satyadev can be regarded as one

self-fashioning,[26] which was amplified by ardent self-promotion, Satyadev's autobiography is filled with anecdotes arguing the importance of brahmacharya, chastity, sexual self-regulation, and celibacy for the anti-colonial struggle. These are connected to his extolling of the physical labour and bodily fitness necessary for the achievement of a specifically Hindu political freedom. In this view of life, sex itself is perceived as inherently negative, the devil within the human physiognomy that must be conquered to show man's mastery of the carnal desires that continuously erode him from within. Combining ancient ideals with the teachings of Dayanand Saraswati, Satydev says:

> What have I learned from the school of Arya Samaj? ... A student's life is celibate, he does not have the right to make eye contact with any woman. Oiling one's scalp head, combing the hair, using an umbrella, and watching any kind of dance or drama is a sin (*ras-rang, naach-tamasha dekhna paap hai*).[27]

In an early chapter titled "Swatantrata ke liye Pehla Yuddh" (First War for Freedom), Satyadev narrates his protest against marriage: "I had pledged in my heart not to marry ever ... One cannot serve one's country when married (*vivahit awastha se desh-seva nahin ho sakti*) ... The fire of protest against marriage erupted in my heart ... I sent a letter to my prospective in-laws ... saying that if they did not marry off their girl, they would suffer for eternity, because I was going to be an ascetic soon."[28] At the end of the chapter he announces: "I was victorious in my first encounter."[29] Having relinquished his ties with his family at an early age, he never allows them to reappear in his work. He provides a reason for renouncing fatherhood: "I will never give birth to an enslaved child" (*main gulam santaan*

---

of the early forerunners of the present politically and economically oriented yogi as he epitomised the message that earning money in combination with values of thrift was central to yogic practices.

[26] Drawing from Greenblatt, *Renaissance Self-Fashioning*.
[27] *SKM*, 31.
[28] Ibid., 29–36.
[29] Ibid., 35.

utpann nahin karoonga);³⁰ this was because it was "a grave sin" to do so in an "enslaved country".³¹

He supports the healing power of nude bathing by expressing admiration for the culture of nudism in Germany.³² He offers covert critiques of sodomy through the story of a murderous constable and the shame and fear experienced by a beautiful boy trapped in "unnatural" relations.³³ The reason for his aversion to the festival of Holi is its obscenities.³⁴ The absence of wet dreams in his life he attributes to the Arya Samaj's influence.³⁵ His distaste for "dirty" cinema, theatre, and obscene songs on the radio is made very clear.³⁶ So is his view of the urgent need for "healthy literature" (*nirog sahitya*) and "energy and freedom of thought" among Hindus.³⁷ And, finally, there is in this Freudian context of revulsion against everything sexual a trenchant denunciation of Rahul Sankrityayan's books and writings for spreading obscenity (*anaachaar*) and preaching "anti-social" messages such as "beef-eating" and the "kissing of young women" (*yuvtiyon se chumma-chaati*).³⁸

Naturally therefore, the "dangerously" hypersexual Muslim is in this vision the absolute Other who embodies the "distorted" notions of sexual freedom in Islam:

> No religion gives as much freedom to pacify psychic disorders and consummate passions as Islam. Islam is completely ignorant of what we call self-control, that is, self-restraint, of which we sing constant glories. Islam's [belief in] physical freedom takes the form of raw abandonment and dances in full view of all, so that its followers become the slaves of their senses like animals and cling to vice like bees. Is there any power attracting people to Islam other than this licence to consumption by the senses?³⁹

---

³⁰ Ibid., 46.
³¹ Ibid., 65.
³² Ibid., 329–32.
³³ Ibid., 418–20.
³⁴ Ibid., 422.
³⁵ Ibid., 561–2.
³⁶ *VSPM*, 115–16.
³⁷ Ibid., 117.
³⁸ Ibid., 116–17, 168.
³⁹ *SKM*, 123–4.

His ethic of physical labour, meanwhile, moves further west to draw inspiration from the classical age of Greece: "That culture teaches us that if we want to imbibe healthy thoughts, our body should be healthy. A community that disrespects the body can never hold beautiful thoughts. Thus, Greece had filled its country with gymnasiums."[40] He is obsessed with his own "beautiful, masculine and healthy body", his loud and robust voice, and his food habits.[41] One of his admirers, Raghubir Sahai, himself a staunch Hindu nationalist, said of Satyadev in an interview: "Well, when Swami Satyadev, immediately after returning from America, joined the DAV High School at Dehradun as its Headmaster, we were very much attracted to him by his fine physique. He was a very sturdy young man with an aquiline nose."[42] This was the physique that delivered all his dynamism; it had kept him free of "the disorder called delusion" (*moh naam ka vikaar*) – by this he meant he had been spared falling in love. In fact, he had merely been prevented from attaining the perfection of a heavenly being by "two or three severe weaknesses", his weak eyes being the major impediment to his full incorporation into the pantheon of divinities; minus these physical deficiencies, he tells us, he "would have achieved the status of a deity" (*devta*).[43] Despite them, he suggests there are cogent reasons for seeing him as the embodiment of earthly perfection: "First class fitness, no bad habits, no wastage of money, no venturing near cinema or theatre, the ability to do all my work myself, and top-grade frugality – these are the natural qualities of my character."[44] Self-fashioning and self-promotion, it could be said in his case, culminate in self-exaltation.

Egoism and Eulogising the Self

It has been suggested that Indian first-person narratives often adopt a modest tone and exhibit a notable reluctance to be open about

---

[40] Ibid., 354.
[41] He wrote extensively on the subject, also publishing pictures of his "beautiful" body doing exercises: Satyadev, "Vyaayaam".
[42] Interview with Raghubir Sahai by Sharma, 9.
[43] *VSPM*, preface.
[44] *SKM*, 429.

deeply personal experiences.[45] "Hindi writers are afraid to reveal themselves. They do not like to make their lives open."[46] Arguably, this generalisation is less true of Satyadev than any other Hindi writer since his autobiography is a straightforward contradiction of this idea of vernacular modesty, reticence, and discretion in the genre. His self-scrutiny is in fact a consummate study in self-love, self-heroism, and ego-history. His immodesty is shameless and spectacular, and the reason for it, or so the author would have us believe, is to satisfy his admirers' "frenzied" demands on account of their passion for his lectures and books, his ascetic practices and muscular body.[47]

As one might expect from such a personality, Satyadev was an unstoppable orator who delivered public speeches across many parts of India, especially Punjab, UP, Bihar, Rajputana, Bombay, and Madhya Pradesh.[48] His lectures, if his self-accolades are to be believed, left the crowds spellbound: hearing him, people broke down and wept aloud (*dahade maar kar rone lage*).[49] So deeply impressed by his lectures on non-cooperation were the many students who heard them that they immediately abandoned their university to join the struggle.[50]

This self-congratulatory rhetoric carries over into the celebration and promotion of his writings and self-published books. It appears from his swelling balances in several banks that many of his works, such as *Rashtriya Sandhya, Sanjeevni Booti, Lekhan Mala*, and *Meri*

---

[45] Kumar, *Writing the First*, 1–21, 211–78; Arnold and Blackburn, *Telling Lives*, 14–16, 54–5.

[46] Zamindar, "Modern Hindi", 117.

[47] *SKM*, 363, 381–2, 407, 412.

[48] For example, it was noted by the government: "He [Swami Satyadev] delivered speeches at Patna, Gaya and Muzaffarpur, which attracted much more popular interest than agitators have found it possible to arouse in recent days. The audience at the first day's meeting numbered only 1000, but rose to 5000 and 6000 at the second, and the addresses were listened to with attention": "Fortnightly Reports: Reports on the Political Situation in India during the second fortnight of August 1922", 18/1922, Part III, Home Poll, NAI, 13.

[49] *SKM*, 234.

[50] Ibid., 235–6.

Kailash Yatra sold 100,000 copies each.[51] Of *Lehsun Badshah*, his most famous book, he boasts that "people went crazy" to read it.[52] Repudiating critical reviews of his autobiography, he defends his life story as the offer of a vicarious habitation to an entire nation: "Hindi magazines should have lapped my autobiography, as a blind and old person was serving the nation through it."[53] He sees himself as a landmark in the collective memory of the nation, ending his second autobiography thus: "I am a pioneer path builder . . . With the release of my autobiography, waves of freedom have started to rise from all corners. Thousands of my fans are reading it with great reverence, writing to me that I am working as a citizen who loves freedom, just like Thomas Paine of America."[54]

Reflecting on Satyadev's domineering projections of his selfhood, Satyabhakt, the Left-Hindi journalist who is the fourth subject of the present book, recalls parts of a humorous rhyme published in the Calcutta magazine *Bharat Mitra*:

naya sadhu amrica gaami, parivrajak sanyasi.
gerua bastar haath kamandal, bagal biraje pustak bundle.
pothi beche kare kaleva, doodh mithai phal aur meva.
sab par veh tuma phatkaare, baba ko bhi poot pukare.

[New sage returned from America, Parivrajak sanyasi.
Saffron clothes, stoup in hand, alongside a bundle of books.
Sells his book, eats a breakfast of milk, sweets, fruits and nuts.
He rebukes all, and even refers to elders as children.[55]]

This satirical view seems much needed when confronting the egotism of a writer who says of his own writing: "As I understand it, probably no Hindi writer working in the field of literature achieved such great success as I did – and entirely through self-reliance."[56]

[51] Ibid., 146, 172.
[52] *Lehsun Badshah* continues in print even now: Satyadev, *Lehsun Badshah*; Interview with Sabhajit Shukla; *SKM*, 519–24.
[53] *VSPM*, 12.
[54] Ibid., 185.
[55] Quoted in Satyabhakt, *Kranti Path*, 420.
[56] *SKM*, 338.

Everything points to this autobiography as a monumental ego-document,[57] a text which glorifies an "indigenous psychology invested in history and individuality."[58] It is evident here that Satyadev's self-praise operates as a strategy to deflect criticism, promote his books, and assert his authority in public arenas. Feelings of material inadequacy catalysed a modern and possessive individualism which could feed and find expression in the genre of autobiography: Satyadev's self-promotion, masquerading as self-cultivation and muscular ascetic nationalism, also fostered his ideas on freedom – to which I now turn.

Conceptualising an Exclusionary Freedom

The *Oxford Handbook of Freedom* associates "positive freedom" with individual "self-mastery" and collective "self-government".[59] It also highlights the inherent tensions between freedom and equality. The concept of freedom was central in Satyadev's thought. The cover and title of his autobiography shows "In Search of Freedom", and the word "freedom" was repeated in the sequel. Satyadev's idiosyncratic conceptualisation of this term shows his longing for a more modern ideal of political freedom running through the autobiography, at the very beginning of which Satyadev champions himself as one whose main aim in life is to spread the ideals of freedom, truth, and knowledge globally: "What is my intention in writing this autobiography? . . . Carrying my ideal of freedom, I have crossed the seas and the earth, and faced fierce obstacles . . . Freedom is the only goal of my life . . . It is the key to opening the doors of divine knowledge" (*daivi gyan ka bhandar kholne ki kunji*).[60] He keeps circling back to this central tenet:

> I came from the new world and had a treasure trove of freedom (*azadi ka bharpoor khazana*). Thirsty people rushed to the banks of river Ravi

---

[57] Dekker, "Introduction".
[58] Eakin, *Writing Life*, 76, 79.
[59] Schmidtz and Pavel, *The Oxford Handbook*.
[60] *SKM*, 2–3.

to quench themselves and were filled with joy on listening to my message of freedom. They found a narrator who sang songs of freedom fearlessly . . . America provided me with ample material for this message of freedom, which I used with ingenuity . . . If I gave a lecture on the Hindi language or spoke on women's education, or even gave a speech on the importance of exercise, I inserted freedom into every aspect.[61]

When the police were attempting to arrest Bhai Parmanand, when Tilak was in jail, when Bengal's youth were victimised and Gandhi hardly known, says Satyadev, "I was spreading the love for freedom" and "beating the trumpet of freedom" (*swadhinta bigul*).[62] But this freedom comes at a price: it cannot exist without self-control: "Not freedom is the need but self-control – freedom begets licentiousness, while self-control gives blissful peace, releasing us from the snares of selfish freedom."[63] This freedom and self-control both blend logically in his mind with asceticism:

> Our people cannot understand the value of freedom right now. Here, it will soon take the form of waywardness (*swachhandata*) and the extreme left path will dominate this country. Therefore, people of this country, who have been sick for centuries, need to be given strong and forceful booster medicines (*balvardhak goliyan*), so that they can gradually gain strength . . . Who is free? The answer is: only he who has subjugated his senses, i.e. he who practices abstinence.[64]

As a normative force, freedom, it has been argued, "remains enmeshed in networks of instruction which ensure that enlightenment always already contains the traces of tutelage as its ground and condition of being."[65] Satyadev upholds this by categorically differentiating between freedom and liberty: the former he equates with waywardness, the latter with self-restraint: "In the word *swatantrata* we can smell *swachhandata* (waywardness), in *swadhinta* (liberty) we can see the light of *atm sanyam* (self-restraint); we must put the

[61] Ibid., 142–3.
[62] Ibid., 148.
[63] Ibid., cover.
[64] Ibid., 555.
[65] Scott, *Spiritual Despots*, 2.

principle of liberty in our life-philosophy."[66] His concept of freedom comes with yet other caveats. In opposition to upholding it as an ideal for all, he outlines a conditional, sectarian, and negative notion of freedom which is meant for some and not all. Hindus and Muslims are rigidly demarcated, with only the former allowed into the sanctum sanctorum of freedom's portals. Clearly what this specious, contorted, illogical, and bogus notion of freedom basically amounts to is a sectarian Hindu negation of equality.

Segmented Freedom and Nationalism: Hindu Sangathan and Muslims

Scholars have shown that a modern cosmopolitan Arya Samaj and Hindu nationalism, even while championing aggressive Hinduism, postulated the idea of self-cultivation, civility, and tolerance as essentially Hindu traits in opposition to an overtly backward, religious, and intolerant Muslim.[67] Hindu nationalism is thus often driven "not by substantive dogma, but rather by practices and affiliations that mark sharp distinctions from other identities,"[68] particularly Muslim. Moreover, the "flexibility, fungibility and ambiguity" exhibited by Hindu nationalism allows an "extremist, parochial, and illiberal ethos" to pass itself off as "moderate, universalist, and enlightened".[69] In similar vein Satyadev's autobiography, written four years after Independence, while apparently adopting a secular, modern, and universalist frame, redefined freedom as an exclusively Hindu freedom – freedom from Muslims who are apparently unsuited by their religion to the true ideals of freedom. It is the Hindu alone who can persuade each of his senses and bodily parts to serve the nation: "My feet work for India. My mouth sings songs of India. My hands serve India. My ears listen to the melody of India. My body wears Indian clothes. My heart is immersed in the love of India. My mind contemplates India's interests and my eyes

[66] *SKM*, 559.
[67] Adcock, *The Limits*, 168–9. Also Gould, *Hindu Nationalism*, 153–4.
[68] Israel and Zavos, "Narratives of Transformation", 354.
[69] Anand, *Hindu Nationalism*, 10.

see Indian pride."[70] Therefore, if you think of India's communities, he says, "Among Hindus, Muslims and Christians, Hindus are the most committed towards their nation. They have the greatest feelings of sacrifice for the country, they are the greatest number in the country, and it is their civilisation and culture which is celebrated by scholars all over the world ... Hindus can be easily and quickly organised to fight for independence."[71] Like the most standard and commonplace of Hindu nationalists, he too laments the contemporary emasculation of Hindus: "The majority of Hindus in India are in deep darkness. They have left their culture, and enlightening their soul requires a massive effort. The minority Muslims will present great obstacles, and the British will make Muslims a means for their empire ... They will constantly try to crush Indian nationality. Indian independence will always be in danger till this problem is solved."[72]

His book *Asahyog*, likewise, exhorts people to non-cooperation with masculine, even phallic, articulations of protest: "You have to do the healing of our society through the syringe of masculinity."[73] The solution he proposes for restoring Hindu masculinity and freedom, and which is much thought out and spoken of in his writing, is Hindu sangathan. With the decline of Non-Cooperation and Khilafat, campaigns to unify Hindus had gained urgency, with the Arya Samaj and Hindu Mahasabha launching programmes of shuddhi and sangathan on a large scale.[74] Satyadev championed these vigorously, envisaging sangathan as an awakening of the Hindu mind, body, and body politic, a means to project Hindu civilisational and cultural unity and promote "Hindu freedom".[75] The years from 1924 to 1927 were crucial in his life, for over this time he published and promoted his book *Sangathan ka Bigul*.[76] He devotes

[70] Satyadev, *Rashtriya Sandhya*, 9.
[71] Satyadev, "Main Kyun Hindu-Sangathan", 422.
[72] *SKM*, 119.
[73] Satyadev, *Asahyog*, 2.
[74] For details, Gupta, *Sexuality, Obscenity*, 222–5, 230–8.
[75] Satyadev, "Main Kyun Hindu-Sangathan".
[76] Satyadev, *Sangathan ka Bigul*.

three chapters of his autobiography to the subject.⁷⁷ In chapter 32, "Sangathan ki Amogh Shakti" (The Infallible Power of Sangathan), he begins by saying that "the year 1926 is called the year of Hindu sangathan in my life."⁷⁸ *Sangathan ka Bigul*, written and published over the time recalled in the autobiography, contains vivid descriptions of his warlike promotion of Hindu sangathan. He refers, with his habitual self-esteem, to the book as the Bible of Hindu sangathan – it should, he says, be "in the pocket of all the soldiers being admitted to the army of Hindu *sangathan*", and in fact no Hindu home should be without a copy of it.⁷⁹ He continues:

> The question of protecting the existence of the Hindu community is superior to all other questions . . . We have to search for new ways to make the Hindu community powerful . . . This is no time to argue for caste divisions . . . We have to bring together all parts of the community to make it a solid whole . . . We have to remove dirty blood and ensure the circulation of pure blood in our veins.⁸⁰

Physical culture among Hindus is argued as exemplary.⁸¹ Inspiration is drawn from yogic cults towards this end. At least six editions of *Sangathan ka Bigul* were published between 1925 and 1927, with print runs of 4000 copies each. A tract of 130 pages, this was extremely popular and sold out rapidly.⁸² A further 20,000 copies were printed and distributed free in the Hindi-speaking regions.⁸³ Satyadev delivered lectures and read abstracts from it at public meetings in Amritsar, Munger, Bhagalpur, Patna, Bankipur, Champaran, Sindh, Basti, Allahabad, and Bombay. His audiences were huge and

---

⁷⁷ *SKM*, 275.
⁷⁸ Ibid., 301.
⁷⁹ Satyadev, *Sangathan ka Bigul*, Preface, v.
⁸⁰ Ibid., ix–xi.
⁸¹ Ibid., 62–70.
⁸² *SKM*, 296, 301–4.
⁸³ The book received wide coverage in newspapers. For example, "Through Indian Eyes: Malignant Microbes", *The Times of India*, 21 December 1925, 10; "Through Indian Eyes: A Tale of Sins", *The Times of India*, 22 February 1926, 10; "Through Indian Eyes: Fourteen Articles", *The Times of India*, 5 July 1926, 8.

packed, with newspapers reporting the event and the government making a careful and detailed note of it in its intelligence reports.

Satyadev's venom against Muslims was unabated all through these many lectures. He had swallowed in its entirety the essentialising of Islam as a religion with "innate characteristics" that were responsible for, among other retrograde practices, the poor quality or lack of women's education, and purdah.[84] A demeaning trope in the Hindu repertoire of prejudices was to consider all Muslims, including the wealthy, as inherently dirty. This was an additional reason for refusing to eat with them. Narrating his stay in the bungalow of a "Khwaja Sahab" with Gandhi in 1919, he says:

> We were staying in Khwaja Sahab's bungalow in Aligarh. He was a very rich and respected man. All the people of Gandhi-ji's party had food at his place, but I did a hunger strike. When Gandhi-ji came to know of this, he called me and asked the reason for it. I smilingly replied: "Bapuji, we believe in such a culture in which cleanliness, meaning purity, has been given a high place. In their kitchens, chickens roam about, their discharges are lying around, broken egg-peels are lying around, flies are scorching the surroundings – think for yourself, how can a man of Aryan culture eat food cooked in such a place? (*unka paka hua bhojan arya sanskriti rakhne vala purush kaise kha sakta hai*)" . . . Gandhi ordered food for me from the house of a Hindu householder.[85]

---

[84] *SKM*, 126. Satyadev also disliked communism, and compared Islam and communism: "Communism is a sect that fills a man with bigotry. It destroys all kinds of progressiveness in a person . . . Communists consider their ideology innocent just like Muslims and are ready to die for it like religious fanatics . . . If a Muslim is killed for his faith, the communist kills others for his ideology": *SKM*, 427. In March 1918 the Bihar and Orissa governments blamed Satyadev for delivering a series of highly inflammatory speeches in support of the anti-cow-killing movement at Motihari in the district of Champaran, in which he allegedly appealed to the Hindu community to protect the cow at all costs and invited them to consider the numerical inferiority of Muslims. Satyadev issued a statement refuting the charges. For details, 22 July 1918, Deposit, Home Poll, NAI; "Swami Satyadeva's Speeches", *Amrit Bazaar Patrika*, 20 March 1918, 6; "Swami Satya Deva's Internment Reply to Government Communique", *The Leader*, 23 March 1918, 4.

[85] *SKM*, 232–3. Gandhi too penned this incident, as follows: "Swami Satyadev and I were Khwaja Sahib's guests. Swami Satyadev did not share my views.

Mohinder Singh shows that in the autobiography of the Arya Samajist Swami Shraddhanand, written in 1924, the trope of civilisation became one of the grounds for the foundations of nationalism and for assertions by the Swami of difference from the West.[86] With Satyadev, the trope of freedom running through his autobiography is the basis for a restricted, anti-secular, anti-Gandhian nationalism hell-bent on the exclusion of Muslims. This makes him a major forerunner of the contemporary propagandists of "love jihad" whose expressions of prejudice take shape as narratives of the abduction of Hindu women and children by Muslims. Islam, says Satyadev, is "responsible for horrific violence, brutal murders, gruesome atrocities and raping of women."[87] In a series of articles on Punjab in *Saptahik Arjun* he says, "a large majority of Muslims were abducting women and children from all corners and slashing the throats of children through rape."[88] In this precursor of Hindutva ideas there is, to quote from a different context, "an obsessive preoccupation with the predatory sexuality of the putative Muslim figure and the dangers to the integrity of the Hindu bodies."[89]

The extremist Hindu view of Partition has long been that it was the best thing to have happened to India. This too is echoed in Satyadev:

> Partition came as a boon to us and a gift due to the infinite grace of God. Well, if you think that in a country where eighty per cent of the Muslims are employed in the police and where there is a population of

---

We argued about them. I told him that holding the views I did, it would be as wrong of me to refuse to partake of the food offered by a Mussalman as it would be on his part to transgress his *maryada*. So, Swami Satyadev was provided with separate cooking arrangements": Gandhi, *Young India*, 651.

[86] Singh, "'A Question of Life'", 467.

[87] *SKM*, 123. Such Islamophobic constructions have an ongoing resilience, for example in the discourse of contemporary "love jihad": Gupta, "Allegories of 'Love Jihad'".

[88] *Saptahik Arjun*, 20 May, 8 July, 19 August, and 18 November 1935, quoted in *SKM*, 349. See also *SKM*, 351.

[89] Anand, *Hindu Nationalism*, 1, 9.

eight crore organised Muslims, could we have trampled Muslim princely states like Hyderabad-Junagadh as we wished? Could Hindi ever have become the national language? . . . The Muslim community fell into three parts with Partition – heads in Pakistan, torso in India, and legs in East Pakistan – this was a misfortune that befell Muslim militancy.[90]

Satyadev's admiration of Hitler and Nazism has been noted. The autobiography, though composed well after Hitler's defeat, continues in its adoration of blatant racism and hatred of the Other. Scholars of Hindutva rightly point to the textual origins of this rabid sentiment in the writings of Golwalkar and Savarkar,[91] but the fact is that there were very many precursors who were influential in laying the foundations of sectarian Hindu nationalism, and Satyadev's autobiography needs recognition as a Hindu riff on *Mein Kampf*. This is also, as I will try to make clear, the ideology most unashamedly clear in its support to Gandhi's assassin Godse.

Gandhi and Godse

Assassinations, it has been said, are "designed to have direct political and symbolic effects."[92] Often, lone assassins are more deadly than conspiracies, which over the long run can become fractious, porous, and difficult to implement.[93] Gandhi's murder by Nathuram Godse for reasons he made clear provides a lens through which to understand fissures and conflicts in the ideological, political, and cultural imagination of India.[94] In our own time there has been, since the dominance of the Hindu Right, a visible shift in the political climate, with increasingly popular and academic attempts to rehabilitate Godse by proclaiming him a patriotic martyr, a Hindu

---

[90] *SKM*, 468–9, 471–3.
[91] For an erudite reading of Savarkar, see Chaturvedi, *Hindutva and Violence*.
[92] Burleigh, *Day of the Assassins*, 5.
[93] Ibid.
[94] For two contrasting views: Setalvad, *Beyond Doubt*; Elst, *Mahatma Gandhi*. For a lucid analysis, Jha, *Gandhi's Assassin*. Also Hardiman, *Gandhi in His Time*, 185–94; Noorani, *Savarkar and Gandhi*; Nandy, *At the Edge*, 70–99.

hero. His birthday has been celebrated by some Hindu Mahasabha members.[95] Pradeep Dalvi's unhistorical play *Mee Nathuram Godse Boltoye* (I Am Nathuram Godse Speaking),[96] and Koenraad Elst's book *Mahatma Gandhi and His Assassin*,[97] are other instances of such revivalism. These are prefigured by Satyadev's autobiography. The portions in it that speak of Gandhi show one of the earliest defences of Godse and his perspective. Gandhi's inclusive Hinduism and nationalism were, in Satyadev's vision, anathema to those in Godse's – which he enthusiastically espoused. This was despite the fact that Satyadev had a close relationship with Gandhi between 1917 and 1922.[98] Letters between the two, and various incidents, testify to their friendship. When Satyadev was jailed for twenty days in a *faujdari* (criminal offence) case in 1918, Gandhi wrote a letter to the Bihar governor in his support. At Gandhi's urging and with his blessings Satyadev spent considerable time in Madras in 1918–19 promoting Hindi, writing a promotional booklet and corresponding with Gandhi about it.[99] In 1919–20 Satyadev toured extensively with Gandhi while campaigning for non-cooperation, even reciting a bhajan in front of 30,000 people at the historic Calcutta Session of the Indian National Congress in 1919.[100] However, after 1920 there was a marked cooling off between the two, as well as between Satyadev and the Congress.[101] According to Raghubir Sahai: "Swami Satyadev had almost given up his connection with the Congress, with Gandhiji and Motilalji towards the latter years of his life. He had become a zealous exponent of Hindi, Arya Samaj and Vedic culture, and he had almost lost faith in Congress ideology."[102]

---

[95] Noronha, "MP: Hindu Mahasabha".
[96] For a critique, Phadke, "The Murderer".
[97] Elst, *Mahatma Gandhi*.
[98] *SKM*, 195.
[99] Satyadev, *The Hindi Propaganda*; *SKM*, 202–4; letters dated 10 January and 6 February 1919 in Gandhi, *The Collected Works, 17*, 257, 277.
[100] "Refusal of a Passport to Satya Deva", 10/XVI/1924, Home Poll, NAI; *SKM*, 227–9.
[101] For example, "Beaten a Hasty Retreat: Swami Satya Deva on Bardoli Resolution", *The Leader*, 22 February 1922, 5.
[102] Interview with Raghubir Sahai by Sharma, 15.

When writing his autobiography more than thirty years later, Satyadev critiques Gandhi retrospectively by showing hostility to Gandhi's support for the dispatch of Indian recruits during World War I – where the Indians were meant to fight for the hated British against his favourite Germans.[103] He also outlines his opposition to the Khilafat struggle, in which a supposedly Hindu Gandhi supported Satyadev's mortal enemy, the Mussalman: "When Mahatma-ji combined the cart of Khilafat with the bull of Bharatvarsha, we were disoriented . . . By agreeing to Gandhi's order, a man like me also drank the bitter pill of Khilafat and joined the Non-Cooperation movement with him."[104] The withdrawal of Non-Cooperation after Chauri Chaura by Gandhi was mistaken too, says Satyadev: "Gandhi-ji's act was an unforgivable crime towards the nation. If he had been in an independent country . . . the agitated subjects would have hanged him (*uttejit praja unhen phaansi par latka deti*)."[105]

The hostility to Gandhi is virtually a leitmotif in the book. Satyadev often refers to himself as a *svavalambi* (self-supporting) sanyasi vis-à-vis Gandhi.[106] He compares and contrasts Gandhi to Hitler and Lenin and counterposes the Mahatma with Tilak: "After returning from South Africa, when Mahatma-ji started studying Indian politics, the popularity of Lokmanya pricked him like a thorn . . . I was a matchless devotee (*ananya bhakt*) of Lokmanya, so listening to Gandhi's words ignited my body with anger (*mere tan badan mein aag lag gayi*)."[107] Comparing Hitler's popularity with Gandhi's, he says:

> They were not illiterate, rustic, ignorant, and fanatical people, but were very well-educated, cultured, truthful, and dear children of parents. These young men were enchanted with Hitler's amazing renunciation, his serene character, his indomitable courage and unwavering patriotism. In India, millions of women and men who followed Mahatma Gandhi did so only emotionally and they might not have made such a huge sacrifice for Gandhi which these millions of German men of

[103] *SKM*, 210.
[104] Ibid., 233–4.
[105] Ibid., 246.
[106] *VSPM*, 207; *SKM*, 236.
[107] *SKM*, 181–2.

German descent did for Hitler the Great . . . No matter how much the world today discredits this peoples' hero of Germany, when the storm of prejudice disappears, the ghost of Communism is buried, and the balance of thought in the world is restored . . . then the world will know that . . . this Emperor Hitler who resided in the hearts of young men and women was indeed a great man who raised the morality of the race and the standard of living. He will be truly praised by later religious ideologues.[108]

Gandhi is declared a failure on various fronts:

1) Mahatma Gandhi did not succeed in any work in his life. His personal-domestic life was not successful. His sons were dissatisfied with him . . . 2) Mahatma Gandhi launched satyagraha in South Africa for the rights of Indians . . . He found no success in it. 3) Mahatma Gandhi raised the movement for Hindu–Muslim unity and fought the Khilafat battle, but all in vain! . . . 4) He marginalised Hindi and became a champion of Hindustani, which nobody could ever accept . . . 5) He ran after khadi . . . The country did not accept this either . . . Gandhi-ji's philosophy was very impractical.[109]

Vindicating Assassination

Written three years after Gandhi's assassination, a key chapter of Satyadev's autobiography is titled "Mahatma Gandhi ko ek Hindu ne Kyon Maara" (Why Did a Hindu Kill Mahatma Gandhi).[110] He asks here: "The question arises why Mahatma Gandhi – a preacher of non-violence, messenger of peace and philanthropist – was killed by a well-educated Hindu young man with his bullet? Why did Nathuram Godse – a worshipper of our culture of sages – kill Mahatma Gandhi while he was going to the prayer ground?"[111] His answer purports to be fatalistic: "When Gandhiji was killed, I came to the

[108] Ibid., 405–6.
[109] Ibid., 493–4. The autobiography is critical of Nehru as well, calling him "excessively emotional", "lacking in reason", "an unbalanced politician", "dictatorial", and "egoistic": *SKM*, 287, 402.
[110] Ibid., 508–18.
[111] Ibid., 506.

conclusion that whatever happened was done by the will and grace of God."[112] He compares the murderers of Swami Shraddhanand and Mahatma Gandhi – Abdul Rasheed and Godse, respectively. His reasoning in condemning the former and validating the latter, given his obvious preferences and prejudices, are unsurprising. Rasheed he sees as a *mazhabi diwana* (religious fanatic), and Godse as a rationalist, full of *tark* (reasoning).[113] "Mahatma Gandhiji must have committed some inexcusable mistake, on account of which a learned man like Nathuram Godse came from Poona to Delhi to kill him ... What was that mistake?"[114] The answer is simple: Gandhi's "favours" and "misconceived" policy of appeasement towards the Muslims, his "skewed" belief in non-violence:

> Gandhi-ji believed in non-violence ... But does non-violence mean that you do injustice to one community while helping another? ... Gandhi-ji started misusing his non-violence ... which became his death knell ... When Pakistan was established and lakhs of Hindus and Sikhs were driven out from Punjab ... the Hindu soul, very much wounded, began to cry. Was it not Mahatma Gandhi's duty to listen to this cry? ... We threatened Hindus and sent Muslim women to Pakistan, but did not do the same for Hindu women ... When 55 crores were given to Pakistan the Hindu heart was shattered ... The little patience which was left in Hindus was also gone ... This was the national insult which Godse embodied in himself and as a representative of pained Hindus came out of Poona to kill Mahatma Gandhi ... Gandhi-ji hit the delicate Hindu heart in its vital parts and on account of this had to give up his life.[115]

From this viewpoint Gandhi is describable by a phrase popularised in our own time by the Hindu Right – an anti-national. For Satyadev the assassin's "martyr-like outrage against Gandhi's principles", and the "punishment" necessary to "save" Hindu India provides the justification for Godse's act.[116] "Therefore, our verdict

---

[112] Ibid., 510.
[113] *VSPM*, 92; Also: *SKM*, 514.
[114] *SKM*, 514–15.
[115] Ibid., 515–17. For a critique, Vaidya, "The Murderer", 62–4.
[116] Setalvad, "Introduction", 13.

is that there was no crime committed by Nathuram Godse. It was our fault which compelled him to act against his culture and the future generation will analyse this important event similarly."[117] In the sequel to his autobiography, Satyadev reiterates that Godse was "innocent".[118]

It is worth recalling the psychological similarities between Godse and Satyadev. Godse was upper caste – a Chitpavan Brahmin from Maharashtra; he was a writer and journalist – editor of the newspaper *Hindu Rashtra*; he had embraced celibacy – he shunned his sexual self and upheld the bachelorhood that was brahmacharya; he was full of moral outrage – against "emasculated" and "soft" Hindus, the kind embodied by Gandhi; his hatred of Muslims was absolute – as was his belief in a violent, masculine Hindu nationalism. His character and predilections, in short, were wholly consonant with Satyadev's. Their subjectivities show a heavy overlap.

Gandhi's assassination has fuelled a large literature. Setalvad calls it "the first act of terror in independent India."[119] Ashis Nandy contends that Gandhi's thought – his argument for de-Brahminisation, inclusive understanding of Hinduism, rejection of a masculine Kshatriya identity, emphasis on non-violence, and re-evaluation of femininity and sexuality – threatened the very foundations of Godse's sense of his own self.[120] Others see the murder as a key turning point in the assertion of state secularism over communalism: Yasmin Khan says it was the critical moment in the consolidation of the Nehruvian state.[121]

Various hostile reviews and reactions to Satyadev's autobiography in the 1950s were only to be expected. Satyadev had set the cat among the pigeons just over the time when militant Hinduism had been encaged. The *National Herald* carried a four-column review against the book.[122] The *Blitz* published a review severely criticising

[117] *SKM*, 515–17.
[118] *VSPM*, 113.
[119] Setalvad, "Introduction", 9.
[120] Nandy, *At the Edge*, 70–99.
[121] Khan, "Performing Peace", 80.
[122] S.S., "A Book that Preached".

the autobiography.¹²³ Nehru's office issued a press note through the Press Trust of India (PTI) against it on 7 April 1952, calling the book "anti-social" and "objectionable" and refuting Satyadev's claim that the book was funded by the Congress government of Bihar at the behest of President Rajendra Prasad.¹²⁴

In the sequel to his autobiography that Satyadev published in 1952 he defended the earlier work by assailing his critics and wove a fanciful story about virtually everyone having discussed his autobiography: that a *bavaal* (tornado) had been unleashed after its publication; that the PTI had blasted a bomb (*bam-gola fata*) against it; that the "venom" and "poison" of newspaper reviews revealed a "bankruptcy of intelligence" (*buddhi ka divalyapan*); that the book had rocked the whole nation and that this had provoked a tide (*jwaarbhaata*) against it; that the editor of *Blitz* was "a snake charmer whose business is to search for dirty feats of human life like Miss Mayo"; that there was a total outcry (*hahaakaar*) in the official circles of Delhi and Lucknow around his book.¹²⁵ It was a matter of great anguish to him and grave injustice to the nation that "such a truthful, honest, courageous and inspiring biography" had been declared anti-social.¹²⁶

An equal if not larger number of reviews, particularly in the vernacular, celebrated the autobiography. On 20 January 1952 *Arya Martand*, a Hindi newspaper from Ajmer, published one of the first reviews, praised it greatly, calling it as interesting as a novel, a "must-read" for young people. The *Nagpur Times* of 10 February 1952 said it was a fabulous autobiography in Hindi of a political sanyasi who had played a prominent part in the Indian struggle. Praises for the autobiography were also published in *Kesari* (5 March 1952), and in the magazine of Gurukul Kangri, *Gurukul Patrika*, which called it crystal clear (*suspasht*) and inspiring (*utsaahak*).¹²⁷

---

¹²³ "Gandhi Deserved His Murder – Godse not at all to blame!", *Blitz*, 29 March 1952. Also *VSPM*, 58–9.
¹²⁴ Quoted in *VSPM*, 66–8.
¹²⁵ *VSPM*, 10, 28, 54–6.
¹²⁶ Ibid., 53, 69–70, 116.
¹²⁷ Quoted in *VSPM*, 14–19, 25–7, 122–4, 127.

The autobiography seems in short a showcasing of contrasting ideas on the organisation of a nation through the figures of Gandhi and Satyadev. Although both upheld a model of renunciation and celibacy, they worked and fashioned themselves in opposed ways. Gandhi was an upholder of femininity, Satyadev celebrated masculinity; Gandhi denounced wealth, Satyadev acquired a substantial amount; Gandhi advocated non-violence, Satyadev was a votary of violence; Gandhi ate frugally, Satyadev was a gourmand; Gandhi's steely resolve was cloaked within a physically feeble persona, Satyadev flourished his tall, masculine, athletic body; Gandhi was a votary of Hindu–Muslim unity, Satyadev of Hindu sangathan. Their belief in asceticism notwithstanding, they were driven in radically dissimilar directions, most crucially in relation to their conceptions of Hinduism.

Satyadev's autobiography, I have tried to show, needs to be rescued from the oblivion into which it has been consigned because, for all its fascist views and pompous self-regard, it is an important contribution to the intellectual history of sectarian Hindi-Hindu literature. Its relevance in our time of Hindutva's ascendance is, ironically, likely to be welcomed by those who are now far less inhibited in celebrating Godse and denigrating Gandhi. There can be no doubt at all that Satyadev's life story is a significant historical resource: it provides a conceptual framework forged by some of the precursors of the monolithic Hindu rashtra under construction since 2014. There has been a much needed and justifiable revival of academic interest in the founding father of Hindutva, V.D. Savarkar. I would argue that in order to properly understand and engage with some of the figures who now rule North India, and who are in the process of upending the political landscape shaped by Gandhi, Nehru, and Ambedkar, it is necessary to also read the work of Swami Satyadev Parivrajak.

IV

SATYABHAKT
(1897–1985)

7

A "Marginal" History of Vernacular Communism

Satyabhakt's historical significance is that he turned many old revolutionaries towards Marxism and mass movements . . . If any one person can be credited with being the founder of the Communist Party, he is Satyabhakt.[1]

In February [1926, M.N.] Roy wrote to a correspondent in India denouncing [Satya] Bhakta as a government spy. In April, he [Satyabhakt] and his group were expelled from the party.[2]

THESE TWO QUOTATIONS convey antithetical views of Satyabhakt, a leading Hindi journalist in early-twentieth-century North India who was the founder-organiser of the first Indian Communist Conference held at Kanpur on 26 December 1925. In this chapter I try to trace what Alan Wald calls the "force field" of communist movements.[3] I do this through the ostensibly ordinary, "paradoxical and discrepant" figure of Satyabhakt – who represents a minoritised and marginalised strand of vernacular communism – and his layered engagements through the Hindi print-public sphere of late colonial India.

The coming of communism and the formation of communist parties in India has been well documented by scholars who have highlighted the movement's international connections and influences from Russia to China; its successes and failures; its grounding in

[1] Sharma, *Bharat mein Angrezi*, 397, 407.
[2] Haithcox, *Communism and Nationalism*, 46.
[3] Wald, *Exiles*, 72.

 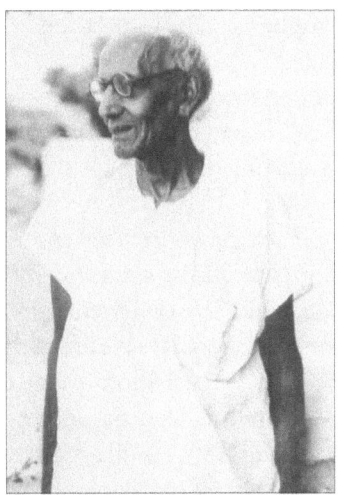

Figs 7.1-i and 7.1-ii: Satyabhakt in middle age and as an old man.

class identities and marginalisation of caste and gender concerns; its layered connections with revolutionary movements and violence; and its circuitous understandings of nationalism, secularism, and modernity.[4] While this scholarship has offered meaningful insights, the arena of "vernacular communism" – i.e. an idea of communism that politically, socially, and culturally drew from India's specific contexts, and which attempted to carve autonomous idioms and sensibilities – has remained little studied. Compounding the problem, histories of communism in India, particularly its canonised versions, are often inundated with the top-heavy dry vocabulary of academic Marxism which largely centres on the ideology's theoretical, economistic, and universal aspects. Recent works, instead,

---

[4] The literature on these various themes is substantial. Some notable examples are Raza, *Revolutionary Pasts*; Overstreet and Windmiller, *Communism in India*; Haithcox, *Communism and Nationalism*; Gupta, *Comintern, India*; Nigam, *The Insurrection*, 258–304; Seth, *Marxist Theory*; Gupta, *Communism and Nationalism*; Maitra, *Marxism in India*; Chowdhuri, *Leftism in India*; Loomba, *Revolutionary Desires*; Menon, *Caste, Nationalism;* Govind, *Between Love*; Maclean, *A Revolutionary History*; Vaidik, *Waiting for Swaraj*.

emphasise the "translation of *meaning-value* from language to language and culture to culture",[5] by which they mean a language widely understood, discussed, sung, symbolically recognised, and spoken. Such linguistic practice makes communism knowable and translatable in the language of the everyday, at the micro and regional levels.[6]

There have also been some fascinating (auto)biographies of leading communist stars and mainstream protagonists of communist ideologies in early-twentieth-century India.[7] A biography of Muzaffar Ahmad weaves his life with the origins of communism in Bengal, the radical transitions made by early communists, the growth of a Muslim intelligentsia, and the emergence of a new political space in a colonial city.[8] In his thought-provoking intellectual biography of M.N. Roy, Kris Manjapra points out that Roy has been regarded as a colonial cosmopolitan icon of the interwar years.[9] At the same time many communists who did not fit the "typical" framework or grand narratives, despite being deeply committed to visions of communism, were removed from the established centres of communist activities, relegated to the margins, almost effaced, and, worse still, demonised. While discussing alternative forms of literacy, Martha J. Cutter reflects that "the dominant discourse may involve integration within hierarchies that denigrate all 'minority' subjectivity and voice, leaving overarching power structures unchanged."[10] A recent history of the left in India makes a persuasive case for studying intermediate and everyday histories of ordinary and "errant" communists.[11] There has also been an implicit regional and linguistic bias, whereby the Hindustani-speaking region has often been sidelined in renderings of Indian communism.

[5] Liu, *Tokens of Exchange*, 2 (emphasis in the original).
[6] Shaikh, "Translating Marx", 65–6.
[7] For example, Communist Party of India (Marxist), *Memoirs*; Chattopadhyay, *An Early Communist*; Ahmad, *Myself and the Communist*; Banerjee, *S.A. Dange*.
[8] Chattopadhyay, *An Early Communist*, 2.
[9] Manjapra, *M.N. Roy*.
[10] Cutter, "Editor's Introduction", 5.
[11] Raza, *Revolutionary Pasts*, 8–13.

This chapter attempts to address some of these concerns through the prism, personality, and writings of Satyabhakt, whose life and ideas of communism show contending discourses while embodying its ordinary histories. He represents a way of imagining, writing, and practising communism in everyday life – a much more mundane articulation which also often draws on local idioms and Hindu spiritual ethics. Satyabhakt was particularly active in the communist movement from 1921 to 1927. Though he established and organised the first Indian Communist Party (ICP) and Conference, authored articles in contemporary magazines, and wrote several leaflets, tracts, and books on communism – some of which were proscribed – his marginal status in communist histories has aggravated his obscurity. With the exception of Karmendu Shishir and Ramvilas Sharma,[12] most Hindi writers on the subject have also thought him inconsequential. There was, as belated recompense, a brief "Satyabhakt Abhinandan Ank" (Commemorative Issue on Satyabhakt) issued via *Navyug Sandesh*, a weekly newspaper in Rajasthan, on 2 October 1981.

While examining the world of communist ideas in Hindi, this chapter offers a politico-historical interpretation of Satyabhakt by looking mainly at a selection of his journalistic writings, books, and fragmentary autobiographies. I begin by considering the times in which he lived in relation to some of the leftist trends in the Hindi nonfictional writings to which he made a significant contribution. The second section provides another context to Satyabhakt's Hindi communist print world by briefly highlighting the dynamics of the first Indian Communist Conference (ICC) and how Satyabhakt's indigenous and nationalist visions of communism were incongruent with international communist politics. I show how this played a role in his marginalisation, and often even downright denunciation. Disputing such a framing, the final section explores some of Satyabhakt's Hindi writings on communism, deliberating on the possibilities and limitations of his interventions and their relationship to a broad leftist arena. My story of Indian communism, as enunciated through Satyabhakt, tries to move beyond the many homogenised accounts of communism in India. Relying on a vernacular frame, I offer a

[12] Shishir, *Satyabhakt*; Sharma, *Bharat mein Angrezi*.

mutant vision. My view is that even if his ideas were at times flawed or amateur, Satyabhakt provides an ethical communist imaginary which needs firmer historicisation.

Historical Antecedents, Hindi and Communism

Political currents in the interwar years had a crucial bearing on Satyabhakt's evolution. The "international moment" signalled by the Bolshevik Revolution became a major inspirational event for the growth of communism in other countries, including India.[13] On the domestic front the advent of M.K. Gandhi signified a new mass turn of the freedom struggle, with the Khilafat Movement also contributing to a communist flowering.[14] In the aftermath of the Russian Revolution, communist literature began entering India, inspiring publications in the regional languages, including Urdu and Hindi. Paranoid British authorities started making serious moves to suppress communist ideas, and the colonial Home Department established a special branch to monitor the growing influence of communism, resulting in the banning of many books on the subject.[15] Between 1922 and 1929 there were three conspiracy trials against communist activities in North India: the Peshawar Conspiracy Case (1922), the Kanpur Bolshevik Conspiracy Case (1924), and the Meerut Conspiracy Case (1929). These had critical political implications, with many newspapers reporting their happenings, magazines publishing articles on communism and its doctrines, and the people of the region reading about this ideology for the first time on such a large scale.

Alongside, the development of the railways, increasing urbanisation, large-scale migrations from villages to cities, and World War I signalled a huge growth of industries and workers in many cities of India. Small communist groups started operation in several scattered

[13] Saha, *The Russian Revolution*, 110–37.
[14] Minault, *The Khilafat Movement*.
[15] Kaye, *Communism in India*; Petrie, *Communism in India*.

regions – Bengal, Bombay, Madras, Punjab, and UP. Significantly, Satyabhakt's most productive and overtly communist phase was between 1923 and 1926 when he moved to Kanpur, one of the most important industrial centres of North India and a key site of communist activities from the 1920s. Kanpur saw an enormous growth in its worker numbers. Casual, migrant, largely rural unorganised labourers and small artisans mingled with a relatively organised and stable industrial and factory working class in the region, with trade unions coming into being and evolving. The social and political milieu of the city was conducive to vibrant workers' movements and communist ideas.[16] The existence of a group of communist workers was noted in Kanpur in January 1923.[17]

In the 1920s and 1930s communist print cultures were thriving in the vernacular and provincial worlds, with many Urdu litterateurs active in the Progressive Writers' Association.[18] In Hindi too there emerged a group of progressive writers, including Premchand, Yashpal, Rahul Sankrityayan, Rambriksh Benipuri, and Sahajanand Saraswati, exemplifying the impact of socialist ideas and ideals on creativity.[19] There had been earlier stalwarts – such as Radhamohan Gokul, Ramashankar Awasthi, Dashrath Prasad Dwivedi, Ganesh Shankar Vidyarthi, and Satyabhakt – most of them relatively unnoticed and unsung. Many of these first-generation anti-colonial communists and left intellectuals writing in Hindi framed utopian projects that led to impressive literary expressions which, in turn, expanded progressive and political subjectivity. These vernacular writers can be seen as adapting Marxism to Indian conditions. They enmeshed their admiration for socialism, rationalism, and leftist thinking within their commitment to swaraj, nationalism, Hindu traditions, and religious idioms.[20] Simultaneously, they drew on decentralised networks

---

[16] For workers' movements in Kanpur, see Joshi, *Lost Worlds*.
[17] "Communist Activities in India", L/PJ/12/132, IOR, BL.
[18] For details, Ahmed, *Literature and Politics*; Jalil, *Liking Progress*.
[19] For the revolutionary in Hindi novels, Govind, *Between Love*.
[20] Scholarship on Hindi print cultures has paid little attention to leftist leanings. For an exception, Govind, *Between Love*. However, he looks only at novels. The authoritative work still remains Sharma, *Bharat mein Angrezi*.

of knowledge, native sensibilities, and new vernacular possibilities, using their poetic licence to confront British imperialism and simplify the language of communism.

Many books on the Russian Revolution – for example, *Rus mein Yugantar* (New Era in Russia), and *Rus ka Punarjanam* (Rebirth of Russia) – were published in Hindi in the 1920s. Ramashankar Awasthi initially worked in the Pratap Press with Ganesh Shankar Vidyarthi (1890–1931), and later became the editor of *Vartman*. He published various articles on the Russian Revolution in *Maryada*.[21] His several books on the subject included *Rus ki Rajya Kranti*, *Bolshevik Jadugar* (probably the first biography of Lenin in Hindi), and *Lal Kranti*.[22] Krishnakant Malaviya, editor of the weekly paper *Abhyudaya* and the magazine *Maryada*, both based in Allahabad, published various writers as well as his own writings on the subject. Between 1918 and 1920 *Maryada* was the foremost regular publisher of sympathetic articles on the Russian Revolution. In fact, the history and spread of Bolshevism in Hindi cannot be understood without acknowledging the role of *Maryada*.[23] Malaviya wrote and published a series in the journal titled "Sansar-Sankat", which outlined and spread the news coming out of Russia. Ganesh Shankar Vidyarthi was another influential journalist of this ilk. A leading light in Kanpur who was editor of the spirited Hindi newspaper *Pratap*, he was also the founder of the Mazdoor Sabha, a workers' organisation in the region. A Gandhian nationalist, he was aligned with Congress and inspired by socialist ideas, his writings, speeches, and work revealing a mix of religious rhetoric upholding Hindu concerns, dedication to workers and the oppressed, and a repudiation of the very communal violence which resulted in his martyrdom – he was killed in Kanpur trying to rescue Muslim women from a rioting mob.[24] Radhamohan Gokul (1865–1935), referred to by some as the "Charvak" of Hindi,[25] and editor of the fiery half-weekly *Pranvir* published from

---

[21] Sharma, *Bharat mein Angrezi*, 266–9.

[22] Awasthi, *Rus ki Rajya*; idem, *Bolshevik Jadugar*; idem, *Lal Kranti*.

[23] Sharma, *Bharat mein Angrezi*, 237–42, 261–5; Singh, *Samajvad*, 22–6.

[24] On Vidyarthi, Salil, *Ganesh Shankar*; Joshi, *Lost Worlds*, 278–87; Orsini, *The Hindi Public*, 351–2.

[25] "Charvak" being a reference to the exemplary philosopher of the tradi-

Nagpur, was a revolutionary, a Sanatani, a social reformer, and a communist. Agnostic, materialist, and steeped in the progressive heritage of Hindu philosophy, he was one of the earliest Hindi litterateurs to pour his life into communist dreams, even while assisting many revolutionaries with finance and inspirational literature. His books and publications ranged from *Desh ka Dhan* (1906) to *Communism Kya Hai* (1927).[26] His pamphlets on socialism and Marxism helped convert a number of young people in Kanpur and elsewhere to the cause of socialism, and he was instrumental in introducing its ideas to, among others, Bhagat Singh.[27] Equally, Hindi magazines and newspapers like *Inqalab* from Lahore, *Pranvir* from Nagpur, *Swadesh* from Gorakhpur, and *Pratap* and *Vartman* from Kanpur were promoting socialist ideas.[28]

Satyabhakt is a critical figure here because his left leanings were embedded in the Hindi sensibility of a vernacular journalist, as well as belief in Hindu spiritualism.[29] However, unlike many others attracted in the same direction, he was also an active contributor on the ground who seemed aware of Marx's dictum that "the task is not just to understand the world but to change it." This is evident from the fact that he felt driven enough to establish a formal communist party. It will not do to dismiss him as an amateur Marxist: his life shows the potential to dream as well as translate some of the dreams into practical organisational realities in the cause of communism – a party, a journal, a series of pamphlets, a newspaper. Describing Satyabhakt by the phrase "Is Yug ka Itihaas Purush" (A Man of History for this Era), Manmath Nath Gupta (1908–2000), the leading Marxist revolutionary writer and a member of the Hindustan Republican Association, said: "The name of Satyabhakt is foremost among the few

---

tion of atheistic philosophy in ancient Hindu thought. A contemporary text which deploys the figure of Charvak (to narrate an anti-Hindutva history of Indian nationalism) is Chatterjee, *The Truths and Lies*.

[26] Gokul, *Communism Kya Hai?* On Gokul, Shishir, *Radhamohan Gokul*; Kaljayee, *Ek the Radhamohan*.

[27] Vaidik, *Waiting for Swaraj*, 50–1.

[28] Shishir, *Satyabhakt*, 11–12.

[29] Satyabhakt's commitment to Hindi was strong: "Hindi Gadya ka Kram Vikas".

people who broke through the darkness ... of imperialism and revealed the reality of the Russian Revolution ... It is undisputed that the credit goes to him for sounding the first trumpet of socialism in the temple of Hindi literature" (*Hindi sahitya ke mandir mein samajvad ka danka pehle pehal bajane ka shrey hai*).[30] Satyabhakt's corpus reveals a multifaceted early grassroots communist who wrote mainly nonfiction and was part of an urban Hindi literati.

Satyabhakt was born as Chakan Lal in Bharatpur, Rajasthan, on 2 April 1897, where he received his earlier education.[31] His father, Kundanlal, was a teacher in a medical school and a firm supporter of swadeshi. Early in his life Satyabhakt was exposed to the weekly *Bharat Mitra*, Gokul's *Satya Sanatan Dharma*, and *Pratap*. He devoured books such as *Desh ki Baat*,[32] Bankim Chandra's famous *Anandamath*, and later *Underground Russia* and *Nihilist Rahasya*, all of which shaped his revolutionary spirit.[33] Between 1912 and 1916 he was deeply impressed by Satyanarayan, a famous poet who wrote on diverse subjects including *sringar* (decorated beauty), bhakti, and nationalism. He also came in contact with two well-regarded Hindi writers, Banarsidas Chaturvedi and Narayan Prasad Arora, an association that continued for a long time. In 1912–13 he tried his hand at making a crude bomb – which burst prematurely, permanently injuring a finger.[34] In 1916, as part of an organisation called the Bharat Sevak Samiti, he worked as a volunteer in Haridwar's Kumbh where he met Gandhi. Like many who were greatly taken by the Mahatma's charisma, Satyabhakt went to live in his ashram for

[30] Gupta, "Agragaami Lekhak", 19. Another writer called Ram Dulari Trivedi remarked: "Satyabhakt was the first man to put the sign board of Communist in our country": Interview with Satyabhakt by Damodaran, 6.

[31] This biographical sketch of Satyabhakt is drawn from: Interview with Satyabhakt by Sharma; Interview with Satyabhakt by Damodaran; Shishir, *Satyabhakt*, 14–33; Satyabhakt, *Kranti Path*, 415–32. Also Singh, "Satyabhakt: Hindi Navjagran".

[32] This was a Hindi translation of the famous *Deshar Katha*, written by Sakharam Ganesh Deuskar in 1904, which was widely read during the partition of Bengal. Also Pande, *Desh ki Baat*.

[33] Stepniak, *Underground Russia*.

[34] Consequently, Satyabhakt was on police watch for the next twenty years.

a few months, where he translated, among others, Gandhi's *Sarvodaya* and *Jail ke Anubhav* into Hindi. Not fully convinced with the doctrine of non-violence and some of Gandhi's other beliefs, he departed from the ashram, harbouring an unease that prevented him being a wholehearted Gandhian.[35] His contact with Gandhi continued all the same and between 1916 and 1920 he started the "Rashtriya Granthmala" (National Book Series), publishing several booklets priced at 1 anna. These were around 15–20 pages each, including *Asahyog* (Non-Cooperation), *Swadeshi par Mahatma Gandhi* (Mahatma Gandhi on Swadeshi), *Schoolon ka Boycott* (Boycott of Schools), *Satyagraha Rahasya* (Satyagraha Secrets), and *Gandhi Charitra* (Gandhi's Biography).[36] Many of them were reprinted several times. In 1921 he took to wearing khadi; moreover, he studiously avoided critiquing Gandhi all his life.[37] It seems apparent that his ideological differences with Gandhi notwithstanding, the Gandhian inspiration persisted throughout: he continued to believe in the principles of simplicity, hard physical labour, and a strong work ethic. In this he resembled the many revolutionaries and communists in colonial India who incorporated into their praxis a Gandhian aesthetic of simplicity, austerity, and renunciation; Indian communism was often "tainted", so to say, by ascetic subtexts and quasi-religious lineages.[38] True to his humble background, Satyabhakt lived an austere

---

[35] In his later years Satyabhakt recollected and compared Gandhian and revolutionary movements, firmly standing with the latter: "I have coincidentally observed both these movements very closely . . . On that basis I have reached the conclusion that if 10–20 lakh or even 50 lakh people participated in Mahatmaji's movement, 90–95 per cent of these went back to their old ways within a year or two . . . In comparison to that, even if the number of people who participated in the revolutionary movement never reached even a thousand, those who came to it came with faith and a sense of self-sacrifice and then could never leave it soon": Satyabhakt, *Kranti ka Agaman*, 12.

[36] These pamphlets have no year or place of publication. Some of them can be accessed here: List B, "List of Private Papers: Satya Bhakta Papers, Acc. No. 287" (hereafter Acc. 287), NAI. He also wrote some articles in praise of Gandhi: "Mahatma Gandhi".

[37] Interview with Satyabhakt by Sharma, 23.

[38] Dasgupta, "The Ascetic Modality". Similarly, a Hindi booklet *Khaddar*

life throughout and seems never to have been tempted into accumulating wealth or property.

He was drawn more powerfully towards revolutionary and leftwing politics. Changing his name to "Satyabhakt" (lit. "worshipper of truth"), he became an active Hindi journalist in 1916. Being a restless sort of soul, he moved constantly from one place and job to another. In 1919 Pandit Sundar Lal, who published a weekly called *Bhavishya* from Allahabad, invited Satyabhakt to join him. There Satyabhakt witnessed a momentous political strike as well as a meeting which had 50,000 people. When *Bhavishya* closed down, Satyabhakt went to work for K.K. Malaviya's *Maryada*. In early 1923 Gokul, a fervent communist and editor of the influential half-weekly *Pranvir* of Nagpur, jailed for six months, noticed the revolutionary edge in Satyabhakt's writings and asked him to be its editor. Satyabhakt remained a great admirer of Gokul all his life and the two enjoyed a close relationship.[39] While in Nagpur, Satyabhakt published a daily bulletin and reports on the famous Flag Satyagraha of 1923 in *Pranvir* and *Pratap*.[40] In September 1923 he decided to move to Kanpur, "the heart of the workers' movement",[41] and this began the

---

Posh Athva Kranti Ki Jai (Khadi-clad or Victory to the Revolution) published in Agra in 1930 depicted armed revolutionary socialists wanting to establish a "revolutionary republic" modelled on Russia, who also become the guardians of the Gandhian movement: Loomba, *Revolutionary Desires*, 76–8.

[39] Gokul greatly helped Satyabhakt in giving a new edge to communism in Kanpur, and in the formation of the party. Satyabhakt also published extensively on Gokul after his death: Satyabhakt, "Swargiya Radhamohan"; idem, *Kranti Path*, 312–412; idem, *Kranti ka Agaman*. The last was a compilation of Gokul's writings, including his famous *Viplav*, with a long introduction by Satyabhakt.

[40] For details on the Satyagraha: "Jhanda Satyagraha Nagpur", PP 5454/1923, Sardar Patel, Digitised Private Papers, NAI. Satyabhakt said: "I used to go to the place of arrest every day and bring news items and prepare the newspaper at night and send it for sales in the morning. I used to send the same news by wire to *Pratap* in Kanpur. This satyagraha continued for three months": Interview with Satyabhakt by Sharma, 15–16.

[41] Interview with Satyabhakt by Sharma, 14–15; Interview with Satyabhakt by Damodaran, 4.

most significant period of his life. For a while he aligned passionately with the labour movement, becoming a member of the Hind Mazdoor Sabha, taking part in labour agitations and issuing socialist pamphlets. Soon he announced the founding of the ICP and called for the first ICC, but left it after a short while due to internal differences.[42] Simultaneously, he wrote books, pamphlets, articles, and reports on communism, ran a "Satyug Press", and for a short while in 1939 published a magazine called *Satyug* which had affinities with Hindu belief. Over this period his several articles in magazines like *Saraswati, Maryada, Matvala, Lalita, Prabha*, and *Chand*, as well as around a hundred books and tracts, covered diverse subjects. Facing financial difficulties, he shifted to Agra in 1927, then to Bombay for a few months. In 1929 he again moved to Allahabad and edited *Chand* for several years.

A secretive aspect of Satyabhakt's life was that while he himself was of the Bania (Vaishya) caste – which he never used as his identity marker – he married a Dalit, possibly a sweeperess, servant, and/or widow, because of which he was ostracised from his family all his life.[43] In 1955, facing poverty, extreme hardship, and familial as well as social marginalisation, he associated himself with a religious body, the Akhand Jyoti Sansthan of Mathura, which was run by one of his old friends. Here he wrote eighty-five very popular short biographical tracts under a series called "Yug Nirman Yojana" (Plan for a New Era). He continued in penury, living in a room in Mathura, where he died on 3 December 1985.

Satyabhakt's chaotic life and writings reveal that, away from atheist and secular alignments, he derived the moral legitimacy of communism through nationalism, vernacularism, and Hindu spiritualism. For him socialism and communism were not abstract doctrines but ideas that had to be understood, interpreted, and practised in everyday life. At various stages, through critical self-reflection, he

[42] "Indian Communist Party: Satya Bhakte's", L/PJ/12/57, IOR, BL (hereafter L/PJ/12/57).

[43] This is not listed anywhere, except a reliable reference in Shishir, *Satyabhakt*, 29. After the marriage, Satyabhakt's relations with his family deteriorated and they adopted a contemptuous attitude towards him: Interview with Karmendu Shishir.

challenged his marginalisation and crafted himself as a proactive participant of communist lineage in India. His books after independence in the 1970s – *Kranti Path ke Pathik* (1973) which was a select history of the freedom movement and communism in India,[44] and *Kranti ka Agaman* (1974) which was largely a compilation of the landmark writings of Gokul[45] – were serious undertakings in the politics of memorialising the self and being remembered as a communist. In his various interviews Satyabhakt downplayed, or even effaced, aspects of his writings and literary activities, preferring to record himself as an active subject and actor in the making of communism in India. He ensured that fragments of his life, particularly his efforts at forming the ICP, and his life between 1923 and 1927, were preserved in the National Archives of India,[46] the Prime Minister's Museum and Library,[47] and the P.C. Joshi Archives of Contemporary History at Jawaharlal Nehru University, all in New Delhi. However, for his disparate engagements in the Hindi literary sphere, and his other substantial but scattered writings, one has to dig into the Hindi magazines of the time, and in the small local libraries of UP.

The First Communist Conference and Satyabhakt's Marginalisation

Satyabhakt was at the forefront of floating the idea of a Communist Party catering to Indian needs. He has been widely regarded as the founder and organiser of the first ICC, held in Kanpur on 26 December 1925.[48] Forming the Bhartiya Samyavadi Dal (the ICP) on 1 September 1924, between 1923 and 1926 he worked continuously for the promotion of both party and conference through pamphlets, bulletins, advertisements, appeals, books, articles, and reports. Although largely due to M.N. Roy's efforts a communist party had

[44] Satyabhakt, *Kranti Path*.
[45] Satyabhakt, *Kranti ka Agaman*.
[46] Acc. 287, NAI.
[47] "List of Small Collections: First Indian Communist Conference Papers 1925, List No. 190 (XXXXV), Acc. No. 299" (hereafter Acc. 299), PMML.
[48] For details, Kaushik and Mitrokhin, "First Indian", 67–71.

been formed in Tashkent in October 1920 soon after the Second Congress of the Communist International (Comintern), the Kanpur Conference was nevertheless seen as the formal launching of a communist party within India, the first open effort to develop a communist network all over the country. While the Communist Party of India (Marxist), i.e. the CPI (M) draws its initial inspiration from the Tashkent formation, the Communist Party of India (CPI) marks its roots from the Kanpur Conference. On 1 September 1924 Satyabhakt declared through newspapers like *Aaj* (Banaras), *Pratap* (Kanpur), and *Bande Mataram* (Calcutta) that an ICP has been formed "with branches at Calcutta, Madras, Bombay and Cawnpore", and that "an All-India Communist Conference will be held in three months' time."[49] The party and conference created quite a buzz initially, especially in the vernacular press of UP. Satyabhakt was quoted in almost all such articles and he himself published widely on the subject.[50] From February 1925 "ICP" appeared as a separate sub-heading in the *Native Newspaper Reports* (*NNR*) of UP.[51]

During the Kanpur Bolshevik Case trial, the court declared it was not illegal to spread communist ideas, and "to have faith in communism in itself is no offense", which motivated Satyabhakt to legally float a communist party with no need for subterfuge.[52] Further, after the arrest and conviction of Shaukat Usmani in the Bolshevik Conspiracy Case, the "mantle" of promulgating communism in UP fell on Satyabhakt.[53] The initial founding members included, among others, Gokul, Narayan Prasad Arora, Hasrat Mohani, Ramashankar Awasthi, Ramprasad Mishra, Shaukat Usmani, and Munnilal Awasthi.[54] In a letter to the *Socialist* in 1924, Satyabhakt mentioned

[49] Satyabhakt, *Bharat mein Samyavad*, 32; Roy, *Communism in India*, 109.
[50] *NNR, 1925–26.*
[51] *NNR*, week ending 14 February 1925, 5.
[52] Petrie, *Communism in India*, 66. In the Kanpur Bolshevik Case, many communists were charged with a conspiracy to separate India from Britain through violent revolution, though the court stated that it was not in itself illegal to propagate communism.
[53] Ibid., 171.
[54] The provisional general rules of the ICP stated their first objective as

some fifty people, "including several prominent personages", having become members of the ICP.[55] It was reported that over the first three months seventy-eight people from diverse occupations and regions filled out membership forms.[56] By March 1925 the membership had risen to 215, of which 139 were residents of UP.[57] Satyabhakt attributed the "slow progress to the lack of intelligent and efficient workers who understand what communism is, and are prepared to devote themselves to its interests."[58] The ICC, held outside the compound where the annual session of the Indian National Congress was taking place, was attended by about 400 delegates. A central committee was formed which decided to establish the party headquarters in Bombay, with branches in Lahore, Kanpur, Madras, and Calcutta.[59] Though Satyabhakt was initially appointed to the executive committee as UP provincial secretary, he soon found himself without influence and therefore left the organisation.[60] Later he reflected on his move away from active communist work, stating his dire economic situation, extreme tiredness, and differences with some of his views: "For me it was just a change of route. My main work earlier

---

being "to secure the freedom of India by all practical means", and "to establish a workers' and farmers' republic through nationalisation of the means and instruments of production and distribution, such as land, mines, factories, railways, tramways, ships etc by and in the interest of the whole community of India": F. 1, Acc. 299, PMML; F. 14, List A, Acc. 287, NAI.

[55] Petrie, *Communism in India*, 67; L/PJ/12/57. There were, of course, some prominent people active in various regions of India, for example, Dange in Bombay, Muzaffar Ahmad in Calcutta, M. Singaravelu in Madras, and Gulam Hussain in Punjab.

[56] Petrie, *Communism in India*, 172; Interview with Satyabhakt by Sharma, 32.

[57] Petrie, *Communism in India*, 172, 174.

[58] L/PJ/12/57.

[59] For further details Chattopadhyay, *An Early Communist*, 147–8.

[60] Divisions appeared over connections with the Comintern between S.V. Ghate, Joglekar, and Muzaffar Ahmad on the one hand, and Hasrat Mohani, Arjanlal Sethi, and Satyabhakt on the other. With the ascendancy of the former group, Satyabhakt's proposals were outvoted and defeated, and he soon left the conference and then the organisation.

too had been to promote [communism] through newspapers and books. And now I started walking on the same path. Unlike leaders, I never gave powerful speeches that could inspire people. That did not suit my basic nature."[61] In another interview he said: "I have worked only for communism, not the communist party. I have faith in communism. The party is a different thing. In a party, there are certain people . . . good and bad."[62]

Various documents, debates, and details are available on the ICC and happenings thereafter.[63] Commentaries on Satyabhakt focus on his role in, and understanding of, the conference and communism in India. All the official communist and left narratives pertaining to Satyabhakt seem in agreement on his dismissal, demonisation, and denunciation. They disparage him for his ill-informed, ideologically deviant, and flawed understandings of communism and Marxism; his breaking away from and antagonism towards the Comintern; his ridicule of M.N. Roy; his insistence on giving the party a legal framework; his faith in Hindu and nationalist idioms; and his enforced distancing from workers and the communist movement.[64]

One of the main grounds of contention between Satyabhakt and others was on the international versus the national perspective of the party, with Satyabhakt representing the latter. This was reflected concretely in the politics of naming the party, with Satyabhakt insisting on the "Indian Communist Party" rather than the "Communist Party of India" in order to underline its distinctly autonomous and nationalist orientation. He strongly opposed interventions and controls from far away, including Russia and England, as well as affiliation to the Comintern. His interest was in establishing an independent, indigenous, national communist party.[65] From the viewpoint of Marxism as an international brotherhood of workers, Satyabhakt's view was deviant: "Satya Bhakta's ignorance of the first

[61] Interview with Satyabhakt by Sharma, 30.
[62] Interview with Satyabhakt by Damodaran, 9–10.
[63] For example: Kaushik and Mitrokhin, "First Indian", 67–71.
[64] For example Adhikari, *Documents of the History*, Vol. II, 406–7, 592–6, 600, 615, 618–20; Karnik, *M.N. Roy*.
[65] Petrie, *Communism in India*, 165–6.

principle of communism – that it is international – was duly exposed ... Satya Bhakta's national communism ... had been somewhat un-Marxian."[66] International communism and its global networks were dominant in colonial India.[67] For Satyabhakt, by contrast, it was critical to ask if universalist ideas and controls from distant contexts worked for Indian communism. Partha Chatterjee sums up the dilemma: "First, there was a universalisation of the Bolshevik model ... Comintern control over revolutionary internationalism meant that other forms of organisation or strategy were neither properly understood nor encouraged. Second ... there was a strong centralisation of the international movement directed from Moscow."[68]

Disapproving communism as an import with overarching control outside the country, the vernacular proponent's view was that communism needed to be home grown. When drafting the manifesto of the ICP Satyabhakt was firm: "We are an absolutely independent body. Our relation with the Third International is of the nature of friendship and mutual sympathy ... but we do not want to take orders or instructions from others."[69] He reiterated similar positions in articles he wrote in newspapers of the time, arguing that an international alliance "would only offer government a pretext to suppress the Indian Communist Party. India cannot adopt a programme of violence, and as a subject country its voice will carry little weight in the International. The most important thing is therefore the freedom of the country without which neither communistic nor any other reforms can be introduced."[70] Marxism needed a distinctly Indian shape and alignment with nationalism. His books reflect the same argument: "Even while firmly believing in communism, due to the differences between our circumstances and culture, it is natural for us and foreign communists to have some

[66] 89/1930, Home Poll, NAI.
[67] Raza, *Revolutionary Pasts*.
[68] Chatterjee, "Nationalism, Internationalism", 328.
[69] *Indian Communist Party: A Manifesto*, F. 9, Acc. 299, PMML. Also L/PJ/12/57; *The Leader*, 28 June 1925, 5.
[70] *NNR*, week ending 7 November 1925, 5.

difference in our ways."⁷¹ His focus was on the particular, the local, and the indigenous, which could entail abandoning the universal and the international. In an interview in 1974 he repeats the idea: "I believed that India's condition was different from other countries. In particular, it had to get rid of a forced foreign rule. Therefore, its communist programme had to be different from others . . . Some young men . . . had started considering internationalism as a big ideal, even if it was not at all practical at that time."⁷²

Satyabhakt was an admirer of Peter Kropotkin (1842–1921), the Russian activist and philosopher who was on the margins of the revolutionary upheaval. Kropotkin was against a centralised Bolshevik leadership and advocated a decentralised anarcho-communist society. Satyabhakt translated Kropotkin's book, *An Appeal to the Young*, as *Navyuvakon se Do Baten* (1927); it was also published in *Vishal Bharat* and widely circulated.⁷³ Despite disparaging the international leanings of communism, he was inspired by the Irish Sinn Fein and its nationalist movement.⁷⁴ He wrote *Ireland ke Gadar ki Kahaniyan* in 1927,⁷⁵ and, with additions, the novel *Gorilla* in 1946, echoing his enthusiasm and support for guerrilla warfare.⁷⁶

Given the tenor of Satyabhakt's views, his differences with M.N. Roy's positions were inevitable. Manjapra begins Roy's intellectual biography by "situating him beyond the regnant binaries of the 'local' versus 'global', or 'subaltern knowledge' versus 'Western episteme'."⁷⁷ And yet when it comes to Satyabhakt, this sounds dubious. Till late 1924 Roy was unaware of Satyabhakt, "a professed Communist of Cawnpore" who was "tolerably well-known in India."⁷⁸ Considering

⁷¹ Satyabhakt, *Bharat mein Samyavad*, 3.
⁷² Interview with Satyabhakt by Sharma, 21.
⁷³ Satyabhakt, *Kranti Path*, 419. The translation is also available in Satyabhakt, *Samyavad ka Sandesh*.
⁷⁴ The Irish Sinn Fein inspired many Indian nationalists: Silvestri, *Ireland and India*; O'Malley, *Ireland, India*.
⁷⁵ Satyabhakt, *Ireland ke Gadar*. On account of its proscription, the book could not be sold freely.
⁷⁶ Satyabhakt, *Gorilla*.
⁷⁷ Manjapra, *M.N. Roy*, xiii.
⁷⁸ Petrie, *Communism in India*, 75.

him a writer of some "bombastic letters to our British comrades," Roy came to regard Satyabhakt with extreme suspicion.[79] He viewed Satyabhakt's reliance on indigeneity as a skewed and inferior understanding of communism and referred to him as an "imposter".[80] Worse, he called him "a government spy" and suggested that Satyabhakt and the ICP were "a ruse of Government to attract people of communist tendencies in order to worm out their secrets." In Roy's view the ICP had been permitted to exist for nearly eighteen months by the government only because it was "organised under official inspiration and was headed by *provocateurs* . . . The object was to use this party as a trap for all Communists, but the strategy failed."[81] He was also "opposed to [the] legalist deviation" of the communist party as he believed that would make it "a harmless nominal entity, unworthy of repression."[82] In his biography of Roy, V.B. Karnik refers to Satyabhakt as "a left-wing Congressman" and "a person of doubtful character."[83] Satyabhakt, in turn, published a leaflet attacking Roy, denouncing him as a British spy, a "self-interested" person, and a "hired agitator" who received "money from Moscow" with the chief object of filling "his pockets".[84] Roy's financial status as well as the apparently enormous sums he received from the Comintern for financing the communist movement in India, and his alleged lack of a moral ethic, made Satyabhakt deeply sceptical of Roy; he felt foreign money was suspect and communism in India needed to be furthered solely by indigenous effort.[85] Quoting from various government reports, books, and documents available now in the National Archives, and combining them with his own views, Satyabhakt's

---

[79] Ibid., 101–4.

[80] "Question of Publication Material about Communist & M. N. Roy Letters", 190/1928, Home Poll, NAI.

[81] Petrie, *Communism in India*, 104, 119.

[82] "Activities in India of Non-Indian Communists", 18/VII, Home Poll, NAI. Roy seems to have played an important role in marginalising Satyabhakt.

[83] Karnik, *M.N. Roy*, 222, 226 fn.

[84] Satyabhakt, *The Indian Communists and M.N. Roy*, Leaflet, Cawnpore, 1 May 1926, F. 6, Acc. 299, PMML; F. 18, List A, Acc. 287, NAI.

[85] L/PJ/12/57; *NNR*, week ending 7 November 1925, 5.

Bharat Mein Samyavad continued the severity against Roy, who was blamed for bungling funds.[86] Some of the charges against Roy appear to have been prompted by spite rather than evidence.[87]

The unstated problem for vernacular intellectuals such as Satyabhakt was a deep-rooted hostility to what they perceived as the airs and graces of the English-centric communist whose language skills allowed him to feel equally at home outside India and which made him relatively indifferent to national boundaries. The brotherhood promised by Marxism was the ideal while the ground reality was, in part, constituted by the unacknowledged class antagonism between specific communists. Some comrades gave out the sense of seeing themselves as more equal than others, for which a major reason was the English language. Linguistic superiority gave the internationalist skilled in English a feeling of social elevation which the indigenous nationalist resented: the obvious analogue of this in our own time is the hostility of Hindi-Hindutva adherents to the English-speaking literati whom they denounce as the "Khan Market Gang".[88] People like Satyabhakt, by contrast, were more grounded, empirical, immediate, and particular on account of their embeddedness within the vernacular and the regional.[89] Satyabhakt's positions, while at times problematic, reflect "the complexity of conflict between local cultures and high theory"; where Roy and others of his ilk were adopting

---

[86] Satyabhakt, *Bharat Mein Samyavad*, 19.

[87] Petrie, *Communism in India*, 109.

[88] A reference to New Delhi's affluent classes who frequent the upmarket shops of Khan Market in the city centre.

[89] Roy has, of course, left behind a rich legacy of intellectual ideas, and was deeply committed to human freedom and dignity. And yet, it has been argued, "Roy was never able to establish his bona fides as an Indian nationalist. His frequent and caustic criticism of Gandhi and Indian tradition stood in the way": Haithcox, *Communism and Nationalism*, 252–3. Ramvilas Sharma argues that "Roy subordinated the original goal of rooting out imperialism, and made destruction of indigenous capitalism his basic goal. Indigenous capitalism was associated with the national independence movement. Roy's strategy was to divide the freedom movement, keep the working class away from that movement and thus help imperialism": Sharma, *Bharat Mein Angrezi Raj*, 415.

a "language of universalism", Satyabhakt was asserting an "ineradicable difference".[90]

Satyabhakt's heterodoxy was not unique: there were many voices expressing socialist and communist ideals in diverse ways and distinct idioms. In 1921 communists like Virendranath Chattopadhyay visited Moscow and presented a thesis to Lenin which was couched in nationalist frames and prioritised the destruction of British imperialism.[91] K. Damodaran (1912–1975) delved deep into ancient Indian philosophical traditions and drew on indigenous and vernacular knowledge found in the *Charaka Samhita* and *Khagol Vidya*, both Sanskrit texts which had the potential to align with communist thought. Sohan Singh Josh (1898–1982), a dynamic communist leader from Punjab, began as an activist in the Sikh Akali movement and became a leading light of the Kirti Kisan Sabha and the Naujawan Bharat Sabha. He "wove together revolutionary nationalism, communist internationalism and regional expressions of politics, together with their linguistic, social, cultural and religious registers."[92] It is in conjunction with such voices that Satyabhakt's needs to be heard.

There were, of course, serious limitations to his vernacular fabric and working methods. He often lacked theoretical rigour and represented a seemingly pedestrian outlook; he was quite an individualist, an isolated voice with a limited base; he often began very enthusiastically but did not have the vision to sustain what he had begun; and ignoring the atheistic worldview of international communism he remained doggedly rooted in a Hindu spiritual ethic. These "flaws" – a term favoured by the dominant to further sideline the already subordinate – do not suffice as reasons to ignore figures such as Satyabhakt. What has been all too often dismissed by the voice of hegemony as ephemeral or incoherent is all too often the voice of the vernacular. The consequence, as I have earlier argued in relation to Santram, Yashoda, and Satyadev, is that a substantial world remains

[90] Nigam, *The Insurrection*, 267.
[91] Gupta, *Comintern, India*, 46–9.
[92] Raza, "Provincializing the International", 142.

unrecorded and unanalysed by the historian. To accept the marginalisation of people such as Satyabhakt by people such as Roy would therefore mean allowing regional and local-language spheres of leftist activities to continue unexamined.[93] The under-acknowledged communist also symbolised the everyday lived lives of those committed to its ethos. So it is necessary to look at Satyabhakt's considerable corpus: he was cheifly an ethical and committed crusader-journalist and communist whose deep commitment to the oppressed and the downtrodden made him try to convey voices from below. For Satyabhakt there was no difference between writing, journalism, social work, and the production of politically conscious literature.[94]

Idioms from Below and Communist Writings

A substantial part of Satyabhakt's literary journey reveals that he was very much a fellow traveller within leftist literary production; that he was one of the earliest Hindi writers to produce extensive work on the subject; and that he could never escape his deliberately separated and personalised communist sensibility. In spite of his political complexities, changing engagements, and a life surrounded by uncertainty, it was centrally communism that gave his life meaning. I focus here on his communist writings, many of which were proscribed, and in which terms like communist, socialist, Bolshevik, leftist, and revolutionary were interchangeable.[95] As a whole his writings were very much within a tradition of social realism, mirroring injustices in society. I also touch here on his articles and reports on civil, democratic, and human rights. In 1919, long before his formal commitment to communism,

[93] Cashbaugh, "A Paradoxical".
[94] Interview with Satyabhakt by Sharma, 29–30.
[95] Some of Satyabhakt's writings directly on communism were *Bhartiya Shramjeeviyon*; *Bolshevism Kya Hai*; *Ireland ke Gadar*; "Samyavad kya Hai?"; *Karl Marx*; "Samyavad ke Acharya"; *Samyavad ke Siddhant*; *Gorilla*; *Bharat mein Samyavad*; *Kranti Path*; *Kranti ka Agaman*.

 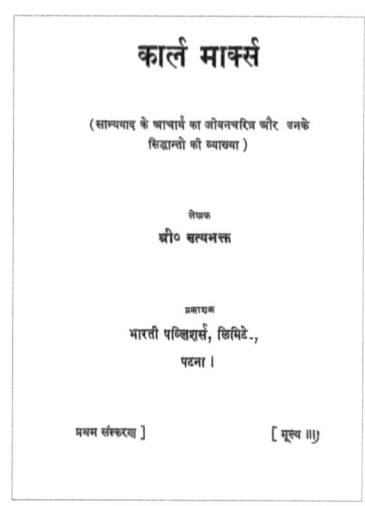

Figs 7.2-i and 7.2-ii: Two books by Satyabhakt – *Bolshevism kya Hai* and *Karl Marx*.

Satyabhakt was moved by the plight of political prisoners in India. In an article entitled "Rajnaitik Kaidi aur Sarkar", written just when the Gandhian movement was picking up, he tore into the British government for the treatment meted out to political prisoners. Describing cases from a jail in Hazaribagh, he spoke of how food had become a symbol and part of the language of protest against inhuman conditions and the violence of the colonial state. He contrasted the state in the Philippines under American rule and India under British rule to make his point.[96] In another article the same year titled "Apradhi Kaun Hai", he translated a speech to prisoners in a jail by Clarence Darrow (1857–1938), the famous Chicago lawyer and leading member of the American Civil Liberties Union. In a powerful advocacy for prisoners' rights, Satyabhakt argued a reformist position by linking increases in crime and incarceration numbers to everyday hardship, capitalist exploitation, and the degradation of daily life among the poor.[97]

[96] Satyabhakt, "Rajnaitik Kaidi".
[97] Satyabhakt, "Apradhi Kaun Hai?"

In a bulletin called *Deshi Rajyon mein Sudhar ka ek Ayojan* he critiqued the princely states; a consequence of the bulletin was that in 1921 he came to know Vijay Singh Pathik of the Rajasthan Sewa Sangh.[98] In 1922 Satyabhakt and Ramnarayan Choudhri, Secretary of the Rajasthan Sewa Sangh, published a report in Hindi and English based on their detailed investigation of the killing of more than fifty Bhils and Grassias; there had been inflicted, besides, injuries on around 150 villagers in the villages of Bhula and Balolia which fell within the princely state of Sirohi in Rajasthan. The oppressors, as usual, were the British authorities and, in this case, the Diwan of the state.[99] Framed in terms of Adivasi civil and political rights, this joint report recorded the statements of 115 villagers and was remarkable in its depth and coverage. One of the villagers interviewed said:

> My name is Poona . . . I am Bhil by caste. I am about forty-five years of age. When the Fauj (troops) ransacked our village, I had fled up the hills with my family. In my absence the troops set fire to my two houses which were consumed to ashes. They also burnt seventy maunds of Makki [corn] . . . I have six mouths to feed, but there is nothing left to clothe or feed them with . . . The soldiers killed my brothers Kana and Lakha who have left behind two widows and eight children . . . May God shower his wrath on these whites and the Diwan who have ruined us totally and compelled us to live as beggars.[100]

Since the report squarely blamed the British government and the Sirohi state for an unlawful and venomous attack, it created quite a stir in national and international circles, with the matter being raised in the British parliament as well.[101] In another report, soon after certain peasant women of Bundi protested against repression and atrocities, Satyabhakt attacked the police and Rajput rulers, thus establishing himself as the quintessential journalist speaking out on behalf of the suppressed voices of those below.[102]

---

[98] Satyabhakt, *Kranti Path*, 426–7; Interview with Satyabhakt by Sharma, 12.
[99] Satyabhakt and Ramnarayan, *The Second Bhil*.
[100] Ibid., 7.
[101] Gupt, "Rajasthan ki Jan-Jagriti".
[102] The report was titled *Bundi mein Striyon par Atyachaar*, and was

As the editor of *Pranvir*, Satyabhakt published several articles "decidedly pro-Bolshevik in tone."[103] In newspapers such as *Aaj, Vartman*, and *Pratap* he railed against the firing at workers during the Kanpur Cotton Mills strike of 1924, comparing it to Jallianwala Bagh.[104] Between 1924 and 1925, while establishing the ICP, Satyabhakt contributed extensively to the Hindi print sphere, publishing leaflets, articles, and books on communism. On 18 July 1924 he wrote an article, "Bharat Mein Samyavad", in the Hindi daily *Aaj*, in which he described communism as the panacea for all ills: "Now it is a recognised fact that communism is the only way for the salvation of the oppressed and suffering people of the world."[105] Writing in *Pratap* in August 1924, he remarked that socialism was the only means for a general emancipation of humanity and the country.[106] In *Vartman* in 1924 he confidently asserted that communism and the propagation of its doctrines could never be described as illegal and the government's opposition to it was altogether unjustified.[107] In another he announced that a communist party had been established in India, and that its "main objective is to remove the grievances of the poor *kisan*s (farmers), labourers, and the educated classes."[108] As secretary of the ICP he released a series of leaflets on various subjects, including the provisional rules, manifesto, and future programme of the party.[109]

Satyabhakt's residence in Kanpur was within the confines of a room 3.5 metres wide, located near workers' homes.[110] It doubled up

---

published on 27 June 1922: Gupt, "Rajasthan ki Jan-Jagriti". Also: Interview with Satyabhakt by Sharma, 13.

[103] Petrie, *Communism in India*, 171; "Bolshevik Conspiracy Case", 261/1924, Home Poll, NAI.

[104] For details Joshi, *Lost Worlds*, 194–8.

[105] Satyabhakt, "Bharat mein Samyavad", *Aaj*, 18 July 1924.

[106] *NNR*, week ending 16 August 1924, 4–5. Also *NNR*, week ending 23 August 1924, 6.

[107] *NNR*, week ending 5 April 1924, 3.

[108] *NNR*, week ending 13 September 1924, 6. Also *NNR*, week ending 4 October 1924, 5.

[109] Acc. 299, PMML.

[110] Interview with Satyabhakt by Sharma, 28.

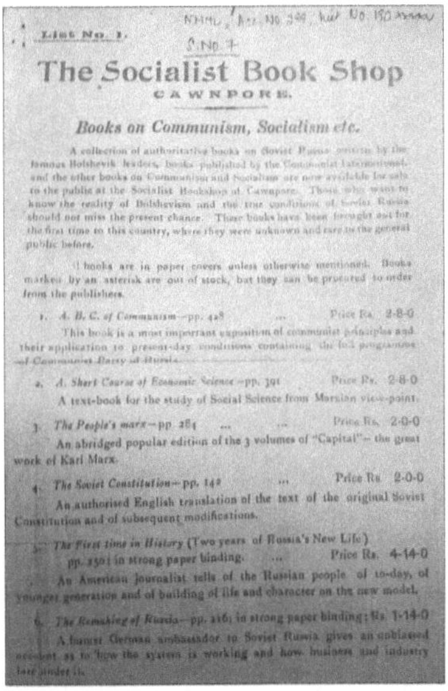
List No. 1.

The Socialist Book Shop

CAWNPORE.

Books on Communism, Socialism etc.

A collection of authoritative books on Soviet Russia written by the famous Bolshevik leaders, books published by the Communist International and the other books on Communism and Socialism are now available for sale to the public at the Socialist Bookshop of Cawnpore. Those who want to know the reality of Bolshevism and the true conditions of Soviet Russia should not miss the present chance. These books have been brought out for the first time to this country, where they were unknown and rare to the general public before.

[illegible] books are in paper covers unless otherwise mentioned. Books marked by an asterisk are out of stock, but they can be procured to order from the publishers.

1. *A. B. C. of Communism*—pp. 428 ... Price Rs. 2-8-0

This book is a most important exposition of communist principles and their application to present-day conditions containing the full programme of Communist Party of Russia.

2. *A Short Course of Economic Science*—pp. 391 Price Rs. 2-8-0

A text-book for the study of Social Science from Marxian view-point.

3. *The People's marx*—pp. 284 ... ... Price Rs. 2-0-0

An abridged popular edition of the 3 volumes of "Capital"—the great work of Karl Marx.

4. *The Soviet Constitution*—pp. 142 ... Price Rs. 2-0-0

An authorised English translation of the text of the original Soviet Constitution and of subsequent modifications.

5. *The First time in History* (Two years of Russia's New Life) pp. 250; in strong paper binding. ... Price Rs. 4-14-0

An American Journalist tells of the Russian people of to-day, of younger generation and of building of life and character on the new model.

6. *The Remaking of Russia*—pp. 216; in strong paper binding; Rs. 1-14-0

A former German ambassador to Soviet Russia gives an unbiased account as to how the system is working and how business and industry fare under it.

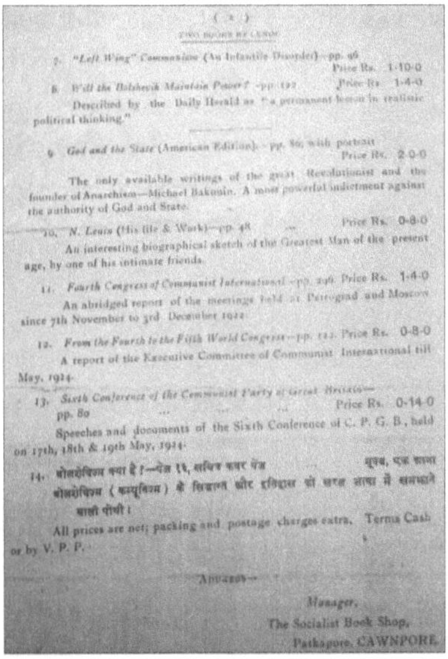
(2)

7. *"Left Wing" Communism* (An Infantile Disorder)—pp. 96 Price Rs. 1-10-0

8. *Will the Bolshevik Maintain Power?*—pp. 192 Price Rs. 1-4-0

Described by the Daily Herald as "a permanent lesson in realistic political thinking."

9. *God and the State* (American Edition)—pp. 86, with portrait Price Rs. 2-0-0

The only available writings of the great Revolutionist and the founder of Anarchism—Michael Bakunin. A most powerful indictment against the authority of God and State.

10. *N. Lenin* (His life & Work)—pp. 48 ... Price Rs. 0-8-0

An interesting biographical sketch of the Greatest Man of the present age, by one of his intimate friends.

11. *Fourth Congress of Communist International*—pp. 296 Price Rs. 1-4-0

An abridged report of the meetings held at Petrograd and Moscow since 7th November to 3rd December 1922.

12. *From the Fourth to the Fifth World Congress*—pp. 122 Price Rs. 0-8-0

A report of the Executive Committee of Communist International till May, 1924.

13. *Sixth Conference of the Communist Party of Great Britain*—pp. 80 ... Price Rs. 0-14-0

Speeches and documents of the Sixth Conference of C. P. G. B., held on 17th, 18th & 19th May, 1924.

14. [illegible]

All prices are net; packing and postage charges extra. Terms Cash or by V. P. P.

Manager,
The Socialist Book Shop,
Pathapore, CAWNPORE.

Figs 7.3-i and 7.3-ii: A list of books available in Satyabhakt's bookshop.

as a venue for procuring communist literature beyond the regimentation of the colonial state. Here he also opened the Socialist Book Shop in 1924, perhaps the first of its kind in North India, which regularly advertised, sold, distributed, and published communist pamphlets, books, tracts, and newspapers, including those that were banned.[111] Satyabhakt recollected that "Bhagat Singh also came [to the bookshop] and purchased the book on the Russian Revolution for Rs 10."[112] It was reported that Satyabhakt "supplied Rs 25 worth of communist literature to the Maharaja of Bikaner" in 1925.[113]

The government soon noted: "There is . . . already the nucleus of a communist organisation in Cawnpore, where communist literature published in Europe is on sale to the public and whence a number of communist pamphlets in the vernacular have already

[111] *The Socialist Book Shop, Cawnpore,* Leaflet, F. 7, Acc. 299, PMML; L/PJ/12/57.

[112] Interview with Satyabhakt by Damodaran, 15.

[113] "Fortnightly Report for UP for second half of September 1925", 112/September 1925, Home Poll, NAI.

been issued."¹¹⁴ Regular raids were carried out by the police on his house and bookshop and the communist literature there was seized. In one such raid on 7 July 1925 the police "recovered some proscribed literature, including 43 copies of the *Workers Weekly.*"¹¹⁵ Satyabhakt challenged these raids: "Has India been reduced to the level of a prison whose inhabitants have lost even the freedom to communicate with the outside world and to read books published in other countries . . . Is it any crime for Indians to be in possession of communist literature?"¹¹⁶ In their fortnightly reports, the UP government referred to Satyabhakt and Gokul as "notorious communists".¹¹⁷

Many leaflets written by Satyabhakt were proscribed by the government under Section 99-A of the Indian Penal Code. For example, on 4 October 1924 a notification ordered the forfeiture of all copies of the Hindi leaflet *Bhartiya Samyavadi Dal* for containing "seditious matter".¹¹⁸ Protesting against the proscription, Satyabhakt wrote in *Vartman*:

> The manner in which the Government has within the last few days proscribed unoffending and unobjectionable books and pamphlets leads us to infer that its legal adviser these days appears to be a raw recruit or one who is inexperienced in the ways of the world. I emphatically declare that this action of the Government is cowardly . . . I for one assert that I am a Communist and that I accept and preach all the principles enunciated in the proscribed pamphlet. I am confident that . . . hundreds of persons . . . in the name of socialism and freedom will kick this order like me.¹¹⁹

---

¹¹⁴ "Term of the Proscription of a Communist Pamphlet: Samyavad ke Premiyon se Appeal", 449/1924, Home Poll, NAI.

¹¹⁵ "Report on the Political Situation in UP for the first half of July 1925", 112/July 1925, Home Poll, NAI.

¹¹⁶ "Indian Communists: Protest Against Raid on Literature", *The Times of India*, 16 July 1925, 7. Also see "Police Raid a House in Cawnpore", *The Times of India*, 1 January 1926, 12.

¹¹⁷ "Fortnightly Reports on the Internal Situation for the months of January, June, July, August and September 1926", 112–IV/1926, Home Poll, NAI.

¹¹⁸ "Proscription of Pamphlets under Section 99–A", 33–II/1924, Home Poll, NAI.

¹¹⁹ *NNR*, fortnight ending 25 October 1924, 6.

He sent a copy of this article to *The Socialist*, Bombay.[120] *Pratap* too condemned the proscription of the leaflet, stating that the action of the government indicated the perversity of its legal intellect.[121] Another pamphlet by Satyabhakt, *Samyavad ke Premiyon se Appeal: Communist Party Kya Chahti Hai?*, published in 1924 and printed at the Sudha Sacharaka Press of Kanpur (which was responsible for printing six proscribed publications, including Satyabhakt's *Agle Sat Sal*), was banned by the government.[122] The pamphlet set out the aims of the Communist party; the government noted in a letter dated 5 December 1924 that its language was "studiously temperate", and yet it was seen as amounting "to preaching disaffection".[123]

A significant part of Satyabhakt's repertoire comprised memoirs and biographies: in 1930 he published a biography of Marx in Hindi.[124] Satyabhakt could not have written it without a working knowledge of *Capital* and *The Communist Manifesto*. The book also dealt with the human, everyday aspects of Marx's life – the poverty and deprivation, the loss of his wife and older daughter, the friendship with Engels. In 1931 Satyabhakt followed it up with a short sketch of Marx in *Chand*.[125] His biography of Lenin remained unpublished.[126] However, between 1968 and 1972, when Satyabhakt published eighty-five popular 32-page life sketches of "well-known personalities who had high ideals" under the Yug Nirman Yojana from Mathura,[127] he included Lenin (*Mahapurush Lenin*) and Marx

[120] Petrie, *Communism in India*, 172.
[121] *NNR*, fortnight ending 25 October 1924, 6.
[122] Satyabhakt, *Samyavad ke Premiyon*.
[123] 449/1924, Home Poll, NAI. Also: "Publications Proscribed under Section 99–A in November & December 1924 & During the Year 1925", 33–III/1925, Home Poll, NAI.
[124] Satyabhakt, *Karl Marx*.
[125] Satyabhakt, "Samyavad ke Acharya".
[126] In a letter to Karmendu Shishir, dated 4 September 1984, Satyabhakt wrote: "My book on Lenin, which is more than 200 pages, is still unpublished as of now." I thank Karmendu Shishir for sharing his correspondence with Satyabhakt.
[127] Priced at 40 or 50 paise, the back cover of each tract stated: "The chronicles of outstanding individuals evoke faith for human idealism in the public mind . . . For the cultivation of revolutionary thought, Yug Nirman Yojana is

(*Maharishi Marx*) in the list, making them accessible to a functionally literate population.

In accordance with the need to reach a subaltern audience with barely tolerable levels of literacy, the vernacular communist had to move away from a chaste, Sanskritised Hindi and instead adopt a simple, colloquial, everyday language. Democratising the language of Hindi and the politics of communism, Satyabhakt made them relatable and retailable to a non-English readership. Ramvilas Sharma noted this: "Satyabhakt used to write in a very simple language, as he understood very well what kind of prose style should be adopted to explain politics to the labourers. This populist and democratic view of language remained with him lifelong."[128]

In May 1923 he started a "Shramjeevi Lekhmala", a series of pamphlets on and for workers, within which he wrote the first bulletin, *Bhartiya Shramjeeviyon ko Sandesh*, consisting of fourteen pages and priced two paise.[129] Distributed in the mill area of the 24 Parganas,[130] the booklet was aligned with labour politics and included episodic tales such as this: "The robber said to Alexander, 'If I have looted some men, you have looted big countries . . . If I have burnt 10–20 villages, you have destroyed many beautiful cities. So, who is

---

bringing out literature in which life characters of great people have been given an important place through its series on the subject. The book presented is one of them." Of the eighty-five tracts, seventy were written by Satyabhakt himself: Satyabhakt, Letter to Karmendu Shishir, 4 September 1984. These included tracts on Indians like Bhagat Singh, Chandrashekhar Azad, Swami Sahajanand, Gandhi, and Bankim Chandra on the one hand, and international ones like Lenin, Marx, and Tolstoy on the other. They were very popular at one point of time but later lost their sheen. Satyabhakt later lamented: "Yug Nirman has now ended the life character series, as their sales are much lower than Gayatri literature. Even then, I will continue to work in some measure with revolutionary martyrs' tracts": Satyabhakt, letter to Karmendu Shishir, 20 September 1984. Fifty-two of these biographies are available in List C, Acc. 287, NAI.

[128] Sharma, *Bharat mein Angrezi*, 397.
[129] Satyabhakt, *Bhartiya Shramjeeviyon*.
[130] Roy, *Communism in India*, 77.

more to blame – you or me?" ... The only solution is for workers to unite and oppose the injustices of the rich ... This is called by several names – Socialism, Communism, Bolshevism, etc."[131] His second bulletin, *Bolshevism Kya Hai*, ran to nineteen pages over which he explained the emancipatory ideologies of Bolshevism and the egalitarian principles of *The Communist Manifesto* in a readable style.[132] The last few pages were in a question-answer style, as for example:

> *Question*: Do you want to translate all the principles of Bolshevism into India? Those people [the Bolsheviks] do not believe in religion. Apart from which, our present conditions, customs and ways of living are also very different.
>
> *Answer*: No, there is no need to carry over all the things of Bolshevism into India ... Our main objective is to remove the injustices done to the poor and to give real rights to all ... If the Bolsheviks of Russia start roaming around naked, we will of course not copy them.[133]

In 1929 Satyabhakt introduced his book entitled *Samyavad ka Sandesh* as "describing some aspects of communism simply."[134] This was a compilation of some of his pamphlets and articles on communism, and an interesting story, "Taalaab ki Kahani" (also published as a booklet), which outlined the chief causes for widespread unemployment and explained terms like *punjipati* (capitalist), bazaar, *adhishesh* (surplus), and *arthik sankat* (economic crisis).[135] Leaflets written by Satyabhakt include Urdu words like *siyasi* (politics), *mukammal irada* (final intention), *usool* (principle), *hamdardi* (empathy), and *aman* (peace).[136] In 1929 when *Chand* wanted to explain the meanings of communism to its readers, Satyabhakt was thought the ideal writer for the article.[137] His essay outlined communism in plebeian terms related to Indian material conditions:

[131] Satyabhakt, *Bhartiya Shramjeeviyon*, 10–13.
[132] Satyabhakt, *Bolshevism Kya Hai*.
[133] Ibid., last page.
[134] Satyabhakt, *Samyavad ka Sandesh*, 3.
[135] Ibid. Also Satyabhakt, *Taalaab ki Kahani*.
[136] For example *Samyavad ke Premiyon*.
[137] Satyabhakt, "Samyavad kya Hai?", 470.

Communism never says that the society or the panchayat will have ownership of my clothes, watch, glasses, table and chair, and food utensils. Because I personally use these things . . . But if I state that a part of the land or mine, railway, or factory is my personal property, then communism opposes it. Because I cannot use these things just personally. I cannot work with land or a mine, the railways or a factory through my labouring body alone.[138]

Summoning diverse sources, Satyabhakt thus forged a discursive vernacular history of communism within a generally accessible vocabulary. Attempting to redefine and expand the pristine meanings of "working class", he also tried to encompass wider solidarities which roped in those engaged in wage and manual labour, not just industrial work. There has been an identity politics-based charge that Marxism equals working class reductionism. Sudipta Kaviraj, for example, while critiquing the marginalisation of caste by Indian Marxists, argues that terms like communist and Marxist "acquired a strangely untroubled currency" for depicting the "aspirations of people in vastly different cultures",[139] but "to be practically effective" such "egalitarianism had to pass through a historical translation."[140] Juned Shaikh emphasises that the Marathi translation of *The Communist Manifesto* in 1931 had to juggle with "the vernacularisation of modern notions of class" and was made "knowable by referencing the particular political, economic and social tensions of the region."[141] Similarly, Satyabhakt's definition of shramjeevi – a non-specific category in the 1920s – was an intersection of overlapping, even competing, categories. He defines the term shramjeevi, the class of "workers" and "proletariat", in broad strokes: "Who are the workers? Every person who works hard with his hands, feet and brain, and eats what he earns through them is a shramjeevi. Then whether it is a farmer, labourer, artisan, clerk, schoolmaster, postman, railway babu or government servant."[142] He goes on: "When we announced the 'Indian Com-

---

[138] Ibid., 471.
[139] Kaviraj, "Marxism in Translation", 173.
[140] Ibid., 179.
[141] Shaikh, "Translating Marx", 65–6.
[142] Satyabhakt, *Bhartiya Shramjeeviyon*, 1.

munist Party' in 1924–25, the understanding and explanation of the proletariat in our mind was based on this. In the party manual thus, along with farmers and labourers, clerks in government and private offices, railway and postal workers, police constables, students of schools and colleges, were also encompassed in the category or class of 'workers' or 'proletariat'."[143] This heterogeneous and expansive meaning of the working class, even though at times overwritten by dogmatic orthodoxy, included all those who worked with their hands: it diluted the quintessential definition of a Marxian proletariat.

When chalking out the outline of *Bhartiya Samyavadi Dal* Satyabhakt said:

> Only those who feed on leisure by cheating and robbing others will keep aloof from it [the ICP]. All who make money by the sweat of their brow and do not prefer to live on ill-gotten gains will find the principles of this agitation to be the *best* [emphasis in the original], especially poor peasants, labourers, clerks, petty government officials, schoolmasters, railway employees, postal hands, orderlies, police constables, press employees, students, *ekka* and *tonga* (horse carriage) drivers, *thelawala*s (cart vendors), petty tradesmen and others who earn by the sweat of their brow, will surely become members of this party, because it alone can secure redressal of their wrongs.[144]

The second, complementary, thing he did was to establish an indissoluble relationship between workers, Shudras, Dalits, slaves, and women, speaking of them interchangeably. Most communist commentaries reified class as *the* category of analysis and exploitation, and undermined caste discrimination, which was submerged within the framework of class. As Aditya Nigam puts it: "Within Marxist scholarship and theorisation of Indian society and politics, caste was blanked out, written over by class to the extent that one would have to look in vain at the writings of Indian Marxists to find its presence even where it was centrally visible in social reality."[145] In

[143] Satyabhakt, *Bharat mein Samyavad*, 2–3.
[144] Satyabhakt, *Bhartiya Samyavadi Dal*, Leaflet, 33–II/1925, Home Poll, NAI.
[145] Nigam, "Hindutva, Caste'", 120.

contrast, a section of thinkers from the non-Brahmin movements of Maharashtra and Tamil Nadu expressed distinct idioms that combined anticaste radicalism with communist ideals. For example, in the late 1920s and early 1930s Dinkarrao Javalkar, a prominent young Satyashodhak non-Brahmin radical leader in Bombay, was attracted to Marxism. As the editor of *Kaivari*, an organ of the Non-Brahmin Party, and author of *Krantice Ranshing* (Battlefield of Revolution), one of the early Marxist books in Marathi, he accused the communist Brahmin leaders of caste elitism and argued that the non-Brahmin movement should not only be socio-religious in its orientation but should launch an economic struggle and fight against capitalism. Though he died early, in 1932, Javalkar opposed capitalists, the British, and Brahmins in that order, and combined anticaste and peasant movements with mill workers, and class struggle with social militancy.[146]

Similarly, Periyar published a Tamil translation of *The Communist Manifesto*, and simultaneously, as part of the Self-Respect Movement, promoted the idea of *samadharma* (equal rights) which was informed by socialist and anticaste principles. The 1930s were the heyday of the marriage of Self-Respect with socialism, which was effective in countering the attractions of religion while subverting the norms of the caste order.[147]

For Satyabhakt the class struggle against capitalism was intrinsically tied up not only with questions of nationalism but also caste and gender. His leaflets noted that no one should be considered achhut or *neech* (lowly).[148] He stated as a matter of fact that in ancient Indian literature workers were referred to as Shudras "who were considered the lowest in *shreni* (class) and *jati* terms", thus combining class with occupational guilds and caste. He added that "the word labourer or worker today implies a low class and caste."[149] He often used workers and women (*shramjeevi aur striyan*) together. For example, drawing analogies between on the one hand the peasants

[146] For details Omvedt, *Cultural Revolt*, 263–7.
[147] Geetha and Rajadurai, *Towards a Non-Brahmin*, 335–7, 402–9.
[148] F. 2, Acc. 299, PMML.
[149] Satyabhakt, "Samyavad Kya Hai?", 472.

and workers of contemporary India, and on the other the slaves and women of ancient Egypt, Greece, Rome, and China, he said that "Women and labourers have always been in a similar plight everywhere in the world."[150] He thus placed caste and gender as "legitimate" subjects of consideration by Marxism and communism; in his understanding, class and labour were not just economic terms but material facts intricately tied to other social identities and ways of being.

He was particularly desirous of possessing a press of his own and publishing a communist newspaper in Hindi. His most serious effort in this direction was the starting of the fortnightly paper *Samyavadi* on 1 January 1926, whose tagline was "Champion of Peasants, Labourers and Service Classes".[151] It advertised its aims:

> 1. Oppose the oppression of farmers. 2. Reveal the poor condition of labourers to the common people. 3. Redress the grievances of postman, rail and telegram worker, schoolmaster, government accountant, clerk, and other low-paid government and private servants. 4. Demand equal rights for those who are called Untouchables. 5. Liberate women from the bondage of social slavery. 6. Narrate descriptions of communist and Bolshevik movements in the country and abroad. 7. Spread knowledge about principles of communism among people.[152]

Priced at Rs 2 for a year's subscription, with each issue running to eight pages, the paper carried no advertisements. Unfortunately, on account of financial difficulties and proscription, only two issues of it appeared. All the same, they were extensively reported on in the native newspapers. One report stated:

> The *Samyavadi*, a new fortnightly organ of the Indian Communists started at Cawnpore by Satyabhakt, publishes a number of articles explaining the aims and objects of communism . . . The oppressed untouchables are becoming alive to the clever practices of the higher

---

[150] Ibid.
[151] Satyabhakt, *Samyavadi*. Only two issues of the paper came out, on 1 January 1926 and 16 January 1926, respectively.
[152] F. 14, 75, Acc. 299, PMML.

classes ... When these hungry and naked people will unitedly proclaim their rights, the capitalists and their parasites, the politicians, will be found nowhere. That will be the day of the victory of communism.[153]

The second issue of the paper too received considerable attention in the native newspapers:

> The *Samyavadi* dwells on the necessity of the adoption of communist principles for the betterment of the lot of the masses of the world and remarks: ... At present the condition of India is in many respects different from that of other countries ... In spite of our sympathy with the communistic parties in other countries it is impossible and harmful to us to establish relations with them. Indian labourers will have to depend upon themselves for their organisation and not upon outsiders ... Mr Singaravelu, writing in the same paper remarks ... that Indians cannot get rid of their afflictions so long as the masses or their unions do not secure control over land, mines, factories, houses and ships, railway trains and the like.[154]

Besides explaining the aims and objects of communism in India in simple language – with articles by M. Singaravelu, Maulana Azad Subhani, Gokul, and others – the two issues carried full-page biographical sketches of Lenin and Marx written by Satyabhakt.[155] Both issues of *Samyavadi* were seized by the government. Upon their seizure, *Matvala* issued a statement of regret at the action.[156]

Satyabhakt's actions and writings thus shed light on several matters. First, his engagements with leftist ideologies are demonstrated through his imprint on the Hindi print-public sphere. Second, the internal dynamics of the first Indian Communist Conference points to Satyabhakt's alignment with a national and indigenous, rather than an international, version of communism – as also on his differences with Roy and his subsequent marginalisation. Third, Satya-

---

[153] *NNR*, week ending 6 February 1926, 5.
[154] *NNR*, week ending 13 February 1926, 4.
[155] Satyabhakt, *Samyavadi*, 1 January 1926, 6; *Samyavadi*, 16 January 1926, 6.
[156] *Matvala*, 6 March 1926.

bhakt placed great importance on the expressive potency of straightforward, everyday language to explain communism and its egalitarian and emancipatory ideas. And, finally, he expanded the meanings of the working class, insisting on the inclusion of discussions on caste and gender.

Debates on communism and its evolution in India have often been routed through a circumscribed and dogmatic validation and legitimation that periodically draw from a Western or internationally defined vocabulary. This is compounded by most studies overlooking the expression of communist ideas in the vernacular, particularly in Hindi, and some of the traditions from which Indian Marxism drew. In fact, the vernaculars absorbed the many promises of communism and modernity to shape a slightly deviant amalgam which needs to be explored more carefully. In the interwar years Satyabhakt, like many others, preferred and forged such a strand of Indian communism. This was a vernacular literary and political project that brought communist thought in touch with workers' movements, a Gandhian ideology, and Congress nationalism. In this vision, nationalism and communism, tradition and modernity, spiritualism and materialism were not contradictory, but a heady mix.

Representing the suppressed heterogeneities of left dissent, Satyabhakt offers a faint yet sympathetic picture of communism in India which has been unjustly overlayered and rendered marginal. His voice, perhaps even more than the voices of Santram, Yashoda, and Satyadev, requires resurrection if only for one very good reason: alone within this quartet, Satyabhakt enjoyed neither fame nor fortune. At no point in his life does he seem to have prospered. Articulate, compassionate, and committed to a distant ideal of egalitarianism which he tried hard to bring closer to India, he lived and died in a poverty and obscurity that he never deserved.

8

Hindu Communism
Apocalypse and Utopian Ram Rajya

> The basic purpose of communism is to establish
> Ram Rajya on earth – Satyabhakt[1]

SATYABHAKT'S WORDS above show him as a Hindu communist yoking together two quite disparate worldviews. Distancing himself from the Marxist orthodoxy of atheistic liberation, his idea of an impending pralay was intended as a warning about the collapse of colonialism and capitalism alongside the hope of a utopian communist future. This was conceived as a romanticised Ram Rajya, presaging the unfolding of a future satyug for India and inspired in part by Gandhi's creative use of Ram Rajya.

Here I look at Satyabhakt's writings while keeping in mind Simone Weil's left mysticism, Enrique Dussel's philosophy of liberation, and Alan Wald's descriptions of lesser-known dissenting communist writers in order to focus on the imaginative *and* troubling congruency of communist ideology with a Hindu faith-based morality.[2] By recalling an important dimension of Satyabhakt's intellectual journey, I try to illuminate the largely uncharted territory of thought identifiable as "Hindu Communism". I suggest that without properly considering this sphere – which is an amalgam of the vernacular,

---

[1] Satyabhakt, *Agle Sat*, 116.
[2] My chief sources here are McCullough, *The Religious Philosophy*; Dussel, *Beyond Philosophy*; and Wald, *Writing from the Left*.

literary and journalistic Hindi, and the Hindu religious sphere – the story and history of communism in India is incomplete. I will also contrast and critique some of the prevailing theoretical assumptions of Marxist discourse in India with certain communist practices on the ground.

Mainstream Marxism and communism, which operate largely in an atheistic, materialist, and enlightenment framework, are often hostile to religion, regarding it as an ideological deviation.[3] Many Indian communists and secular historians also agree with such atheistic assertions since they believe in a clear separation between religion and politics. Given the meteoric rise of Hindutva politics in India, they have persuasively argued against the use of Hindu religious symbolism in the political-public sphere and made a strong case for Marxist secularism.[4] As Neeladri Bhattacharya observes: "To critique the communalist valorisation of the religious, secular historians have tried to see in every action only the play of non-religious interests – either political or economic."[5] But the difficulty, perhaps even futility, of attempting to dismantle militant Hindutva has only shown the resilience and pervasiveness of religious idioms and Hinduism in India, suggesting thus that the counternarratives to communalism may not lie in secularism alone. An alternative may exist and be sought in a range of histories and writings between the two, some of which are based in humanist religious ideas and terminologies.[6] No religion is monolithic or singular, and this perhaps holds greater valance for Hinduism. Its diverse texts, doctrines, and practices carry connecting and competing voices which have been historically variable and culturally reconfigured in fluid, pluralistic terms.[7] In spite of claims about its homogeneity, ideals of equality and practices of inequality have long existed within it in tension

[3] For an overview, McLellan, *Marxism and Religion*.

[4] For example Vanaik, *Hindutva Rising*.

[5] Bhattacharya, "Predicaments", 65.

[6] For nuanced critiques of secularism, Madan, *India's Religions*; Bhargava, *Secularism*.

[7] For an outline of layers of Hinduism, Frazier, "History and Historiography".

with one another; caste hierarchies have been variously solidified, and yet rebellious and contentious strands of Hinduism continue to thrive amongst many so-called lower jatis. While Brahmanical scriptures and rituals have upheld and strengthened unequal conceptions of varnashramdharma and patriarchies, many groupings – including women, lower-caste movements, and sects of tantric yoga and bhakti – have reshaped the meanings of Hinduism and stressed its multivocality. The *Manusmriti* sits alongside the *Kamasutra*, while a variety of elevated shankaracharyas and Manu coexist with dissenters such as Kalidasa, Meera, and Kabir. In short the Hindu scenario is one in which purity collides with impurity, where the hardening of religious identities does not eliminate syncretic practices, and where celibacy, asceticism, and yogic detachment mingle unproblematically with belief in desire, eroticism, and sensuality.[8] Despite the contemporary dominance of Hindutva, humane, plural, contingent, and everyday strands of Hinduism continue to find outlets.

Equally, communism is not always bound by the rules of atheism or shaped by a secular teleology. Liberation theology has promoted a fusion between religion and Marxism.[9] However, its focus has been overwhelmingly dependent upon Christianity, and to some extent Islam, Judaism, and Buddhism.[10] In comparison, Hindu liberation theology is a neglected field, perhaps because religions like Christianity and Islam have been considered more amenable to left readings and translations.[11] Back in 2002 Ruth Vanita thus underscored the continuing presence of the Christian left and the Islamic left in different parts of the world while lamenting the lack of a Hindu left and critiquing "secular left's almost paranoid stance on anything that savored of Hinduism."[12] Satyabhakt complicates such a standpoint in exemplifying the quintessential figure of this lost Hindu left.

[8] Menon, *Infinite Variety*.
[9] For an overview, Rowland, *The Cambridge Companion*.
[10] For an exception, Timani and Ashton, *Post-Christian Interreligious*.
[11] There is some work on Hindu Advaita Vedanta as a philosophy of social justice: Rambachan, *A Hindu Theology*.
[12] Vanita, "Whatever Happened to the Hindu Left?"

Resurgent religious idioms and cultural traditions were reworked in everyday public life by a variety of constituencies – social reformers, nationalists, Hindu and Muslim organisations, subalterns, peasants, Dalits, women, workers, writers, and communists – for very different ends and purposes. In North India over the 1920s and 1930s, subaltern movements and a section of progressive left intellectuals saw no problem aligning with religion, ethical tradition, and morality in their search for inspiration and vocabularies of dignity, equality, a just polity, and social liberation. Hindi writers and journalists like Radhamohan Gokul, Krishnakant Malaviya, Ramashankar Awasthi, Ganesh Shankar Vidyarthi, and Satyabhakt sought to create a socialist Hindi print sphere which engaged with the religious traditions and philosophical currents of popular and classical Hinduism. Naturally, this sometimes had ambiguous implications.

It is in this milieu that Satyabhakt needs to be seen. His thoughts suggest that the meanings of communism, far from being fixed, were much more dynamic, flexible, and open to interpretation in the 1920s, as "the Left created, appropriated, and translated" communist idioms in familiar and everyday social, cultural, and religious terms.[13] Aditya Nigam draws attention to the fact that a considerable number of early communists saw communism as "primarily a political imaginary that did not demand a subordination of their spiritual world to the political", and "did not entail the epistemological rupture, the abandonment of old ways of making sense of the world and the adoption of the standpoint of High Rationalism."[14] Satyabhakt went a step further: he not only saw no discrepancy between communism and religious spiritualism but also actually regarded them as supplementary and complementary when dreaming of an egalitarian India.

Satyabhakt's grandfather had often narrated tales to him of ghosts and Hindu mythology.[15] The grandson became well versed in the Puranas, particularly the *Bhagavata Purana* and the *Garuda Purana*,

[13] Raza, *Revolutionary Pasts*, 12.
[14] Nigam, *The Insurrection*, 271.
[15] Satyabhakt, *Marne ke Bad*, 5.

and was much moved by the *Ramcharitmanas*, viewing its impact as having been as widespread as the Bible's.[16] Though Satyabhakt formally dissociated himself from organised left politics, his commitment to communism was lifelong. His many articles in Hindi magazines and books on communism have been noted earlier; what is worth remarking on here is that almost half of his journalistic and literary output was dedicated to the business of death and rebirth, Hindu customs and beliefs, past and future predictions, dystopia and utopia, destruction and creation, pralay and satyug. Through many of these, Satyabhakt's intention was to offer visionary alternatives that might reshape the world through his focused projection of Ram Rajya. This strand was not peripheral but central to his persona and worldview. A substantial cluster of his writings thus appear, prima facie, to repudiate his leftist affiliations, being based on apparently depoliticised and culturalist portrayals of past, present, and future. However, it seems to me that even these writings allude to his communist beliefs and testify to his progressive vision and leftist conscience. It has been cogently argued that "Texts need to be read symptomatically, as representations of repressed political allegiances and buried historical realities around which an author cannot quite wrap his conscious mind: that, in short, there is such a thing as the political unconscious, and it warrants close critical attention."[17] This insight persuades us to recognise that even those of Satyabhakt's writings that were infused with Hindu ethics and sensibilities carry subtexts redolent of communist idioms and imprints.

I focus here on these allusions and tendencies in his texts. The first section briefly considers Satyabhakt's interest in eschatology, divinity, and Hindu customs and superstitions, as well as in similar beliefs prevalent in other cultures and countries. The second section shows his deployment of messianic Hinduism in communist writings, where his left leanings coexist with a social spirit deriving from his Hindu sensibility. The third section deliberates on his obsession with prophecies and predictions of pralay, catastrophe, and apocalypse as

---

[16] Satyabhakt, "Sapt Dwip", 37; idem, "Ramayan mein Stri", 296.
[17] Foley, "Biography and the Political", 654.

precursors of revolutionary change. The concluding section discusses his utopian political desire for a synthesis of his vernacular communist vision with a wider conceptualisation of Ram Rajya.

Even when erratic and uneven, his writings in this Hindu religious mode suggest a move from dystopia to utopia, pessimism to optimism, bondage to freedom, and capitalism to communism.

An Eclectic Hindu Worldview

Oscillating between religion and rationality, belief and scepticism, Hindu myths and the scientific temperament, Satyabhakt embraced these dualities and could be perceived in the rubric of – to borrow a term from Gregg Frazer – "theistic rationalism".[18] His hybrid belief system resembled the reframing of tradition to accommodate the inflow of new ideas by many Indian social reformers.[19] In grappling with universal questions arising out of genesis, eschatology, and superstition he was fascinated by, and drew from, the deistic and positivist framework of Herbert Spencer (1820–1903); the evolutionary theory of Social Darwinism; James Frazer's (1854–1941) global comparisons between magical, mythological, and religious belief; the divine and colourful occult findings of the palmist and astrologer Cheiro (1866–1936); and, as mentioned earlier, the Russian communist anarchist Peter Kropotkin's idea of co-operation rather than competition as an evolutionary mechanism in human societies.[20] In an article entitled "Vishwa Rachna", Satyabhakt says: "The emergence of any creature on the planet, whether human or animal, did not happen accidentally or in a supernatural way . . . To believe in the divine origin of the world and its creatures is only possible through blind faith."[21] In another, "Manushya ka Avirbhav", he says humans are not God's creations but have evolved through stages;

[18] For an expansion of the term, Frazer, *The Religious Beliefs*.
[19] Chakrabarty, "Radical Histories", 752.
[20] As mentioned in the preceding chapter, in 1927 Satyabhakt also translated Kropotkin's book *An Appeal to the Young* as *Navyuvakon se Do Baten*, which was widely circulated: Satyabhakt, *Kranti Path*, 419.
[21] Satyabhakt, "Vishwa Rachna", 171.

that this "fact is supported not only by science but also by legends"; and that "religious sentiments" are not so "delicate" that they can be "undermined by histories of evolution".[22] In two sequential articles he explains the arrival of deities, including the Hindu gods, and the emergence of temples, idols, priests (*mandir*s, *murtis, pujaris*). His two essays, he says, are "meant to awaken the power of independent thought within human beings rather than blind faith."[23] Casting doubt on the omnipotence of gods, he says that, often "ordinary spirits were transformed into gods", and that the Hindu gods of the past were very much like humans: "Similar to human beings, the deities of the Hindu Puranas were filled with feelings of jealousy and revenge, and on many occasions they were also scared of other potent humans. Many times, these gods were also defeated by humans."[24]

While reformist movements like the Arya Samaj, and the British Orientalists who were influenced by Enlightenment perspectives, regarded the Puranic tradition as degraded and corrupt and in need of replacement by the pristine Vedic knowledge of the classical "golden age", Satyabhakt was sceptically unpersuaded. Without offering an aggressive defence of Hindu tradition, he maintained a distance from organisations like the Hindu Mahasabha and the Arya Samaj; equally, he distanced himself from the supposed virtues of Vedic antiquity and instead often upheld Puranic ethics. The Puranas, being authorless texts that incorporated a Sanskrit textual heritage and folk religion, were implicitly seen by Satyabhakt as the carriers and transmitters of dharma in everyday life. Often evident in the vernacular, their communicative appeal was a pendulum linking the Brahmanical elite with humbler audiences. Or, to put it in the words of Rosalind O'Hanlon, they linked "Sanskrit and vernacular languages, text and oral performance, local histories and all-India gods."[25]

The early caste *vamsavali*s (genealogical histories) of Chamars, written in accessible Hindi in the early twentieth century, drew from

[22] Satyabhakt, "Manushya ka Avirbhav", 31, 38.
[23] Satyabhakt, "Devtaon ki Utpatti", 516. Also Satyabhakt, "Ishwar ki Utpatti".
[24] Satyabhakt, "Devtaon ki Utpatti", 519.
[25] O'Hanlon, "Performance in a World", 98.

itihaas-puranic traditions to reinterpret mythical Hindu pasts and claim the dignity of a Kshatriya status for themselves.[26] Revealing his emotional bond with the Puranas, its legends and their interplay of truth and falsehood, Satyabhakt defended them for explaining human values in a simple and entertaining language through easily understandable idioms: "Goswami Tulsidas' *Ramayan*, which is propagated today in every home, has been largely compiled from the *Purana*s . . . the Arya-Samaj often condemns them, calling them the main reason for the prevalence of hypocrisy and Gurudom . . . But in fact . . . there is much historical material in the Puranas that is not available anywhere else."[27]

A recurring theme in Satyabhakt's writings is the use of a comparative framework between past and present Hindu customs, beliefs and superstitions, and those existing in other parts of the world. Such juxtapositions illuminate the complementarities, similarities, elasticities, fusions, thematic parallels, and shared practices among multiple beliefs and religious customs in the everyday life of different regions and communities. Between 1932 and 1934, he composed a series of such articles in *Chand*, in one of which he chronicled the varied forms of *shradh* (custom to honour deceased ancestors) in various parts of the world;[28] in another, when describing the ancient system of marriage in India, he connected it to those in other countries and lamented that the modern system "eliminates the primacy of the woman . . . [and makes the] marriage relationship more rigid, where if a woman tries to use her cohabitation-related ancient rights again, she is far more harshly punished." Vindicating ancient practice, he said that the modern system was not necessarily "superior or beneficial".[29] In yet another piece, he showed that Hindu customs of grain worship were prevalent in different forms in many countries.[30] Similarly, he outlined the congruence of

---

[26] For example Raghuvanshi, *Chanvar Purana*. For details: Rawat, *Reconsidering Untouchability*, 123–31.
[27] Satyabhakt, "Sapt Dwip", 37.
[28] Satyabhakt, "Sansar ke Vibhinn".
[29] Satyabhakt, "Prachin Kal ki Vivah", 400.
[30] Satyabhakt, "Ann Dev ki Puja".

superstitions in varying regions.³¹ These writings are based on his understanding of cultures of intimacy, pluralism, cohabitation, reciprocity, syncretism, and dialogue. They deny that Hindu customs can be sharply differentiated from similar practices elsewhere.³² They also undermine the idea of a secular, enlightened, civilised, modern, and rationalist West vis-à-vis a backward, superstitious, religious, and irrational East.³³

In 1918, early in his journalistic career, Satyabhakt wrote a three-part series in *Stri Darpan* titled "Bhut Rahasya". Here he questioned beliefs in ghosts and spirits.³⁴ Many of his writings in this vein criticise Hindu superstition on the basis of evidence drawn from science, modernity, and rationality: they are an appeal for the eradication of ignorance and illusionary fear. At the same time, he foresaw many possibilities. Thus, in 1947 he wrote a book on the afterlife titled *Marne ke Bad*.³⁵ It has been argued that a ritual attention to the dead occupies much of Hinduism as it signals a liberation of the soul.³⁶ Satyabhakt reiterated his deep interest in and fascination with the mysteries of soul, death, and rebirth because he "constantly read, pondered over, thought and wrote on the subject."³⁷ *Marne ke Bad* is a collection of his stories on *parlok* (paradise), *punarjanam* (rebirth), and spirits of the dead; it betrays the influence of the famous occultist Cheiro. The stories allure readers with magical and transcendental descriptions of supernatural encounters. The last part of the book attempts to substantiate the claims made in the stories by narrating some "true" incidents of rebirth, and provide supporting opinions

[31] Satyabhakt, "Andhvishwas".

[32] At places one can also discern an implicit preservation of a Hindu order and an ambivalence towards Muslims. Communists, like others, may not always be above sectarian identities, and we sometimes see traces of it in Satyabhakt as well. For example Satyabhakt, "Andhvishwas", 504.

[33] Scholars have critiqued assumptions that the West civilised and brought light to the East, which was backward because of its superstitious beliefs in religion, magic, and sorcery: Nigam, *The Insurrection*, 263.

[34] Satyabhakt, "Bhut Rahasya".

[35] Satyabhakt, *Marne ke Bad*.

[36] Blackburn, "Death and Deification".

[37] Satyabhakt, *Marne ke Bad*, 6.

from Hindu scriptures, an Indian scientist, and a meditating ascetic (*samadhisth yogi*).[38] Grappling with the limits of human perception, and blurring the boundaries between the living and the dead, Satyabhakt interweaves motifs of fear and dread on the one hand, and pleasure and wonderment on the other. This shows his distance from a soulless atheistic secularism: his Hindu religiosity involved understanding the common person's difficulty in accepting neat separations of belief and disbelief, and an acknowledgement of their acceptance of the coexistence of the supernatural and the natural in everyday life.

Indian Traditions and Hinduism in Dialogue with Communism

Satyabhakt's attachment to indigenous, diverse, and ecumenical Hindu values and culture was in sharp contrast to dominant communist ideals as well as to those of communists like M.N. Roy and Muzaffar Ahmad. In early 1927, mainly targeting Satyabhakt, Ahmad remarked in a letter to Roy that communists were forced to "capture" the First Communist Conference at Kanpur since many "masquerading" as communists were linked with Hindu and Muslim communal organisations. This "insult" to the communist ideology forced the "real" communists to corner the reactionary elements and prevent the launching of a fake organisation.[39] Demeaning Satyabhakt's Hindu leanings, Ahmad further stated that he saw Satyabhakt in Western clothes but with a *safa* (turban) which he perhaps wore to hide the chutia on his head. Such patronising, condescending dismissals of Satyabhakt as a Hindu communal reactionary is a disservice to the pluralities and complexities of communist ideologies, and even more to the intelligence of believers in the left, particularly in the context of colonial India.

Many of the early communists never thought of leaving Hinduism or Islam. In fact, the everyday political practices of early left leaders, organisations, and workers drew from Hindu and Islamic

[38] Ibid., 101–28.
[39] Quoted in Chattopadhyay, *An Early Communist*, 147–8.

religious-cultural traditions when mobilising people. Class conflicts and political ideologies were often presented via the use of expressive religious idioms and iconographies even by some of the most radical socialist authors and labour activists, and yet these leaders had no concept of themselves as anything but non-communal.[40] In Punjab in the 1920s there was little, if any, contradiction in Akali activists joining the ranks of avowedly socialist and communist bodies, and a fair number were affiliated to both Sikh and socialist/communist parties.[41] Sahajanand Saraswati, the revolutionary sanyasi, saw no contradiction in being a Hindu sanyasi and simultaneously being a peasant leader fighting for justice for poor peasants. He asserted in his *Gita Hridaya* (1948) – his Marxist interpretation of the *Bhagvad Gita* – that "there is no contradiction between the moral stance of the *Gita* and that of the Marxists."[42] *Havan*s (ritual offerings), *katha*s (Hindu tales), the chanting of Vedic verses, and the distribution of *prasad* (propitiatory offerings) were often popular aspects within the political activities of trade unions to create bonds between workers that did not usually lead to exclusivist positions.[43] In Kanpur, magic lantern demonstrations organised by the Mazdoor Sabha used religious characters, such as the mythical tyrant Kansa, to describe British oppression. Sudarshan Chakr, a communist worker and writer based in the region in the 1920s–40s, in his book *Communist Katha*, replicated the structure of the *Ramayan* with its seven chapters. His chapter titles were "Marx Kand", "Rus Kand", etc., these being reminiscent of the *kand*s (segments) of the epic. He also linked Ram and Krishna with Marx and Lenin as great social levellers: *"Krishna hee Karl Marx ban gaye, vahi Lenin ban kar tan gaye. Vahi the Stalin avatar, gaya jisse Hitler tak har"* (Krishna was he who became Karl Marx; he also became Lenin and stood firm. He too was

---

[40] Gooptu, *The Politics*, 391–2.

[41] Raza, "Provincializing the International", 143. To take another example, the martyrdom images of Bhagat Singh were often anchored in religious imaginaries and visuals, repeatedly featuring Hindu gods or Bharat Mata, also revealing the undercurrents between revolutionary politics and a Hindu framework: Maclean, *A Revolutionary History*, 223.

[42] Quoted in Nadkarni, "Does Hinduism Lack?", 1848.

[43] Joshi, *Lost Worlds*, 189, 243.

the incarnation of Stalin, against whom even Hitler lost).[44] Popular cultural and religious beliefs included emancipatory motifs familiar to the working class, so it made sense to deploy them in the fight for a just socio-economic order.

Creatively arguing the pros and cons of ancient and medieval systems of production in India based on sanghas and *udyog* (manufacturing), and comparing them with the occupational systems (*vyavsaya pranali*) of capitalism, Satyabhakt argued that the scales were tipped in favour of the former, "a flourishing stage of our business that was maintained till the arrival of the British."[45] In a context of Hindu hegemony, refashioning moral critiques of capitalism more or less required the explicatory power of religious idiom. Satyabhakt therefore recommended the traditional system, the work ethic of which seemed to him fairer in several ways – the recognition and appreciation of skills; fairer distribution whereby a skilled artisan could become a master artisan; and a perspective on work better aligned not so much with profit but with ways of earning and living (*jeevika ka ek sadhan*). By contrast, the modern system increased the gap between *malik aur naukar* (master and servant), capitalists and workers. Contrasting past *karigar*s (artisans) with present *mazdoor*s (workers) he says:

> There is no doubt that the fate of these artisans of the Middle Ages was far better than the workers of the present age . . . As long as trade was in the hands of sanghas, the only way to become a master was to gain maximum skill in workmanship. But now, in this present new situation, instead of mastery, machines have started being considered central and the person who has the money to buy them becomes the owner . . . With this, the difference between the owner and the artisan has become much more explicit and direct . . . The greatest virtue of past practice was that it did not create the kind of inequality in society we are seeing today.[46]

No doubt some of this is an aestheticised, romantic, and nostalgic vision of a precolonial and precapitalist time of unalienated labour when wage labour did not dominate work relationships; all the same,

[44] Quoted in ibid., 244.
[45] Satyabhakt, "Prachin Kal ki Vyavsay", 463.
[46] Ibid., 465–8.

its purpose was to show up the iniquities introduced into factories and workplaces by the imperial and capitalist division of labour. It is also noticeable that Satyabhakt's notion of a harmonious past is not sectarian: it blends the ancient Hindu system with medieval and Mughal systems of production. Michael Lowy sums it up well when arguing that people can draw "inspiration from Marxist and messianic sources" and use "nostalgia for the past as a revolutionary method for the present" because the aim of revolutionary romanticism "is not a *return* to the past, but a *detour* through the past on the way to a utopian future."[47]

In Satyabhakt's *Samyavad ke Siddhant* (1934), "Om" appears written just above the main title.[48] It shows that Satyabhakt's spiritualism and identity as a Hindu and nationalist sat comfortably with his communism. Celebrating Marx and Marxism, Avijit Pathak suggests that one needs to go beyond ideology to recognise the "intuitive music of the soul" – this is visible in Tagore's "aesthetically enriched religiosity" and Gandhi's "journey to the inner world", both of which transformed "politics into an act of love and *sarvodaya*."[49] Satyabhakt's texts are open to such readings. They render a Hindu faith-based ethical morality compatible with a humanist communist ideology which seeks to touch people's hearts and emotions: "While working for the promotion of communism, I kept in mind the specificities and specialities of Indianness and characteristics of culture . . . If the Indian public is interested in spirituality, then it is not a mistake to keep this feature in the propagation of communism."[50]

Early Muslim leftists like Hasrat Mohani and Maulana Azad Subhani, pioneering figures in histories of labour and left struggles in urban UP, seem analogous with Satyabhakt in constantly using

[47] Lowy, *Fire Alarm*, 2, 5.
[48] It was common practice in the epistolary culture to inscribe a religious symbol on top of a letter or a book. Bhagat Singh too wrote a postcard to his grandfather in 1918 with "Om" inscribed on top: Vaidik, *Waiting for Swaraj*, 74.
[49] Pathak, "A Non-Marxist's Gratitude".
[50] Satyabhakt, *Bharat mein Samyavad*, 19.

religious symbolism to further radical egalitarianism.[51] Hasrat Mohani regarded himself as a Communist Muslim. His preaching was that socialism and Islam were one in sharing the cardinal principles of anti-landlordism, anti-capitalism, and equality.[52] Slightly later, the Muslim litterateurs and intellectuals of the Progressive Writers' Association cannot be described reductively as "religious" or "secular" merely because they drew from Indo-Persian traditions and Islamic religious ethics to articulate their anti-imperialist, leftist, and feminist politics.[53] Recollecting how communism was relatively new for Indians in the 1920s, Satyabhakt began his book *Bharat mein Samyavad* thus: "As such, in our culture, since ancient times, there was a feeling of unity and harmony, which developed and reached the idea that 'all people are spiritual', but it was mostly confined to the metaphysical-ideological field."[54] He stressed the social and humane aspects of Hinduism rather than its theological and metaphysical dimensions, which enabled him to drape communist social equality in the attire of Hindu morality and tradition: "It has been firmly stated in our shastras that not eating one's own bread and giving it to someone else is a very high characteristic of humanity."[55] The hierarchies of caste Hinduism are strategically ignored by quoting from the *Atharvaveda*: "All drink water from the same *piau* (tap) and share food with all others in a single dining session . . . This is the main principle and real ideal of communism."[56] A selective display of Hindu texts thus provides a messianic hope of liberation and justice.[57] In fact, his communism is epitomised as his Indianness and Hinduness:

[51] Both Mohani and Subhani were close to Satyabhakt and active in the First Communist Conference at Kanpur.
[52] Gooptu, *The Politics*, 278–84.
[53] For details Waheed, *Hidden Histories*.
[54] Satyabhakt, *Bharat mein Samyavad*, 3.
[55] Ibid., 13.
[56] Ibid., 14.
[57] Satyabhakt travelled easily between his left and Hindu beliefs. For example, in a letter dated 15 March 1985, he wrote to Karmendu Shishir: "These days I write something or the other on communism and politics. However, this

Listen to the essence of religion and practice it in your life. What you do not like yourself, desist from with others. What could be more a principle of communism than this? If we do not want our hard-earned money to be snatched away by others, we can naturally never think of taking possession of the wealth of others. If we do not relish others behaving harshly and disrespectfully with us, we will need to be sweet and benign in our behaviour. This is the true essence of religion. People who understand religion to mean the worshipping of gods and the feeding of food to ants, pigeons, and monkeys are misguided.[58]

This variety of belief system, it has been said, threw the "secular universalism of Marxism into repeated crisis."[59] Left Hinduism cherry-picks ancient Hindu beliefs for modern inspiration and reclaims their humane heritage for the cause of communism.[60] Satyabhakt's version of communism shows this most clearly.

Apocalyptic Predictions and Future Prophecies

The calamitous effects of COVID-19 have again reminded us that apocalypse is an integral part of our myth and history, and one that shows remarkable resilience.[61] In the 1920s and 1930s the dystopia of Nazism and the imminence of World War II fuelled the apocalyptic imagination of many writers who tried to come to terms with

---

topic may not be particularly appropriate for your journal *Kabir*. Therefore, I may send an article on Tulsidas ji." Courtesy Karmendu Shishir.

[58] Satyabhakt, *Bharat mein Samyavad*, 14.

[59] Nigam, *The Insurrection*, 263.

[60] As mentioned in the previous chapter, his eighty-five life narratives, published under the "Yug Nirman Yojana", again reflect his hybridised and eclectic make-up, as they included on the one hand "Hindu" nationalists like Tilak, Madan Mohan Malaviya, Maharana Pratap, and Bankim Chandra, and on the other revolutionary martyrs, socialists, and communists like Bhagat Singh, Chandra Shekhar Azad, Radhamohan Gokul, Raja Mahendra Pratap, Lenin, and Marx.

[61] For an overview of apocalyptic literature and scholarship, Al-Bagdadi, Marno, and Riedl, *The Apocalyptic Complex*.

HINDU COMMUNISM 299

the failures of civilisation.⁶² Meanwhile the aftermath of the Russian Revolution (1917–23) engendered dreams of a future world of communism. A prelude to the socialist utopia was thought of as a period of mass destruction, and since World War I was the context of the initial Bolshevik savagery against the tsarist regime, carnage was often seen as a necessary precondition for the coming into being of a new order. Marx's writings, too, were frequently based in a tradition of prophecy. For communist enthusiasts apocalypse was not necessarily negative, it was organic to the process of social transformation. Satyabhakt's millenarianism captures these moods of the age, giving expression to ecological, technological, and political crisis as the precursor of communist egalitarianism.⁶³ He was fascinated by clairvoyants, chiliasts, and fortune tellers, acknowledging his propensity for blends of the occult and the political: "The thing is that from the beginning I had a hobby for political prophecies."⁶⁴ Some of his articles and books – such as *Agle Sat Sal* and *Samvat Do Hazar* – were in line with apocalyptic literature.⁶⁵ Published as "Samyavadi Pustak Mala, Sankhya 1" (Communist Book Series, Number 1), which clearly delineates its tenor, *Agle Sat Sal: San 1924 se 1931 Tak Hone Wali Khand Pralay ka Varnan* (1924) offers a summary of its contents on the very first page:

> Description of the catastrophe that will take place from 1924 to 1931: in which the future of Europe, destruction of the Empire of England, the great war of Asia and Europe, the independence of India, the re-establishment of Muslim rule in India, the coming of extreme political and natural crisis in the world, and finally the propagation of communism and the salvation of the world by some great man or avatar, is described with proof.⁶⁶

---

⁶² Berger, "Introduction", 389. Otherwise, too, a considerable section of the world literature of the early twentieth century was saturated with apocalyptic images: Bulfin, "The Natural Catastrophe".
⁶³ Pralay has also often been used in Hindi writings in the context of the 1857 revolt, a *gadar* or a *kranti*.
⁶⁴ Interview with Satyabhakt by Sharma, 18.
⁶⁵ Satyabhakt, *Agle Sat*; idem, *Samvat Do Hazar*.
⁶⁶ Satyabhakt, *Agle Sat*.

The book drew partial inspiration from the Reverend Michael P. Baxter's (1834–1910) *Forty Future Wonders of Scripture Prophecy*, a hugely popular work of speculation first published in 1866 which saw repeated runs with altered titles such as *Future Wonders of the World*.[67] The crux of the Book of Revelation in the Bible is the prediction of a future Christian paradise, and this spawned a rich tradition of Christian revelatory writings.[68] Baxter's book was based on biblical prophecies and apocalyptic predictions of coming perils and pleasures for the years 1867–75. The author was a "nonconformist minister and philanthropist" and editor of *The Christian Herald*, a London-based evangelical weekly newspaper.[69] Creatively remoulding Baxter's book to serve its own ends, *Agle Sat Sal* based itself on the conviction that the world, more specifically India, had reached a critical juncture and was awaiting something unique and important to unfold that would have profound implications for all future time.

Satyabhakt divided this work into two main parts. The first gave a summary of Baxter's book but took full liberties in condensing and reworking it to suit contemporary situations since the period of predictions covered in the two books was completely different. This first part also had chapters on topics such as World War I, the League of Nations, and People's Red Rule in European Countries. Most interestingly, there was one on the "40th Wonder"; this had been reformulated as "Ek Hazar Varsh tak Prithvi par *Ram Rajya* ya Samyavadi Shasan" (Ram Rajya or Communist Rule on Earth for a Thousand Years). Inspired by Baxter's image of Jesus as a prophet of apocalypse and resurrection, Satyabhakt focused chiefly on the brute force of capitalist modernity to proclaim that "the present rule of European countries will be destroyed, and in its place communist or Bolshevik (workers') rule will be established."[70]

Part II of the book carried predictions of the future by famous political thinkers, writers, scientists, and *jyotish*is (astrologers), which

[67] Baxter, *Coming Wonders*.
[68] For scholarly readings, Hvidt, *Christian Prophecy*; Hamori, *Women's Divination*.
[69] Curtis, "There Are No Secular", 82.
[70] Satyabhakt, *Agle Sat*, 117.

HINDU COMMUNISM 301

ranged from Chand Bardai (the author of *Prithviraj Raso*) to literary notables such as Tolstoy and Byron, all of whose writings were interpreted as heralding the coming of communism.

A final section of the book, titled "Bharat ka Bhavishya" (Future of India), combined Satyabhakt's own ideas and beliefs with a robust and enthusiastic view of the communist future. Finding its prediction of the end of British rule and the coming of communism seditious, *Agle Sat Sal* was soon seized and banned by the government.

Similarly, Satyabhakt's *Samvat Do Hazar, athva Bhavi Mahabharat* (1936) is based on catastrophic changes in society and predicts what the world was going to be over 1937–44, again looking at a span of seven years. Since his *Agle Sat Sal* had been proscribed, he published *Samvat Do Hazar* under the pseudonym "Bhartiya Yogi" (Indian Ascetic) from his Satyug Press.[71] This became his most famous and popular book: a fourth edition of it came out in 1942.[72] Written a little before World War II, it described in detail the manufacturing of weapons of mass destruction, the horrors of modern warfare, the destructive power of technology, and the barbarous cruelty of Nazi Germany; but it also relied on astrology:

> Before the beginning of a new era, there is a great degree of turbulence and violence in the world, in which most of the opponents change their views or are eliminated . . . At such times natural calamities like earthquakes, storms and famines also erupt in a terrible form, further helping in cleansing the world . . . Shri Krishna has also said this clearly in the Gita . . . The second thousandth year of the Vikram Samvat is about to end and the third thousandth is about to begin, which is a very big event . . . Some people say that the Kalki avatar is absolutely certain to appear in Samvat 2000.[73]

He also describes "strange" recent happenings signifying a major upheaval, such as the "rain of blood" in Etawah, and mango trees in Allahabad bearing fruits three times within five months.[74] Reviewing

[71] The Hindu calendar's Samvat 2000 coincides with the Gregorian calendar's March–April 1943 to February–March 1944.
[72] Satyabhakt, *Samvat Do Hazar*.
[73] Ibid., 14–15.
[74] Ibid., 15–18.

the book, *The Leader* noted that it "contains [a] mine of information about military preparations, use of electricity, poisonous gases and other new instruments of destruction . . . In the course of his discussion he [the author] shows that the predictions contained in the *Holy Bible* and the *Mahabharat* as well as the prophecies made by some eminent western and eastern astrologers tend to establish the same truth."[75]

These themes in Satyabhakt's books are echoed in various articles that he wrote. In one entitled "Sapt Dwip" he drew from the Puranas to illustrate pralay as a prelude to the new:

> Though man has conquered many natural forces and is working through them for his benefit and pleasure, when nature assumes an angry form man has no power to control it . . . Although the work of nature appears cruel from above, in truth it is for the ultimate welfare of human kind, and only because of it is this creation maintained. When the weight of the earth becomes unbearable, and its fertility decreases drastically because of the toll on it of its constant care of human beings and animals, nature shows mercy and creates a new fertile earth for the abode of mankind. It immerses the present under water, so that in a million years it can again attain its fertility and become habitable for humans. If we think from this perspective, the metaphor of the Puranas, in which . . . the earth takes the form of a cow and goes to Brahma for salvation, is a description of pralay.[76]

Another article is titled "Pralay"; it explains the idea of apocalypse "scientifically" and argues that for the creation of nature pralay is a necessity (*srishti ke liye pralay ka hona avashyak hai*).[77]

This fascination with Hindu myths of pralay and catastrophe leads Satyabhakt into repeated combinations and recombinations of man-made disasters and struggles – e.g. global wars, military invasions, freedom struggles, nationalist protests, domestic upheavals, and the end of the British Empire – with natural disasters such as floods, earth-

---

[75] *Leader*, 24 November 1936. Quoted in Satyabhakt, *Samvat Do Hazar*, last page; Satyabhakt, *Kranti Path*, 432.

[76] Satyabhakt, "Sapt Dwip", 40.

[77] Satyabhakt, "Pralay".

quakes, volcanic eruptions, and climatic changes. Present immorality, which includes blatantly exploitative practices against the natural world, are the unavoidable forerunners of ruin – but only until a resurrection, which too is inevitable in the shape of the communist Ram Rajya.

Satyabhakt's echo of his own *nom de plume* when christening his Satyug Press, as well as his magazine *Satyug*, shows his deep yearning for the arrival of a higher Truth – an event that he hopes to catalyse through spiritually predictive and communist-idealist writings. As he says, "*Satyug* was also published for this purpose. In that, too, I used to preach, indirectly, how the world would be completely transformed by war, famine, epidemics and other catastrophes, and a new era would begin, based on religion, justice and equality."[78]

Communism as a Utopian Ram Rajya

Ruth Levitas categorises utopia as the imaginary reconstitution of society (IROS).[79] The genre of utopia often functions "as a critique of contemporary society, and often in a transparent way."[80] As a concept it often has its "religious roots in paradise" and "political roots in socialism".[81] Moreover, "utopian visions are never arbitrary. They always draw on the resources present in the ambient culture and develop them with specific ends in mind that are heavily structured by the present."[82] Sandeep Banerjee looks at some of the literary imaginations in colonial India and shows how these "counter-colonial spatial imaginaries" were "utopian in their negation of colonialism" in plural and contradictory ways.[83] A necessary corollary of Satyabhakt's idea of apocalypse was a communist utopian dream, which in his case was expressed through the idiom of Ram Rajya.

The political meaning of Ram Rajya has interested many scholarly commentators. Sheldon Pollock argues that the concept of Ram

---

[78] Interview with Satyabhakt by Sharma, 18.
[79] Levitas, *Utopia as Method*.
[80] Hartley, *The Abyss*, 150.
[81] Gardin, Tilley, and Prakash, "Introduction", 1.
[82] Ibid., 4.
[83] Banerjee, *Space, Utopia*, 9.

Rajya aids a "construction and representation of reality through a more or less systematic historical fantasy."[84] Philip Lutgendorf says that "Ramraj has been viewed both as a harmonious but hierarchical order, in which the privileged confidently enjoy their status and the dispossessed keep within their limits, or conversely, as a kingdom of righteousness, in which the possibilities of freedom are made accessible to all."[85] Paula Richman observes how an ancient narrative tradition like the *Ramayan*, with its conception of Ram Rajya, has served as a central organising political metaphor, aiding a range of discourses and providing an imaginative framework for modern India.[86] Other scholars and historians too draw our attention to how Hindu religious texts and traditions, particularly revolving around the *Bhagvad Gita* and the *Ramayan*, furnished the key literary sources that were invoked for the Hindu nationalist imagination and the Indian freedom struggle.[87] It was believed that "If Indians could live according to the high ideals of this text [the *Ramayan*], they would be able to overcome poverty, untouchability, and foreign rule."[88] The language of Tulsidas' *Ramcharitmanas*, the cult of Rama, and the political ideals of Ram Rajya have a deep resonance with Hindu audiences and readers.

Indeed, the conceptualisation of a Hindu political imagination was on the agenda of many nationalist ideologues in the early twentieth century. Their ideas were often developed in response to the colonial dismissal of the existence of any sort of political culture in India. They utilised the concept of Ram Rajya in distinct ways to reinforce their political ideals and views. The term was most effectively and successfully adopted and extended to modern ideologies of nationalism by Gandhi: "If the word Ram Rajya offends anyone, then I shall call it 'Dharmarajya'."[89] He gave Ram Rajya a new meaning, equating

[84] Pollock, "Ramayana and Political", 280.
[85] Lutgendorf, "Interpreting Ramraj", 267.
[86] Richman, "A Tamil Modernist's Account". Also Pollock, "Ramayana and Political".
[87] Gould, *Hindu Nationalism*, 51–5, 71–3.
[88] Veer, *Imperial Encounters*, 126.
[89] Gandhi, *The Collected Works: 43*, 112.

it with his ideas of freedom, khadi, refusal to pay the salt tax, and swaraj. Ram Rajya meant a "moral government based upon truth and non-violence, in other words universal religion," an ideal social order under which "the poor will be fully protected, everything will be done with justice, and the voice of the people will always be respected."[90] In North India, particularly, this Gandhian idea as a just form of political rule "had an almost millenarian impact on the Hindu population."[91] Baba Ramchandra, a dynamic leader of the farmers of Awadh, also radically interpreted Ram Rajya and the *Ramcharitmanas* to mobilise peasants against exploiters.[92] The veneration of Ram became a means of expressing social equality and the dignity of labour by some agricultural castes.[93] As Peter van der Veer argues, unlike China, "in India traditions were made into resources in the anti-imperialist struggle against a material modernisation that culturally and politically subjected India to Western power."[94]

Keeping the concept of Ram Rajya alive and ticking in contemporary times, many celebratory and crude idealisations have aligned it with Brahmanical and Hindutva politics.[95] In his book *Ram Rajya and Its Ideals*, the Kanpur-based Hindutva scholar L.P. Chaturvedi says: "During the period of Sri Ram . . . [the] aspect of town planning was fully developed, medical science and astrology were fully matured . . . the civilisation of the period of Ram was fully matured in the spheres of goodness and demonic world."[96] By contrast, the writer Prem Nath Bazaz argues that the concept of Ram Rajya is reactionary, communal, and undemocratic.[97]

---

[90] Ibid. For details, Lutgendorf, "Interpreting Ramraj", 253–4.
[91] Veer, *Imperial Encounters*, 126.
[92] Kumar, "The *Ramcharitmanas*".
[93] Pinch, *Peasants and Monks*, 81–114. Further, in the towns of UP, the Shudra poor celebrated festivals like Holi and viewed Krishna as a saviour of the oppressed and the underprivileged: Gooptu, *The Politics*, 211–13.
[94] Veer, "Spirituality in Modern", 1115.
[95] For some examples, Pollock, "Ramayana and Political"; Lutgendorf, "Interpreting Ramraj", 272–8.
[96] Chaturvedi, *Ram Rajya*.
[97] Bazaz, *The Shadow of Ram Rajya*.

The relationship between imaginings stimulated by Ram Rajya and beliefs in Marxism and communism has been ambiguous, to say the least. In 1957 Karpatri Maharaj (1907–1982) – a monk in the Hindu Dasanami monastic tradition and founder of the Ram Rajya Parishad, an orthodox Hindu religious political party – wrote a book of 816 pages, *Marxvad aur Ram Rajya*, which was published by the famous Gita Press.[98] Reflecting on the political theories of Western philosophy and its thinkers, one of the central purposes of this book was to demolish Marxism and communism by pronouncing it completely antithetical to Ram Rajya and Hindu political formulations. Maharaj argued that Ram Rajya could only be based on rules of shastric and Sanatani religion, that it was the only way in which the will of the people could be ensured:

> The principle of personal property cannot be called a principle of exploitation . . . Anarchist communists and socialists are always clamouring for great revolutions and changes. In consonance with scriptures and traditions . . . Ram Rajya does not wish even an iota of change in the principles of Sanatani culture, religion, and politics . . . Supporters of Ram Rajya consider God, religion, and soul as the fundamental base . . . A Marxist says that an individual can get freedom only through people's will . . . Believers of Ram Rajya consider the harmonious prosperity of every good person or class as superior. Class-struggle is sheer propaganda . . . It does not work for good people.[99]

The book is saturated with other such ideas in a heavily Sanskritised Hindi, as for instance "rich investors guided by religion were the main reason for the welfare of the nation"; the "communist move-

---

[98] Maharaj, *Marxvad aur Ram Rajya*. Karpatri Maharaj and his party Ram Rajya Parishad, founded in 1948, were at the forefront of trying to block the Hindu Code Bill. Maharaj also held a huge *yagya* (prayer ceremony) to prevent the entry of Dalits into the Vishwanath Temple of Banaras and was sent to jail for this. His party, ultimately, merged with the Bharatiya Jan Sangh. For further details, Lutgendorf, "Interpreting Ramraj", 273–4; Mukul, *Gita Press*, 185–6, 336–8. Articles against communism and atheism also appeared at regular intervals in the journal *Kalyan* published by the Gita Press: Mukul, *Gita Press*, 328–40.

[99] Maharaj, *Marxvad aur Ram Rajya*, 245–7.

ment was dependent on pure malice and jealousy"; "the wealth of individuals is protected in *Ram Rajya*"; "Marxism directly abducts religion, wealth, life, and property"; "religion is eternal, caste system, faithful and chaste wifehood are also eternal"; and "Marxism and theism cannot exist together".[100] The writer supported sati, child marriage, and purdah. In response Rahul Sankrityayan wrote a sarcastic critique, *Ram Rajya aur Marxvad*, which was published by the People's Publishing House in January 1959. In it he attacked Maharaj's support of exploitative moneyed magnates, his reprehensible views on slavery, caste, and women, his support of Ram Rajya and critique of Marxism: "Karpatriji Maharaj is propagating a pro-capitalist rule in the name of Ram Rajya ... The Ram Rajya of Karpatriji is controlled by religion ... he wishes to establish mysticism by refuting Marx's philosophy."[101]

This was the general context of Satyabhakt's earlier conceptualisation of Ram Rajya, an idea open to "appropriation by both power-wielding elites and disenfranchised lower orders."[102] Satyabhakt's utopia connected communist ideas of equality with Ram Rajya's model of happiness; it was no more and no less than a strategy to make communism intelligible and acceptable to a Hindi-Hindu audience. The conceptualisation was idealised and utopian to the point of unreality: Ram Rajya presaged a sublime world without arms, military might, wars, oppression, crime, exploitation, hunger, suffering, pain, poverty, and inequality – as in one of the millenarian chapters of *Agle Sat Sal*:

> At the end of these seven years, the condition of earth will change completely. Millions of people will be reduced from the population of the earth and the world will look deserted. But after this, when Jesus Christ and his fellow saints start governing the earth, all miseries and sufferings will be removed, and the number of human beings will increase greatly in a few years ... War will stop forever. Everybody will cultivate land and work hard to earn their bread ... In this age, rule will be in

[100] Ibid., 280, 299, 301, 338, 360–1, 414, 560.
[101] Sankrityayan, *Ram Rajya aur Marxvad*, 35, 40, 47, 94.
[102] Lutgendorf, "Interpreting Ramraj", 255.

the hands of those whose character is pure; and those who are humble, courteous and love the poor.[103]

The excesses of such idealisations apart, Satyabhakt's writings show his immersion in traditions of learning unconfined by India. In his article "Ram Rajya ki Adhunik Kalpana", he reinterprets Ram Rajya by connecting it directly to Plato's *Republic* and Thomas More's *Utopia*.[104] The article widens the scope of utopia by proposing a broader and more pluralist vision.[105] It shows an awareness also of early Christian writers who had harboured similar utopian dreams. The bulk of the article, however, is a description of More's *Utopia* (1516).[106] Satyabhakt sees More's concept as analogous with Ram Rajya in presaging the construction of communist ideals. The essay ends:

> This type of ideal society has not been conceived by More alone, but many writers of countries like England, France, and Italy have written similar stories. Although communists today do not value these stories and consider them merely the imagination of Sheikh Chilli,[107] we come to the conclusion from his study that even though the tendency of mankind is often to be selfish with other people, the seeds of love and fraternity are contained within humanity, which, from time to time, we glimpse. This is the reason why we see various forms of this [utopian] imagination from a devotional poet like Tulsidas to the Bolsheviks of the present times! When exactly this imagination is to be translated into reality cannot be said, but we believe that human society is constantly moving towards it and will reach the goal at some point or the other.[108]

Satyabhakt's amalgam of communism and Hindu ethics was imaginative no doubt, and moreover non-sectarian in relation to Muslims, but in relation to caste Hinduism we find him floundering.

[103] Satyabhakt, *Agle Sat*, 114–15.

[104] Satyabhakt, "Ram-Rajya ki Adhunik", 153–7.

[105] For a broad overview of utopia and its multiple meanings, Rusen, Fehr, and Rieger, *Thinking Utopia*. On Marxism and utopia, Berg, *The Immanent Utopia*, 43–76.

[106] More, *Utopia*.

[107] A character from folklore, a daydreamer who thoughtlessly concocts grandiose ideas.

[108] Satyabhakt, "Ram-Rajya ki Adhunik", 157.

The Brahmanical hegemony obvious in textual Hinduism, and its upholding of hierarchy and exclusion in the formulation of varnashramdharma, were never clearly addressed by Satyabhakt.[109] In very considerable mitigation of this failing, it has to be said in his favour that he married a Dalit woman and did not retreat in face of the consequent social ostracism.[110] In fact, his Ram Rajya-cum-communism show his belief in the need for striving towards gender equality. He objected, for instance, to Tulsidas' misogynistic view of women (*stri jati ke sambandh mein anuchit akshep*), calling it completely "unjustified and contemptible".[111] And although extreme hardship drove him to spend his last thirty years at the ashram of the Akhand Jyoti Institute in Mathura, he refused to participate in the daily prayers performed there despite attendance being deemed compulsory.[112]

The entanglement of religious idioms with political rhetoric could unleash complex questions of identity and give rise to ambiguities open to divergent interpretations – at times progressive, at times sectarian and ethnic. For all this, the spiritual and ethical idioms of a mythical Ram Rajya helped validate and translate communism into distinctly Indian circumstances, vernacularising it and making it more flexible and comprehensible. Satyabhakt's creative fusion of religion and communism says much about the everyday terrain of popular plebeian desires and communist dreams within

[109] For example, feminist and Dalit discourses have rightly challenged the idea of a utopian Ram Rajya and the victimisation of Sita and Shambuk.

[110] Shishir, *Satyabhakt*, 29. Unfortunately, we do not know anything more about this subject.

[111] Satyabhakt, "Ramayan mein Stri Jati". In fact, in *Stri Darpan*, Satyabhakt wrote quite a few articles pro-women in tone. He wrote "Prachin Bharat mein Striyon", which ran over four issues of *Stri Darpan* from January to April 1918, and cited examples from history to support the women's movement. In another article he vociferously asked Indian women to declare themselves "strong, free and independent" (*sabal, swadheen aur swatantra*): Satyabhakt, "Bhartiya Striyon ko Sandesh". At times, puritanical and sexually conservative stances can also be discerned in his writings. For example, Satyabhakt, "Bharatvarsha mein Ashlilta". Satyabhakt also translated into Hindi the infamous American author Katherine Mayo's *Slaves of the Gods* as *Devtaon ke Gulam* in 1929.

[112] Shishir, *Satyabhakt*, 30.

which no neat boundaries separate the religious and the secular, the spiritual and the material.

My purpose in this chapter and its predecessor has been partly to excavate an eccentric and sometimes wrong-headed yet genuine and interesting thinker. But, more than that, it is to suggest that an examination of the intertwining of communism and Hinduism can provide insights into these worldviews by complicating singular and dogmatic interpretations of both. I have also tried to open up normative issues on the nature and meanings of modernity, political idealism, and religiosity in India. Circumscribed communist vocabularies of validation and legitimation often perceive the views of figures like Satyabhakt as promiscuous meanderings or distorted versions of communism, or as flowing from irrational belief, superstition, and outmoded religious idiom. It can of course be argued that idealism allied with great commitment, as manifest in Satyabhakt, is not necessarily intellectually noteworthy, that it shows clear ideological limits and perhaps merely a layperson's simplistic understanding of communism. I would counter such an argument by pointing out that the nobility of thought, the compassion, and the courage that Satyabhakt showed over the course of his whole life makes him truly remarkable. Moreover, he transcended and refashioned both Marxism and Hinduism to make a malleable compound. His creative use of two conjoined terms suggests that the subject of "Hindu Communism" has had, and continues to have, multiple resolutions. This marrying of communism with a reinterpreted ethical and egalitarian Hinduism generated new forms of affect. Troublesome to proponents of atheism, secular communism, *and* communal Hindutva, leftists like Satyabhakt embodied complex and hybrid social identities that released psychic and emotional energies for change. Historiography has accustomed us to remember the great reformers – Rammohan Roy, Jyotiba Phule, Dhondo Keshav Karve, etc. – and by implication to view even the exceptional subaltern struggle to articulate thought and initiate social change as quixotic or curious or unremarkable or subsumable within a generalised plebeian *Weltanschauung*. By focusing on figures like Santram, Yashoda, Satyadev, and Satyabhakt I have tried to suggest that there are intermediate, or more truly intermediary, figures who can be discerned and identified as thinkers and achievers of substance in their own right. The admittedly fragmentary, incomplete, sometimes amateur, and "minor" nature of the social philosophies and interpretive understandings of such middling and perhaps unclassifiable figures does not deserve them the oblivion in which they exist.

Three obvious common denominators are apparent in the world my quartet inhabited: vernacular print cultures, dreams and desires of freedom, and the deployment of Hindu ideas to project a utopian dream. They drew upon the rhythms of ordinary life, the daily experiences of lived realities, and ubiquitous popular Hindu practices. Their plural Hindi and Hindu notions of belonging, while problematic, represent a complexity of layered nuances, hidden transcripts, forgotten histories, and a range of possibilities that reside within the intellectual legacies of Hindi and Hinduism.

This book has tried to excavate, rescue, and resurrect four figures within the bounds of a small space and a short period of time. Each of them functioned as a representative of one key idea or concept that flourished in and helped shape Hindi and Hindu practices, behaviours, attitudes, predilections, and prejudices in critical ways. It can only be conjectured with confidence that there are very many more such, especially women, awaiting the arrival of historians into their several archives.

Glossary

achhut	literally "untouched"; an alternative and less negative term for "untouchable"
Ad Dharm	a popular Dalit movement in early-twentieth-century Punjab, led by Mangoo Ram
Adi Hindu	a popular Dalit movement in early-twentieth-century UP, led by Swami Acchutanand
Arya Samaj	activist Hindu revivalist organisation founded in 1875
ashlil	obscene, indecent
ashram	monastery; stage of one's life
aushadhalaya	(ayurvedic) dispensary
aushadhi	(ayurvedic) herbal medicine
azadi	freedom
Bania	used for members of castes associated with commerce, trade, and money-lending
bhabhi	elder sister-in-law
bigul	trumpet
brahmachari	celibate (man)
brahmacharya	male celibacy; sexual self-restraint
Brahmin	member of the highest Hindu caste in the fourfold varna scheme, with priestly traditions

GLOSSARY

Chamar	a major Dalit caste of North India, sometimes associated with leather work, but historically agriculturists; "Chamar" is a pejorative term; the caste is also known as "Jatav"
crore	ten million
Chhayavad	a dominant movement in Hindi poetry between 1918 and 1935, which stressed the poet's individual sensibility
chikitsa	cure; therapy
chikitsak	medical practitioner; doctor
churna	(ayurvedic) powder
chutia	knot of hair on head of Hindus; identified usually with Brahmins
dai	mostly an "untouchable" midwife
dampati	a married couple
dawa / dawaiyan / dawaein	medicines
desi	indigenous
devi	lady; goddess
dharma	religion; moral order
dhoti	cloth worn by men around lower torso
dvija	twice-born; pure-caste Hindu. Twice-born indicates a physical first birth and a second spiritual birth
ghar ka vaid	household doctor
gharelu	domestic; household
ghummakkad	a travel enthusiast; wanderer; traveller
grh	home; household
grhini	lady; mistress of the house

hakim	doctor; usually one practising the unani system of medicine
Harijan	literally "child of God"; term propagated by Gandhi for the "untouchables"
Hindu Mahasabha	all-India Hindu body founded in 1915
Hindutva	a militant concept of Hindu identity; term popularised from the 1920s by the ideologue V.D. Savarkar
hookah-pani	literally, smoking pipes and drinking; social intercourse
itihaas	history
jati	basic unit of Hindu caste; a subcaste
Jat-Pat Torak Mandal	"Organisation to Break Caste", founded in 1922
kaliyug	in Hindu mythology the fourth and most degenerate age of human history
kama vasna	carnal desire; libido
kama vigyan	sexual sciences
kama	sex; pleasure; desire; erotic love
Kamasutra	literally, "principles of love"; the classic Sanskrit manual on sex
kamashastra	science of sex
Kayastha	Hindu caste of North India (mainly), connected with administrative and scribal traditions
khadi	homespun cloth popularised by Gandhi
Khatri	Hindu caste of North India (mainly), associated with military and scribal traditions
kokashastra	treatise on sex

GLOSSARY

Kshatriya	Hindu upper caste, placed just below the Brahmin in the fourfold varna scheme, connected with kingly and warrior traditions
Kumhar	a Shudra, OBC caste of Punjab, traditionally potters; a section of Hindu Kumhars honorifically call themselves Prajapati
Nagari Pracharini Sabha	"Society for the Promotion of Nagari", founded in 1893 in Banaras
nuskhe	recipes
pak shastra	culinary science
panchayat	court of arbitrators (in a village), usually consisting of a community's elders, often elected
pandit	person (usually Brahmin) with knowledge of Hindu scriptures; used often by upper-caste learned Hindus as a suffix to their names
parivrajak	traveller
pralay	catastrophe; end of the world
pratilom	literally, "against the grain"; hypogamy; here signifies marriage between a "superior-caste" female and an "inferior-caste" male
Purana	collection of Hindu sacred texts, generally dating from the first millennium AD
Ram Rajya	the righteous reign of Ram
ramban	panacea; arrow of Ram, sweeping away all evil
rashtra	nation

rati/riti shastra	body of knowledge on the art of love-making
rishi	sage
roti-beti	food and marriage; bread and bride ties
Sanatani	one who believes in ancient, orthodox Hindu belief and practice
sangathan	organisation; here used for Hindu organisation in defence of "Hindu" interests
sangha	guild
santati shastra	knowledge of childcare
sanyasi	ascetic
satyug	blissful era of truth; an earlier age of piety, as opposed to *kaliyug*
savarna	dominant caste
seva	service; caring
shastra	a body of knowledge and writings, usually of ancient Hindu scriptures
shastric	classical; ancient sacred knowledge
shramjeevi	wage earner; worker
shuddhi	purification; Hindu movement in the late nineteenth and twentieth centuries to reclaim and reconvert those who had converted from Hinduism to other religions
Shudra	lowest Hindu caste in the fourfold varna scheme; caste with labouring traditions
stri	woman
swadeshi	manufactured and belonging to one's own country; the Swadeshi Movement asked for a ban on the import of foreign goods to India

swami	title given to a renowned sage
swaraj/swarajya	self-rule; independence
swatantrata	freedom
vaid/vaidya	ayurvedic (an Indian medical system) doctor
vaigyanik	scientific
Vaishya	third in the Hindu fourfold varna scheme, usually designating commercial livelihood
varna	literally "colour"; denoting the four traditional castes of Hinduism, viz. Brahmin, Kshatriya, Vaishya, and Shudra
varnashramdharma	duties performed according to the system of four varnas and four ashrams
varnavyavastha	caste system
vigyan	science
yogi	ascetic
zenana	upper-caste women's seclusion zone

Bibliography

The first part of the bibliography contains articles, followed by books, written by the four central subjects of the book. The year/edition mentioned first indicates the one I have used, unless otherwise stated.

Santram BA

"30 June 1948 ke Pehle aur Baad" (Before and After 30 June 1948), *Saraswati*, July 1947, 46–9.
"Aajkal ki Sundriyan" (Beauties of Today), *Sudha*, January 1939, 604–8.
"Abolish Castes to Be Free", *The Northern India Observer*, January 1943, 45.
"Achhuton ko Kya Karna Chahiye?" (What Should the Untouchables Do?), *Sudha*, August 1940, 189–91.
"Antarjatiya Vivah Pratha ki Aavyashakta" (Need for Inter-Caste Marriage), *Chand*, September 1935, 525–8.
"Antarjatiya Vivah" (Inter-Caste Marriage), *Sudha*, July 1929, 596–608.
"Bhartiya Jeevan ke Kuch Shochniya Drishya" (Some Sad Scenes of Indian Life), *Madhuri*, January 1925, 792–7.
"Byah Shaadi mein Nritya–Gaan ka Nishedh" (Prohibition of Singing–Dancing in Marriages), *Saraswati*, February 1938, 169–71.
"Chaturvarna Ved–Moolak Nahin" (The Caste System is Not Rooted in the Vedas), *Sudha*, August 1938, 103–12.
"Hindi aur Hindu ki Raksha ka Prashn" (The Question of Protecting Hindi and Hindu), *Saraswati*, February 1945, 72–5.
"Hindi ka Swaroop" (Form of Hindi), *Saraswati*, February 1940, 192–6.
"Hindi Mein Striyon ke Liye Upyogi Sahitya" (Useful Literature for Women in Hindi), *Sudha*, May 1928, 441–3.
"Hindu aur Swarajya" (Hindus and Independence), *Sudha*, February 1936, 2–9.
"Hindu Manovritti ke Kuch Namune" (Some Samples of the Hindu Mentality), *Chand*, November 1936, 47–51.
"Hindu Manovritti" (Hindu Mentality), *Sudha*, May 1929, 423–5.
"Hindu Rishis and the Caste", *Tribune*, 28 February 1936, 6.
"Hindu Sangathan ke Kuch Upay" (Some Measures for Hindu Sangathan), *Sudha*, May 1937, 275–84.

"Hindu Striyon ke Apharan ke Mool Karan" (Main Reasons for the Abduction of Hindu Women), *Saraswati*, October 1936, 373–8.
"Hindu Striyon mein Islam ka Prachaar" (Propagation of Islam among Hindu Women), *Chand*, September 1929, 593–5.
"Hindu Vinash ke Marg Par" (Hindus on the Path of Destruction), in *Jati Todo* (Break Caste) (Speeches Delivered at Akhil Bhartiya Jati Todo Mahasammelan, 1966) (Lucknow: Bahujan Kalyan Prakashan, 1981, 4th edn).
"Hamari Swatantrata ka Karyakram" (Our Programme for Freedom), *Saraswati*, June 1946, 506–10.
"Isse Anek Logon Ne Hindi Likhna Seekha" (Many People Learned to Write Hindi from This), in Narayan Chaturvedi, ed., *Saraswati Hirak Jayanti Ank, 1900–53* (Allahabad: Indian Press, 1961), 49–50.
"Jati–Panti ke Dushparinam" (The Ills of Casteism), *Sudha*, September 1927, 219–22.
"Jati–Panti ya Mritu?" (Casteism or Death), *Sudha*, February 1941, 26–30.
"Jat-Pat Torak Mandal ka Sandesh" (The Message of JPTM), *Madhuri*, February 1927, 60–3.
"Jat-Pat Torak Mandal", *Indian Social Reformer*, 36, 1 May 1926, 550.
"Jullundur Kanya Mahavidyalaya" (Girls' College in Jullundur), *Prabha*, June 1921, 344–6.
"Kamashastra aur Dharmik Pakshpat" (Sexual Science and Religious Sectarianism), *Sudha*, February 1932, 76–80.
"Kranti ki Lehar" (Wave of Revolution), *Saraswati,* September 1927, 1032–5.
"Ku-Klux-Klan ki Netri" (Leader of Ku-Klux-Klan), *Prabha*, January 1922, 37–9.
"Lahore ka Jat-Pat Torak Mandal" (Lahore's JPTM), *Saraswati*, February 1929, 188–93.
"League to Abolish Caste System", *Indian Social Reformer*, 33 (20), 13 January 1923, 320.
"Naagar–Sarvasvam", *Madhuri*, April 1923, 396–9.
"Naziyon ke Manovaigyanik Akraman" (Psychological Attacks of the Nazis), *Saraswati*, May 1941, 340–3.
"Place of Harijans in Caste System", *Tribune*, 17 December 1935, 10.
"Prem ka Satya Swaroop" (True Nature of Love), *Madhuri,* March 1939, 180–7.
"Punjab Kaumi Vidyapeeth" (Punjab Community College), *Prabha*, June 1923, 423–7.
"Punjab Mein Bhasha ka Prashn" (Question of Language in Punjab), *Saraswati*, October 1929, 425–30.
"Punjab Mein Hindi Par Sankat" (The Crisis of Hindi in Punjab), *Saraswati*, August 1931, 152–5.
"Purushon ke Anand" (The Pleasures of Men), *Chand*, January 1938, 270–2.
"Rashtriya Shiksha ka Swaroop" (The Nature of National Education), *Saraswati*, October 1922, 206–10.

"Rati Rahasya" (Secrets of Sex), *Madhuri,* December 1924, 601–5.
"Sahitya Sansaar mein Anuvaadkarta ka Sthaan" (The Place of Translators in the World of Literature), *Madhuri,* April 1942, 252–7.
"Sampradayik Ekta ki Samasya" (Problem in Communal Unity), *Sudha,* August 1941, 61–5.
"Sanskrit Sahitya Mein Kamashastra ka Sthan" (The Position of Sexual Science in Sanskrit Literature), *Madhuri,* July 1924, 789–95.
"Sanyukt Prant ki Hindi" (The Hindi of UP), *Saraswati,* June 1919, 324–7.
"Stri ke Saath Kaise Nibaha Ja Sakta Hai?" (How to Maintain Good Relations with a Woman), *Saraswati,* June 1936, 576–80.
"Subharya" (Accomplished Wife), *Saraswati,* April 1928, 398–407.
"Supati" (The Ideal Husband), *Madhuri,* April 1927, 308–15.
"Swami-ji: Jaisa Maine Unhen Dekha" (Swami-ji: As I Saw Him), in *Sri Swami Satya Dev,* 12–16.
"Swargiya Babu Chintamani aur Unka Mahatv" (The Late Babu Chintamani and His Importance), *Saraswati,* September 1928, n.p.
"Taunted and Scoffed by Orthodoxy: Anticaste Movement in the Punjab: Experiences of a Social Reform Leader", *The Sunday Observer,* 13 July 1952, 2–7.
"The Real Cause of Pakistan", *Indian Social Reformer,* 29 May 1957, 237–8.
"Varna Vyavastha ka Vastavik Swaroop" (The Real Nature of the Caste System), *Sudha,* April 1930, 292–4.
"Varna Vyavastha" (The Caste System), *Sudha,* August 1940, 117–21.
"Veshya Samajik Paheli" (Prostitute: A Social Puzzle), *Prabha,* September 1923, 190–1.
"Veshyavritti" (Prostitution), *Prabha,* August 1923, 110–16.
"Vidhi ka Vidhaan" (The Fate of Rites), *Hans: Atmakatha Ank,* January–February 1932, 42–4.
"Vivah ka Bhavishya" (The Future of Marriage), Parts I & II, *Sudha,* October & November 1931, 302–10 and 469–74, respectively.
"Vivahit Prem" (Marital Love), *Madhuri,* August 1940, 73–8.

Adarsh Pati (Ideal Husband) (Lahore: Rajpal & Sons, 1932; 1924, 2nd edn).
Adarsh Patni (Ideal Wife. A Book Advising Women on Matters of Love and Sex) (Delhi: Rajpal & Sons, 1950, 13th edn; 1924).
Agar Kashti Dubi tau Duboge Saare (Everyone will Drown if the Boat Drowns) (Hoshiarpur: Jat-Pat Torak Mandal, 1974; Delhi: Samyak Prakashan, 2008).
Alberuni ka Bharat, 3 vols (trans. of Alberuni's *Tarikh-al-Hind*) (Prayag: Indian Press Limited, 1926–8).
Antarjatiya Vivah hi Kyun? (Why Only Inter-Caste Marriages) (Hoshiarpur: Jat-Pat Torak Mandal, 1959).

Arya Samaj aur Varna Vyavastha (Arya Samaj and Caste System) (Lahore: Sahitya Sadan, n.d.).
Bharat mein Bible, 2 vols (trans. of Louis Jacolliot's *The Bible in India: Hindoo Origin of Hebrew and Christian Revelation*) (Lucknow: Ganga Pustakmala Karyalaya, 1928).
Caste Must Go: A Word About the Jat-Pat Torak Mandal, Lahore (Lahore: Jat-Pat Torak Mandal, 1938).
Dayanand (Prayag: Indian Press, 1930).
Ekagrata aur Divyashakti (trans. of O. Hashnu Hara's *Concentration and the Acquirement of Personal Magnetism*) (Bombay: Gandhi Hindi Pustak Bhandar, 1917).
Hindi Gadya Vatika (comp. & ed., Selection of Hindi Prose. Meant for Hindi Proficiency Examination, Punjab) (Lahore: Sahitya Sadan, 1936).
Hindu aur Jat–Pat (Hindus and Casteism) (Hoshiarpur: Jat-Pat Torak Mandal, 1967, 2nd edn).
Hindutva jo Hinduon ko hi Le Duba (Hindutva – which Ruined Hindus) (Hoshiarpur: Jat-Pat Torak Mandal, 1962; Delhi: Samyak Prakashan, 2008).
Hamara Samaj (Our Society) (Bombay: Nalanda Prakashan, 1949; Delhi: Samyak Prakashan, 2007, 3rd edn).
Hamare Bachhe (Our Children) (Hoshiarpur: Vishweshwaranand Vaidik Sansthan, 1950).
Itsing ki Bharat Yatra (trans. of I-Tsing's *A Record of the Buddhist Religion: As Practised in India and the Malay Archipelago, A.D. 671–695*) (Prayag: Indian Press Limited, 1925).
Jatibhed ka Uchhed (trans. of B.R. Ambedkar's *Annihilation of Caste*) (Lahore: Jat-Pat Torak Mandal, 1937).
Jati–Bhed Prashnotri (Question–Answers on Caste Discrimination) (Delhi: Bhartiya Dalit Varg Sangh, 1946).
Jativaad ka Janaza (The Funeral of Casteism) (New Delhi: Samyak Prakashan, 2006).
Jat–Pat ke Sambandh Mein Kuch Kadve–Kasaile Anubhav (Bitter Experiences of the Caste System) (Hoshiarpur: Jat-Pat Torak Mandal, 1958).
Kama Kunj (Garden of Sex. A Sex Manual for Women and Men) (Lucknow: Naval Kishore Press, 1929).
Karmyog (trans. of O. Hashnu Hara's *Practical Yoga*) (Lucknow: Ganga Pustakmala Karyalaya, 1939, 2nd edn).
Lok Vyavhaar arthat Mitra Banane aur Janta ko Prabhavit Karne ki Vidhiyan (trans. of Dale Carnegie's *How to Win Friends and Influence People*) (Prayag: Indian Press Limited, 1940, 5th edn; Bombay: D.B. Taraporevala, 1959).
Manav Jeevan ka Vidhaan (trans. of Robert Dodsley's *The Economy of Human Life*) (Prayag: Indian Press, 1923).

Mere Jeevan ke Anubhav (Experiences of My Life) (Varanasi: Hindi Pracharak Pustakalya, 1963; 1974, 2nd edn; rpntd Delhi: Gautam Book Centre, 2008).

Pakistan ki Sthapna mein Hinduon ka Haath (The Role of Hindus in the Establishment of Pakistan) (Hoshiarpur: Jat-Pat Torak Mandal, 1969).

Rashtriya Ekta aur Jatibhed (National Unity and Caste-Division) (Hoshiarpur: Jat-Pat Torak Mandal, 1963).

Rati Vigyan (Sexual Science) (Bombay: Bharatvarsh Prakashan, 1950, 2nd edn).

Rati Vilas (trans. of Marie Stopes' *Enduring Passion*) (Lahore: Rajpal, 1931).

Sahitya Sudha (Literary Nectar) (Lahore: Das Brothers, 1927, 3rd edn).

Santan Sankhya ka Seema-Bandhan arthat Dampati Mitra (Limiting the Number of Children, i.e. A Friend of the Couple, trans. of Marie Stopes' *Contraception*) (Lahore: Rajpal, 1926).

Sukhi Parivar (Happy Family) (Bombay: Bharatvarsh Prakashan, 1950).

Yugantar (ed.; Hindi Monthly Anticaste Journal) (Lahore, 1932–5).

Vinaash ka Marg Chodiye (Leave the Path of Destruction) (Hoshiarpur: Jat-Pat Torak Mandal, 1971).

Vivahit Prem (trans. of Marie Stopes' *Married Love*) (Lahore: Rajpal, 1925).

Yashoda Devi

Achaar ki Kothri arthat Achaar, Murabba, Chutney Banane ki Vidhi (Room of Pickles, i.e. A Guide to Making Pickles, Marmalades, Chutneys) (Allahabad: Stri Aushadhalaya, 1929, 2nd edn).

Adarsh Pati–Patni aur Santati Sudhar (Ideal Husband–Wife and Child Reform) (Allahabad: Banita Hitaishi Press, 1924, 2nd edn; 1913).

Arogya Vidhan Vidyarthi Jeevan (Student Life. A Handbook Especially Intended for Students, Treated from a Medical and Hygienic Point of View. An Attack on Masturbation Particularly – No. 1 of "Arogya Vidhan Sankhya" Series) (Allahabad: Banita Hitaishi Press, 1929).

Bharat ka Nari Itihaas (History of Women in India) (Allahabad: Sri Ram Sharma, 1921).

Dampati Arogyata Jeevanshastra arthat Ratishastra Santati Shastra aur Devi Anubhav Prakash (The Science of a Healthy Conjugal Life, or the Science of Sexual Intercourse and Procreation, and Light of Devi's Knowledge) (Allahabad: Devi Pustakalaya, 1931, 3rd edn; 1927, 2nd edn).

Dampatya Prem aur Ratikriya ka Gupt Rahasya (Secret of Love and Sex Between the Married Couple) (Allahabad: Banita Hitaishi Press, 1933).

Garbh Raksha Vidhan (Statutes for Safe Pregnancy. A Quasi Medical Tract – No. 4 of "Nari Kartavya Granthavali" Series) (Allahabad: Sri Ram Sharma, 1911; 1912, 2nd edn; 1912, 3rd edn; 1916, 4th edn; 1927, new edn).

Ghar ka Vaid (Household Doctor. A Medical Tract Intended for Indian Housewives – No. 14 of "Nari Kartavya Granthavali" Series) (Allahabad: Banita Hitaishi Press, 1912; 1913, 2nd edn; 1917, 3rd edn).

Grhini Kartavya Shastra Arogyashastra arthat Pakshastra (Manual for the Housewife on Vegetarian Cooking with Ayurvedic Instructions) (Allahabad: Sri Ram Sharma, 1913; 1915, 2nd edn; 1924, 3rd edn; 1932, 5th edn).

Kanya Gyan Vatika (ed.; Garden of Knowledge for Girls) (Allahabad: Devi Pustakalaya, 1939).

Kanya Kartavya (Duties of Girls) (Allahabad: Banita Hitaishi Press, 1925).

Kanya Sarvasva (ed.; Hindi Monthly Literary Journal for Girls) (Allahabad, 1930–6).

Nari Dharmashastra Grh-Prabandh Shiksha (Education on Home Management for Women) (Allahabad: Devi Pustakalaya, 1931).

Nari Sharir Vigyan Stri Chikitsa Sagar: Sambhog Vigyan (Women's Physiology and Women's Medical Treatment: The Science of Intercourse) (Allahabad: Devi Pustakalaya, 1938).

Nari Svasthya Raksha: Arogya Vidhan arthat Stri Rog Chikitsa (Women's Health Care, i.e. The Treatment of Women's Diseases. A Manual of Ayurvedic Medicines for Women's Diseases) (Allahabad: Stri Aushadhalaya, 1926).

Nari–Niti Shiksha (Teachings on Ethics for Women – No. 2 of "Nari Kartavya Granthavali" Series) (Allahabad: Banita Hitaishi Press, 1910; 1922, 2nd edn; 1926, 4th edn).

Pradar Rog Chikitsa (Treatment of Leukorrhea) (Allahabad: Sri Ram Sharma, 1940).

Ritu Dosh (Masik Dharmake Rog): Nidaan aur Chikitsa (Cures for Menstrual Disorders) (Allahabad: Sri Ram Sharma, 1940).

Shishu Raksha Vidhan Arthat Bal Rog Chikitsa: Pratham Bhag (Protection of Children, or the Treatment of Juvenile Diseases: Part I – No. 16 of "Nari Kartavya Granthavali" Series) (Allahabad, 1912; 1924, 2nd edn).

Stri Chikitsak (ed.; Hindi Monthly Journal Devoted to the Treatment of Female Diseases) (Allahabad, 1913–38, 5000 copies per month).

Stri Dharma Shikshak (ed.; Hindi Monthly Journal Dealing with Female Education and Social Issues) (Allahabad, 1909–31).

Vaidik Ratn Sangrah arthat Devi Anubhav Prakash (A Collection of Ayurvedic Medical Gems, or the Illustration of Devi's Medical Experience) (Allahabad: Banita Hitaishi Press, 1930, 2nd edn; 1927).

Vaidik Shastra ka Asli Kokshastra (Sexual Science as Dealt with in Ayurvedic Medical Science) (Allahabad: Sri Ram Sharma, 1929).

Vivah Vigyan (Science of Marriage) (Allahabad: Sri Ram Sharma, 1928).

Swami Satyadev Parivrajak

"A Country Fair in Germany", *The Rural India*, June 1940, 357–9.

"Aakaash Mein Meri Pehli Udaan" (My First Air Flight), *Saraswati,* November 1928, 529–40.
"America ka Rashtriya Din" (National Day of America), *Maryada,* September–October 1912, 395–7.
"Amrica Bhraman" (American Excursion), *Saraswati,* May 1911, 216–18.
"Amrica ke Kheton par Mere Kuch Din" (My Few Days on an American Farm), *Saraswati,* May 1908, 218–26.
"Amrica ki Striyan" (American Women), *Saraswati,* March 1908, 130–5.
"Amrica Mein Vidyarthi Jeevan" (Student Life in America), *Saraswati,* October 1908, 450–5.
"Ashcharyajanak Ghanti" (Amazing Bell), *Saraswati,* April 1908, 150–5.
"Bijli ki Railgadi" (Electric Railway), *Saraswati,* April 1907, 150–2.
"Chicago ka Ravivaar" (Sunday in Chicago), *Saraswati,* June 1907, 238–43.
"Chicago Mein Meri Pratham Ratri" (My First Night in Chicago), *Saraswati,* February 1907, 56–9.
"Chicago Vishwavidyalaya" (Chicago University), *Saraswati,* March 1907, 103–10.
"Geneva Jheel ki Sair" (Excursion on Lake Geneva), *Saraswati,* October 1907, 402–9.
"German Dictator Hitler", *Saraswati,* February 1934, 180–3.
"Germanon ki Pyari Rhine Nadi" (Beloved Rhine, River of the Germans), *Madhuri,* August 1929, 28.
"Hindi Sahitya aur Hamara Kaam" (Hindi Literature and Our Work), *Saraswati,* October 1909, 460–4.
"Kirti Kalima" (Glory and Disgrace), *Saraswati,* August 1908, 352–63.
"Main Dubara Germany Kaise Pahuncha" (How I Reached Germany Again), *Saraswati,* August 1928, 171–84.
"Main Kyun Hindu-Sangathan ka Pakshpaati Hoon" (Why I Am a Supporter of Hindu Sangathan), *Madhuri,* September 1929, 420–5.
"Mala" (Necklace), *Saraswati,* July 1911, 317–22.
"Mera Europe Prasthan" (My Departure to Europe), *Saraswati,* June 1934, 602–3.
"Meri Doosri Aakaash Yatra" (My Second Air Flight), *Saraswati,* December 1928, 650–7.
"Miss Parker ka School" (Miss Parker's School), *Maryada,* August 1911, 153–5.
"Nayi Duniya ke Samachar" (News from the New World), *Saraswati,* June 1907, 249–50.
"Nayi Duniya ki Khabren" (News from the New World), *Saraswati,* August 1907, 332–4.
"New York Nagri mein Veer Garibaldi" (Brave Garibaldi in New York), *Saraswati,* September 1907, 345–50.
"Nivedan" (Request), *Saraswati,* May 1910, 240.
"Paris Mein Do Raaten" (Two Nights in Paris), *Saraswati,* November 1929, 482–92.

"United States of America ki Prasidh Rajdhani Washington Shahar" (The United States' Famous Capital, Washington City), *Maryada,* June 1911, 61–4.
"Vyaayaam" (Exercise), *Saraswati,* August 1933, 118–25.

Amrica Bhraman: Pratham Bhag (An Excursion to America: Part I. Satya Granth Mala, 6) (Allahabad: Standard Press, 1913; 1916, 2nd edn; 1921, 3rd edn; 1926, new edn).
Amrica Digdarshan (An Account of the Author's Experiences of American Life and Institutions) (Allahabad: Satya Granth Mala, 1916, 2nd edn; Allahabad: Sahityaodaya Karyalaya, 1912; Agra: Mardana Book Depot, 1922; Patna and Prayag: 1926, rev. and enl. edn).
Amrica ke Nirdhan Vidyarthiyon ke Parishram (Diligence of Poor Students of America. Satya Granth Mala, 4) (Banaras: Satya Granthavali, 1912; Agra: Ramprasad Garg, 1917, 3rd edn; 1924, 4th edn).
Amrica ke Svavalambi Vidyarthi (Self-Supporting Students of America) (Jwalapur: Satya Gyan Niketan, 1957).
Amrica Path Pradarshak (A Guide Book for Indian Visitors to America) (Lucknow: Naval Kishore Press, 1911; Prayag: Sudershan Press, 1918, 2nd edn; Prayag: Sahityodaya Karyalaya, 1922, 4th edn).
Amrica Pravas ki Meri Adbhut Kahani (The Amazing Story of My Stay in America) (Jwalapur: Satyagyan Prakashan, 1957).
Asahyog (Non-Cooperation) (Ahmedabad: Atmtilak Granth Society, 1921).
Ashcharyajanak Ghanti tatha Anya Rochak Kathaein (The Amazing Bell and Other Interesting Stories) (Agra: Ramprasad Garg, 1921, 3rd edn).
Europe ki Sukhad Smritiyan (Sweet Memories of Europe) (Jwalapur: Satya Gyan Niketan, 1937).
Germany Mein Mere Aadhyatmik Pravachan arthat Meri Paanchvi Germany Yatra (My Spiritual Talks in Germany, i.e. My Fifth Trip to Germany) (Jwalapur: Satya Gyan Niketan, 1960).
Hindi ka Sandesh (The Message of Hindi) (Patna: Rajpali Press, 1926, 10th edn; 1922, 8th edn).
Lehsun Badshah (The King of Garlic) (Varanasi: Nagari Pracharini Sabha, 2013, 10th edn).
Meri German Yatra (My Journey to Germany. Satya Granth Mala, 15) (Dehradun: Sudarshan Press, 1926; 1925, 2nd edn).
Meri Kailash Yatra (My Pilgrimage to Kailash. Satya Granth Mala, 8) (Prayag: Satyadev, 1916; 1924, 2nd edn; 1926, new edn).
My Experiences in America: Part I, trans. A. Rama Iyer (Srirangam: Sri Vani Vilas Press, 1922).
Nayi Duniya ke Mere Adbhut Sansmaran (Reminiscences of My Student Life in America) (Jwalapur: Satya Gyan Niketan, 1939).
Rashtriya Sandhya (Hindu National Prayers) (Agra: Sahitya Ratn Bhandar, 1925).

Sangathan ka Bigul (Trumpet of Sangathan) (Dehradun: Satya Granth Mala, 1926, 3rd edn; 1925, 2nd edn).
Sanjeevni Booti (Immortalising Herb) (Bombay: Satyadev, 1926; 1914, 2nd edn).
Swatantrata ki Khoj Mein arthat Meri Atm Katha (In Search of Freedom, An Autobiography) (Jwalapur: Satya Gyan Niketan, 1951).
The First Hindi Reader: Hindi Bhasha ki Pehli Pustak: Hindi Prachar Series, Pamphlet No. 2 (Madras: Hindi Prachar Office, 1922).
The Hindi Propaganda: Hindi Prachar Series, Pamphlet No. 1 (Madras: Hindi Prachar Office, 1918).
Vichaar Swatantrya ke Prangan Mein: My Autobiography – Critics Answered (Jwalapur: Satya Gyan Niketan, 1952).
Yatri Mitra (Travelling Friend) (Jwalapur: Satya Gyan Niketan, 1936).

Satyabhakt

"Andhvishwas" (Superstition), *Chand*, September 1932, 499–504.
"Ann Dev ki Puja" (Worship of the God of Grain), *Chand*, December 1933, 253–9.
"Apradhi Kaun Hai?" (Who Is the Criminal?), *Chand*, June 1929, 180–8.
"Bharatvarsha mein Ashlilta ki Vriddhi" (The Growth of Obscenity in India), *Stri Darpan*, April 1919, 199–205.
"Bhartiya Striyon ko Sandesh" (Message to Indian Women), *Stri Darpan*, June 1920, 331–7.
"Bhut Rahasya" (The Mystery of Ghosts), *Stri Darpan*, July 1918, 40–8.
"Devtaon ki Utpatti" (The Origin of Gods), *Chand*, September 1933, 516–23.
"Hindi Gadya ka Kram Vikas" (The Chronological Development of Hindi Prose), *Saraswati*, March 1919, 139–46.
"Ishwar ki Utpatti" (The Origin of God), *Chand*, October 1933, 627–32.
"Mahatma Gandhi ki Jivani par Ek Drishti" (A Reflection on Mahatma Gandhi's Life), *Maryada*, May 1918, 229–36.
"Manushya ka Avirbhav" (The Emergence of Humankind), *Chand*, May 1933, 31–8.
"Prachin Bharat mein Striyon ke Adhikar", 4 Parts (The Rights of Women in Ancient India), *Stri Darpan*, January to April 1918.
"Prachin Kal ki Vivah Pratha" (Marriage Practices in Ancient Times), *Chand*, August 1933, 393–400.
"Prachin Kal ki Vyavsay Pranali" (The Occupational System in Ancient Times), *Chand*, February 1934, 463–8.
"Pralay" (The End of the World), *Chand*, July 1933, 290–9.
"Rajnaitik Kaidi aur Bharat Sarkar" (Political Prisoners and the Government of India), *Maryada*, May 1919, 241–5.
"Ramayana mein Stri Jati" (Women in the Ramayana), *Stri Darpan*, December 2017, 296–302.

"Ram–Rajya ki Adhunik Kalpana" (The Modern Imagining of Ram Rajya), *Chand*, November 1933, 153–7.
"Samyavad ke Acharya: Karl Marx" (The Master of Communism: Karl Marx), *Chand*, April 1931, 703–6.
"Samyavad kya Hai?" (What is Communism?), *Chand*, August 1929, 470–2.
"Sansar ke Vibhinn Deshon mein Shradh-Pratha" (The Custom of Honouring Deceased Ancestors in Various Countries), *Chand*, June 1932, 169–74.
"Sapt Dwip" (Seven Islands), *Chand*, November 1932, 37–40.
"Swargiya Radhamohan Gokulji ki Yaad Mein" (In Memory of the late Radhamohan Gokulji), in Shivprakash Pachauri, ed., *Radhamohan Gokulji Smarika* (Remembering Radhamohan Gokulji) (Agra, January 1983), 53–9.
"Vishwa Rachna" (World Formation), *Chand*, June 1933, 164–71.

Agle Sat Sal: San 1924 se 1931 Tak hone Wali Khand Pralay ka Varnan (The Next Seven Years: A Description of the Holocaust from 1924 to 1931. Samyavadi Pustak Mala 1) (Kanpur: Satyabhakt, 1924).
Bharat mein Samyavad: Indian Communist Party ka Arambhik Itihaas (Communism in India: Early History of the Indian Communist Party) (Agra: Prakashchandra, 1973).
Bhartiya Shramjeeviyon ko Sandesh (A Message to the Indian Proletariat) (Nagpur: Satyabhakt, 1923).
Bolshevism Kya Hai (*What is Bolshevism?*) (Kanpur: Socialist Bookshop, 1924).
Devtaon ke Gulam (trans. Katherine Mayo's *Slaves of the Gods*) (Kanpur: Socialist Bookshop, 1929).
Gorilla (Allahabad: Satyug, 1946).
Ireland ke Gadar ki Kahaniyan (Stories of the Irish Revolution) (Kanpur: Socialist Bookshop, 1927).
Karl Marx ka Jeevan Charitra (A Biography of Karl Marx) (Patna: Bharti Publishers, 1930).
Kranti ka Agaman: Sri Radhamohan Gokulji tatha anya Krantikari Mahamanavon ki Yug Parivartankari Vichardhara (ed.; Coming of Revolution: The Age-Altering Ideology of Radhamohan Gokul and Other Great Revolutionaries) (Bareilly: Sanskriti Sansthan, 1974).
Kranti Path ke Pathik (Travellers of the Revolutionary Path) (Bareilly: Sanskriti Sansthan, 1973).
Marne ke Bad (After Death) (Kanpur: Bhishm & Brothers, 1947).
Samvat Do Hazar, athva Bhavi Mahabharat (pseud., Bhartiya "Yogi". Samvat 2000, or The Coming Mahabharat) (Allahabad: Satyug Press, 1942, 4th edn).
Samyavad ka Sandesh (Message of Communism) (Allahabad: Navyuk Pustak Bhandar, 1929, 3rd rev. edn; 1934).

Samyavad ke Premiyon se Appeal: Communist Party Kya Chahti Hai (An Appeal to the Lovers of Communism: What Does the Communist Party Want) (Kanpur: Sudha Sacharaka Press, 1924).
Samyavad ke Siddhant (Principles of Communism) (Prayag: Tarun Bharat Granthavali, 1934).
Samyavadi (ed.; The Communist. Fortnightly Newspaper), 1 January 1926 & 16 January 1926.
Taalaab ki Kahani (The Story of a Pond) (Kanpur: Socialist Bookshop, 1927).
The Second Bhil Tragedy in Sirohi State: Report (with Ramnarayan) (Ajmer: Rajasthan Sevasangha, 1922).

Other Published Sources

Adcock, C.S., *The Limits of Tolerance: Indian Secularism and the Politics of Religious Freedom* (New York: Oxford University Press, 2014).
Adhikari, G., ed., *Documents of the History of the Communist Party of India, Vol. II, 1923–25* (Delhi: People's Publishing House, 1974).
Adolph, Andrea, *Food and Femininity in Twentieth Century British Women's Fiction* (England: Ashgate, 2009).
Agarwal, Kanhaiya Lal, *Grhini Chikitsa* (The Treatment of Women's Diseases) (Allahabad: Granthkar, 1922).
Ahluwalia, Sanjam, "'Tyranny of Orgasm': Global Governance of Sexuality from Bombay, 1930s–1950s", in Fuechtner, Haynes and Jones, eds, *A Global History of Sexual Science*, 353–73.
Ahluwalia, Sanjam, *Reproductive Restraints: Birth Control in India, 1877–1947* (Urbana: University of Illinois Press, 2008).
Ahmad, Muzaffar, *Myself and the Communist Party of India, 1920–9* (Calcutta: National Book Agency, 1970).
Ahmed, Talat, *Literature and Politics in the Age of Nationalism: The Progressive Episode in South Asia, 1932–56* (London: Routledge, 2009).
Ahuja, Ravi, "Authoritarian Shadows: Indian Independence and the Problem of Democratisation", *Social Scientist*, 46 (5–6), May–June 2018, 3–20.
Ainslie, Whitelaw, *Materia Indica, II* (London: Longman, 1826).
Alam, Muzaffar, and Sanjay Subrahmanyam, *Indo-Persian Travels in the Age of Discoveries, 1400–1800* (Cambridge: Cambridge University Press, 2007).
Alavi, Seema, *Islam and Healing: Loss and Recovery of an Indo-Muslim Medical Tradition, 1600–1900* (Ranikhet: Permanent Black, 2007).
Al-Bagdadi, Nadia, David Marno, and Matthias Riedl, eds, *The Apocalyptic Complex: Perspectives, Histories, Persistence* (New York: Central European University Press, 2018).
Ali, Daud, "Padmasri's 'Nagarasarvasva' and the World of Medieval Kamasastra", *Journal of Indian Philosophy*, 39 (1), February 2011, 41–62.

Alter, Joseph S., *Gandhi's Body: Sex, Diet and the Politics of Nationalism* (Philadelphia: University of Pennsylvania Press, 2000).
Alter, Joseph S., *The Wrestler's Body: Identity and Ideology in North India* (Delhi: Oxford University Press, 1993).
Ambedkar, B.R., *Annihilation of Caste: Speech Prepared for the Annual Conference of JPTM of Lahore but Not Delivered* (Bombay: B.R. Kadrekar, 1936).
Anand, Dibyesh, *Hindu Nationalism in India and the Politics of Fear* (New York: Palgrave, 2011).
Anand, S., "Sanskrit, English and Dalits", *Economic and Political Weekly*, 34 (30), 24 July 1999, 2053–6.
Anandhi, S., "Reproductive Bodies and Regulated Sexuality: Birth Control Debates in Early Twentieth Century Tamilnadu", in Mary E. John and Janaki Nair, eds, *A Question of Silence? The Sexual Economies of Modern India* (New Delhi, 1998), 139–66.
Anon., "Book Review of Swami Satya Deva's *In Search of Freedom: An Autobiography*", *The Sunday Tribune (Magazine Section)*, 17 February 1952, IV.
Appadurai, Arjun, "How to Make a National Cuisine: Cookbooks in Contemporary India", *Comparative Studies in Society and History*, 30 (1), 1988, 3–24.
Arendt, Hannah, *The Human Condition* (Chicago: Chicago University Press, 2018, 2nd edn).
Arnold, David, and Stuart Blackburn, "Introduction: Life Histories in India", in David Arnold and Stuart Blackburn, eds, *Telling Lives in India*, (Delhi: Permanent Black, 2004), 1–28.
Arnold, David, and Stuart Blackburn, eds, *Telling Lives in India: Biography, Autobiography, and Life History* (Delhi: Permanent Black, 2004).
Arnold, David, *Colonizing the Body: State Medicine and Epidemic Disease in Nineteenth-Century India* (Berkeley: University of California Press, 1993).
Arnold, David, *Science, Technology and Medicine in Colonial India: The New Cambridge History of India III.5* (Cambridge: Cambridge University Press, 2000).
Arondekar, Anjali, and Geeta Patel, "Area Impossible: Notes toward an Introduction", *GLQ: A Journal of Lesbian and Gay Studies*, 22 (2), 2016, 151–71.
Arondekar, Anjali, *Abundance: Sexuality's History* (Durham: Duke University Press, 2023).
Arondekar, Anjali, *For the Record: On Sexuality and the Colonial Archive in India* (Durham: Duke University Press, 2009).
Aryabhasha Pustakalay ka Suchipatra, Vol. 1 (List of Books at Nagari Pracharini Sabha Library) (Kashi: Nagari Pracharini Sabha, 1941).
"Atmakatha Ank" (Autobiography Issue), *Hans*, January–February 1932, rpnt, with an introduction by Purushottam Das Modi (Varanasi: Vishwavidyalaya Prakashan, 2010; 2008).
Auxiliary Committee of the Indian Statutory Commission, *Review of the Growth of Education in British India* (Delhi: Government of India Press, 1930).

Awasthi, Ramashankar, *Bolshevik Jadugar, Arthat Lenin ki Jivani aur Uske Vichaar* (Bolshevik Magician, Meaning Biography of Lenin and His Thoughts) (Calcutta: Bharat Pustak Bhandar, 1921).
Awasthi, Ramashankar, *Lal Kranti: Bolshevik Kranti ka Sachitra Itihaas* (Red Revolution: Illustrated History of Bolshevik Revolution) (Calcutta: Mukundlal Verma, 1928).
Awasthi, Ramashankar, *Rus ki Rajya Kranti* (Russian Revolution) (Kanpur: Pratap Pustakalay, 1920).
Bachchan, Harivansh Rai, *In the Afternoon of Time: An Autobiography*, ed., and trans., Rupert Snell (New Delhi: Penguin, 1998).
Bai, Satyabhama, *Dhatri Vidya* (The Art of Midwifery) (Allahabad: Stri Aushadhalaya, 1913).
Bai, Satyabhama, *Jeevan Raksha* (Preservation of Life) (Allahabad: Stri Aushadhalaya, 1912).
Baishya, Anirban K. and Darshan S. Mini, "Translating Porn Studies: Lessons from the Vernacular", *Porn Studies*, 7 (1), 2020, 2–12.
Balfour, Margaret I., and Ruth Young, *The Work of Medical Women in India* (London, H. Milford, 1929).
Ballabh, Radha, *Marnonmukhi Arya Chikitsa* (Treatment of the Dying Ayurvedic System) (Aligarh: Banke Lal, 1922, 2nd edn).
Banerjee, Gopal, ed., *S.A. Dange: A Fruitful Life* (Kolkata: Progressive Publishers, 2002).
Banerjee, Prathama, *Elementary Aspects of the Political: Histories from the Global South* (Durham: Duke University Press, 2020).
Banerjee, Sandeep, *Space, Utopia and Indian Decolonization: Literary Pre-Figurations of the Postcolony* (New York: Routledge, 2019).
Banerjee, Sikata, *Make Me a Man: Masculinity, Hinduism and Nationalism in India* (Albany: SUNY Press, 2005).
Bapu, Prabhu, *Hindu Mahasabha in Colonial North India, 1915–1930: Constructing Nation and History* (London: Routledge, 2013).
Basu, Tapan, *Hindi Dalit Literature in the United Provinces: Swami Acchutanand and Chandrika Prasad Jigyasu, 1900–1930* (New Delhi: Bloomsbury, 2023).
Bauer, Heike, "'Not a Translation but a Mutilation': The Limits of Translation and the Discipline of Sexology", *The Yale Journal of Criticism*, 16 (2), Fall 2002, 381–405.
Bauer, Heike, *English Literary Sexology: Translations of Inversion, 1860–1930* (New York: Palgrave Macmillan, 2009).
Baxter, Rev. M., *Coming Wonders Expected Between 1867 and 1875* (London: E.A. Taylor, 1867).
Bayly, Susan, *Caste, Society, and Politics in India: From the Eighteenth Century to the Modern Age* (Cambridge: Cambridge University Press, 1999).
Bazaz, P.N., *The Shadow of Ram Rajya over India* (Delhi: Spark, 1980).

Berg, Axel van den, *The Immanent Utopia: From Marxism on the State to the State of Marxism* (Princeton: Princeton University Press, 1988).
Berger, James, "Introduction: Twentieth Century Apocalypse: Forecasts and Aftermaths", *Twentieth Century Literature*, 46 (4), Winter 2000, 387–95.
Berger, Rachel, "Alimentary Affairs: Historicizing Food in Modern India", *History Compass*, 16 (2), 2018, 1–10.
Berger, Rachel, "Between Digestion and Desire: Genealogies of Food in Nationalist North India", *Modern Asian Studies*, 47 (5), 2013, 1622–43.
Berger, Rachel, "Clarified Commodities: Managing Ghee in Interwar India", *Technology and Culture*, 60 (4), 2019, 1004–26.
Berger, Rachel, *Ayurveda made Modern: Political Histories of Indigenous Medicine in North India, 1900–1955* (New York: Palgrave, 2013).
Berlant, Lauren and Jay Prosser, "Life Writing and Intimate Publics: A Conversation with Lauren Berlant", *Biography*, 34 (1), Winter 2011, 180–7.
Berlant, Lauren, *Desire/Love* (New York: Punctum Books, 2012).
Bhabha, Homi, "Unsatisfied: Notes on Vernacular Cosmopolitanism", in L. Garcia-Moreno and P.C. Pfeiffer, eds, *Text and Narration: Cross-Disciplinary Essays on Cultural and National Identities* (Columbia: Camden House Press, 1996), 191–207.
Bhagwandas, Bhakt, *Ras Vyanjan Prakash* (Light on Delicious Dishes) (Bombay: Venkateshwar Press, 1902).
Bhargav, Mohanlal, *Vyanjan Prakash, arthat Sab Prakaar ke Bhojan Banane ki Vidya* (Recipe Knowledge, Meaning the Method of Preparing Food of all Kinds) (Lucknow: Naval Kishore Press, 1938, 3rd edn; 1924, 2nd edn).
Bhargava, Rajeev, *Secularism and Its Critics: Themes in Politics* (Delhi: Oxford University Press, 1999).
Bharti, Kanwal, "Santram BA: A Committed Anticaste Warrior", *Forward Press*, 26 July 2017, https://www.forwardpress.in/2017/07/santram-b-a-a-committed-anti-castewarrior/, accessed 21 October 2017.
Bhattacharji, Shobhana, ed., *Travel Writing in India* (New Delhi: Sahitya Akademi, 2008).
Bhattacharya, Neeladri, "Predicaments of Secular Histories", *Public Culture*, 20 (1), 2008, 57–73.
Blackburn, Stuart, and Vasudha Dalmia, "Introduction", in Stuart Blackburn and Vasudha Dalmia, eds, *India's Literary History: Essays on the Nineteenth Century* (Delhi: Permanent Black, 2004).
Blackburn, Stuart, "Death and Deification: Folk Cults in Hinduism", *History of Religions*, 24 (3), February 1995, 255–74.
Blackburn, Stuart, *Print, Folklore, and Nationalism in Colonial South India* (Delhi: Permanent Black, 2003).
Botre, Shrikant, and Douglas E. Haynes, "Sexual Knowledge, Sexual Anxieties: Middle-Class Males in Western India and the Correspondence in *Samaj Swasthya*, 1927–53", *Modern Asian Studies*, 51 (4), 2017, 991–1034.

Botre, Shrikant, and Douglas E. Haynes, "Understanding R.D. Karve: *Brahmacharya*, Modernity, and the Appropriation of Global Sexual Science in Western India, 1927–1953", in Veronika Fuechtner, Douglas E. Haynes, and Ryan M. Jones, eds, *A Global History of Sexual Science, 1880–1960* (California: University of California Press, 2018),163–85.

Brandt, Susan H., *Women Healers: Gender, Authority, and Medicine in Early Philadelphia* (Philadelphia: University of Pennsylvania Press, 2022).

Brass, Paul R., "The Politics of Ayurvedic Education: A Case Study of Revivalism and Modernization in India", in Susanne Hoeber Rudolph and Lloyd I. Rudolph, eds, *Education and Politics in India: Studies in Organisation, Society, and Policy* (Delhi: Oxford University Press, 1972), 342–71.

Brueck, Laura, *Writing Resistance: The Rhetorical Imagination of Hindi Dalit Literature* (New York: Columbia University Press, 2014).

Bulfin, Ailise, "The Natural Catastrophe in Late Victorian Popular Fiction: How Will the World End?", *Critical Survey*, 27 (2), 2015, 81–101.

Burleigh, Michael, *Day of the Assassins: A History of Political Murder* (London: Picador, 2021).

Burton, Antoinette, *At the Heart of Empire: Indians and the Colonial Encounter in Late Victorian Britain* (Berkeley: University of California Press, 1998).

Burton, Antoinette, *Burdens of History: British Feminists, Indian Women and Imperial Culture. 1865–1915* (Chapel Hill: The University of North Carolina Press, 1994).

Burton, David, *The Raj at the Table: A Culinary History of the British in India* (London: Faber and Faber, 1993).

Butler, Judith, *Bodies that Matter: On the Discursive Limits of 'Sex'* (London: Routledge, 1993).

Cashbaugh, Sean, "A Paradoxical, Discrepant, and Mutant Marxism: Imagining a Radical Science Fiction in the American Popular Front", *Journal for the Study of Radicalism*, 10 (1), Spring 2016, 63–106.

Census of India, 1911, Punjab, XIV (I), Report by Pandit Harikishan Kaul (Lahore: Civil and Military Gazette Press, 1912).

Census of India, 1911, UP, XV (I), Report by E.A.H. Blunt (Allahabad: Government Printing, 1912).

Census of India, 1921, Punjab and Delhi, XV (I), Report by L. Middleton and S.M. Jacob (Lahore: Civil and Military Gazette Press, 1923).

Census of India, 1931, Bengal & Sikkim, V (I), Report by A.R. Porter (Calcutta: Central Publication Branch, 1933).

Census of India, 1931, Jammu & Kashmir State, XXIV (I), Report by Rai Bahadur Pt Anant Ram (Jammu: Government Press, 1933).

Census of India, 1931, Punjab, XVII (I), Report by Khan Ahmad Hasan Khan (Lahore: Civil and Military Gazette Press, 1933).

Census of India, 1931, UP, XVIII (I), Report by A.C. Turner (Allahabad: Printing and Stationery, 1933).

Chaddha, Gargi, "Unki Yaden aur Chhoti-Chhoti Baten" (His Memories and Snippets), *Vishwajyoti (Sri Santram BA Smriti Ank)*, September 1988, 28–34.

Chakrabarty, Dipesh, "Radical Histories and Question of Enlightenment Rationalism: Some Recent Critiques of *Subaltern Studies*", *Economic and Political Weekly*, 30 (14), 8 April 1995, 751–9.

Chakrabarty, Dipesh, *Provincializing Europe: Postcolonial Thought and Historical Difference* (Princeton: Princeton University Press, 2000).

Chakraborty, Chandrima, *Masculinity, Asceticism, Hinduism: Past and Present Imaginings of India* (Ranikhet: Permanent Black, 2011).

Chakravarti, Uma, *Gendering Caste Through a Feminist Lens* (Calcutta: Stree, 2003).

Chatterjee, Partha, "Introduction: History in the Vernacular", in Raziuddin Aquil and Partha Chatterjee, eds, *History in the Vernacular* (Ranikhet: Permanent Black, 2008), 1–24.

Chatterjee, Partha, "Nationalism, Internationalism, and Cosmopolitanism: Some Observations from Modern Indian History", *Comparative Studies of South Asia, Africa and Middle East*, 36 (2), 2016, 320–34.

Chatterjee, Partha, *The Truths and Lies of Nationalism – as Narrated by Charvak* (Ranikhet: Permanent Black, 2021).

Chattopadhyay, Suchetana, *An Early Communist: Muzaffar Ahmad in Calcutta 1913–29* (New Delhi: Tulika Books, 2011).

Chaturvedi, L.P., *Ram Rajya and Its Ideals* (Nagpur: Vishwa Bharti Prakashan, 1992).

Chaturvedi, Pankaj, *Atmakatha ki Sanskriti* (New Delhi: Vani Prakashan, 2011).

Chaturvedi, Shailkumari, *Navin Pak-Shastra* (Novel Culinary Science) (Mathura: Adarsh Hindu Pustakalaya, 1939).

Chaturvedi, Vinayak, *Hindutva and Violence: V.D. Savarkar and the Politics of History* (Ranikhet: Permanent Black, 2022).

Chaudhari, Shaukat Rai, *Ayurveda ka Vaigyanik Svarup* (Scientific Basis of Ayurveda) (Kangri: Gurukul Press, 1918).

Chiang, Howard, *After Eunuchs: Science, Medicine, and the Transformation of Sex in Modern China* (New York: Columbia University Press, 2018).

Chiang, Howard, ed., *Sexuality in China: Histories of Power and Pleasure* (Seattle: University of Washington Press, 2018).

Chopra, Radhika, Caroline Osella, and Filippo Osella, eds, *South Asian Masculinities: Context of Change, Sites of Continuity* (Delhi: Women Unlimited, 2004).

Choudhury, Ishani, "A Palatable Journey through the Pages: Bengali Cookbooks and the 'Ideal' Kitchen in the Late Nineteenth and Early Twentieth Century", *Global Food History*, 3 (1), 2017, 24–39.

Chowdhry, Prem, *Contentious Marriages, Eloping Couples: Gender, Caste and Patriarchy in Northern India* (Delhi: Oxford University Press, 2007).

Chowdhuri, Satyabrata Ray, *Leftism in India, 1917–1947* (New York: Palgrave, 2007).
Chudal, Alaka Atreya, *A Freethinking Cultural Nationalist: A Life History of Rahul Sankrityayan* (New Delhi: Oxford University Press, 2016).
Chudal, Alka Atreya, "A Life of the 'Other' and a Story of the 'Self': Shivrani Devi in *Premcand Ghar Me*", *Cracow Indological Studies*, 20 (2), 2018, 145–62.
Collingham, E.M., *Imperial Bodies. The Physical Experience of the Raj, c.1800– 1947* (Cambridge: Polity Press, 2001).
Communist Party of India (Marxist), *Memoirs: 25 Communist Freedom Fighters* (Delhi: People's Democracy, 2005).
Constable, Philip, "Sitting on the Verandah: The Ideology and Practice of 'Untouchable' Educational Protest in Late Nineteenth-Century Western India", *The Indian Economic and Social History Review*, 37 (4), 2000, 383–422.
Curtis, Heather D., "'There Are No Secular Events': Popular Media and the Diverging Paths of British and American Evangelicalism", in David Hempton and Hugh McLeod, eds, *Secularization and Religious Innovation in the North Atlantic World* (Oxford: Oxford University Press, 2017), 80–102.
Cutter, Martha J., "Editor's Introduction: Translation and Alternative Forms of Literacy", *MELUS: Multi-Ethnic Literature of the US*, 34 (4), Winter 2009, 5–13.
Daechsel, Markus, *The Politics of Self-Expression: The Urdu Middleclass Milieu in Mid-Twentieth Century India and Pakistan* (New York: Routledge, 2006).
Dalmia, Vasudha, *Fiction as History: The Novel and the City in Modern North India* (Ranikhet: Permanent Black, 2017).
Dalmia, Vasudha, *The Nationalization of Hindu Traditions: Bharatendu Harischandra and Nineteenth-century Banaras* (Delhi: Oxford University Press, 1997).
Dalton, Dennis, *Indian Ideas of Freedom* (Delhi: HarperCollins India, 2023).
Danton, Robert, "Book Production in British India, 1850–1900", *Book History*, 5, 2002, 239–62.
Das, Bhagwan, *In Pursuit of Ambedkar: A Memoir* (Delhi: Navayana, 2009).
Dasgupta, Probal, "Sanskrit, English and Dalits", *Economic and Political Weekly*, 35 (16), 15 April 2000, 1407–12.
Dasgupta, Rajarshi, "The Ascetic Modality: A Critique of Communist Self-fashioning", in Nivedita Menon, Aditya Nigam, and Sanjay Palshikar, eds, *Critical Studies in Politics: Exploring Sites, Selves, Power* (Delhi: Orient BlackSwan, 2014), 67–87.
Dekker, Rudolf, "Introduction", in Rudolf Dekker, ed., *Egodocuments and History: Autobiographical Writing in Its Social Context since the Middle Ages* (Hilversum: Verloren, 2002), 7–20.
Derrida, Jacques, "The Law of Genre", trans. Avital Ronell, *Critical Inquiry*, 7 (1), 1980, 55–81.

Devi, Anant, *Vyanjan Prakash* (Culinary Wisdom) (Kanpur: Lala Pooranmal Bookseller, 1910).
Dharmvir, *Dalit Chintan ka Vikas* (Development of Dalit Thought) (New Delhi: Vani Prakashan, 2008).
Dhingra, Tekchand, "Rajnaitik Sanyasi" (Political Ascetic), in *Sri Swami Satya Dev*, 6–11.
Dimitrova, Diana, *Hinduism and Hindi Theatre* (New York: Palgrave, 2016).
Dirks, Nicholas B., *Castes of Mind: Colonialism and the Making of Modern India* (Princeton: Princeton University Press, 2001).
Doniger, Wendy, "From Kama to Karma: The Resurgence of Puritanism in Contemporary India", *Social Research,* 78 (1), Spring 2011, 49–74.
Dube, Deo Narayan, *Santan Vigyan* (Science of Procreation) (Banaras: Bhargav Press, 1930).
Dube, Devi Prasad, ed., *A Guide to Mothers or, How to Preserve the Health of Children* (Agra: Sat Brat, 1899).
Dupee, Jeffrey N., *British Travel Writers in China: Writing Home to a British Public, 1890–1914* (Lewiston: The Edwin Mellen Press, 2004).
Dussel, Enrique, *Beyond Philosophy: Ethics, History, Marxism and Liberation Theology,* ed. Eduardo Mendieta (Lanham: Rowman & Littlefield Publishers, Inc., 2003).
Dutt, Narayan, ed., *Banarsidas Chaturvedi ke Chuninda Patra: Ek Lambe Yug ki Jhankiyan, Vol. 1* (Selected Letters of Banarsidas Chaturvedi: Glimpses of a Long Era) (Delhi: Rajkamal, 2006).
Dutt, Udoy Chand, *The Materia Medica of the Hindus, with a Glossary of Indian Plants by George King* (1870; rpntd Varanasi: Chowkhamba, 1980, 3rd edn).
Eakin, Paul John, "Foreword", in Philippe Lejeune, *On Autobiography,* trans. Katherine Leary (Minneapolis: University of Minneapolis Press, 1989), vii–xxviii.
Eakin, Paul John, *Writing Life Writing: Narrative, History, Autobiography* (New York: Routledge, 2020).
Eaton, Richard M., *A Social History of the Deccan, 1300–1761: Eight Indian Lives* (Cambridge: Cambridge University Press, 2005).
Editor, "Daktari Dawaein" (Allopathic Doctor's Medicines), *Chand*, November 1922, 62–72.
Editor, "Jati-Pati Torak Sansthan" (Organisation to Break Caste), *Chand*, January 1923, 174–5.
Elst, Koenraad, *Mahatma Gandhi and His Assassin* (New Delhi: Voice of India, 2015).
Ender, Evelyne, *Architexts of Memory: Literature, Science and Autobiography* (Ann Arbor: University of Michigan Press, 2005).
Ernst, Waltraud, ed., *Plural Medicine, Tradition and Modernity, 1800–2000* (London: Routledge, 2002).

Fallon, S.W., ed., *Hindustani–English Dictionary of Idioms and Proverbs* (New Delhi: Star Publications, 1991; 1886).

Fischer-Tiné, Harald, Julia Hauser, and Ashok Malhotra, "Introduction: Feeding Bodies, Nurturing Identities: The Politics of Diet in Late Colonial and Early Post-Colonial India", *South Asia: Journal of South Asian Studies*, 44 (1), 2021, 107–16.

Fisher, Michael H., *Counterflows to Colonialism: Indian Travellers and Settlers in Britain, 1600–1858* (Delhi: Permanent Black, 2004).

Foley, Barbara, "Biography and the Political Unconscious: Ellison, Toomer, Jameson, and the Politics of Symptomatic Reading", *Biography*, 36 (4), Fall 2013, 649–71.

Foucault, Michel, *The History of Sexuality: Vol. 1*, trans. Robert Hurley (New York: Vintage, 1990).

Fox, Richard, *Gandhian Utopia: Experiments with Culture* (Boston: Beacon Press, 1989).

Frazer, Gregg L., *The Religious Beliefs of America's Founders: Reason, Revelation, and Revolution* (Kansas: University Press of Kansas, 2012).

Frazier, Jessica, "History and Historiography in Hinduism", *The Journal of Hindu Studies*, 2, 2009, 1–16.

Freitag, Sandria B., *Collective Action and Community: Public Arenas and the Emergence of Communalism in North India* (Berkeley: University of California, 1989).

Fuechtner, Veronika, Douglas E. Haynes, and Ryan M. Jones, "Introduction: Toward a Global History of Sexual Science: Movements, Networks, and Deployments", in Veronika Fuechtner, Douglas E. Haynes, and Ryan M. Jones, eds, *A Global History of Sexual Science, 1880–1960* (California: University of California Press, 2018), 1–25.

Fuechtner, Veronika, Douglas E. Haynes, and Ryan M. Jones, eds, *A Global History of Sexual Science, 1880–1960* (California: University of California Press, 2018).

Gajarawala, Toral Jatin, *Untouchable Fictions: Literary Realism and the Crisis of Caste* (New York: Fordham University Press, 2012).

Gandhi, Mahatma, *The Collected Works of Mahatma Gandhi, 98 Vols (Electronic Book)* (New Delhi: Publications Division Government of India, 1999).

Gandhi, Mahatma, *Young India: 1924–1926* (Madras: S. Ganesan, 1927).

Gaur, Ganeshdutt Sharma, *Santan Shastra* (Science of Child Management) (Allahabad: Hindi Sahitya, 1928, 2nd edn).

Gazetteer of the Hoshiarpur District, 1883–4 (Lahore: Civil and Military Gazette Press, 1885).

Geetha, V., and S.V. Rajadurai, *Towards a Non-Brahmin Millennium: From Iyothee Thass to Periyar* (Kolkata: Samya, 2011; 1998).

General Review, *The Jat-Pat Torak Mandal* (Organisation to Break Caste) (Lahore: Lion Press, 1939).

Ghanekar, Bhaskar Govind, *Aupsargik Rog* (Infectious Diseases) (Banaras, 1937).
Gharelu Chikitsa (Household Cure), Anek Suvikhyaat Doctor tatha Anubhavi Stri–Purush (Many Eminent Doctors and Experienced Men and Women) (Allahabad: Chand Karyalaya, 1929, 3rd edn; 1927).
Ghose, Indira, ed., *Memsahibs Abroad: Writings by Women Travellers in Nineteenth Century India* (Delhi: Oxford University Press, 1998).
Ghosh, Anindita, ed., *Power in Print: Popular Publishing and the Politics of Language and Culture in a Colonial Society, 1778–1905* (Delhi: Oxford University Press, 2006).
Ghosh, Durba, *Sex and the Family in Colonial India: The Making of Empire* (Cambridge: Cambridge University Press, 2006).
Giddens, Anthony, *The Transformation of Intimacy: Sexuality, Love, and Eroticism in Modern Societies* (Stanford: Stanford University Press, 1992).
Gilroy, Paul, *The Black Atlantic: Modernity and Double Consciousness* (London: Verso, 1993).
Girdavar, Sannulal Gupt, *Stri Subodhini* (Manual on the Ideal Conduct of a Woman) (Lucknow: Naval Kishore Press, 1922).
Girija, K.P., *Mapping the History of Ayurveda: Culture, Hegemony and the Rhetoric of Diversity* (London: Routledge, 2022).
Gokul, Radhamohan, *Communism Kya Hai?* (What is Communism?) (Kanpur: Socialist Bookshop, 1927).
Goodrick-Clark, Nicholas, *Hitler's Priestess: Savitri Devi, the Hindu-Aryan Myth, and Neo-Nazism* (New York: New York University Press, 1998).
Gooptu, Nandini, *The Politics of the Urban Poor in Early Twentieth Century India* (Cambridge: Cambridge University Press, 2001).
Gopal, Madan, "A Hundred Years of Writing", *Times of India*, 16 February 1987, 8.
Gordin, Michael D., Helen Tilley, and Gyan Prakash, "Introduction: Utopia and Dystopia Beyond Space and Time", in Michael D. Gordin, Helen Tilley, and Gyan Prakash, eds, *Utopia/Dystopia: Conditions of Historical Possibility* (Princeton: Princeton University Press, 2010), 1–17.
Gould, William, *Hindu Nationalism and the Language of Politics in Late Colonial India* (Cambridge: Cambridge University Press, 2005).
Govind, Nikhil, *Between Love and Freedom: The Revolutionary in the Hindi Novel* (Delhi: Routledge, 2014).
Graham, James Reid, "The Arya Samaj as a Reformation in Hinduism with Special Reference to Caste", Unpublished PhD Dissertation (New Haven: Yale University, 1943).
Gramsci, Antonio, *Selections from the Prison Notebooks*, ed. and trans. Quintin Hoare and Geoffrey Nowell Smith (New York: International Publishers, 1971).
Granoff, Phyllis, *Monks and Magicians: Religious Biographies in Asia* (Oakville: Mosaic Press, 1988).

Green, T. H., *Lectures on the Principles of Political Obligation* (Kitchener: Batoche Books, 1999).
Greenblatt, Stephen, *Renaissance Self-Fashioning: From More to Shakespeare* (Chicago: University of Chicago Press, 1980).
Guha, Ambalika, *Colonial Modernities: Midwifery in Bengal, c.1860–1947* (London: Routledge, 2018).
Guha, Ramachandra, *India After Gandhi: The History of the World's Largest Democracy* (Delhi: Picador, 2007).
Gunaji, Nagesh Vasudev, trans., *Americantil Garib Vidyarthi* (Poor Students of America, trans. in Gujaratu of Satyadev's Book) (Belgaon: Manoranjak Granthprasarak Mandali, 1914).
Gupt, Ganga Prasad, *Gupt Prachin Kok Shastra* (Secret Ancient Treatise on Sex) (Aligarh: Jagat Vinod Press, 1916, 2nd edn).
Gupt, Mataprasad, *Gud–Pak–Vigyan Mithai* (Jaggery Knowhow and Culinary Desserts) (Lucknow: Naval Kishore Press, 1940).
Gupt, Mataprasad, *Pakprakash aur Mithai* (Knowledge of Cuisine and Sweets), ed. and comp. Ramakant Tripathi "Prakash" (Lucknow: Naval Kishore Press, 1937, 2nd edn; 1929).
Gupt, Shobhalal, "Rajasthan ki Jan-Jagriti Mein Shri Satyabhakt ji ka Yogdaan" (The Contribution of Satyabhakt in the Public Awakening of Rajasthan), *Navyug Sandesh*, 2 October 1981, 26.
Gupta, Brahmananda, "Indigenous Medicine in Nineteenth and Twentieth Century Bengal", in Charles Leslie, ed., *Asian Medical Systems: A Comparative Study* (Berkeley: University of California Press, 1976), 368–78.
Gupta, Charu, "Allegories of 'Love Jihad' and *Ghar Vapasi*: Interlocking the Socio–Religious with the Political", *Archiv Orientalni: Journal of African and Asian Studies*, 84 (2), 2016, 291–316.
Gupta, Charu, "Malleability of the Vernacular: Personal Anecdotes", *South Asian Review*, 41 (2), 2020, 197–9.
Gupta, Charu, "Procreation and Pleasure: Writings of a Woman Ayurvedic Practitioner in Colonial North India", *Studies in History*, 21 (1), 2005, 14–44.
Gupta, Charu, "Vernacular Sexology from the Margins: A Woman and a Shudra", *South Asia: Journal of South Asian Studies*, 43 (6), 2020, 1105–27.
Gupta, Charu, Laura Brueck, Hans Harder, and Shobna Nijhawan, "Introduction: Literary Sentiments in the Vernacular: Gender and Genre in Modern South Asia", *South Asia: Journal of South Asian Studies*, 43 (5), 2020, 803–16.
Gupta, Charu, *Sexuality, Obscenity, Community: Women, Muslims and the Hindu Public in Colonial India* (Delhi: Permanent Black, 2001).
Gupta, Charu, *The Gender of Caste: Representing Dalits in Print* (Ranikhet: Permanent Black, 2016).
Gupta, D.N., *Communism and Nationalism in Colonial India, 1939–1945* (London: Sage, 2008).

Gupta, Manmath Nath, "Agragaami Lekhak Satyabhakt" (Progressive Writer Satyabhakt), *Navyug Sandesh*, 2 October 1981, 19.

Gupta, Saumya, "Culinary Codes for an Emergent Nation: Prescriptions from *Pak Chandrika*, 1926", *Global Food History*, 9 (2), 2023, 175–93.

Gupta, Sobhanlal Datta, *Comintern, India and the Colonial Question, 1920–37* (Calcutta: Centre for Studies in Social Sciences, 1980).

Haithcox, John Patrick, *Communism and Nationalism in India: M.N. Roy and Comintern Policy 1920–1939* (Bombay: Oxford University Press, 1971).

Hamori, Esther J., *Women's Divination in Biblical Literature: Prophecy, Necromancy, and Other Arts of Knowledge* (New Haven: Yale University Press, 2015).

Hamzic, Vanja, *Sexual and Gender Diversity in the Muslim World: History, Law and Vernacular Knowledge* (London: I.B. Tauris, 2016).

Hansen, Kathryn, *Stages of Life: Indian Theatre Autobiographies* (Ranikhet: Permanent Black, 2011).

Hansen, Thomas Blom, *The Saffron Wave: Democracy and Hindu Nationalism in Modern India* (Princeton: Princeton University Press, 1999).

Hardiman, David, and Projit Bihari Mukharji, eds, *Medical Marginality in South Asia: Situating Subaltern Therapeutics* (London: Routledge, 2012).

Hardiman, David, *Gandhi in His Time and Ours* (Delhi: Permanent Black, 2003).

Harrison, Mark, *Public Health in British India: Anglo-Indian Preventive Medicine 1859–1914* (Cambridge: Cambridge University Press, 1994).

Hartley, George, *The Abyss of Representation: Marxism and the Postmodern Sublime* (Durham: Duke University Press, 2003).

Hauser, Julia, *A Taste for Purity: An Entangled History of Vegetarianism* (New York: Columbia University Press, 2023).

Haynes, Douglas E., "Gandhi, Brahmacharya and Global Sexual Science, 1919–38", *South Asia: Journal of South Asian Studies*, 43 (6), 2020, 1163–78.

Haynes, Douglas E., "Selling Masculinity: Advertisements for Sex Tonics and the Making of Modern Conjugality in Western India, 1900–1945", *South Asia*, 35 (4), 2012, 787–831.

Haynes, Douglas E., *The Emergence of Brand-name Capitalism in Late Colonial India* (London: Bloomsbury, 2023).

Heath, Deana, *Purifying Empire: Obscenity and the Politics of Moral Regulation in Britain, India and Australia* (Cambridge: Cambridge University Press, 2010).

Hodges, Sarah, *Contraception, Colonialism and Commerce: Birth Control in South India, 1920–1940* (Aldershot: Ashgate, 2008).

Holland, Sharon Patricia, *The Erotic Life of Racism* (Durham: Duke University Press, 2012).

Hunt, Sarah Beth, *Hindi Dalit Literature and the Politics of Representation* (New Delhi: Routledge, 2014).

Hussain, Syed Ejaz, and Mohit Saha, eds, *India's Indigenous Medical Systems: A Cross-Disciplinary Approach* (Delhi: Primus, 2015).

Hvidt, Niels Christian, *Christian Prophecy: The Post-Biblical Tradition* (New York: Oxford University Press, 2007).
Ilaiah, Kancha, *Why I Am Not a Hindu: A Sudra Critique of Hindutva Philosophy, Culture, and Political Economy* (Kolkata: Samya, 2002).
Imam, Hasan, "Satya Dev 'Sanyasi': Biographical Sketch of a Forgotten Political Activist", *Proceedings of the Indian History Congress*, 70, 2009–10, 713–23.
Indian Kanoon, http://indiankanoon.org/doc/.
Israel, Hephzibah, and John Zavos, "Narratives of Transformation: Religious Conversion and Indian Traditions of 'Life Writing'", *South Asia: Journal of South Asian Studies*, 41 (2), 2018, 352–65.
Jaffrelot, Christophe, *The Hindu Nationalist Movement: 1925 to the 1990s* (New Delhi: Penguin, 1999).
Jalil, Rakhshanda, *Liking Progress, Loving Change: A Literary History of the Progressive Writers' Movement in Urdu* (Delhi: Oxford University Press, 2014).
Jha, Dhirendra K., *Gandhi's Assassin: The Making of Nathuram Godse and His Idea of India* (Delhi: Penguin, 2022).
Jigyasu, Rajendra, *Dharma ki Balivedi Par: Mahashya Rajpal ji ki Balidan Gatha* (On the Altar of Religion: The Tale of Mr Rajpal's Sacrifice) (Delhi: Rajpal & Sons, 1998).
Jones, Kenneth, *Arya Dharm: Hindu Consciousness in 19th-Century Punjab* (New Delhi: Manohar, 2006; 1976).
Joshi, Chitra, *Lost Worlds: Indian Labour and Its Forgotten Histories* (Delhi: Permanent Black, 2003).
Joshi, Girish Chandra, *Adarsh Pak Vidhi* (Ideal Cooking Method) (Kashi: Hind Pustak Agency, 1938).
Joshi, Sanjay, *Fractured Modernity: Making of a Middle-Class in Colonial North India* (Delhi: Oxford University Press, 2001).
Juergensmeyer, Mark, *Religious Rebels in the Punjab: The Ad Dharm Challenge to Caste* (New Delhi: Navayana, 2009; 1982).
Kala, Sheoji Lal, *Santan Palan* (Rearing of Children) (Moradabad: Lakshmi Narayan, 1916).
Kaljayee, Kishen, ed., *Ek the Radhamohan Gokul* (There Was One Radhamohan Gokul) (Delhi: Ananya Prakashan, 2015).
Karlekar, Malavika, *Voices from Within: Early Personal Narratives of Bengali Women* (Delhi: Oxford University Press, 1991).
Karnik, V.B., *M.N. Roy: Political Biography* (Bombay: Nav Jagriti Samaj, 1978).
Kaushik, Devendra, and L.V. Mitrokhin, "First Indian Communist Conference at Kanpur (1925)", *Mainstream*, 8 (1, 2, 3), 1967, 67–71.
Kaviraj, Sudipta, "Marxism in Translation: Critical Reflections on Indian Radical Thought", in Richard Bourke and Raymond Geuss, eds, *Political Judgement: Essays for John Dunn* (Cambridge: Cambridge University Press, 2009), 172–200.

Kaviraj, Sudipta, *The Invention of Private Life: Literature and Ideas* (New York: Columbia University Press, 2015).
Kaviraj, Sudipta, *The Trajectories of the Indian State: Politics and Ideas* (Ranikhet: Permanent Black, 2010).
Kaye, Cecil, *Communism in India* (Delhi: Government of India Press, 1926).
Keck, Stephen L., "Picturesque Burma: British Travel Writing 1890–1914", *Journal of Southeast Asian Studies*, 35 (3), October 2004, 387–414.
Khan, Yasmin, "Performing Peace: Gandhi's Assassination as a Critical Moment in the Consolidation of the Nehruvian State", *Modern Asian Studies*, 45 (1), January 2011, 57–80.
Khare, R.S., ed., *The Eternal Food: Gastronomic Ideas and Experiences of Hindus and Buddhists* (Albany: SUNY Press, 1992).
King, Christopher R., *One Language, Two Scripts: The Hindi Movement in Nineteenth Century North India* (Bombay: Oxford University Press, 1994).
Kothari, Rita, *Uneasy Translations: Self, Experience and Indian Literature* (New Delhi: Bloomsbury, 2022).
Kshirsagar, R.K., *Dalit Movement in India and Its Leaders (1857–1956)* (New Delhi: M.D. Publications, 1994).
Kudaisya, Gyanesh, *India in the 1950s: A Republic in the Making* (New Delhi: Oxford University Press, 2017).
Kumar, Deepak, ed., *Science and Empire: Essays in Indian Context, 1700–1947* (Delhi: Anamika Prakashan, 1991).
Kumar, Kapil, "The *Ramcharitmanas* as a Radical Text: Baba Ram Chandra in Oudh, 1920–1950", in Sudhir Chandra, ed., *Social Transformation and Creative Imagination* (Delhi, 1984), 311–33.
Kumar, Krishan, "Aspects of the Western Utopian Tradition", in Jorn Rusen, Michael Fehr, and Thomas W. Rieger, eds, *Thinking Utopia: Steps into Other Worlds* (New York: Berghahn Books, 2005), 17–31.
Kumar, Krishna, *Political Agenda of Education: A Study of Colonialist and Nationalist Ideas* (New Delhi: Sage, 1991).
Kumar, Raj, *Dalit Personal Narratives: Reading Caste, Nation, and Identity* (New Delhi: Orient BlackSwan, 2011).
Kumar, Udaya, "Writing the Life of the Guru: Chattampi Swamikai, Sree Narayana Guru, and Modes of Biographical Construction", in Vijaya Ramaswamy and Yogesh Sharma, eds, *Biography as History: Indian Perspectives* (New Delhi: Orient BlackSwan, 2009), 53–87.
Kumar, Udaya, *Writing the First Person: Literature, History and Autobiography in Modern Kerala* (Ranikhet: Permanent Black, 2016).
Lackey, Michael, *Biofiction: An Introduction* (New York: Routledge, 2021).
Lal, Hazari, comp., *Vaidyak Sar* (The Essence of Ayurvedic Medicine) (Banaras: Raj Rajeshwari, 1910).

Lal, Maneesha, "The Politics of Gender and Medicine in Colonial India: The Countess of Dufferin's Fund, 1885–1888", *Bulletin of the History of Medicine*, 68 (1), March 1994, 29–66.

Lal, Shrikrishna, and Karunapati Tripathi, eds, *Hirak Jayanti Granth* (Golden Jubilee Volume) (Kashi: Nagari Pracharini Sabha, 1957; 1954).

Lambert-Hurley, Siobhan, Daniel Majchrowicz, and Sunil Sharma, eds, *Three Centuries of Travel Writing by Muslim Women* (Bloomington: Indiana University Press, 2022).

Langford, Jean M., *Fluent Bodies: Ayurvedic Remedies for Postcolonial Imbalance* (Durham: Duke University Press, 2002).

Larkosh, Christopher, ed., *Re-Engendering Translation: Transcultural Practice, Gender/Sexuality and the Politics of Alterity* (London: Routledge, 2011).

Leng, Kirsten, *Sexual Politics and Feminist Science: Women Sexologists in Germany, 1900–1933* (Ithaca: Cornell University Press, 2018).

Leong, Elaine, *Recipes and Everyday Knowledge: Medicine, Science and the Household in Early Modern England* (Chicago: University of Chicago Press, 2018).

Leong-Salobir, Cecilia, *Food Culture in Colonial Asia: A Taste of Empire* (London: Routledge, 2011).

Leslie, Charles, "Interpretations of Illness: Syncretism in Modern Ayurveda", in Charles Leslie and Allan Young, eds, *Paths to Asian Medical Knowledge* (Berkeley: University of California Press, 1992), 177–208.

Levine, Philippa, *Prostitution, Race, and Politics: Policing Venereal Disease in the British Empire* (New York: Routledge, 2003).

Levitas, Ruth, *Utopia as Method: The Imaginary Reconstitution of Society* (England: Palgrave, 2013).

Liu, Lydia H., ed., *Tokens of Exchange: The Problem of Translation in Global Circulations* (Durham: Duke University Press, 1999).

Loomba, Ania, *Revolutionary Desires: Women, Communism, and Feminism in India* (London: Routledge, 2019).

Lowy, Michael, *Fire Alarm: Reading Walter Benjamin's 'On the Concept of History'*, trans. Chris Turner (London: Verso, 2005).

Lubin, Alex, *Romance and Rights: The Politics of Interracial Intimacy, 1945–1954* (Jackson: Mississippi University Press, 2005).

Lutgendorf, Philip, "Interpreting Ramraj: Reflections on the 'Ramayan', Bhakti, and Hindu Nationalism", in David N. Lorenzen, ed., *Bhakti Religion in North India: Community, Identity and Political Action* (Albany: SUNY Press, 1995), 253–87.

Maclean, Kama, *A Revolutionary History of Interwar India: Violence, Image, Voice and Text* (London: Hurst, 2015).

Madan, T.N., ed., *India's Religions: Perspectives from Sociology and History* (New Delhi: Oxford University Press, 2004).

Maharaj, Karpatri, *Marxvad aur Ram Rajya* (Marxism and Ram Rajya) (Gorakhpur: Gita Press, 1957).

Maitra, Kiran, *Marxism in India: From Decline to Debacle* (Delhi: Roli Books, 2012).

Majchrowicz, Daniel, *The World in Words: Travel Writing and the Global Imagination in Muslim South Asia* (Cambridge: Cambridge University Press, 2023).

Majeed, Javed, *Autobiography, Travel and Postnational Identity: Gandhi, Nehru and Iqbal* (New York: Palgrave, 2007).

Malhotra, Anshu, and Siobhan Lambert-Hurley, eds, *Speaking of the Self: Gender, Performance, and Autobiography in South Asia* (Durham: Duke University Press, 2015).

Mani, Preetha, *The Idea of Indian Literature: Gender, Genre, and Comparative Method* (Evanston: Northwestern University Press, 2022).

Manjapra, Kris, *M.N. Roy: Marxism and Colonial Cosmopolitanism* (New Delhi: Routledge, 2010).

Mankekar, Purnima, "Dangerous Desires: Television and Erotics in Late Twentieth century India", *The Journal of Asian Studies,* 63 (2), May 2004, 403–31.

Markovits, Rahul, *A Passage to Europe: The Global Politics of Mobility in the Age of Revolutions* (Ranikhet: Permanent Black, 2023).

McCullough, Lissa, *The Religious Philosophy of Simone Weil: An Introduction* (London: I.B. Tauris, 2014).

McLellan, David, *Marxism and Religion: A Description and Assessment of the Marxist Critique of Christianity* (London: Macmillan, 1987).

Menon, Dilip M., *Caste, Nationalism and Communism in South India: Malabar 1900–1948* (Cambridge: Cambridge University Press, 1994).

Menon, Madhavi, *Infinite Variety: A History of Desire in India* (New Delhi: Speaking Tiger, 2018).

Mills, James H., and Satadru Sen, *Confronting the Body: The Politics of Physicality in Colonial and Post-Colonial India* (London: Anthem Press, 2004).

Mills, Sara, *Discourses of Difference: An Analysis of Women's Travel Writing and Colonialism* (London: Routledge, 1991).

Minault, Gail, *The Khilafat Movement: Religious Symbolism and Popular Mobilisation in India* (New York: Columbia University Press, 1982).

Mishra, Kripanath, *Videsh ki Baat* (Foreign Affairs) (Prayag: Indian Press Limited, 1935).

Mitra, Durba, "Sexuality and the History of Disciplinary Transgression", *South Asia: Journal of South Asian Studies,* 43 (6), 2020, 1216–27.

Mitra, Durba, *Indian Sex Life: Sexuality and the Colonial Origins of Modern Social Thought* (Princeton: Princeton University Press, 2020).

Mitra, N., *The Indian Literary Year Book and Authors' Who is Who* (Allahabad: Panini Office, 1918).

Mitta, Manoj, *Caste Pride: Battles for Equality in Hindu India* (Chennai: Westland Books, 2023).

Mody, Sujata S., "Literature, Language, and Nation Formation: The Story of a

Modern Hindi Journal 1900–1920", PhD Dissertation (Berkeley: University of California, 2008).

Mody, Sujata S., *The Making of Modern Hindi: Literary Authority in Colonial North India* (New Delhi: Oxford University Press, 2018).

Mohanty, Sachidananda, ed., *Travel Writing and the Empire* (New Delhi: Katha, 2003).

Mongia, Radhika, *Indian Migration and Empire: A Colonial Genealogy of the Modern State* (Durham: Duke University Press, 2018).

More, Thomas, *Utopia*, eds Edward Surtz and J.H. Hexter (New Haven: Yale University Press, 1965).

Mukharji, Projit Bihari, *Doctoring Traditions: Ayurveda, Small Technologies, and Braided Sciences* (Chicago: University of Chicago Press, 2016).

Mukharji, Projit Bihari, *Nationalizing the Body: The Market, Print and Daktari Medicine in Colonial Bengal, 1860–1930* (London: Anthem Press, 2009).

Mukherjee, Sujata, *Gender, Medicine, and Society in Colonial India: Women's Health Care in Nineteenth and Early Twentieth Century Bengal* (Delhi: Oxford University Press, 2017).

Mukhopadhyay, Aparajita, *Imperial Technology and 'Native' Agency: A Social History of Railways in Colonial India, 1850–1920* (London: Routledge, 2018).

Mukhopadhyay, B., "Writing Home, Writing Travel: The Poetics and Politics of Dwelling in Bengali Modernity", *Comparative Studies in Society and History*, 44 (2), April 2002, 293–318.

Mukhopadhyay, Kirankumar, comp., *Dadi ke Nuskhe arthat Ghar ka Doctor* (Grandmother's Recipes, i.e. The Household Doctor) (Allahabad: Kirankumar, 1929).

Mukul, Akshaya, *Gita Press and the Making of Hindu India* (Noida: Harper Collins, 2015).

Mukul, Akshaya, *Writer, Rebel, Soldier, Lover: The Many Lives of Agyeya* (Gurugram: Penguin, 2022).

Murugkar, Lata, *Dalit Panther Movement in Maharashtra: A Sociological Appraisal* (Bombay: Popular Prakashan, 1991).

Muthu, David C., *A Short Account of the Antiquity of Hindu Medicine* (London: Bailliere, 1927, 2nd edn).

Nadkarni, M.V., "Does Hinduism Lack Social Concern?", *Economic and Political Weekly*, 42 (20), 19 May 2007, 1844–9.

Naim, C.M., *Zikr-i Mir: An Eighteenth-Century Autobiography* (New Delhi: Oxford University Press, 1999).

Nala, Maharaja, *Pakadarpanam* (Culinary Mirror), ed., Vamacarna Bhattacarya (Varanasi: Chaukhambha, 1983, 2nd edn).

Nandy, Ashis, *At the Edge of Psychology: Essays in Politics and Culture* (Delhi: Oxford University Press, 1980).

Nandy, Ashis, *The Intimate Enemy: Loss and Recovery of Self Under Colonialism* (Delhi: Oxford University Press, 1983).

Native Newspaper Reports of the United Provinces (NNR), 1870–1940 (Allahabad: Superintendent, Government Press, 1870–1940).
Naye Varsh ka Suchipatra (Catalogue of New Year) (Lahore: Rajpal & Sons, n.d.).
Nigam, Aditya, "Hindutva, Caste and the 'National Unconscious'", in Vishwas Satgar, ed., *Racism After Apartheid: Challenges for Marxism and Anti-Racism* (Johannesburg: Wits University Press, 2019), 118–36.
Nigam, Aditya, *The Insurrection of Little Selves: The Crisis of Secular-Nationalism in India* (Delhi: Oxford University Press, 2005).
Nijhawan, Shobna, *Hindi Publishing in Colonial Lucknow: Gender, Genre, and Visuality in the Creation of a Literary 'Canon'* (Delhi: Oxford University Press, 2018).
Nijhawan, Shobna, *Women and Girls in the Hindi Public Sphere: Periodical Literature in Colonial North India* (Delhi: Oxford University Press, 2012).
Nirala, Suryakant Tripathi, "Varnashram-Dharma ki Vartman Sthiti" (The Present State of the Caste System), *Madhuri*, December 1929, 836–43.
Niranjana, Tejaswini, *Siting Translation: History, Post-Structuralism, and the Colonial Context* (Berkeley: University of California Press, 1992).
Nirta, Caterina, *Marginal Bodies, Trans Utopias* (London: Routledge, 2018).
Noorani, A.G., *Savarkar and Gandhi: The Godse Connection* (Delhi: Leftword Books, 2002).
Noronha, Rahul, "MP: Hindu Mahasabha Celebrates Nathuram Godse's Birth Anniversary in Gwalior, Congress Attacks BJP Govt", *India Today*, 20 May 2020.
O'Hanlon, Rosalind, "Performance in a World of Paper: Puranic Histories and Social Communication in Early Modern India", *Past & Present*, 219, May 2013, 87–126.
O'Malley, Kate, *Ireland, India and Empire: Indo-Irish Radical Connections, 1919–1964* (Manchester: Manchester University Press, 2008).
Omvedt, Gail, *Cultural Revolt in a Colonial Society: The Non-Brahman Movement in Western India, 1850–1935* (Poona: Scientific Socialist Education Trust, 1976).
Orsini, Francesca, "Vernacular: Flawed but Necessary?", *South Asia Review*, 41 (2), 2020, 204–6.
Orsini, Francesca, *The Hindi Public Sphere 1920–1940: Language and Literature in the Age of Nationalism* (Delhi: Oxford University Press, 2002).
Osborne, Peter, *Travelling Light: Photography, Travel and Visual Culture* (Manchester: Manchester University Press, 2000).
Overstreet, Gene Donald, and Marshall Windmiller, *Communism in India* (Berkeley: University of California Press, 1959).
Paik, Shailaja, "Mahar–Dalit–Buddhist: The History and Politics of Naming in Maharashtra", *Contributions to Indian Sociology*, 45 (2), 2011, 217–41.
Pande, Ishita, "Introduction to 'Translating Sex: Locating Sexology in Indian History'", *South Asia: Journal of South Asian Studies*, 43 (6), 2020, 1093–1104.

Pande, Ishita, "Time for Sex: The Education of Desire and the Conduct of Childhood in Global/Hindu Sexology", in Veronika Fuechtner, Douglas E. Haynes, and Ryan M. Jones, eds, *A Global History of Sexual Science, 1880–1960* (California: University of California Press, 2018), 279–301.

Pande, Ishita, *Sex, Law and the Politics of Age: Child Marriage in India, 1891–1937* (Cambridge: Cambridge University Press, 2020).

Pande, Manager, ed., *Desh ki Baat* (National Affairs) (Delhi: National Book Trust, 2005).

Pandey, Gyanendra, *A History of Prejudice: Race, Caste, and Difference in India and the United States* (Cambridge: Cambridge University Press, 2013).

Pandey, Gyanendra, *The Construction of Communalism in Colonial North India* (New Delhi: Oxford University Press, 1990).

Pandey, Sudhakar, ed., *Banga Mahila Granthavali* (Collection of Articles by Banga Mahila) (Varanasi: Nagari Pracharini Sabha, 1988).

Pandian, M.S.S., "Writing Ordinary Lives", *Economic and Political Weekly*, 43 (38), September 2008, 34–40.

Panikkar, K.N., "Indigenous Medicine and Cultural Hegemony: A Study of the Revitalisation Movement in Keralam", *Social History*, 8 (2), 1992, 288–95.

Parekh, Bhikhu, *Colonialism, Tradition and Reform: An Analysis of Gandhi's Political Discourse* (New Delhi: Sage, 1989).

Pascal, Roy, *Design and Truth in Autobiography* (Cambridge: Harvard University Press, 1960).

Paswan, Sanjay, and Paramanshi Jaideva, eds, *Encyclopaedia of Dalits in India: Leaders, Vol. 4* (Delhi: Kalpaz Publications, 2004).

Pathak, Avijit, "A Non-Marxist's Gratitude for Karl Marx", *The Wire*, 9 May 2018. https://thewire.in/politics/karl–marx–marxism, accessed 7 June 2020.

Pati, Biswamoy, and Mark Harrison, eds, *Health, Medicine and Empire: Perspectives on Colonial India* (New Delhi: Orient Longman, 2001).

Peers, Douglas, "'The Habitual Nobility of Being': British Officers and the Social Construction of the Bengal Army in the Early 19th Century", *Modern Asian Studies*, 25 (3), 1991, 545–69.

Petrie, David, *Communism in India, 1924–1927* (Calcutta: Government of India Press, 1927).

Pettit, Philip, *Republicanism: A Theory of Freedom and Government* (Oxford: Oxford University Press, 1997).

Phadke, Y.D., "The Murderer as Martyr: The Glorification of Gandhiji's Murderers", in Teesta Setalvad, comp. & intro., *Beyond Doubt: A Dossier on Gandhi's Assassination* (New Delhi: Tulika Books, 2015), 67–86.

Pinch, William R., *Peasants and Monks in British India* (New Delhi: Oxford University Press, 1996).

Pohl, Nicole, *Women, Space and Utopia, 1600–1800* (England: Ashgate, 2006).

Pollock, Sheldon, "Cosmopolitan and Vernacular in History", *Public Culture*, 12 (3), 2000, 591–625.

Pollock, Sheldon, "Ramayana and Political Imagination in India", *The Journal of Asian Studies*, 52 (2), May 1993, 261–97.

Pradhan, Ramchandra, ed., and trans., *The Struggle of My Life: Autobiography of Swami Sahajanand Saraswati* (Delhi: Oxford University Press, 2018).

Prajapati, Mahesh, comp. and ed., *Santram BA: Pratinidhi Vichaar* (Santram BA: Representative Ideas) (Shahjahanpur: Santram BA Foundation, 2022).

Prakash, Gyan, *Another Reason: Science and the Imagination of Modern India* (Princeton: Princeton University Press, 1999).

Prakashan Suchi (List of Publications) (Varanasi: Nagari Pracharini Sabha, n.d.).

Prasad, Karthik, *Pakraj* (King of Cuisine) (Banaras: Friend and Company, 1908, 2nd edn).

Prasad, Leela, *The Audacious Raconteur: Sovereignty and Storytelling in Colonial India* (Ithaca: Cornell University Press, 2020).

Prasad, Srirupa, *Cultural Politics of Hygiene in India, 1890–1940: Contagions of Feeling* (Basingstoke: Palgrave Macmillan, 2015).

Prashad, Vijay, *Untouchable Freedom: A Social History of a Dalit Community* (New Delhi: Oxford University Press, 2000).

Pratapsingh, Kaviraj, ed., *Ayurveda Mahamandal ka Rajat Jayanti Granth* (Banaras: Ayurveda Mahamandal, 1936).

Pratt, Mary Louise, *Imperial Eyes: Travel Writing and Transculturation* (London: Routledge, 1992).

Prem, Dhaniram, "Guptendriya Ang" (Secret Organs), *Chand*, April 1933, 708–11.

Prem, Dhaniram, "Samaj Sudhar tatha *Chand*" (Social Reform and *Chand*), *Chand*, August–September 1930, 389–93.

Procida, Mary, "Feeding the Imperial Appetite: Imperial Knowledge and Anglo-Indian Domesticity", *Journal of Women's History*, 15 (2), 2003, 123–49.

Puri, Jyoti, "Concerning 'Kamasutras': Challenging Narratives of History and Sexuality", *Signs*, 27 (3), Spring 2002, 603–39.

Raghuvanshi, U.B.S., *Chanvar Purana* (Puranic History of the Chamars) (Aligarh: Uday Bir Singh, 1916).

Rai, Alok, *Hindi Nationalism* (Hyderabad: Orient Longman, 2001).

Rai, Saurav Kumar, "Gendering Late Colonial Ayurvedic Discourse: United Provinces, *c.* 1890–1937", *History and Sociology of South Asia*, 10 (1), 2016, 21–34.

Rai, Saurav Kumar, "Invoking 'Hindu' Ayurveda: Communalisation of the Late Colonial Ayurvedic Discourse", *The Indian Economic & Social History Review*, 56 (4), 2019, 411–26.

Ram, Kalpana, and Margaret Jolly, eds, *Maternities and Modernities: Colonial and Postcolonial Experiences in Asia and the Pacific* (Cambridge: Cambridge University Press, 1998).

Ramakrishnaiya, P., *Ayurveda and Its Merits* (Mangalore: Lakshmi, 1922).

Ramaswamy, Vijaya, and Yogesh Sharma, eds, *Biography as History: Indian Perspectives* (New Delhi: Orient BlackSwan, 2009).
Ramaswamy, Vijaya, "Introduction", in Vijaya Ramaswamy and Yogesh Sharma, eds, *Biography as History: Indian Perspectives* (New Delhi: Orient BlackSwan, 2009), 1–15.
Rambachan, Anantanand, *A Hindu Theology of Liberation: Not-Two is Not One* (Albany: SUNY Press, 2015).
Ramlal, *Nutan Pak Prakash* (New Cooking Wisdom) (Mathura: Sukh Sancharak Company, 1909).
Rancière, Jacques, *The Politics of Literature*, trans. Julie Rose (Cambridge: Polity Press, 2011).
Rao, Anupama, ed., *Gender and Caste* (Delhi: Kali for Women, 2003).
Rao, Anupama, *The Caste Question: Dalits and the Politics of Modern India* (Ranikhet: Permanent Black, 2010).
Rawat, Ramnarayan, *Reconsidering Untouchability: Chamars and Dalit History in North India* (Ranikhet: Permanent Black, 2012).
Ray, Avishek, "The Aesthetic Gaze: Siting Nineteenth Century Indian Travel Writing", *Rupkatha Journal on Interdisciplinary Studies in Humanities*, 8 (4), 2016, 122–9.
Ray, Krishnendu, and Tulasi Srinivas, eds, *Curried Cultures: Globalization, Food, and South Asia* (Berkeley: University of California Press, 2012).
Ray, Utsa, *Culinary Culture in Colonial India: A Cosmopolitan Platter and the Middle-Class* (Delhi: Cambridge University Press, 2015).
Raza, Ali, "Provincializing the International: Communist Print Worlds in Colonial India", *History Workshop Journal*, 89, Spring 2020, 140–53.
Raza, Ali, *Revolutionary Pasts: Communist Internationalism in Colonial India* (Cambridge: Cambridge University Press, 2020).
Rege, Sharmila, *Against the Madness of Manu: B.R. Ambedkar's Writings on Brahmanical Patriarchy* (Delhi: Navayana, 2013).
Rege, Sharmila, *Writing Caste/Writing Gender: Narrating Dalit Women's Testimonies* (Delhi: Zubaan, 2006).
Report of the Unemployment Committee, 1935, UP (Allahabad: Printing and Stationery, 1936).
Report on the Administration of UP, 1907–25 (Allahabad: Government Press, 1908–26).
Richman, Paula, "A Tamil Modernist's Account of India's Past: Ram Raj, Merchant Raj, and British Raj", *The Journal of Asian Studies*, 66 (1), February 2007, 35–62.
Rose, H.A., comp., *A Glossary of the Tribes and Castes of the Punjab and North-West Frontier Province, Vol. II* (Lahore: Civil and Military Gazette Press, 1911).
Rowland, Christopher, ed., *The Cambridge Companion to Liberation Theology* (Cambridge: Cambridge University Press, 2007).

Roy, Kumkum, "Unravelling the *Kamasutra*", in Mary E. John and Janaki Nair, eds, *A Question of Silence? The Sexual Economies of Modern India* (New Delhi: Kali for Women, 1998), 52–76.

Roy, Parama, *Alimentary Tracts: Appetites, Aversions, and the Postcolonial* (Durham: Duke University Press, 2010).

Roy, Subodh, comp. and ed., *Communism in India*, Sir Cecil Kaye; *with Unpublished Documents from National Archives of India, 1919–1924* (Calcutta: Editions Indian, 1971).

Rusen, Jorn, Michael Fehr, and Thomas W. Rieger, eds, *Thinking Utopia: Steps into Other Worlds* (New York: Berghahn Books, 2005).

S.S., "'A Book that Preached Communalism': Book Review of Swami Satya Deva's *Swatantrata ke Khoj Mein*", *National Herald* (Magazine Section), 24 February 1952, 2.

Sadana, Rashmi, *English Heart, Hindi Heartland: The Political Life of Literature in India* (Ranikhet: Permanent Black, 2012).

Saha, Panchanan, *The Russian Revolution and the Indian Patriots* (Calcutta: Man Sanyal, 1987).

Salil, Suresh, ed., *Ganesh Shankar Vidyarthi aur Unka Yug* (Ganesh Shankar Vidyarthi and His Era) (New Delhi: Anamika Publishers, 2014).

Sankrityayan, Rahul, *Ghummakkad Shastra* (Wanderer's Manual, or the Science of Wandering) (Allahabad: Kitab Mahal, 2004; 1948).

Sankrityayan, Rahul, *Jinka Main Kritagya* (To Those Whom I Am Grateful) (Allahabad: Kitab Mahal, 1957).

Sankrityayan, Rahul, *Meri Tibbet Yatra* (My Tibet Journey) (Prayag: Chatrahitkari Pustakmala, 1937).

Sankrityayan, Rahul, *Ram Rajya aur Marxvad* (Ram Rajya and Marxism) (Delhi: People's Publishing House, 1959).

Sankrityayan, Rahul, *Volga se Ganga* (From Volga to Ganga) (Delhi: Kitab Mahal, 2018; 1943).

Santaemilia, Jose, ed., *Gender, Sex and Translation: The Manipulation of Identities* (London: Routledge, 2014).

Sargent, Lyman Tower, "The Necessity of Utopian Thinking: A Cross-National Perspective", in Jorn Rusen, Michael Fehr, and Thomas W. Rieger, eds, *Thinking Utopia: Steps into Other Worlds* (New York: Berghahn Books, 2005), 1–14.

Sarkar, Sumit, *Modern Times: India, 1880s–1950s* (Ranikhet: Permanent Black, 2014).

Sarkar, Tanika, *Hindu Wife, Hindu Nation: Community, Religion and Cultural Nationalism* (Delhi: Permanent Black, 2001).

Sarkar, Tanika, *Religion and Women in India: Gender, Faith, and Politics 1780s–1980s* (Ranikhet: Permanent Black, 2024).

Sarkar, Tanika, *Words to Win: The Making of Amar Jiban; A Modern Autobiography* (Delhi: Kali for Women, 1999).
Satchidanandan, K., "Travel Writing in India: An Overview", in Shobhana Bhattacharji, ed., *Travel Writing in India* (New Delhi: Sahitya Akademi, 2008).
"Satyabhakt Abhinandan-Ank" (Commemorative Issue on Satyabhakt), *Navyug Sandesh*, 2 October 1981.
Savary, Luzia, "Vernacular Eugenics? Santati–Sastra in Popular Hindi Advisory Literature (1900–1940)", *South Asia: Journal of South Asian Studies*, 37 (3), 2014, 381–97.
Savary, Luzia, *Evolution, Race and Public Spheres in India: Vernacular Concepts and Sciences (1860–1930)* (London: Routledge, 2019).
Sayeed, Syed, *Understanding B.R. Ambedkar's 'Annihilation of Caste'* (Ranikhet: Permanent Black, 2023).
Schaffner, Anna Katharina, *Modernism and Perversion: Sexual Deviance in Sexology and Literature, 1850–1930* (New York: Palgrave, 2012).
Schmidtz, David, and Carmen E. Pavel, eds, *The Oxford Handbook of Freedom* (New York: Oxford University Press, 2018).
Schomer, Karine, *Mahadevi Varma and the Chhayavad Age of Modern Hindi Poetry* (Berkeley: University of California Press, 1983).
Schweizer, Bernard, *Radicals on the Road: The Politics of English Travel Writing in the 1930s* (Charlottesville: University of Virginia Press, 2001).
Scott, J. Barton, *Spiritual Despots: Modern Hinduism and the Genealogies of Self-Rule* (Chicago: University of Chicago Press, 2016).
Selvamony, Nirmal, "Vernacular as Homoarchic Mode of Existence", *South Asian Review*, 41 (2), 2020, 194–6.
Sen, Simonti, *Travels to Europe: Self and Other in Bengali Travel Narratives, 1870–1910* (Delhi: Orient Blackswan, 2005).
Sengupta, Indira Chowdhury, *The Frail Hero and Virile History: Gender and the Politics of Culture in Colonial Bengal* (Delhi: Oxford University Press, 1998).
Sengupta, Jayanta, "Nation on a Platter: The Culture and Politics of Food and Cuisine in Colonial Bengal", *Modern Asian Studies*, 44 (1), 2010, 81–98.
Setalvad, Teesta, comp. & intro., *Beyond Doubt: A Dossier on Gandhi's Assassination* (New Delhi: Tulika Books, 2015).
Seth, Sanjay, *Marxist Theory and Nationalist Politics: The Case of Colonial India* (Delhi: Sage, 1995).
Shahani, Gitanjali, *Tasting Difference: Food, Race, and Cultural Encounters in Early Modern Literature* (Ithaca: Cornell University Press, 2020).
Shaikh, Juned, "Translating Marx: *Mavali*, Dalit and the Making of Mumbai's Working Class, 1928–1935", *Economic and Political Weekly*, 46 (31), 2011, 65–73.
Shankar, S., and Charu Gupta, eds, *Caste and Life Narratives* (Delhi: Primus, 2019).

Shankar, S., "The Vernacular: An Introduction", *South Asian Review*, 41 (2), 2020, 191–3.
Shankar, S., *Flesh and Fish Blood: Postcolonialism, Translation, and the Vernacular* (Delhi: Orient BlackSwan, 2012).
Sharma, Dinanath, *Swami Satyadev Parivrajak: Vyaktitva evam Sahityik Krititva* (Swami Satyadev Parivrajak: His Personality and Literary Accomplishments) (Delhi: Rajpal and Sons, 1984).
Sharma, Hanumanprasad, *Aahaar Vigyan* (The Science of Food) (Banaras: Mahashakti Sahitya, 1931).
Sharma, Hanumanprasad, *Sukhi Grhini* (A Happy Wife. A Book on Women's Health) (Banaras: Nageshwar Prasad, 1931).
Sharma, Harihar, "Madras Mein Hindi-Prachaar" (The Propagation of Hindi in Madras), *Vishal Bharat,* January 1929, 85–8.
Sharma, Jagannath, *Pak Vigyan* (The Science of Cooking) (Kashi: Laksmi Pustakalaya, 1933).
Sharma, Kanhaiya Lal, *Kok Shastra athva Yauvan Bilas* (Treatise on Sex or Youthful Pleasure) (Moradabad: Jagannath Prasad, 1900).
Sharma, Kshetrapal, *Bhartiya Vanaspatiyon par Vilayati Doctoron ka Anubhav* (Experience of Foreign Doctors on Indian Flora) (Mathura: Ram Narayan, 1905).
Sharma, Madhuri, *Indigenous and Western Medicine in Colonial India* (Delhi: Foundation Books, 2012).
Sharma, Mangaldev, "Bhranti ki Lehar" (Wave of Fallacy), *Madhuri,* October 1927, 414–19.
Sharma, Maniram, *Kanya Pakshastra* (Cooking for Girls) (Prayag: Onkar Press, 1915).
Sharma, Maniram, *Pak Chandrika* (Culinary Moonlight), ed. and comp., Vidyawati Sehgal (Allahabad: Chand Karyalaya, 1926; 1934, 4th edn).
Sharma, Maniram, *Pak Vidya va Bhojan Banane ki Vidhi* (Cookery Education and Methods for Preparing Food) (Prayag: Ramnarayanlal Bookseller, 1915).
Sharma, Mukul, *Caste and Nature: Dalits and Indian Environmental Thought* (New Delhi: Oxford University Press, 2017).
Sharma, Ramvilas, *Bharat mein Angrezi Raj aur Marxvad, 2 Vols* (Colonial Rule and Marxism in India) (Delhi: Rajkamal, 1982).
Sharma, Shiv, *The System of Ayurveda* (Bombay: Venkateshwar Press, 1929).
Sharma, Suresh, ed., *Benipuri Granthavali: Vol. 4* (Delhi: Radhakrishna Prakashan, 1998).
Sharma, Thakurdutt, *Dugdh aur Dugdh ki Vastuen* (Milk and Milk Products) (Lahore: Amritdhara Aushadhalaya, 1926).
Shastri, Ram Narayan Vaidya, *Janan Vigyan ya Garbhadan Rahasya* (The Science of Procreation, or the Mystery of Conception) (Kanpur: Ram Narayan Verma, 1931).

Shastri, Saligram, *Ayurveda Mahatv* (The Greatness of Ayurveda) (Lucknow: Naval Kishore Press, 1926).
Shishir, Karmendu, ed., *Radhamohan Gokul Samagra, 2 Vols* (Collection of Radhamohan Gokul's Writings) (Delhi: Anamika, 2009).
Shishir, Karmendu, *Satyabhakt aur Samyavadi Party* (Satyabhakt and the Communist Party) (Delhi: Lokmitra, 2010; 1982).
Shree, Geetanjali, "Hindi Against Hindi", *The Indian Express*, 7 November 2023, 15.
Shridharani, Krishnalal, *My India, My America* (New York: Duell, Sloan and Pearce, 1941).
Shukl, Jagannath Prasad, *Ayurveda ka Mahatv* (The Greatness of the Indian Science of Medicine) (Allahabad: Ram Das Vaish, 1910, 2nd edn).
Shukl, Pandit Nrisinghram, *Vrihad Pak Vigyan: Vegetarian and Non-Vegetarian, yaani Niraamish Aur Aamish* (Comprehensive Cooking Guide: Vegetarian and Non-Vegetarian) (Mathura: Hindi Pustakalaya, 1938).
Shukl, Veni, *London–Paris ki Sair* (A Trip to London and Paris) (Prayag: Indian Press Limited, 1925).
Shukl, Vidyabhaskar, "Ek Phool Jo Khilne Nahin Paya" (A Flower that Did Not Bloom), *Balsakha*, September 1928, 318–21.
Silvestri, Michael, *Ireland and India: Nationalism, Empire and Memory* (New York: Palgrave, 2009).
Singer, Margot, and Nicole Walker, "Introduction", in Margot Singer and Nicole Walker, eds, *Bending Genre: Essays on Creative Nonfiction* (New York: Bloomsbury Academic, 2023, 2nd edn), 1–6.
Singh, Ayodhya, *Samajvad: Bhartiya Janta ka Sangharsh* (Socialism: The Struggle of the Indian People) (Delhi: Anamika, 2007).
Singh, Kamlesh, *Hindi Atmakatha: Swarup evam Sahitya* (Hindi Autobiography: Form and Literature) (New Delhi: National Publishing House, 1989).
Singh, Krishan Pratap, "Satyabhakt: Hindi Navjagran ke Albele Sainani" (Satyabhakt: The Brave Fighters of Hindi Renaissance), *The Wire*, 2 April 2018.
Singh, Maina Chawla, *Gender, Religion, and 'The Heathen Lands': American Missionary Women in South Asia, 1860–1940s* (New York: Garland Publishing, 2000).
Singh, Mohinder, "'A Question of Life and Death': Conversion, Self and Identity in Swami Shraddhanand's Autobiography", *South Asia: Journal of South Asian Studies*, 41 (2), 2018, 452–67.
Singh, Naath, "Kya Hindi-Pathak Kaamuk aur Vyabhichaari Hain?" (Are Hindi Readers Promiscuous and Adulterous?), *Saraswati*, May 1934, 503–5.
Singh, Ramjee, and S. Sundaram, eds, *Gandhi and the World Order* (New Delhi: APH Publishing Corporation, 1996).
Singh, Satnam, *Santram BA krit Mere Jeevan ke Anubhav: Dalit Sahitya ki Pehli Sva-Jeevni* (The Experience of My Life by Santram BA: The First Autobiography of Dalit Literature) (Delhi: Samyak Prakashan, 2008).

Sinha, Mrinalini, *Colonial Masculinity: The 'Manly Englishman' and the 'Effeminate Bengali' in the Late Nineteenth Century* (Manchester: Manchester University Press, 1995).
Sivaramakrishnan, Kavita, *Old Potions, New Bottles: Recasting Indigenous Medicine in Colonial Punjab, 1850–1945* (New Delhi: Orient Blackswan, 2006).
Slate, Nico, *Gandhi's Search for the Perfect Diet: Eating with the World in Mind* (Seattle: University of Washington Press, 2019).
Smith, Sidonie, and Julia Watson, *Reading Autobiography: A Guide for Interpreting Life Narratives* (Minneapolis: University of Minnesota Press, 2001).
Smith, Sidonie, *Moving Lives: Twentieth Century Women's Travel Writing* (Minneapolis: University of Minnesota Press, 2001).
Snell, Rupert, "A Hindi Poet from Allahabad: Translating Harivansh Rai Bachchan's Autobiography", *Modern Asian Studies*, 34 (2), May 2000, 425–47.
Snell, Rupert, "Confessions of a 17th-Century Jain Merchant: The *Ardhakathanak* of Banarasidas", *South Asia Research*, 25 (1), 2005, 79–104.
Spivak, Gayatri Chakravorty, "Teaching Literature Today", in Ruth Vanita, ed., *India and the World: Postcolonialism, Translation and Indian Literature* (New Delhi: Pencraft International, 2014), 17–34.
Sreedhar, Darshana, and Anirban K. Baishya, "Transgressions in Toonland: *Savita Bhabhi, Velamma* and the Indian Adult Comic", *Porn Studies*, 7 (1), 2020, 115–31.
Sreenivas, Mytheli, *Wives, Widows and Concubines: The Conjugal Family Ideal in Colonial India* (Bloomington: Indiana University Press, 2008).
Sri Swami Satya Dev Parivrajak (A Collection of Essays on Parivrajak) (Patiala: Bhasha Vibhag, Punjab, 1959).
Srivastava, Sanjay, "'Ghummakkads', a Woman's Place, and the LTC-Walas: Towards a Critical History of 'Home', 'Belonging' and 'Attachment'", *Contributions to Indian Sociology*, 39, 2005, 375–405.
Stark, Ulrike, *An Empire of Books: The Naval Kishore Press and the Diffusion of the Printed Word in Colonial India* (Ranikhet: Permanent Black, 2007).
Statement of Newspapers and Periodicals Published in the United Provinces, 1934 (Allahabad: Superintendent, Government Press, 1935).
Statement of Particulars Regarding Books and Periodicals Published in the United Provinces, 1882–1945 (Allahabad: Government Press, 1882–1945).
Stengers, Jean, and Anne van Neck, *Masturbation: The History of a Great Terror*, trans. Kathryn Hoffmann (New York: Palgrave, 2001).
Stepniak, *Underground Russia: Revolutionary Profiles and Sketches from Life* (New York: John W. Lovell Company, 1883).
Steves, Rick, *Travel as a Political Act* (New York: Nation Books, 2009).
Stopes, Marie C., *Married Love* (London: A.C. Fifield, 1918).
Suartika, Gusti Ayu Made, and Julie Nichols, eds, *Reframing the Vernacular: Politics, Semiotics, and Representation* (Switzerland: Springer, 2020).

Tandon, Ramnarayan, ed., *Hindi Sevi Sansar, Vol. 1* (Lucknow: Vidya Mandir, 1951, 2nd edn).
Thakur, Jyotirmayi, *Aahaar aur Aarogyata* (Food and Health) (Banaras: Sahitya Sevak Karyalaya, 1948).
Thakur, Jyotirmayi, *Gharelu Shiksha tatha Pakshastra* (Home Remedies and Cooking) (Prayag: Sahitya Niketan, 1945, 3rd edn).
Thakur, Jyotirmayi, *Gharelu Vigyan* (Domestic Science) (Prayag: Adarsh Granthmala, 1932).
Thakur, Jyotirmayi, *Stri aur Saundarya* (Women and Beauty) (Prayag: Mahila Hitkari Pustak Mala, 1933).
Tharakeshwar, V.B., "Empire Writes Back? Kannada Travel Fiction and Nationalist Discourse", in Sachidananda Mohanty, ed., *Travel Writing and the Empire* (New Delhi: Katha, 2003), 126–49.
Thruvengadam, P., "Sant Ram", *The Indian Rationalist*, 2 (6), June 1954, 65–7.
Timani, Hussam S., and Loye Sekihata Ashton, eds, *Post-Christian Interreligious Liberation Theology* (Switzerland: Palgrave-Macmillan, 2019).
Tiwari, Rama Devi, *Pak Prabhakar* (Cooking Insights) (Prayag: Surendra Mani Tiwari, 1939, 2nd edn).
Tiwari, Vishwa Mohan, *Hindi ka Yatra Sahitya: Ek Brihangam Drishti* (Travel Literature in Hindi: A Bird's Eye View) (Delhi: Alekh Prakashan, 2004).
Torpey, John C., *The Invention of the Passport: Surveillance, Citizenship and the State* (Cambridge: Cambridge University Press, 2018, 2nd edn).
Trautmann, Thomas R., *Aryans and British India* (New Delhi: Oxford University Press, 1997).
Trivedi, Chotelal, *Vyanjan Prakaar* (Types of Dishes) (Agra: Hakim Ramchandji, 1941).
Uma, Alladi, K. Suneetha Rani, and D. Murali Manohar, "Introduction", in Alladi Uma, K. Suneetha Rani, and D. Murali Manohar, eds, *English in the Dalit Context* (Hyderabad: Orient BlackSwan, 2014), 1–9.
Upadhyay, Gangaprasad, *Hum Kya Khaaven: Ghaas ya Maans?* (What Should We Eat: Vegetables or Meat?) (Prayag: Kala Press, 1945).
Vaidik, Aparna, *Waiting for Swaraj: Inner Lives of Indian Revolutionaries* (Cambridge: Cambridge University Press, 2021).
Vaidya, Babu Haridas, *Chikitsa Chandrodaya: Pehla Bhag* (Healing Practices: Part I) (Agra: Satya Vratt Sharma, 1935, 4th edn).
Vaidya, Chunibhai, "The Murderer as Martyr: Gandhi or Godse?", in Teesta Setalvad, comp. & intro., *Beyond Doubt: A Dossier on Gandhi's Assassination* (New Delhi: Tulika Book, 2015), 61–6.
Vaidya, Jagannathprasad Shukl, *Arogyavidhan athva Bharat Mein Mandagni* (Health Solutions, or Dyspepsia in India) (Prayag: Standard Press, 1921, 2nd edn).
Vaidyaraj, Radhavallabh, *Aupsargik Sannipat* (Plague) (Aligarh: Arogyasindhu Karyalaya, 1916).

Vanaik, Achin, *Hindutva Rising: Secular Claims, Communal Realities* (Delhi: Tulika Books, 2017).
Vanchu, M.P., "Santati Nirodh aur Bharat" (India and Birth Control), *Yugantar*, February 1935, 20–1.
Vanina, Eugenia, "The *Ardhakathanaka* by Banarasi Das: A Socio-Cultural Study", *Journal of the Royal Asiatic Society of Great Britain and Ireland*, 5 (2), July 1995, 211–24.
Vanita, Ruth, "Whatever Happened to the Hindu Left?", *Seminar*, 512, April 2002.
Veer, Peter van der, "Spirituality in Modern Society", *Social Research*, 76 (4), 2009, 1097–1120.
Veer, Peter van der, *Imperial Encounters: Religion and Modernity in India and Britain* (Princeton: Princeton University Press, 2001).
Venkatachalapathy, A.R., *In Those Days There Was No Coffee* (New Delhi: Yoda Press, 2006).
Venkatachalapathy, A.R., *The Province of the Book: Scholars, Scribes, and Scribblers in Colonial Tamilnadu* (Ranikhet: Permanent Black, 2012).
Venuti, Lawrence, ed., *The Translation Studies Reader* (London: Routledge, 2000).
Verma, Pandey Ramsharanlal, *Pakprakash* (The Art of Cooking) (Allahabad: Indian Press Ltd, 1919).
Vidyalankar, Jay Chandra, "Swami Satyadev ki Rashtra ko Den" (Swami Saytadev's Contribution to the Nation), in *Sri Swami Satya Dev*, 1–5.
Vidyarthi, Sudhir, "Jat–Pat ke Khilaf Santram BA ka Jihad Khatm Nahin Hua" (Santram BA's Never-ending Crusade Against Casteism), *Vishwajyoti (Jat-Pat Torak Ank 2)*, June–July 1985, 142–3.
Vidyavachaspati, Indra, "Sri Swami Satyadev Parivrajak", in *Sri Swami Satya Dev*, 10–11.
Visvanathan, Shiv, "Narendra Modi's Symbolic War", *Economic and Political Weekly*, 49 (22), 31 May 2014, 10–13.
Waheed, Sarah Fatima, *Hidden Histories of Pakistan: Censorship, Literature, and Secular Nationalism in Late Colonial India* (Cambridge: Cambridge University Press, 2022).
Wald, Alan M., *Writing from the Left: New Essays on Radical Culture and Politics* (New York: Verso, 1994).
Wald, Alan, *Exiles from a Future Time: The Forging of the Mid-Twentieth Century Literary Left* (Chapel Hill: University of North Carolina Press, 2002).
Walsh, Judith, *Domesticity in Colonial India: What Women Learned When Men Gave Them Advice* (Delhi: Oxford University Press, 2004).
White, David Gordon, *The Alchemical Body: Siddha Traditions in Medieval India* (Chicago: University of Chicago Press, 1996).
Whitehead, Judy, "Bodies Clean and Unclean: Prostitution, Sanitary Legislation and Respectable Femininity in Colonial North India", *Gender History*, 7, 1995, 41–63.

Winichakul, Thongchai, *Siam Mapped: The History of the Geo-Body of a Nation* (Honolulu: University of Hawaii Press, 1994).

Wise, T.A., *Commentary on the Hindu System of Medicine* (Calcutta: Thacker & Co., 1845).

Zachariah, Benjamin, "At the Fuzzy Edges of Fascism: Framing the *Volk* in India", *South Asia: Journal of South Asian Studies*, 38 (4), 639–55.

Zamindar, N.C., "Modern Hindi Biographies and Autobiographies", *Indian Literature*, 17 (4), October–November 1974, 114–17.

Zamindar, Pyarelal, *Kok Shastra* (Treatise on Sex) (Aligarh: Hindustani Book Depot, 1905, 7th edn).

Zavos, John, *The Emergence of Hindu Nationalism in India* (New Delhi: Oxford University Press, 2000).

Archival Sources

Prime Ministers Memorial Museum and Library, New Delhi

"List of Small Collections: First Indian Communist Conference Papers 1925", List No. 190 (XXXXV), Acc. No. 299.

"Individual Collections: Papers of Santram BA", List 430.

National Archives of India

Proceedings and Files of the Government of India: Home Dept, 1900–1926; Home Poll, 1910–38.

Private Papers, Satyabhakta, Acc. No. 287.

Archives on Contemporary History, JNU

1922–26 Documents on "Communist Activities in India".

Patna Archives

"Satya Dev Sanyasi", File No. 139/1914, Confidential, Govt of Bihar.

Criminal Investigation Department Office, Lucknow

(Secret) Police Abstracts of Intelligence of UP Government, 1922–40 (PAI)

Letters in Private Collections

Letters of Ambedkar to Santram BA, Courtesy: Shanti Swaroop Bauddh (Nanak Chand Rattu, "Dr Ambedkar Paper Collections").

Letters of Satyabhakt to Karmendu Shishir, Courtesy: Karmendu Shishir.

British Library, London

Public and Judicial Records, L/PJ Series, India Office Records.
Stopes Papers, MSS no. ADD 58578, Department of Manuscripts, British Library.

Magazines and Newspapers (Select Issues)

Balsakha, 1928–44.
Chand, 1922–44.
Kanya Sarvasva, 1913–36.
Madhuri, 1922–40.
Maryada, 1910–23.
Prabha, 1921–23.
Samyavadi, 1926.
Saraswati, 1900–41.
Stri Chikitsak, 1913–38.
Stri Darpan, 1910–27.
Stri Dharma Shikshak, 1909–31.
Sudha, 1927–41.
Vishal Bharat, 1930–40.
Vishwajyoti, 1985–8.
Yugantar, 1932–4.

Interviews

Interview with Jayaprakash Narayan by Hari Dev Sharma, 29 June 1972, Acc. No. 393, Oral History Transcript, PMML.
Interview with Karmendu Shishir, Delhi, 13 June 2018.
Interview with Madhu Chaddha, Daughter of Gargi Chadha and Grand-daughter of Santram BA, Delhi, 25 January 2016.
Interview with Rachna Sharma, Grand-daughter-in-law of Yashoda Devi, Allahabad, 12 March 2023.
Interview with Raghubir Sahai by Hari Dev Sharma, 1 January 1970, Acc. No. 178, Oral History Transcript, PMML.
Interview with Sabhajit Shukla, Additional Assistant Secretary, Nagari Pracharini Sabha, Banaras, 5 March 2019.
Interview with Samir Sharma, Greatgrandson of Yashoda Devi, Allahabad, 12 March 2023.
Interview with Santram by Shyam Lal Manchanda, 15 May 1971, Acc. No. 238, Oral History Transcript, PMML.
Interview with Santram by Mark Juergensmeyer, Purani Bassi, Hoshiarpur, 18 April 1971.

Interview with Satnam Singh, Delhi, 9 February 2016.
Interview with Satyabhakt by Com. Damodaran, 1974, Interview 3, ACH, JNU, Archives of Contemporary History, Jawaharlal Nehru University.
Interview with Satyabhakt by Hari Devi Sharma, 13 July 1974, Acc. No. 214, Oral History Transcript, PMML.
Interview with Sripat Sharma, Grandson of Yashoda Devi, Allahabad, 14 August 2000.
Interview with Sudha Sharma, Granddaughter of Yashoda Devi, Delhi, 19 May 2023.

Index

Aaj 54, 261, 272
Abhyudaya 2, 20, 151, 195, 200, 254
Acchutanand, Swami 21, 45, 65
achhut 59–60, 280. *See also* Dalit
Ad Dharm movement 42, 51–2, 55, 58, 60, 64–5, 78
Adi Hindu movement 21, 65
Adityanath, Yogi 226
advertisements 88, 106, 115, 119–20, 123, 137–8, 170, 181, 196, 206, 260, 281
Agra 56, 115, 122, 179, 258–9
Agyeya 16, 21, 189
Ahmad, Muzaffar 250, 262, 293
ailments 119, 126, 147, 154, 158, 161, 171. *See also* illness
Akhand Jyoti Sansthan 259, 309
alcohol/alcoholism 150, 164, 190
Aligarh 87, 224, 237
Allahabad 1, 3, 5, 7, 16, 114–16, 154, 156–7, 180, 236, 254, 258–9, 301
allopathic/allopathy 118, 120, 159–60, 177–8. *See also* biomedicine
Ambedkar, Bhimrao 6, 15, 20, 32–4, 40–3, 55, 58, 63–4, 66–9, 72–3, 78, 89, 246; letters to Santram 67–8
America 36, 62, 90, 184–5, 189, 191, 193, 195–203, 205–6, 209–12, 218, 223, 229, 231, 233; students of 191, 205–6
anticaste 1, 3, 6, 14–15, 20–3, 29, 34–5, 40–3, 45, 55–6, 58, 62, 67–9, 74, 78, 80–1, 91–2, 102–3, 106, 109, 145, 280
aphrodisiacs 106, 137, 138
apocalypse/apocalyptic 3, 35, 284, 288–9, 298–303. *See also pralay*
archives 2, 7–8, 10–11, 13, 24, 27, 78, 81–2, 159, 181, 185, 260, 266–7, 311
Arya Samaj 2, 4, 15, 21, 23, 28, 40, 42–3, 45, 48, 51–6, 58–60, 62–4, 66, 69–71, 76, 78, 92, 104, 107, 121, 150–1, 157, 192–3, 224–5, 227–8, 234–5, 240, 290–1
ascetic/asceticism 3, 5, 23, 31, 36, 64, 215, 218, 222, 225–7, 230, 232–3, 246, 257, 286, 293, 301. See also *brahmacharya*, celibacy
ashlil/ashlilta 84, 94, 102, 305–6, 309
astrologer/astrology 289, 300–2, 305
Atharvaveda 297
atheism/atheistic 35, 254–5, 259, 268, 284–6, 293, 306, 310
aushadhi 115, 176, 178, 180
autobiography(ies) 23–7, 29–31, 40–7, 50–1, 55, 64, 69, 71, 78,

189, 217, 220–5, 227, 230–2, 234, 236, 238–42, 244–5, 246, 250–1
Awasthi, Ramashankar 253–4, 261, 287
ayurveda/ayurvedic 1, 3–4, 6–7, 15, 22, 27, 29, 34–6, 82–4, 112–17, 129–30, 133–4, 143–8, 151, 158–60, 162, 164–6, 170, 172–7, 181; and West 112–13, 117, 119–21, 125; as resistance 120; communalisation of 121–2; glorification of ancient 119–22, 124, 126–7, 144, 151, 158–9, 162, 164; in print 118–20, 160; knowledge 3, 22, 123, 130, 148, 159, 176; links to food and remedies 115, 146–8, 158–60, 162, 165–6, 170, 172–3, 175–7; male control over 122–3, 126, 129, 144, 159–60; practitioners 36, 113–15, 118, 125; professionalisation of 119–20, 126, 177, 181; training 120, 122; usefulness for women of 123–6, 129–30, 143, 159–60, 172, 174. *See also* home remedies, Yashoda Devi
Ayurvedic Mahamandal 123

Bachchan, Harivansh Rai 26, 189, 222
Bai, Satyabhama 132, 138
Banaras 7, 16, 115, 179, 261, 306
Banita Hitaishi Press 17, 115
barrenness 130, 143
Bauddh, Shanti Swaroop 47–8, 67
Baxter, Michael P. 300

beauty/beautiful 36, 99, 171, 174, 176, 184–5, 187–8, 197, 201–3, 207, 211, 213, 215, 219, 223, 228–9, 256, 276
beef 150, 228
Bengal 16, 19, 57, 92, 162, 233, 250, 253, 256
Bengali 22, 24, 149, 155, 166, 186
Benipuri, Rambriksh 21, 189, 222, 253
Bhagvad Gita 294, 301, 304
Bhai Parmanand 26, 56, 63, 72, 74, 89, 233
Bhumanand 55, 72
Bhartiya Samyavadi Dal 260, 274, 279. *See also* Indian Communist Party
Bible 89, 236, 288, 300, 302
Bihar 114, 223–4, 230, 237, 240, 245
biography(ies) 24, 26–7, 45, 55, 127, 148, 222, 245, 250, 254, 265–6, 275–6, 282
biomedicine/biomedical 11, 112–14, 117–18, 120–1, 126–7, 130, 160, 172–3, 181. *See also* allopathy
birth control 5, 35, 83, 85, 98–9, 106–8, 122
body/bodies/bodily 3, 29, 31–2, 35–6, 57, 69–70, 80, 100–1, 106, 108–9, 113, 117, 122, 136–47, 150, 152, 154, 162, 166, 171–2, 178, 181, 187–8, 197, 205, 213, 217, 219, 226, 238; ascetic and masculine 31, 103–4, 136, 152, 185, 187–8, 205, 207, 213–15, 217, 225–6, 229–30, 235, 246; caste 78,

INDEX

82, 151; control, care and cure 29, 32, 34–6, 117, 127–8, 144–5, 147, 150–1, 171–2, 176–8; desires 31, 101, 140; female 3, 69, 101–2, 107–8, 113–14, 117–18, 127, 139–41, 181; perfect 36, 136, 138, 162, 184, 187–8, 197, 207, 213–15, 227, 229, 234; weak 152, 214. *See also* masculinity, sexuality

Bolshevik/Bolshevism 254, 264–5, 269–70, 272, 277, 281, 299, 300, 308; Conspiracy Case (Kanpur, 1924) 252, 261, 272; Revolution 252

Bombay 207, 230, 236, 253, 259, 261–2, 275, 280

brahmacharya/brahmachari 5, 23, 31–2, 52, 83–4, 99, 103–7, 118, 138, 150, 153, 192, 197, 214–15, 217, 227, 244. *See also* asceticism, celibacy

Brahmin/Brahmanical 3, 20, 47–8, 56, 59–62, 66, 71–2, 74–6, 92, 103–4, 114, 145, 164, 167, 177, 193, 244, 280, 286, 290, 305, 309

British 7, 11, 58, 62, 75, 84, 113, 122, 128, 150–1, 154, 163–4, 172, 181, 208, 235, 261, 270–1, 280, 290, 295, 301–2

Buddha/Buddhist 27–8, 33, 41–2, 64, 89–90, 286

Calcutta 231, 240, 261–2
capitalism/capitalist 35, 57, 84, 153, 180, 267, 270, 277, 280–2, 284, 289, 295–7, 300, 307

caste(s) 1, 3–4, 28–9, 35, 37, 40–78, 80–3, 91–2; and gender 1, 44, 68–78, 91–2; birth-based 57, 63, 71, 75; critique of 4, 6, 12–13, 22, 28, 34–5, 40–4, 46, 50–1, 53–8, 60–2, 66–9, 102; hierarchy 5, 9, 15, 19, 22, 34, 44, 46, 48–51, 54, 59–60, 63–4, 68, 77, 81, 92, 103, 148, 151, 181, 192, 249, 278–9, 286; lower 22, 46, 51–2, 57, 59–60, 80, 102, 109, 132, 152, 286; reform 35, 42–4, 57, 59–60, 157; suffering 29, 42, 78; system 41, 57, 61, 63–4, 67, 70–1, 92, 307; taboos 43, 72; upper 13, 20–1, 52, 58–9, 68, 72, 80–2, 85, 92, 102, 104, 114, 129, 148, 152, 162–3, 209, 212, 244. *See also* anticaste, Santram BA

celibacy/celibate 31, 36, 105, 139, 192, 197, 215, 225–7, 244, 246, 286. *See also* asceticism, *brahmacharya*

censorship 12, 35, 135

Chakan Lal 28, 256. *See also* Satyabhakt

Chand 20, 54, 56, 106, 154, 156–7, 160–1, 177–8, 259, 275, 277, 291

Chand Karyalaya 154, 161

Charaka Samhita 119, 268

Chatterjee, Bankim Chandra 256, 276, 298

Chaturvedi, Banarsidas 91, 256

Cheiro 289, 292

child/children 55, 71, 74, 76–7, 79, 83, 101, 104–5, 107–8,

118, 128, 130, 134, 136, 146, 161, 167, 172, 174, 191, 205, 216, 227, 231, 241, 271, 307; abduction of 238; male 134
Christ 300, 307
Christian/Christianity 10, 61, 89, 212, 235, 286, 300, 308
citizen/citizenship 30, 74, 137, 184, 196, 213–14, 219, 231
class(es) 3, 12, 15–16, 22, 37, 52, 72, 86, 103, 112–13, 118, 128, 143, 148, 150, 152, 154, 164, 181, 188, 211, 253, 267, 272, 278–80, 281–3, 295; working 253, 267, 278–9, 283, 295
clean/cleanliness 66, 118, 127–8, 164, 203, 205, 207, 237
colonial/colonialism 1, 6, 10–13, 23, 25, 31, 33–4, 43, 50, 57, 82–4, 86, 99–100, 106, 113, 116–17, 122, 136, 144, 149–50, 154, 158, 164, 170, 172, 181–2, 186–7, 199, 209, 217, 219, 248, 257, 264, 270, 273, 284, 293, 303
communal/communalism 7, 62, 164, 210, 220, 224, 244, 254, 285, 293–4, 305, 310
communism 1, 3–4, 6–7, 11, 13–14, 21, 23, 27, 29, 37, 220, 237, 242, 248–52, 254–5, 257–69, 272, 275–8, 281–9, 293, 296–9, 301, 303, 306–10; Hindu 6, 268, 284–311; histories of 249–50, 285; Indian 37, 250–1, 257, 260–2, 264–6, 268, 283, 285, 296–7, 309; vernacular 29, 37, 248–9, 254, 266, 276–8, 283

communist 3, 36, 268–9, 250–5, 283–94; activists 250, 254–5, 258, 260; ideologies 250–3, 261, 268–9, 280, 283–4, 293, 307–8; literature 3, 21, 251–3, 255–6, 263, 269, 272–5, 277, 281–2, 288; movement 248, 251, 263, 266, 281, 306; utopia 3, 6, 13, 23, 35, 253, 303, 306
Communist International (Comintern) 35, 249, 261–4, 266, 268
Communist Party 5, 15, 248, 250–1, 255, 259–61, 263–4, 266, 272, 275, 278–9
conjugal/conjugality 31, 80, 83, 85, 88, 92, 94, 97, 98–100, 127, 129, 135, 143, 153
conversions 61, 66–7, 69
cook/cooking 69–70, 119, 127–8, 147, 150–2, 155, 162–7, 169–71, 181, 237–8
cookbooks 3, 36, 148, 154–8, 162, 164, 166–7, 169–72
copyright 5, 17, 83, 97, 195; violations 87–8
cosmopolitan/cosmopolitanism 6, 8–9, 11, 20, 30, 96, 188, 207, 218–19, 234, 250
culinary 3, 148, 151, 153, 162–3, 167, 181; knowledge 128, 146, 148, 156, 166, 169, 172; texts 119, 146, 148, 156–8, 164, 166
cure/curing 32, 36, 98, 123–4, 126, 129–31, 135, 139, 146, 159–61, 172–4, 176–8, 181; home 159–60, 173–4
custom 163, 203, 212, 277, 288, 291–2; burning the dead 212;

fasting 150; grain worship 291; Hindu 288, 291–2

dai 113–14, 128
Dai, Ganga 132
Dalit 2, 7, 9, 16, 21, 24, 25, 26, 28, 30, 40 44, 45, 46, 47, 48, 50, 51, 56, 64, 65, 68, 69, 74, 75, 78, 80, 82, 150, 151, 163, 219, 279, 287, 306, 259, 309; literature 21, 26, 45–50; publishing 45–6
Dayanand Saraswati, Swami 27, 51, 104, 224–5, 227
desire 13–14, 23, 30–2, 35, 69, 77–9, 81–2, 85–6, 88, 93, 99–102, 105, 108–9, 113, 140, 153, 155, 163, 165, 170, 187, 196, 199, 210, 213, 227, 286, 289, 309, 311; bodily 31, 101, 140; sexual 30–1, 79, 81, 86, 102, 108, 153; utopian 13, 23, 32, 289
Devi Pustakalaya 17, 115
diet/dietary 147, 149–50, 152, 163–5, 171–2
diseases 6, 29, 36, 73, 77, 84, 98, 105, 113, 118–19, 124, 126–8, 130–1, 133, 137, 141, 143, 146, 151, 161, 164, 166, 171, 173–4, 177–8; cholera 151, 161; cough 160–1, 176; diarrhoea 161, 174; earache 160, 174; eye 161, 174; fevers 154, 160–1, 174, 176–8; gonorrhoea 139, 176; infections 130, 137, 164, 176; infertility 130, 137, 143, 176; leukorrhea 129–31, 161; malaria 161, 174; menstrual pains 130, 176; pain 29, 44, 161, 174, 307; plague 151, 161; snakebite 161, 173; venereal 84, 105, 113, 131, 141; wounds 176
doctors 56, 97, 113–14, 125, 138, 147, 149, 160–1, 175, 177; ayurvedic 121–2; domestic 147–9; male 114; Western 121. *See also* ayurveda, *vaid*
domestic/domesticity 2, 32, 34, 122, 128–9, 136, 151, 153, 155, 159, 141, 153, 155, 159, 164, 174, 178, 182; remedies 148, 188; violence 141
dreams 1, 6, 21, 32, 137, 213, 218–19, 222, 228, 255, 299, 308–9, 311; communist 255, 309; utopian 32, 303, 308, 311; wet 137, 228
Dwivedi, Mahavir Prasad 16, 26, 53, 190, 195, 199–200, 212
dystopia 1, 33–4, 145, 152, 288–9, 298

economy/economic 18, 147, 165, 181, 226, 262, 278, 280–1, 285, 295; agency 181–2; crisis 277; domestic 153, 178; political 149, 177
education 3, 50, 74, 81, 100, 116, 128, 155, 188–9, 192, 204–6, 210–11, 217–18, 233, 237, 256; sex 81, 100
egalitarian/egalitarianism 15, 21, 23, 52, 108, 277–8, 283, 287, 297, 299, 310

ego/egoism 30, 221, 229–31, 232, 242
Ellis, Havelock 94, 97, 105
embodiment 32, 78, 121, 155, 163, 165, 229
endogamy/endogamous 13, 22, 44, 69, 73, 75–8, 81, 103
England 62, 154, 199, 207, 215, 263, 299, 308
English 6, 9, 11–14, 20, 49, 53, 81–3, 85–6, 88, 91–4, 98, 119, 155, 185, 191, 196, 201, 212, 221, 267, 271, 276
epidemics 118, 141, 152, 303
equality 23, 35, 37, 52, 58, 61, 66, 74, 76, 109, 232, 234, 285, 287, 297, 303–5, 307, 309
erotic/eroticism 23, 31, 83–8, 90, 92, 96–7, 100, 106, 108, 133, 170, 179, 219, 286
ethic(s) 3, 5, 33–4, 66, 79, 83, 93, 99–102, 128, 135, 139, 144, 210, 229, 251, 257, 266, 268, 288, 290, 295, 297, 308; heterosexual 3, 5, 79, 83, 99, 100, 102, 135, 144
eugenics 76, 83, 85, 94, 104, 106, 108, 122, 136, 162
Europe 3, 19, 25, 36, 60, 80, 90, 184–7, 190–1, 193, 196–9, 201–2, 204–5, 207–10, 212–18, 273, 299
everyday 14, 29, 117, 147, 155, 186, 221, 251, 259, 290–1, 293
exclusion 13, 22, 44, 59, 69, 238, 309

family 6, 20, 24, 29, 35, 43, 48, 55, 60, 72, 77, 106, 109, 114–15, 118, 120, 127–8, 139, 130, 143, 146–7, 153–4, 159, 165, 167, 171, 178, 180, 191–2, 215, 226–7, 259, 271
fantasy 170, 184, 187, 219, 226, 304
fascism 184, 187
female 114, 123–4, 126, 130, 135, 139, 167, 171, 173, 178–9, 200; body 3, 102, 114; sexuality 31, 81–2, 100–2, 131, 136, 143
feminist 9, 21, 107, 113–14, 141, 297, 309
femininity 117, 149, 166, 244, 246
fiction 10, 17, 18, 34, 45, 108, 188, 189, 190, 256
fit/fitness 104, 184, 187, 205, 207, 214, 219, 225–7, 229
food 23, 127, 134, 146–7, 150, 162, 171; and ayurveda 151, 172; and caste 51, 53, 68–70, 73, 151, 164; and class 152–3, 164–5; and gender 166–71; habits 171, 201, 229, 297–8; healthy 36, 152–3, 172; histories of 36, 148–9; *kaccha/ pukka* 152; politics of 70, 148–54, 162–3, 270; recipes 115, 155–7, 172. *See also* cookbooks, vegetarian, Yashoda Devi
foreplay 102, 140
France 62, 193, 197, 207, 208, 215, 308
freedom 1, 6–7, 11, 32–6, 59, 62, 73, 76, 93, 104, 108–9, 177, 187–8, 196, 199, 203–4, 207, 209–11, 213–16, 218–23,

225–8, 231–5, 238, 252, 260, 262, 264, 267, 274, 289, 302, 304–6, 311; ideals of 6, 32, 34, 213, 222, 232, 234, 305; movement 104, 260, 267; personal 204, 210; political 33, 34, 227, 232; sectarian 35–6, 220, 222, 225, 232, 234; sexual 93, 109, 228; utopian 6, 32, 34, 35; vernacular 1, 6, 187
frugality 153, 229
fruits 134, 157, 162, 172, 231, 301

Gandhi, Mahatma 6, 29–30, 32–3, 36, 42, 55, 66, 74, 78, 84, 104, 106, 136, 150–1, 189, 201–2, 220–6, 233, 237–46, 252, 256–7, 267, 276, 284, 296, 304–5; and Ambedkar 6, 42, 55, 66, 78; assassination of 220, 223–4, 242, 244
Ganga Devi 54, 69, 72
Ganga Pustak Mala 16, 89, 154
gender/gendered 1–3, 6–7, 12–15, 20, 22, 24, 29, 35, 36–7, 44, 69, 78, 81–2, 84, 86, 99–100, 108–9, 112–14, 117, 122–3, 126–8, 143–4, 148–9, 151, 167, 173, 182, 187, 249, 280–1, 283, 309; relations 36, 84, 99–100, 108, 126
genre 1, 3–4, 17–18, 21, 25–7, 36, 94, 118, 129, 143, 148, 154, 174, 186, 188–90, 194, 218, 223, 230, 232, 303
Germany 75, 94, 129, 188, 190–1, 193, 199, 202, 207–10, 212–18, 220, 228, 242, 301
ghee 152–3

girls 60, 72, 74, 103, 125, 128, 169, 205, 215, 227
Gita Press 16, 223, 306
Godse, Nathuram 224, 226, 239–40, 242–6
Gokul, Radhamohan 21, 253–6, 258, 260–1, 274, 282, 287, 298
Gupt, Mataprasad 157, 163, 167, 169
Gurukul Kangri 54, 76, 245

*hakim*s 87, 121–2, 175
Hans 7, 26, 46, 54
Harischandra, Bharatendu 16–17, 194
healing 34, 36, 144, 149, 159–60, 172–3, 177, 228, 235
health 3, 22–3, 28–9, 36, 84–5, 104, 113–19, 122–3, 126–30, 138–9, 141, 143–4, 146–9, 152–5, 158, 170–3, 179–81, 197–8, 205, 207, 211
heteronormative 69, 100, 103, 135, 145
heterosexual/heterosexuality 3, 5, 31, 34, 79, 83, 99, 102, 144, 226
Hindi 4, 7, 19–21, 27, 44, 84–5, 119, 148, 256; and Dalit 21, 45–6, 50; and Hindu 1–2, 7–8, 15–16, 18–19, 20–1, 23, 26–7, 32, 36, 188, 222–3, 267, 311; as a language of unity 4, 19, 21, 187; communist ideas in 251; eclectic 4, 6, 19, 20–1, 160, 222, 298; Khari Boli 4, 18, 26, 198; medical writings in 159; print culture 1–2, 4–6, 15–16, 19–21, 26, 54, 85, 106–7, 117, 129, 148, 154,

158–9, 181, 195, 231, 248, 251, 253, 255, 260, 272, 282, 285, 287–8; recipes in 36, 148, 155, 162, 164, 166; Sanskritised 4, 19–20, 276, 306; sex literature in 85–6; travel writing 185; vernacularisation of 4, 9, 20, 85, 87, 119, 124, 155

Hindi Sahitya Sammelan 16

Hindu(s) 1–2, 5–6, 20, 22–3, 30, 59, 61–3, 64–5, 127, 211–13, 218–19, 225–6, 246; and caste 2 ; and Muslims 16, 21, 23, 33, 61–2, 150, 234, 242, 246, 287, 293; ascetic 23, 225, 226; beliefs 23, 28, 155, 297–8; bodies 31, 181, 213, 226; communalism 16, 222, 224–5; communism 1, 3, 6, 13, 23, 284, 310; cooking traditions 162; emasculated 244; Left 23, 286; masculine 3, 31, 162, 185; nationalism 2, 4, 6–7, 20–1, 27, 36, 57, 60, 127, 150, 162–3, 181, 188, 214–15, 217, 219, 221–2, 224–5, 234, 239, 243–4; orthodoxy 43, 59, 66, 205; patriarchies 1, 31, 77, 81, 109, 211, 286; pluralities 5, 7, 13, 22–3; political 31, 185–7, 227; religious 21, 34, 57, 107, 163, 285; Right 239, 243; women 13, 36, 60, 127, 238, 243

Hinduism 3, 5–6, 16–17, 20, 22–3, 35, 42, 55, 66–7, 70, 78, 84, 86, 121, 164, 197, 212, 219, 222, 225, 234, 240, 244, 246, 255, 259, 285–8, 292–4, 297–8, 308–11; egalitarian 35, 212, 225, 240, 287–8, 310; kitchen 164; masculine 36, 136, 188, 218, 235; middle classes and 22, 150, 152, 188; militant 219, 234, 244; multiplicity of 23; Sanatani 43, 66, 70

Hindu Mahasabha 15, 20, 21, 69, 150, 235, 240, 290

Hindutva 6, 23, 54, 187, 216, 226, 238–9, 246, 255, 267, 279, 285–6, 305, 310

histories 1–2, 4, 6–7, 11, 13, 15, 19, 21, 23–7, 29–32, 34–7, 42–4, 46, 48, 55, 65, 68, 77–8, 80, 84, 108, 113, 116, 122, 130, 148, 159, 170, 185, 194, 203, 209, 212, 220–2, 230, 232, 246, 249–51, 254–5, 260, 278, 285, 290, 296, 298, 309, 311; anticaste 15, 29; social 27, 32, 35; writing 11, 15

historiography 11, 149, 185, 285, 310

Hitler, Adolf 187–8, 213, 215–18, 220, 239, 241–2, 294–5. See also Nazi

home remedies 34, 36, 115, 119, 146, 147–8, 154, 158–61, 172–5, 177

Hoshiarpur 3, 48–9, 52, 54, 64

hospitals 113, 120, 122, 144

hotels 152, 198, 205

household 3, 34, 36, 49, 101, 114–15, 117–18, 122, 125,

127–9, 139–40, 146, 153–5, 158–61, 164–7, 173–6, 178, 181; management 127, 153, 174; work 101, 165
housewife 117, 125, 127, 148, 153, 155, 166, 169, 172, 174, 178; as *ghar ka vaid* 172; ideal 127, 148, 153, 155
hunger 68, 108, 200, 237, 307
husband(s) 17, 28, 34, 76, 79, 101, 115, 132, 135, 137, 140, 141, 142, 169; tyranny of the 34, 101, 137, 141–2
hygiene 84, 118, 127, 128, 144, 151, 153, 159, 164

identity/identities 1, 2, 5, 6, 12, 16, 20–2, 24, 25, 28, 31, 36, 43–4, 61, 64, 75, 80, 83, 99, 112, 117, 119, 120, 122, 123, 127, 136, 144, 148–51, 155, 158, 164, 162, 181, 209, 211, 213, 224, 234, 244, 249, 259, 278, 281, 286, 292, 296, 309, 310; community 20, 119; cultural 120, 127, 136, 144, 158; gender 99, 148; Hindu 119, 122; nationalist 117, 122, 127, 144; religious 2, 12, 16, 21–2, 61, 148–9, 181, 286; social 5, 281, 310
ideology/ideologies 52, 60, 64, 75, 77, 92, 216, 221, 237, 239, 240, 249–50, 252, 277, 282, 283, 284, 293, 294, 296, 304; communist 282, 284, 293, 296
idioms 1, 8, 10, 12–13, 25, 61, 68, 78, 98, 188, 198, 210, 249, 251, 253, 263, 268, 280, 285, 287–8, 291, 294–5, 303, 309–10; communist 287, 288; religious 61, 253, 285, 287, 294–5, 309–10
ill/illnesses 29, 36, 106, 123–4, 128, 135–7, 139, 140–1, 145–7, 149, 152, 154, 166, 171–2, 174, 176, 181, 263, 279
images and cartoons 2, 60–1, 8, 114, 124, 127, 155, 203, 212, 217, 294, 299
impotent/impotency 105, 107, 137
Indian Communist Conference (ICC) 5, 36, 248, 251, 259–63, 282, 293, 297
Indian Communist Party (ICP) 5, 251, 259–64, 266, 272, 278–9
Indian National Congress 15, 21, 240, 245, 254, 261–2, 283
Indian Social Reformer 57, 70–1
indigenous 9, 14, 22–3, 29, 34, 97, 123, 128, 158, 160, 187, 196, 218, 222, 232, 267; communism 37, 251, 263, 265–6, 282, 293; food 162–3, 165, 178; knowledge 10, 112, 268; medicine 112–14, 117, 124–6, 144, 153, 172, 177; practitioners 119–20, 122, 126
intellectual(s) 9, 11, 22, 26, 33–4, 36–7, 45, 50–1, 194, 210, 216, 246, 250, 253, 267, 287
intercaste marriages 1, 3, 5, 31, 35, 40, 43–4, 53, 55, 57, 59–60, 62, 65, 68–78, 81, 103, 108–9
intercourse 79, 88, 97, 100–1, 105, 108, 129, 133, 135–8, 140
inter-dining 57, 59, 69–70, 72, 151

internationalism 37, 213, 264–5, 268
interwar years 250, 252, 283
intimacy 18, 44, 55, 77, 78, 82, 108, 171, 292
Islam 61, 113, 120, 228, 237–8, 286, 293, 297
Italy 193, 207–8, 308

Jacolliot, Louis 89
jati 77–8, 280, 286, 309
Jat–Pat Torak Mandal (JPTM) 5, 17, 40, 43–4, 47, 54–60, 63–8, 70–2
Jigyasu, Chandrika Prasad 21, 45, 90, 107
Jinnah, Muhammad Ali 62, 224
journalists/journalism 3, 19–21, 36, 47, 50, 116, 201, 231, 244, 248, 254–5, 258, 269, 271, 287
Jullundur 50, 54, 64

Kabir 286, 298
kama 85, 87, 91, 107; *shastra* 35, 82, 85, 91, 93–5, 97, 99–100, 102, 105–8, 133, 137; *vasna* 91, 107; *vigyan* 87, 91
Kamasutra 83, 86–7, 90, 93, 96, 286
Kanpur (Cawnpore) 2, 5, 7, 158, 248, 252–5, 258, 260–2, 265–6, 272–5, 281, 293–4, 297, 305
Kanya Sarvasva 119, 124, 128
Karpatri Maharaj, Swami 306–7
Karve, R.D. 80, 105–6
Kashi 56, 121, 193, 206
khadi 242, 257, 305
Khilafat Movement 235, 241, 242, 252

kiss/kissing 100–1, 140, 228
kitchen 36, 51, 63, 69, 133, 147–50, 162, 164–7, 169–72, 175, 180, 237; pharmacists 36, 146, 148–9, 175; recipes 148
koka 85; *shastra* 85, 87, 92–3
Kokkok (Koka Pandit) 90, 93–4, 96
Kranti 54, 56, 68
Krishna, Lord 27, 74, 294, 301, 305
Kropotkin, Peter 265, 289
Kumhar 47–9, 51

labour/labourer(s) 60, 77, 130, 147, 169–70, 199, 205, 206, 212, 227, 229, 253, 257, 259, 272, 276, 278–2, 294–6, 305
Lahore 50, 53–4, 56, 59, 65–6, 71, 76, 87, 90, 192, 255, 262
languages and literatures 3, 4, 6, 8–10, 12, 16, 19–21, 30, 34, 36, 53, 93, 106, 109, 119, 189, 199, 228, 239, 246, 255, 269, 276, 298–9; Arabic 18; Awadhi 19, 164; Bengali 24; Bhojpuri 19; Braj 19; French 14, 28, 89, 195; Gujarati 53, 88, 103, 191; Gurumukhi 42; Khari Boli Hindi 4, 18, 26, 198; Latin 8; Malayalam 24; Marathi 21, 53, 88, 191, 278, 280; Persian 9, 12, 14, 18–20, 53, 88, 186, 297; regional 14, 25, 194, 252; Russian 14, 21, 252, 254, 256, 265, 273, 289, 299; sexology 3, 78, 85, 88, 101–2; Tamil 11, 67, 280, 304; Telugu 45; vernacular 14–15, 100

Leader, The 237, 240, 264, 302
left/leftist 23, 253, 255, 286–8, 297
Lenin 241, 254, 268, 275–6, 282, 294, 298
letters 4, 27–9, 67, 91, 93, 104, 115, 117, 123, 130, 135–7, 179, 200, 240, 266
liberty 33, 210–11, 233–4
life 5, 20, 25, 29, 40, 45, 117, 136, 153, 234; history 23, 26, 29, 44; individual 25, 28, 30, 77; narratives 1, 24, 26, 28, 42, 44–6, 57, 78, 298; ordinary 43, 311; public 33, 44, 151, 221, 287; sexual 35, 79, 82, 133, 139; writing 24–5, 35, 60
literacy 12, 250, 276
love 22, 42, 44, 53, 60, 68, 82, 85, 88, 90, 92, 97–8, 102–3, 108, 128, 133–5, 138, 201, 203, 217, 229–30, 233–4, 238, 296, 308; jihad 238
Lucknow 7, 90, 154, 245

Madhuri 20, 54, 65, 94, 95
Madras 202, 240, 253, 261, 262
Mahabharat 22, 74, 301, 302
Malaviya, Krishnakant 2, 254, 258, 287
male 100, 141, 144, 213; body 102, 136, 138, 187, 215; sexuality 32, 102, 136
male–female/man–woman 79, 93, 96, 98, 108–9, 115, 118, 130, 143, 200, 242
Mangoo Ram 52, 64–5, 68
manhood/manliness 106, 136, 152, 218, 226. *See also* masculinity

Manu 73, 286
margin/marginalised/marginality 2, 9, 12, 14–15, 21, 30, 37, 40, 62, 80, 88, 112–13, 122, 129, 172–3, 242, 248–9, 251, 259–60, 269, 278, 282–3
market(s) 4, 12, 88, 104, 106, 122, 133, 152, 163, 170, 179, 181, 198, 210
marriages 1, 3, 5, 22–3, 31, 35, 40, 43–4, 53, 55, 57, 59–62, 65, 68–79, 81–3, 85, 88, 98, 100, 102–5, 108–9, 114–15, 133, 135, 141, 143–4, 215, 227, 259, 280, 291, 307. *See also* intercaste marriages
Marx, Karl 20, 27, 250, 255, 269–70, 275–8, 280, 282, 294, 296, 298–9, 307
Marxism 248–9, 253, 255, 263–4, 267, 278, 280–1, 283, 285–6, 296, 298, 306–8, 310
Maryada 191, 195, 200, 254, 258–9
masculine/masculinity 5, 31, 36, 76, 81, 104, 106, 117, 136, 139–40, 149, 162, 184–5, 187–8, 213–15, 217–18, 222, 225–6, 229, 235, 244, 246
masturbation 5, 31–2, 104, 106, 129, 136–9, 176
Matvala 259, 282
Mayo, Katherine 62, 309
meat 150, 163–4
medical 6, 112–14, 117–18, 120, 123, 125–6, 128, 132, 136, 147, 149, 152, 158–9, 173–4, 181; folk practices 9, 30, 112, 159, 166, 172–3, 177, 290; indigenous systems 124, 126,

144, 172; knowledge 36, 114, 117, 147, 159, 161, 174, 179, 181; practitioners 112, 122, 124, 139; recipes 158, 161, 164, 173, 178; remedies 153, 173, 178; science 119, 144, 146, 305; traditions 125, 161, 172; unani 112–13, 120–2, 126; Western 113–14, 172. *See also* ayurveda

medicines 4, 13, 23, 36, 98, 112–14, 116–23, 125–7, 138, 143–4, 147, 149, 151, 158–9, 165, 173–8, 180–1, 233; allopathic 177–8; indigenous 112, 114, 117, 177

memories 24, 29, 42, 44–5, 51, 80, 185, 202, 210, 231

menopause 108

menstrual/menstruation 129–30, 134, 161; pains 130, 161, 176; taboos 132

middle class(es) 5, 12, 16, 20–2, 36, 80, 82, 85, 101, 113–14, 117–19, 125, 127–9, 134, 143–4, 148–50, 152–5, 162, 164–6, 169, 170, 173–4, 178, 182, 187–8, 194, 219; educated 36, 85, 118, 148, 173–4; Hindu 22, 36, 127, 148, 150, 152, 155, 169, 182, 187–8, 219; urban 119, 164, 173

midwife 113–14, 127, 130, 132, 173, 180

milk 152–3, 167, 176, 231

miscarriages 129–30, 173

missionary/missionaries 10, 61, 113, 209

modernity/modernisation 12, 17, 19–20, 25, 34, 43, 55, 72, 74, 76, 82–3, 97, 102, 125, 139, 144–5, 150, 153, 158, 186, 194, 199, 226, 249, 283, 292, 300, 305, 310

Modi, Narendra 226

Mohani, Hasrat 261–2, 296–7

monk 25, 31, 226, 305–6

morality 31, 37, 82, 85, 92, 99, 109, 118, 128, 139, 167, 171, 212, 242, 244, 284, 287, 296–7

More, Thomas 308

Moscow 264, 266, 268

mother tongue 10, 19

movements/struggles 2, 45, 56, 68, 127, 220, 227, 248–9, 257, 264, 268, 280, 305–6; anticaste 68, 280, 286; cow-protection 7, 150; Gandhian 257–8, 270; non-cooperation 230, 235, 240–1, 257; subaltern 287, 310

Muslims/Mussalman 6, 13, 16, 21–3, 29, 33, 35–6, 58–62, 69–70, 122, 150–1, 163, 218–19, 221–5, 228, 234–5, 237–9, 241–4, 246, 250, 254, 287, 292–3, 296–9, 308

myth/mythology 23, 51, 143, 60, 105, 287, 289, 298, 302

Nagari Pracharini Sabha 5, 16, 118, 202, 222

Nala, Maharaja 166

Narayan, Jayaprakash 33, 189, 222

narratives 1–4, 7, 14, 17, 24–30, 35–6, 42–6, 57, 64, 75–8, 82, 84, 98, 108–9, 144, 147–8, 150, 171, 196, 225, 229,

238, 250, 263, 298, 304; personal 25, 30, 43, 148, 229
nation/national/nationalist/nationalism 2, 4, 6–7, 16–17, 19–22, 25, 29, 31, 33, 36–7, 43, 54, 57, 60, 65, 75–7, 97, 109, 114, 117, 127, 136–9, 144, 150–1, 155, 162–3, 165–6, 181, 185, 187–8, 191, 211–17, 219, 221–6, 231–2, 234–5, 238–40, 241, 244–6, 248–9, 253, 255–6, 259, 264, 267–8, 280, 283, 204, 306; bodies of 188, 214; boundaries 211, 213; colonised 38, 187, 222; conservative 17, 29, 127, 213, 238; independence 33, 265, 267, 283; linguistic 19, 54; muscular 150, 187, 219; rhetoric 6, 121, 209
National Herald 220, 244
Naval Kishore Press 16, 90, 120, 128, 154, 157
Nazi 75, 187, 213, 220, 239, 298, 301. *See also* Hitler
Nehru, Jawaharlal 29, 74, 221, 242, 245–6
newspapers and magazines 2, 8, 12, 17–18, 20, 26, 28, 40, 46–7, 54–6, 62, 65, 68, 88, 90–1, 94, 102, 124, 128, 138, 154, 156–7, 178, 191, 194, 206–7, 231, 236–7, 245, 251–2, 254–5, 259–61, 263–4, 272–3, 281–2, 288, 303
"Nirala", Suryakant Tripathi 59–60
nonfiction/nonfictional 1–2, 4, 18, 251, 256

non-vegetarianism 150. *See also* beef, meat
non-violence 33, 151, 242–4, 246, 257, 305
North India 1–2, 5, 7, 16, 22, 35, 37, 43, 80, 96, 123, 150, 152, 154, 159, 164, 223, 246, 248, 252–3, 273, 287, 305
nocturnal emission 106, 137, 139, 176
novels 12, 17–18, 103, 137, 199, 222, 245, 253, 265
nuskhe 146–8, 175, 178

obscene/obscenity 1, 7, 12, 16–18, 22, 31, 35, 84–5, 88, 91, 93–4, 100, 102, 104, 106–7, 109, 122, 133, 136, 153, 170, 222–3, 228, 235, 251, 283
old age/old people 162, 172, 214
oral 120, 154, 290
orgasm 80, 102, 140
orthodoxy 43, 59, 66, 73, 193, 279, 284

Pakistan 54, 58, 62, 239, 243
Pak Chandrika 157, 162–5, 167, 169–70
pamphlets 2, 3, 17–18, 32, 119, 175, 255, 257, 259–60, 273–7
Partition 220, 238–9
Patna 115, 179, 189, 192, 230, 236
patriarchy/patriarchal 1, 77, 81, 109, 117, 143–4, 170, 182, 286
peasants 69, 163, 279, 280, 287, 294, 305
Phule, Jyotiba 78, 310

physical/physicality 137, 188, 202, 219, 229, 236; fitness 104, 188, 207, 213–14
Pillay, A.P. 80–1, 106
pleasure 31, 35–6, 44, 82, 84–5, 88, 92, 96, 98–102, 108–9, 112, 116, 118, 133, 135, 137, 140–1, 175, 185, 188, 190, 197, 202, 216, 293, 300, 302
plural/pluralism 6–7, 11, 13, 80, 86, 125, 149, 159, 172, 178, 224–5, 285–6, 292–3, 303, 308, 311
poem/poetry/poets 17, 19, 43, 53, 93, 201–2, 205, 210, 214
political/politics 6–7, 11–12, 14, 21, 28, 24–5, 31–3, 36–7, 42–3, 48, 66, 68, 70, 74, 85–6, 99, 101, 106, 119, 139, 148–9, 164, 166, 219, 224, 241, 251–2, 258, 260, 263, 268, 276–9, 285, 287–8, 294, 296–7, 305–6; revolutionary 36, 251, 258, 294; *sanyasi* 20, 31, 188, 222, 226, 245
pollution taboos 49, 69, 133, 151–2, 201
pornographic 84–6
poverty 49, 55, 102, 216, 259, 275, 283, 304, 307
power 14–15, 22, 28, 31–2, 62, 76, 81–2, 92, 104, 109, 112, 130, 136, 154, 159, 173, 209, 214, 226, 250, 295, 301, 305
Prabha 54, 259
practitioners 36, 112–14, 118, 120–2, 124–6, 129, 139, 144, 159–60, 173
Prajapati 47–8, 64

pralay 284, 288, 299, 302. *See also* apocalyptic
Pranvir 254–5, 258, 272
Prasad, Rajendra 222, 224, 245
Pratap 254–6, 258, 261, 272, 275
predictions 244, 288, 298, 300, 302, 311
pregnancy 106, 128
prejudice 51, 60, 224, 237–8, 242–3, 311
Premchand, Munshi 17, 19, 21, 26, 253
Press Trust of India (PTI) 245
print 15–16, 21, 50, 83–4, 86, 88, 155, 159, 253; cultures 1, 12, 21, 25, 35, 45, 83, 86, 96, 125, 148, 194, 253, 311; Hindi 1, 21, 45, 53, 148, 253; market 4, 12, 25, 117, 181, 194; presses 12, 15, 16, 80; public sphere 7, 16–17, 21, 37, 44, 53, 86, 129, 194, 248, 282, 285; technologies of 21, 84, 88, 155
procreation 82, 93, 112, 116, 133, 140, 144
progeny 76–7, 134. *See also* child
Progressive Writers' Association 253, 297
proletariat 278–9. *See also* working class
propaganda 21–2, 42, 57, 60, 306
property 5, 109, 202, 223, 258, 278, 306–7
prophecy/prophecies 288, 298–300, 302. *See also* predictions
prose 4, 6, 12, 17–18, 20, 25, 27, 194, 276; growth of 18, 25
prostitutes/prostitution 74, 83, 102, 113

INDEX 373

publishing houses 12, 15–17, 27, 45–6, 90, 115, 118, 154, 195
Punjab 3, 9, 19, 40, 42–4, 48–53, 57, 59, 192, 230, 238, 243, 253, 262, 268, 294
*Purana*s 23, 287, 290–1, 302
purdah 124, 212, 237, 307
purity 59, 65, 69, 81, 94, 102–3, 108, 141, 150–1, 164, 191, 201, 237, 286

race/racism 11, 29, 75, 81, 113, 150, 207, 212, 217–18, 239, 242
Rai, Lala Lajpat 63, 93
railway 88, 152, 211, 278–9, 282
Rajasthan 3, 251, 256, 271–2
Rajasthan Sewa Sangh 271
Rajpal 90, 107; Rajpal & Sons 90
Ram, Lord 27, 161, 217, 294, 305
Ramayan 102, 288, 291, 294, 304, 309
ramban 123, 146, 161
Ramchandra, Baba 163, 305
Ramcharitmanas 288, 291, 304–5
Ram Rajya 6, 23, 35, 284, 288–9, 300, 303–9
Ram Rajya Parishad 306
rationalist/rationality 13, 41–2, 58, 73–4, 76, 95, 128, 136, 243, 287, 253, 289, 292
readers/readership/reading 4, 9, 12, 20, 24, 34–5, 91–3, 101, 124, 155, 166, 173, 184, 194, 196–200, 202, 204, 209, 211, 219, 223, 276–7, 292, 309
recipe(s) 3, 23, 27, 35–6, 115, 119, 146–9, 154–6, 157, 158–66, 169–82, 188, 225; household 3, 154, 158, 161, 174, 176, 181; printed 148, 154, 173, 181. *See also* cookbooks, home remedies
reforms/reformers/reformists 16, 22, 25, 33, 35, 42–3, 57–8, 60, 64–5, 66, 69–70, 78, 84, 87, 93, 99, 102, 113, 117, 129, 139, 145, 151, 157, 211, 218, 226, 264, 287, 289–90, 310; caste 35, 42–3, 60, 157; social 33, 66, 70, 93, 102, 211, 218, 287, 289
religion/religious 3, 15, 19, 24–5, 29, 34, 37, 57, 69–71, 89, 94, 100, 105, 108, 112–13, 121, 163, 166, 173, 189, 216, 228, 234, 237, 242, 277, 280, 285–7, 289–90, 292–3, 296, 298, 303, 305–7, 309–10
remedies 29, 34, 36, 115, 119, 123, 125, 130, 135, 148–9, 153–4, 158–61, 172–6, 178–9, 181, 188. *See also* home remedies
renunciation 226, 241, 246, 257
reproduction 78, 82, 88, 102, 107, 113, 118, 133–4, 161
resistance 11, 13, 21, 44–5, 50, 78, 106, 109, 120, 166, 181–2; forms of 44, 50, 78, 120
rights 44–5, 58, 65, 74, 87, 101–2, 211, 242, 269–71, 277, 280–2, 291
romance/romantic 44, 61, 124, 189, 296
roti–beti 43, 59–60, 68–9
Roy, M.N. 33, 248, 250, 260, 263, 265–7, 269, 282, 293

Russia 215, 220, 248, 254, 256, 258, 263, 277; Russian Revolution 21, 252, 299

Saddharma Pracharak 53, 54
Sahai, Raghubir 197, 229, 240
Sahajanand Saraswati, Swami 21, 253, 276, 294
salvation 203, 272, 299, 302
Samyak Prakashan 45, 46, 47
Samyavadi 260, 274, 279, 281–2, 299–300
sangathan 3, 4, 52, 60, 65, 188, 235–6, 246
Sankrityayan, Rahul 19, 21, 55, 108, 188–9, 194, 228, 253, 307
Sanskrit 9, 11–12, 14, 19–20, 31, 81–3, 85–6, 88, 90–4, 96–7, 119, 122–4, 155, 193, 198, 225, 268, 290; sex classics 9, 31, 81, 83, 88, 90, 92–3, 96
santati shastra 123, 134
Santram BA 1, 3–6, 9, 11, 13–15, 17, 20–3, 26, 28–32, 34–5, 40–84, 86, 88–109, 124, 129, 141, 144–5, 222, 268, 283, 311; and Arya Samaj 54, 63–4; and Dalits 64; and education 50; as anticaste crusader 3, 6, 40–4, 51, 53–8, 60, 62, 71, 80–1, 91–2, 102–3; as Hindi promoter 53–4, 67, 82; as journalist and writer 42, 44, 47, 50, 53–4, 56, 59, 68, 81, 84, 92, 96, 100, 103, 108; as a polyglot 53, 88; as sexologist 81–2, 91–2, 95, 97, 103, 109; as advocate of intercaste marriages 1, 3, 5, 35, 40, 43–4, 53, 55, 62, 65, 68–78, 81, 103, 108; as translator 3, 89, 90, 93, 98; attacks on 59–60, 65–6, 72, 91; autobiography of 29–30, 35, 40–7, 51, 55, 57, 64, 69, 71, 76, 78, 189, 221–3, 225, 230–2, 236, 238, 241, 244–5; caste discrimination of 48, 50–1; on birth control 83, 90, 99, 106–7; on *brahmacharya* 103–7; Shudra status 43, 51. *See also* anticaste, intercaste marriages, JPTM
Santram BA, books *Adarsh Pati* 90, 100, 124, 126–7; *Adarsh Patni* 87, 90, 100; *Antarjatiya Vivah hi Kyun* 53–4, 68, 75–7; *Hamara Samaj* 45, 47–8, 53, 59, 67, 73–5, 102; *Kama Kunj* 90–1, 94–5, 100–2; *Mere Jeevan ke Anubhav (MJKA)* 40–3, 45–6, 48, 50–1, 53–7, 59, 61–3, 69–72, 74–5, 77, 88, 92, 104, 107; *Rati Vigyan* 80, 90, 93, 94, 95, 97, 98, 99, 100, 103; *Santan Sankhya ka Seema Bandhan* 90, 106–7; *Vivahit Prem* 90, 95–9, 101–2
sanyasi 20, 31, 188–9, 192, 197, 217, 222–3, 225–6, 231, 241, 245, 294
Saraswati 20, 53–4, 65, 191, 195, 199–200, 211–12, 217, 259
Satyabhakt 3–6, 11, 13, 15, 17, 20–1, 23, 28–30, 32, 36, 231, 248–9, 251–3, 255–84, 286–303, 307–11; and the Indian Communist Party 5, 251, 259–62, 264, 266, 272,

275, 279; as a biographer 254, 275–6; as a journalist 3, 36, 231, 248, 251, 255–6, 258–60, 269–72, 282, 288; communist beliefs 6, 36, 251, 255, 264, 269, 272–81, 288, 298; conceptualisation of Ram Rajya 284, 300, 307–9; Hindu leanings 251, 255, 287–93; marginalisation of 251, 260; on M.N. Roy 265–6; writings on communism 21, 251, 259, 263, 269, 272–81, 302
Satyabhakt, books *Agle Sat Sal* 275, 284, 299–301, 307–8; *Bharat mein Samyavad* 261, 265, 267, 269, 272, 279, 296–8; *Bhartiya Shramjeeviyon ko Sandesh* 269, 276–8; *Bolshevism Kya Hai* 269, 277; *Gorilla* 265, 269; *Ireland ke Gadar ki Kahaniyan* 265, 269; *Karl Marx ka Jeevan Charitra* 269–70, 275, 294; *Kranti ka Agaman* 257–8, 260, 269; *Kranti Path ke Pathik* 231, 256, 258, 260, 265, 269, 271, 289, 302; *Marne ke Bad* 287, 292; *Samvat Do Hazar* 299–302; *Samyavad ka Sandesh* 265, 277; *Samyavad ke Siddhant* 269, 296
Satyadev Parivrajak 3–6, 9, 11, 13, 15, 17, 20, 23, 28–32, 35–6, 184–246, 311; admiration of Hitler and Nazism 189, 216–17, 220, 239, 241–2; and Gandhi 201–2, 220, 223–5, 237, 239–4, 246; anti-Muslim venom 3, 6, 193, 209–10, 223, 237; as a nationalist 211, 214; as a political *sanyasi* 188, 222, 226, 241, 245; as a powerful orator 188–9, 223, 230, 236–7; as a virulent Hindu 188, 217, 219, 226; as Hindi advocate 188, 202, 240; autobiography of 31, 192, 221, 223–5, 227, 234, 239–40, 242, 244, 246; experiences of America 184, 189, 191, 193–5, 197, 199, 200–3, 205–6, 210–11; idealisation of masculinity and physicality 188, 207, 213–14, 218, 235, 246; naming of 28, 189, 193; perception of freedom 35, 187–8, 199, 213–14, 219, 222, 228, 232–5; refusal of passport to 207–8; supporter of *brahmacharya* 192, 197, 214–15, 222, 225–7, 233; travel writings and admiration of the West 36, 185, 187–8, 190–1, 196–200, 200–2, 207, 210–11, 213–19, 223, 225; travels to Germany 191, 199, 207–8, 210, 213–16; writings of 186–7, 190–1, 195–6, 199, 200–2, 204, 213, 221, 224–5, 230, 238
Satyadev Parivrajak, books *Amrica Bhraman* 184, 193, 212; *Amrica Digdarshan* 191, 196, 202–3; *Amrica ke Nirdhan Vidyarthiyon ke Parishram* 191, 206; *Amrica Pravas ki Meri Adbhut Kahani* 193, 202, 205; *Asahyog* 235, 257; *Europe ki Sukhad Smritiyan* 185, 191, 197–8, 201–2, 207, 210,

214–18; *Germany Mein Mere Aadhytmik Pravachan* 190, 193, 202, 209, 213, 215; *Meri German Yatra* 190–1, 193, 195, 197, 205, 212, 215; *Meri Kailash Yatra* 191, 204, 230–1; *Sangathan ka Bigul* 222, 235–6; *Swatantrata ki Khoj Mein arthat Meri Atm Katha (SKM)* 192–3, 200, 210, 214–15, 217, 221, 223, 225–32, 234–44; *Vichaar Swatantrya ke Prangan Mein (VSPM)* 221, 228–9, 231, 241, 243–5; *Yatri Mitra* 191, 196, 198

satyagraha 33–4, 242, 258
Satyagyan Niketan 5, 17, 195
Satyug 28, 35, 259, 284, 288, 303
Satyug Press 5, 17, 28, 259, 301, 303
Savarkar, V.D. 216, 219, 239, 246
savarna 9, 58, 82, 92, 103, 151
science 10, 31, 45, 74–5, 79–82, 84–5, 88, 91–2, 94–5, 97, 105, 113, 119–22, 127, 133, 144, 146–7, 154–5, 159–60, 164, 166–7, 169, 181, 290, 292, 305
scriptures 31, 93, 96–7, 102, 286, 293, 306
secularism 35, 224, 244, 249, 285, 293
self 3–4, 24–5, 29, 31–2, 43, 45, 50, 65, 74–6, 112, 118–19, 122, 135, 137–8, 150, 152, 173, 187, 190–1, 196, 209, 215, 230–1, 259–60, 280; control 105, 135–6, 151–2, 171, 227–8, 233, 257; fashioning of 2, 4, 23–5, 27, 28–30, 32–3, 45, 197, 199, 217–18, 227, 229–30, 232, 234, 236, 246; reliance 65, 75, 178, 188, 191, 206, 231; writings 7, 23, 26, 28–9, 30, 46
semen 104–5, 134, 136–8, 226
sentiment 65, 94–5, 219, 290
sex/sexual 9, 12–15, 22–3, 31, 35, 68–9, 77, 78–86, 88, 90–3, 95–105, 107–9, 113, 115, 117, 122–4, 129, 133–6, 138–41, 144–5, 150, 164, 167, 225, 227, 233; classics 9, 81, 83, 88, 90, 92; desires 30, 79, 97, 102, 108, 153; pleasure 85, 88, 92, 99–101, 108–9, 135, 140–1, 197; pre-marital 22, 79; problems 109, 126–7, 129–30, 140–1; sciences 31, 79, 82, 84, 88, 91–4, 96–7, 99–101, 105, 108–9, 118, 133; writings on 80–1, 83–5, 90–1, 103, 133
sexology 3, 5, 10, 14, 27, 31, 35, 78–88, 90–3, 95–7, 100, 102–3, 108, 115–18, 122, 129–30, 141, 145; vernacular 14, 80, 83, 85
sexuality 1, 5, 7–8, 12, 16–18, 22, 31–2, 69, 81–4, 86, 100–2, 104, 106, 108–9, 114, 118, 122, 127, 129, 133, 136, 145, 153, 170, 222–3, 226, 235, 238, 244; conjugal 31, 81–2, 100, 102, 136
Sharma, Maniram 156, 162, 167. See also *Pak Chandrika*
Sharma, Ramvilas 251, 267, 276
Sharma, Sri Ram 17, 114–16

shastras 74, 85, 92, 121, 123–4, 146, 166, 177, 297
Shastri, Saligram 120, 122, 134
Shishir, Karmendu 3, 251, 255–6, 259, 275–6, 297–8, 309
Shraddhanand, Swami 53, 200, 238, 243
Shridharani, Krishnalal 201
shuddhi 22, 52, 60, 235
Shudra 3, 9, 40, 42–3, 48–9, 51, 52, 58–9, 62, 65–6, 72, 74–5, 78, 80–2, 92, 279–80, 305
Sikhs 42, 58, 69, 192, 243, 268, 294
Singh, Bhagat 226, 255, 273, 276, 294, 296, 298
Singh, Satnam 45–7, 49–50, 64
sisterhood 126, 147, 172, 178
slave/slavery 8, 36, 62, 74, 58, 198, 207, 209–10, 218, 228, 279, 281, 307
socialism 216, 253, 255–6, 259, 272, 274, 277, 280, 297, 303
Socialist Bookshop 5, 17, 273
soldiers 113, 216, 236, 271
songs 93, 102, 214, 228, 233–4
sovereignty 27, 33–4, 154
spices 149, 162, 170, 172, 177
spiritual/spiritualism 25, 28, 33, 37, 76, 103, 163, 193, 210, 219, 222, 251, 255, 259, 268, 283, 287, 296–7, 309–10
sports 10, 205
Stalin 294, 295
Starling, E.H. 95, 97
Stopes, Marie 5, 9, 20, 35, 80, 83, 88, 90, 94, 96–9, 104–6
Stri Aushadhalaya 5, 114–15, 125–6

Stri Chikitsak 119, 124, 158, 175, 178
Stri Darpan 292, 309
Stri Dharma Shikshak 114, 119, 124, 130, 158, 175
subaltern 10, 14, 31, 42, 44–5, 50, 117, 158, 173, 199, 265, 276, 287, 310
Sudha 54, 72, 75, 89, 90, 91, 154, 156, 160
suffering 42, 44–5, 78, 105, 135, 141, 172, 272, 307
Sukh Dayal 28, 192. *See also* Satyadev Parivrajak
Sunder Bai Pradhan 71–3, 88
superstition 289, 291–2, 310
swaraj 33–4, 253, 305
sweeper 59–61, 64, 66, 259

Tagore, Rabindranath 32–3, 186–7, 296
technology(ies) 21, 88, 113, 125, 147, 155, 160, 194, 301
temperance 127, 153, 171
Thakur, Jyotirmayi 2, 127, 158, 164, 171, 174
theatre 16–17, 24, 25, 137, 228–9
thrift 127–8, 153, 227
Tilak, Bal Gangadhar 233, 241, 298
Times of India, The 236, 274
Tolstoy, Leo 276, 301
touch 7, 59, 73, 82, 103, 140, 220, 269, 283, 296
trade unions 253, 294
translation 3–4, 6, 8–9, 13–14, 26–7, 31, 35, 45, 68, 80–3, 86, 88–90, 93–9, 106, 124, 156, 191, 206, 209, 250, 256–7,

265, 270, 278, 280, 286–7, 289, 308–9
travel 1, 3–4, 7, 12–13, 18, 23, 25, 27, 30, 35–6, 55, 184–91, 193–200, 204, 207, 209, 213–15, 218–19, 222–3, 225; accounts 12, 18, 186–7, 194, 199, 204; and masculinity 187; writings 186–7, 194, 209, 218
travelogues 3, 27, 30, 36, 185, 188–9, 191–2, 195–6, 204
Tribune, The 57, 58, 68, 207
Tulsidas, Goswami 51, 291, 298, 304–5, 308–9

unani 112–13, 120–2, 126
unemployment 152–3, 277
United States (US) 3, 193, 199–201, 203, 210–11. *See also* America
untouchables/untouchability 45, 50, 52, 58–9, 62–3, 65–6, 74–5, 103, 151, 212, 281, 291, 304
Upadhyay, Gangaprasad 2, 26, 150
urbanisation/urbanity 12, 83, 102, 149, 252
Urdu 16, 18, 20, 24, 53–4, 59, 68, 88, 119, 122, 150, 191, 252–3, 277
Usmani, Shaukat 261
utensils 164, 165, 278
utopia/utopian 3, 10, 23, 34, 79, 108, 288, 289, 299, 303, 307–8
United Provinces (UP, Uttar Pradesh) 12, 15–16, 21, 47, 53, 58, 65, 84, 114–16,

118–19, 128, 148–50, 152, 157, 172–3, 223, 230, 253, 260–2, 273–4, 296, 305

*vaid*s 20, 97, 114, 120–3, 126, 129, 147, 160, 175–6, 177
Vaidya, Babu Haridas 119, 122, 174
*varna*s 3, 66, 72, 76, 77–8; Brahmin 3, 20, 47, 56, 60–2, 66, 71–2, 74, 76, 92, 114, 177, 244, 280; Kshatriya 3, 66, 72, 74, 76, 244, 291; Shudra 3, 9, 40, 42–3, 48, 49, 51–2, 59, 62, 72, 78, 80–1, 92, 305; Vaishya 3, 66, 71, 103, 157, 259
varnashramdharma 59–60, 286, 309
varnavyavastha 59, 63, 76
Vartman 254, 255, 272, 274
Vatsyayan 20, 90, 96, 99
Vedvratt 54
vegetarian/vegetarianism 52, 60, 150, 163
vernacular 7–13, 16–17, 31, 88, 96, 147–8, 155, 158, 166, 182, 185, 194, 248–9, 259, 281, 268, 278, 290; communism 248, 249; freedom 6, 187; print 7, 12, 83, 85–6, 261, 311; sexology 14, 79–80, 83, 85, 116
Vidyarthi, Ganesh Shankar 21, 44, 253–4, 287
vigyan 91, 94, 95, 121
violence 45, 69, 141, 150–1, 187, 216, 222, 238, 242–4, 246, 249, 254, 257, 264, 270, 301, 305

Vivekananda, Swami 32–3, 104, 136, 226

warfare 18, 216, 265, 301
wealth 17, 157, 180–1, 202, 217, 222, 225, 246, 258, 298, 307
West/Western 6, 13, 33, 80–1, 166, 181, 197, 222, 265; medicine 112–14, 117, 119–20, 124–6, 127, 138, 158–9; sexual knowledge 85, 94, 114
widow 6, 72, 153, 259
wife/wives 107, 126–7, 132, 135, 137–8, 141, 143, 147, 307. See also housewife
wisdom 6, 154, 159, 161, 173–4, 217
Wise, Dr T.A. 118, 121
women 27–9, 61, 101–2, 113, 116–17, 123–4, 127–8, 140, 143–4, 148, 167, 169–71, 178, 180, 190, 197, 211, 233, 237–8, 309; American 202, 211; and ayurveda 1, 36, 114–15, 119, 124, 126–7, 143; and cooking 148–9, 155, 169; and men 22, 25, 33, 35–6, 77, 79, 90, 99–100, 117, 133, 143, 160, 181, 194, 241; as active partners 83, 100–1; as domestic healers 126, 132, 147–9, 155, 159–60; as entrepreneurs 147; bodies 69, 101, 107, 113; disciplining 102, 107, 167; desires 100–2, 140; educated 36, 148, 173; health 115–19, 126, 128, 146, 170; magazines 90, 154, 156; medical practitioners 113–14, 122, 126, 129, 139, 144, 177;
middle-class 36, 114, 117, 128–9, 134, 148, 153, 169, 173, 182; sexual problems 127, 129–30, 141
workers 37, 102, 113, 152, 169, 252–4, 258, 262–3, 272–3, 276–81, 283, 287, 293–5, 300; movements 37, 253, 283
World War I 241, 252, 299–300
World War II 298, 301
worship 59, 214–15, 225, 291
writers 10, 12, 80, 184; Christian 308; communist 253, 255, 284; Dalit 46, 68; Hindi 17, 26, 40, 59, 188–9, 200, 220, 230–1, 251, 256, 269, 287; travel 3, 188, 194; women 116, 158
writings 2–3, 11, 34, 251, 300; anticaste 41, 43, 81, 91, 103; autobiographical 24, 36; communist 21, 269, 288, 303; Hindi 17, 54, 194, 251, 253, 299; sexology 5, 80, 92, 103

Yashoda Devi 1, 3–6, 9, 11, 13, 15, 17, 22–3, 28–32, 34, 36, 114–17, 119–30, 132–41, 143–9, 155, 158, 162–3, 165–7, 169–72, 175–80, 182, 188, 268, 283, 311; against masturbation 129, 136, 137–8; and ayurveda 3, 114, 117, 120, 122–6, 130, 148; and women 115, 123–7, 129, 132, 134, 139; and biomedicine 126–7, 130, 181; as sexologist 115–16, 144, 129–30, 145; male critique by

136–43; marginalisation of 122–3; mastery and popularity 123–4, 132, 143; recipes and remedies 130, 135, 139, 147, 155, 162, 166, 171–2, 178, 188; writings 114, 117, 119, 123–5, 127–9, 132, 136, 141, 143–4, 148–9, 155, 172. *See also* ayurveda

Yashoda Devi, books *Achaar ki Kothri* 158; *Adarsh Pati–Patni* 124, 126–7; *Arogya Vidhan Vidyarthi Jeevan* 136–8; *Bharat ka Nari Itihaas* 124, 127; *Dampati Arogyata Jeevanshastra* 114, 123–7, 130, 133–4, 137–9, 141, 147, 155, 175–7, 179; *Dampatya Prem aur Ratikriya ka Gupt Rahasya* 124, 126–7, 130, 132–4, 136–8, 140–1, 143; *Ghar ka Vaid* 175; *Grhini Kartavya Shastra Arogyashastra arthat Pakshastra* 135, 146, 158, 162, 165–7, 169–71; *Kanya Kartavya* 115, 127; *Nari Dharmashastra Grh-Prabandh Shiksha* 115, 126, 128, 176, 178; *Nari Sharir Vigyan* 114–15, 124, 126–7, 130, 132, 137, 140–1, 177; *Vaidik Ratn Sangrah* 175–6; *Vaidik Shastra ka Asli Kokshastra* 133; *Vivah Vigyan* 125, 128, 138

yoga 201, 286
yogi 197, 226–7, 293
Yugantar 54–6, 60–1, 107, 254
Yug Nirman Yojana 259, 275, 298

Zamindar, Babu Piare Lal 26, 85, 87, 230
zenana 113, 139

www.ingramcontent.com/pod-product-compliance
Lightning Source LLC
Chambersburg PA
CBHW031411230426
43668CB00007B/279